691-4574

Psychodynamics and Cognition

Psychodynamics and Cognition

Edited by Mardi J. Horowitz

The University of Chicago Press • Chicago and London

MARDI J. HOROWITZ, M.D., is Professor of Psychiatry at
the University of California, San Francisco, where he
directs the Center for the Study of Neuroses and the
Program on Conscious and Unconscious Mental
Processes of the John D. and Catherine T. MacArthur
Foundation.

The University of Chicago Press, Chicago 60637
The University of Chicago Press, Ltd., London
© 1988 by The University of Chicago
All rights reserved. Published 1988
Printed in the United States of America
97 96 95 94 93 92 91 90 89 88   54321

The University of Chicago Press gratefully
acknowledges a subvention from the John D. and
Catherine T. MacArthur Foundation in partial support
of the costs of production of this volume.

Library of Congress Cataloging-in-Publication Data

Psychodynamics and cognition.

    Based on papers presented at a workshop sponsored
by John D. and Catherine T. MacArthur Foundation.
    Bibliography: p.
    Includes index.
    1. Psychoanalysis—Congresses.   2. Cognition—
Congresses.   I. Horowitz, Mardi Jon, 1934-
II. John D. and Catherine T. MacArthur Foundation.
RC506.P784   1988   616.89'17   87-25505
ISBN 0-226-35368-0

Contents

Preface vii
Contributors ix

Part 1. Consciousness and Unconscious Formative Processes

1 Psychodynamic Phenomena and Their Explanation 3
   Mardi J. Horowitz, M.D.
2 Problems and Directions in the Study of
   Consciousness 21
   George Mandler, Ph.D.

Part 2. A Clinical Psychodynamic Perspective

3 Unconsciously Determined Defensive Strategies 49
   Mardi J. Horowitz, M.D.
4 Issues in the Study of Unconscious and Defense
   Processes: Discussion of Horowitz's Comments, with
   Some Elaborations 81
   Matthew Hugh Erdelyi, Ph.D.
5 Steps Toward a Lexicon: Discussion of "Unconsciously
   Determined Defensive Strategies" 95
   Peter H. Knapp, M.D.

Part 3. An Experimental Psychodynamic Perspective

6 Unconscious Conflict: A Convergent Psychodynamic
   and Electrophysiological Approach 117
   Howard Shevrin, Ph.D.
7 Electrophysiology and Meaning in Cognitive Science
   and Dynamic Psychology—Comments on
   "Unconscious Conflict: A Convergent Psychodynamic
   and Electrophysiological Approach" 169
   Anthony J. Marcel, Ph.D.

8 A Response to Marcel's Discussion 191
   Howard Shevrin, Ph.D.
9 Exploring the Form of Information in the Dynamic
   Unconscious 203
   Ray Jackendoff, Ph.D.

Part 4. Omissions of the Expectable from Consciousness

10 Recurrent Momentary Forgetting: Its Content and Its
    Context 223
    Lester Luborsky, Ph.D.
11 Momentary Forgetting: An Alternative
    Formulation 253
    Donald P. Spence, Ph.D.
12 Take a Moment to Really Look at the Little Lawful
    World of Momentary Forgetting—A Reply to
    Spence 265
    Lester Luborsky, Ph.D.
13 Momentary Forgetting as a "Resetting" of a Conscious
    Global Workspace Due to Competition between
    Incompatible Contexts 269
    Bernard J. Baars, Ph.D.

Part 5 Understanding Conscious Experience

14 Sampling Ongoing Consciousness and Emotional
    Experience: Implications for Health 297
    Jerome L. Singer, Ph.D.
15 Prolegomena for the Study of Access to Mental Events:
    Notes on Singer's Chapter 347
    R. B. Zajonc, Ph.D.

Part 6. Conclusions

16 Agreements and Disagreements: Indications for
    Research 363
    Mardi J. Horowitz, M.D.

Author Index 377
Subject Index 383

Preface

This book contains the results of a carefully planned workshop in which major presentations were followed by formal discussions. These statements were prepared in advance and reviewed by all participants. This permitted extensive informal discussions that were taped, transcribed, and provided in summary to the authors. They rewrote chapters, adding responses to key issues. This workshop led to a subsequent workshop on the specific topic of person schemas[1] where a paper presented by George Mandler provided a good historical platform. This paper therefore became one of the two introductory chapters in Part 1 of this volume. Part 2 focuses on key issues at the level of psychodynamic clinical case formulation. Part 3 examines experimental tests of the validity of such formulations. Part 4 focuses on the important construct of repression or omissions from consciousness. Part 5 continues on issues of what can be consciously known, especially about the meanings that evoke emotions. Part 6 is a summary chapter.

The workshop was sponsored by the John D. and Catherine T. MacArthur Foundation's Program on Conscious and Unconscious Mental Processes which I direct. The Center for Advanced Study in the Behavioral Sciences at Stanford University provided an apt location. I am deeply appreciative of a fellowship year at the Center for Advanced Study in the Behavioral Sciences, which provided for the planning of this work. John Conger, Ph.D., William Bevan, Ph.D., Howard Shevrin, Ph.D., Jerome Singer, Ph.D., Lester Luborsky, Ph.D., Idy Gittelson, Ph.D., and Denis Prager, Ph.D., have made invaluable contributions throughout. Visionary ideas, especially from Murray Gell-Mann, Ph.D., and Jonas Salk,

1. The classical plural of *schema* is *schemata;* however, modern usage tends increasingly toward *schemas.* The choice is left to the individual authors in this work. The meaning of *schemata* and *schemas* is the same.

M.D., sparked the effort. Nancy Wilner, Jannie Dresser, and Julio Ruffini, Ph.D., helped edit the contributions to this volume. Charles Stinson, M.D., Sandra Tunis, Ph.D., and Jess Ghannam, Ph.D., read final drafts. Susan Silva served admirably during many word-processing revisions. I thank them all.

Mardi Horowitz, M.D.

Contributors

BERNARD J. BAARS, PH.D., is an Associate Professor at The Wright Institute in Berkeley, California, has been a Sloan Cognitive Science Scholar at the Center for Human Information Processing, University of California, San Diego, and a Visiting Scientist at the Program on Conscious and Unconscious Mental Processes at the Center for the Study of Neuroses, University of California, San Francisco. His publications include *The Cognitive Revolution in Psychology, A Cognitive Theory of Consciousness, The Psychology of Error: A Window on the Mind,* and "Conscious contents provide the nervous system with coherent, global information," in *Consciousness and Self-Regulation.* He is a member of the Cognitive Society and co-chair of the Society for Cognition and Brain Theory.

MATTHEW HUGH ERDELYI, PH.D., received his Ph.D. from Yale University in 1969 and is currently Professor of Psychology at Brooklyn College and The Graduate Center of the City University of New York. His most recent publication is *Psychoanalysis: Freud's Cognitive Psychology.*

MARDI J. HOROWITZ, M.D., is Professor of Psychiatry at the University of California, San Francisco, where he directs the Center for the Study of Neuroses and the Program on Conscious and Unconscious Mental Processes of the John D. and Catherine T. MacArthur Foundation. He is the author of the books *Image Formation and Psychotherapy, Stress Response Syndromes, States of Mind, Introduction to Psychodynamics,* first author of *Personality Styles and Brief Psychotherapy,* and editor of *Hysterical Personality.* He is a Fellow of the American College of Psychiatrists, the American College of Psychoanalysts, and the American Psychiatric Association, which presented him the Foundation's Fund Prize for research on stress response syndromes.

RAY JACKENDOFF, PH.D., is Professor of Linguistics and Chairman of the Program in Linguistics and Cognitive Science at Brandeis University. He received his Ph.D. in linguistics from MIT, where he was a student of Noam Chomsky and Morris Halle. He is the author of *Semantic Interpretation in Generative Grammar, X-Bar Syntax: A Study of Phrase Structure, Semantics and Cognition, Consciousness and the Computational Mind,* and with Fred Lerdahl, *A Generative Theory of Tonal Music,* as well as numerous articles in linguistics, psychology, and music theory.

PETER H. KNAPP, M.D., is Professor of Psychiatry at the Boston University School of Medicine and a Training Psychoanalyst at the Boston Psychoanalytic Institute. He is a former president of the American Psychosomatic Society and author of numerous papers, including "Psychological aspects of asthma." His background is in psychosomatic medicine, and he has special interest in the application of research technique to psychoanalytic material.

LESTER LUBORSKY, PH.D., is Professor of Psychology in Psychiatry at the Medical School, University of Pennsylvania. He is Director of the Center for Personality and Psychotherapy Research. His books include *Personality Patterns of Psychiatrists,* co-authored with Robert Holt; *Research in Psychotherapy, co-authored with Hans Strupp; Principles of Psychoanalytic Psychotherapy;* and, *Psychotherapy: Who Will Benefit and How?* co-authored with Paul Crits-Cristoph, Jim Mintz, and Arthur Auerbach. His research has been in the areas of subliminal perception, defenses and their influence on memory, momentary forgetting, factors influencing the outcomes of psychotherapy, and psychosomatic interactions.

GEORGE MANDLER, PH.D., is Professor of Psychology and Director of the Center for Human Information Processing at the University of California, San Diego. He received his Ph.D. from Yale University and has taught at Harvard University and at the University of Toronto. His major theoretical and research interests have been memory, emotion, and the role of consciousness in cognitive theory. His most recent books are *Mind and Body,* which received the William James Award in 1986, and *Cognitive Psychology.*

ANTHONY J. MARCEL, PH.D., is affiliated with the Medical Research Council of Great Britain, Applied Psychology Unit in

Cambridge, England, and is an Honorary Fellow in Neurology at Addenbrooks Hospital, Cambridge. Among his publications is *Consciousness in Contemporary Science*, co-edited with E. Bisiach.

HOWARD SHEVRIN, PH.D., is Director of the Psychotherapy Evaluation and Treatment Laboratory, Department of Psychiatry, University of Michigan. His most recent publication, entitled *Mind and Behavior*, is in press. He is also the author of many articles, including "The fate of the five metapsychological principles," "Refuseniks: The internal refugees of Russia," and "Glimpses of the unconscious."

JEROME L. SINGER, PH.D., is Professor of Psychology and Director of the Graduate Program in Clinical Psychology at Yale University. He has been the director of numerous research projects involved with such topics as fantasy, imagination, health psychology, and television. Among his publications are *The Power of Human Imagination, Mind Play: The Creative Uses of Daydreaming, Television, Imagination, and Aggression, Teaching Television, Getting the Most Out of Television, The Inner World of Daydreaming, The Stream of Consciousness,* and *The Child's World of Make-Believe.*

DONALD P. SPENCE, PH.D., is Professor of Psychiatry at Teachers College, Columbia University, and has also served as Professor of Psychology at New York University. He is affiliated with the Robert Wood Johnson Medical School, UMDNJ, in Piscataway, New Jersey. His primary research interest is in psychoanalytic theory and subliminal perception. His publications include *Narrative Truth and Historical Truth,* and he edited *The Broad Scope of Psychoanalysis: The Collected Papers of Leopold Bellak* and *Psychoanalysis and Contemporary Science,* vol. 4.

R. B. ZAJONC, PH.D., is the Charles Horton Colley Distinguished Professor of Social Science and Director of the Research Center for Group Dynamics at the University of Michigan, Ann Arbor. He is the author of numerous articles in the field of social psychology, including "Social psychology: An experimental approach." In 1978, he received the American Psychological Association's Distinguished Scientific Contribution Award.

1 Consciousness and Unconscious Formative Processes

This section has introductory chapters from two perspectives, the first from a psychodynamic theorist, the second from a cognitive psychology theorist. The goal is to frame a potential dialogue between these domains of knowledge about human mental processes, especially as they concern the larger issues of meaning, life tasks and choices, and conflictual themes of high emotional relevance.

The first chapter deals with intrusions and omissions, phenomena that are deflections from rational conscious experiences. The second chapter continues to address these phenomena; it summarizes salient theories about how conscious experiences are formed as well as the relevant utilities and limitations of consciousness.

A debate emerges in these chapters that concerns motivation. The first chapter explains intrusions and omissions in terms of unconscious intentions of and for the self. The second chapter questions whether such unconscious purposes are valid psychological mechanisms and suggests that in many instances such inferred motives may be secondary commentaries made by the self to make consciousness and behavioral patterns appear more sensible and rational than is actually the case. The chapters agree that the representation and schematic organization of thought are key issues to address in an effort to improve theory and resolve the debate about how to explain intrusions and omission. These are issues that Part 2 will address in more detail.

1   Psychodynamic Phenomena and Their Explanation

Mardi J. Horowitz, M.D.

Clinicians working within a psychodynamic perspective have developed theories of the formation of neurotic symptoms. These theories involve wishes, fears, and unconscious conflict. They also involve information processing, a theory of unconscious mental processes aimed at reducing potential anxiety by instituting a variety of defensive avoidances. The validity of these explanations has yet to be established scientifically. Nonetheless, the phenomena of interest within psychodynamics are of great importance, for the episodes of experience involve human passion.

Psychodynamic theory had its major root in Freud's psychoanalytic theory. Much has been added since then, and the theory is in need of upgrading and revision. Efforts to revitalize psychodynamic theory may be aided by a rapprochement with cognitive psychology, especially in view of the return in academic psychology to an interest in issues of thought and the subjective experiences of memory, personal intention, and emotion.

The issue of unconscious emotional conflict now lies not only within the domain of psychoanalysis but in what might be called a gap between psychodynamics and information-processing sciences such as cognitive psychology (Wegman 1985; Bowers and Meichenbaum 1984; Edelson 1984; Erdelyi 1984). A bridge across this gap might now be built to the advantage of both disciplines. This chapter looks toward that gap and some ideas for bridging it from the psychodynamic perspective; the next chapter, by George Mandler, addresses some of the same issues from a cognitive psychology perspective. The ensuing chapters are varied plans toward a possible architecture for such bridges.

In this chapter, I shall review some salient features at the core of contemporary psychodynamic work. In particular, I will address the problem of inferring unconscious and defensively aimed processes regulating the conscious representation of thought and emotion. A possible convergence with the theoretical construct

3

of mental schemas[1] will be a part of that introduction. Then I will discuss the omissive and intrusive phenomena that have long been anchoring points of efforts at psychoanalytic types of explanation. I will provide an overview of some major explanations, giving definitions for terms likely to be part of an eventual lexicon to be used in common as part of a dialogue across disciplines.

Contemporary Psychodynamic Issues

Major disagreements within psychoanalytic theory have centered on issues of how to describe inferred unconscious mental processes. The attempts at description began within an id psychology that emphasized unconscious instinctual drives. An ego psychology followed that emphasized unconscious defensive operations. A structural model that emphasized conflict between reality, ego, id, and superego factors seemed for a time to work to explain interaction of forces impacting on the subjective experiences and action choices of the individual. Then controversies emerged between this classical dynamic point of view and the object relations schools, which held a variety of views centered on unconscious schemas of self and others. A new synthesis between classical psychodynamics and object relations perspectives is now being attempted in the field, and the key issues are summarized elsewhere (Kernberg 1976; Greenberg and Mitchell 1983; Horowitz 1987). This synthesis requires a finer level of theorizations about the specifics of inferred conflict and how the mental phenomena of interest are formed. Cognitive psychology may help to provide the theory and language useful in this enterprise, just as psychodynamic observations may provide cognitive psychology with a useful classification theory of phenomena suggestive of emotional conflict and intrapsychic stress.

I am using the term *psychodynamic* because the word *psychoanalytic* is often used to refer to particularly Freudian theory, practice, and modes of training clinical practitioners. Psychodynamic theory contains psychoanalytic theory and additional perspectives or revisions, such as those of Jung, Sullivan, Kelly, and members of later generations. The key sectors of psychodynamic theory in need of refinement and change have to do

---

1. I use the modern plural of *schema*, *schemas* instead of the classical plural, *schemata*. As mentioned in the preface, the choice is left to the individual authors in this work.

with emotion, especially defenses against unwanted moods, emotional pangs, or surges of dangerous desire.

What is psychodynamics? The word itself has come to imply a conflict of impulsive aims and moral values. Psychodynamics concerns configurations of interaction between wishes, the threats anticipated to arise if wishes are expressed, and the regulatory processes used to cope with or defend against this conflictual situation. The impulsive and defensive aims of a psychodynamic configuration influence conscious experience and motoric action. Yet important elements in this configuration are believed to remain beyond the conscious recognition of the subject even when they may be readily recognized or strongly inferred by an observer. We need more theory about the nature, function, and layers of the unconscious mental processes involved.

Cognitive psychology has turned attention to how unconscious or preconscious information processing takes place. Theory from cognitive psychology may help in the resolution of problems in psychodynamic theory. One obstacle is that the theories involved in cognitive psychology are often tested in studies of response to stimuli that emphasize memory or performance tasks. The situations often involve neutral stimuli or contrived analogies of social and emotional contexts. The subjects are often normal college students. Much might be gained by extending this arena to include persons caught up in the stress of neurotic conflicts, enmeshed in dilemmas evocative of high emotion and experiencing lapses of volitional, conscious control over their own representational consciousness. Some observations may be made on the mind in conflict that cannot be made when the mind, in less conflict, is integrating diverging forces.

The Unresolved Issue of Unconscious Defensive Operations

As it happens, there exists in psychodynamic theory a theme that is not well represented in many current cognitive science theories: the theme of defensive aims, processes, and outcomes; the area encompassed by the term *defense mechanisms*. Defense mechanisms include repression, suppression, undoing, reaction formation, role reversal, isolation, projection, regression, and denial. The validity of the entire theory of unconscious defense is widely supported in psychodynamics, yet many scholars working in cognitive science would challenge the validity of that theory.

Defenses are believed to be heightened in the conditions of high emotion, stress, and conflict that characterize the phenomenon of interest in psychodynamics. The integration of cognitive perspectives into psychodynamic theory will require attention to these conditions and to the validity of revised ways of examining the general topic of defensive operation.

Defensive operations can be described in terms of levels of conscious self-awareness. A person may be conscious of certain ideas and feelings and be most reluctant to communicate them, even in a frank and direct conversation with a relatively safe companion. Because of the nature of the situation, the person may want to reveal, even confess, the theme and yet at the same time may want to avoid the threat of embarrassment that might come as a consequence of communicating inner ideas and feelings. The person in this conflict may bring up the theme and yet consciously inhibit the expression of facets of it. These inhibitions may be guards on the words selected for speech, the facial muscles used to form expressions, the visual images conjured as metaphors. Although such defenses are conscious efforts at suppression, there may be unconscious processes that leak expressions into any of these modes, leading to slips of the tongue, micromomentary facial grimaces, and give-away metaphors.

Despite the unintended giveaways of what is consciously thought in a communicative situation, this type of defensiveness is not at the core of theories about what is often called "the dynamic unconscious." The core psychodynamic theories of defense infer much more in the way of unconscious motives and processes. These unconscious motives affect not only communications but intrapsychic, conscious representations. The motives include the wish to avoid unpleasant, overwhelming, or out-of-control states of mind. In effect, some unconscious processes anticipate such outcomes. To prevent the displeasure or threat anticipated, ideas and emotions are inhibited from a conscious representation that would otherwise occur. Such theories imply a great deal of computation within a dynamic sector of unconscious mental processes, dynamic in the sense that it deals with wishes, fears, and conflicts between goals.

This type of inhibition before consciously representing a motivated train of ideas that otherwise could and would become conscious has been regarded as the prototype of *repression*. Even though Freud ([1900] 1953) provided a cognitive model of how repression might operate, most dynamic explanations of phenomena suggestive of repression have focused on *why* the inhibition occurs rather than *how* ideas are prevented from becoming episodes of self-reflective awareness. Explaining why a defensive maneuver might occur is valuable, but much may be gained by adding to such efforts explanations of how defensive operations outside awareness might be accomplished. For example, we know that there are several modes of representation:[2] image and enactive systems as well as lexical ones are included. How are inhibitions distributed across modes for conscious representation? Are inhibitions of translation of information from one system of representation to another mode included in a repressive effort? What are the effects of nonrepresentation versus the immediate forgetting of what has been consciously represented? How might defensive inhibitions relate with equally defensive facilitations or dysinhibitions of substitutive thoughts or feelings? Can the facilitation of some emotional themes reciprocally inhibit the arousal of other emotion systems? These questions would be of equal interest to cognitive psychologists were the theoretical constructs of unconscious defensive operations seen as having potential validity.

The potential validity of a theoretical construct would be supported by its power in explaining phenomena that were hard to account for in other ways. Phenomena of psychodynamic relevance are ones that have been believed to demand this type of explanation.

Phenomena of Psychodynamic Relevance

Psychodynamic clinicians have indicated the types of phenomena that suggest unconscious conflict between impulsive and defensive aims. These would be the phenomena to explore in research attempting to converge psychodynamic and cognitive points of view. These phenomena possess the same feature: they are deflections from ordinarily intended flows of conscious awareness. That is, they are *intrusions* of the unexpected or *omissions* of the representations expected from conscious awareness.

OMISSIVE PHENOMENA

Some omissions of representation suggest the possible operation of unconscious inhibitory processes because the missing expe-

2. A glossary of definitions of some key terms such as *repression* and *representation* will be found at the end of this chapter.

riences can be accessible to conscious experience in other states of mind. In addition, the person may consciously wish to form the missing experience, but the intention is unsuccessful for a time. Omissive phenomena include such experiences as the following:

1. *Repressive or Dissociative Episodes in Awareness*
These phenomena consist of being unable to recall memories or to organize and produce information in one state of mind to the degree that the information can be represented in another state of mind. Among the important phenomena are a loss of memory for significant events that ought to be remembered, as occurs during experiences during periods called fugue states or dissociative episodes. In multiple personality cases, the memories of one "personality" may not be available when another self is dominant. In hypnosis, age regression may be used to recapture memories that otherwise cannot be formed by volitional conscious effort. The everyday aspects of this type of omissive phenomena include the forgetting of dreams that are later recalled and momentary forgetting, as in tip-of-the-tongue phenomena. Slips of the tongue are not just intrusions of the wrong name or word, they sometimes involve significant omissions of the word or phrase the person planned to say. Blocks in normally flowing creative efforts are also a variety of omissive experience.

2. *Segregated Episodes in Awareness.*
These phenomena consist of being unaware in one modality of an expression in another mode of representation. One example is not understanding in word representation the meaning of a current, vivid, self-produced visual image. Another example is being reflectively unaware of making certain bodily gestures or of exhibiting certain physiological arousal patterns that have a clear, emotional impact on others. In other instances, the person may be unaware of responding to a trigger stimulus with emotional arousal or derailment of ongoing thought, even when others can observe and understand the apparent cause-and-effect sequence.

3. *Conspicuous Inattention*
These phenomena include avoidance or forgetfulness with respect to important issues. An important example is the denial of stressful news. Another example is neglecting work on projects about which one feels in conflict. In addition, some persons at times conspicuously fail to learn the actual traits of companions interacting with them and so do not adapt to recurrent difficult situations impeding a mutually gratifying engagement.

INTRUSIVE PHENOMENA

Intrusions suggest the probability of unconscious motives and unconscious inhibitory effects as well. An unbidden experience is intrusive not only because it is out of joint with the immediately preceding conscious thought and feeling tone in an important way, but because the person either does not like the intrusion or is very surprised by it. In addition, conscious defensive efforts to dispel the intrusive idea by suppression may be unsuccessful. Intrusive phenomena include such experiences as the following:

1. *Peremptory Ideation*

These phenomena include the unbidden repetition of unwelcome ideas and feelings. Such intrusive ideas may occur in any mode of representation. Recurrent obsessional worries and paroxysms of doubt often take a lexical form. Repetitions of traumatic events often take form in the imagery system of the original perception: auditory images repeating memories of explosions, visual imagery repeating memories of gruesome scenes or the face of a deceased relative, olfactory imagery repeating the smells of burning flesh. Intrusive emotions are often felt in bodily terms, not as pure affect but as complex constellations of emotion and vague ideas as in nameless dread, searing pangs of remorse, shimmering waves of potential shame. Repetitions of warded-off but insistent wishes may take the form of bodily representations, perhaps in disguised form as in certain tics and mannerisms that repeat themselves in spite of conscious efforts at suppression. Recurrent bad dreams, slips of the tongue, and bad turns to what began as pleasant reveries are everyday aspects of thinking in ways contrary to volitional intentions. What is true of thought is of course true of action, and peremptory actions include temper tantrums, child abuse, compulsive eating, and an immense variety of purposive but consciously unintended, unsuccessfully suppressed, or unsuccessfully repressed behaviors.

2. *Repetitive Irrational but Systematic Views*

These phenomena include shifts in one's conception(s) of self or others from views relatively appropriate to actual situations to specifically distorted or irrational views. One example is attributing unwanted aspects of self to others. A common intrusive experience is the sudden shift from feeling competent to feeling the self as incompetent in a situation. Compulsive reenactments of specific maladaptive interpersonal relationship patterns are seen throughout the psychiatric personality disorders.

Unconscious Fantasies

The intrusion of situationally inappropriate and rationally un-wanted and unfounded views of self and others often contains a pattern. The specific pattern may have occurred in the relation-ships of the developmental past. The schemas involved may have been formed first in early childhood. Although within psycho-dynamic theory there is unresolved debate over what kinds of early transactions lead to subsequent adult neurotic personality disorders, there is general consensus about the importance of early experiences in leading to important, influential, persisting, but unconscious fantasies or role relationship models about the attributes of self and others and their scripts for interaction.

Explanations of Intrusions and Omissions That Involve the Dynamic Unconscious

Explanations for some intrusions and omissions include as factors the effects of high emotion, conflicting intentions, and resultant stress. Cognitive explanations tend to focus on the loss of capacity or the overload of systems as a result of these conditions. These systems are not conscious, and might be called the *organizational and computational unconscious.* Psychodynamic explanations allude to similar derailments of smooth information processing but tend to skip over any details of how such deviations from ordinary consciousness might occur. In addition, psychodynamic explanations emphasize processes inferred to be an aspect of what is often called the *the dynamic unconscious,* because it postulates wishful motives, and defensive ones as well, in con-flictual but active configuration. Some omissions and intrusions are seen as purposive results stemming from disguised wishes or unconscious defenses rather than only as errors in unconscious formative processes due to stress and overload. Three types of theory about the dynamic unconscious have been of interest: the signal anxiety theory, the special states theory, and the schematic repertoire theory.

1. *Signal Anxiety Theory*

According to this theory, it is assumed that unconscious wishful fantasies or traumatic memories in need of mastery *could* be-come conscious representations except that such expressions are inhibited by the forces of regulation motivated by antici-pated threats and defensive aims. That is, because of signal anxiety (unconsciously anticipating a threat if conscious representation, emotional expression, or action occurs), maneuvers such as *repression* are instigated. This has been called Freud's ([1926] 1959) second theory of anxiety and is fundamental to current psychodynamic theory. The sectors of cognitive science that are most relevant to the signal anxiety theory of unconscious defense are those that concern memory and associational networking, especially as organized by emotion (e.g. Anderson and Bower 1973; Bower 1981). These cognitive theories, however, deal with defense, if at all, in terms of conscious intentions such as efforts at thought *suppression* once a representation has formed, so they do not overlap with the psychodynamic concept of inhibition of contents prior to representation on the basis of an unconscious appraisal of threatening consequences were representation to occur.

2. *Special States Theory* Another view is that at least some "unconscious fantasies" are formed in a *special state of consciousness*, perhaps one induced by psychic trauma. These fantasies recur only in a repetition of that state. The reason is that these special states may utilize a different organization of systems than those subsuming ordinary states of consciousness. Called the "hypnoid state" by Breuer, a mentor and colleague of Freud, this special mode is described in their joint work on the traumatic causation of hysteria (Breuer and Freud [1895] 1958). Freud later rejected this explanatory principle. The special state was also called "co-consciousness" by Prince and referred to as dissociation by Janet and others, as summarized by Ellenberger (1964). More recently, other works from cognitive psychology have utilized such concepts in models of memory nodes and networks (e.g., Hilgard 1977; Kihlstrom 1984).

3. *Schematic Repertoire Theory* Yet another view is that "unconscious fantasies" are formed by inner motives or situational triggers that can activate specific schematic propositions in the repertoire of organizers of the individual. This repertoire of person schemas contains archaic components that can never be erased. Such early schemas of self and others are held in check (in terms of acting as organizers of conscious representations) by later developments. For example, mature concepts of self will modulate, contain, and integrate immature self schemas. Mature *role relationship models*, mapping attributes of self and other and the sequence of interactions,

modulate and integrate more primitive ways of handling issues such as those of sex and power. Nonetheless, in a kind of parallel processing, earlier forms continue an unconscious appraisal of current events, possibly following primitive association and sequencing rules such as the magic-logic of "primary process" thinking. Freud formed but did not develop such theory; Jung (1959) focused more in this direction. It was elaborated within psychoanalysis by such diverse theoreticians as Klein (1948), Fairbairn (1954), Jacobson (1964), Kernberg (1980), Knapp (1981), Gedo and Goldberg (1973), Kohut (1977), and Horowitz (in press). This schema theory is also called object relations theory.

At the deepest level of unconscious processes involved in motivation, the schematic forms might be based on how genetic codes unfold. These codes would be instinctive or "wired-in" givens for attachment bonding, fight-flight behavior, sexual behavior and other biologically based drives for meeting organismic and species survival needs. In development, various types of learning would affect how these *built-in unconscious schemas* evolved into an adult repertoire of schemas.

Information organized by such unconscious schemas could enter into the arousal of bodily organ systems and thereby gain conscious representation as a sensation of felt emotion or as self-observation of muscle tensions. Access to conscious symbol systems such as images and words might occur only through this indirect route or as in a person recognizing and symbolically naming the overall state of mind organized by a prevailing *self schema* or *role relationship model*.[3]

The schematic repertoire theory is not incompatible with the special states or signal anxiety theories of how unconscious motives, conflicts, and defenses might lead to some omissive or intrusive phenomena in conscious experience. Rather, it supposes an additional level and provides a structural explanatory construct for the special states theory, in the idea of multiple self schemas in the repertoire of a single individual. This additional level of schemas has also been proposed as an explanatory construct in the parallel distributive-processing theories of cognitive psychology (Rummelhart et al. 1986).

Within psychodynamic perspectives it may be necessary to

3. As mentioned earlier, some underlined terms are found in a lexicon at the end of this chapter.

describe how defenses may work in terms of not only inhibitions of conscious representations but inhibitions of schemas. Memories, ideas, fantasies, and emotions in an *inhibited dynamic unconscious* might be motivated toward and capable of conscious representation but successfully sealed from direct expression by such inhibitions. (Of course, other forms of regulation and control such as facilitation or dysinhibition of reciprocal inhibitors of that which is warded off could also occur. For clarity, just inhibition will be mentioned here.) Schemas such as those of self, others, and scripts for interactive sequences might be motivational and capable of organizing a state of mind of the individual, and yet successfully sealed from doing so in a *deep dynamic unconscious*, a different level of expressive tendency countered by defense than the *inhibited dynamic unconscious*. Once again, the latter contains configurations pressing toward but prevented from representation, while the former contains configurations pressing toward but prevented from a status of organizing and patterning a state of mind.

The schematic repertoire theory of psychodynamics may be able to use and eventually converge with the schema theories of cognitive psychology. The issues of defense as a valid unconscious aspect of information organization at the schematic level would have to be addressed. Meanwhile, as a further introduction to key themes in the works that follow, we may consider the apparent properties of the schematic level of unconscious mental operations.

Properties of Schemas

The properties of schemas that seem relevant to both psychodynamics and cognitive psychology can be summarized from ones suggested by such authors as Bartlett (1932); Asch (1946); Piaget (1979); Neisser (1976); Markus (1977); Hastie (1981); Bandura (1982); Marcel (1983a, 1983b); Taylor and Crocker (1981); Ostrom, Pryor, and Simpson (1981); Krumhansl and Castellano (1983); Horowitz and Zilberg (1983); Lubrosky (1984); Horowitz (1987); and Rummelhart et al. (1986).

1. Schemas summarize past experience into holistic, composite forms, thus allowing incoming information to be measured against the existing composite for "goodness of fit." In forming a conscious experience of thought, information from the internal

composite may be used to fill out forms missing from the external stimulus information. Although this may enable rapid perception in some ways, it may also lead to patterned and recurrent errors in interpreting and responding to stimuli that are actually different from the schematic forms.

2. Schemas that accord well with real stimuli permit a more rapid organization of incoming information than those that match poorly with the actual situation. Therefore, schemas enhance stimuli that fit the schematic view and impede recognition of stimuli that do not.

3. Schemas of self and others enhance a sense of temporal continuity and coherence of identity. Conversely, aschematic conditions seem to lead to a loss of coherence of identity, experienced subjectively and symbolically as fragmentation of self and a loss of location of self in time.

4. As an encapsulation or a composite view of a role, a person schema can be named. Hence, it may be possible to represent consciously by symbols a meaning form that usually operates unconsciously. Naming and conscious reflection may facilitate changes in how schemas are used in appraisals, decisions, and plans and may lead to rehearsals that can build new schemas or that integrate schemas into supraordinate forms. Such deliberate trials and rehearsals may lead to changes in automatic behavioral sequences. This is believed to be a change process in dynamic, cognitive, and behavioral psychotherapies.

5. Multiple schemas may be applied simultaneously and unconsciously to the interpretation of a given stimulus such as a changing social situation. Multiple parallel channels operate in unconscious information processing, but conscious thought tends to proceed in one or only a few channels. As a result, there may be competition for priority and goodness of fit among these multiple schemas as information processing results approach channels for conscious representation. The outcome of the competition determines which derivatives of schemas and information processing gain conscious recognition.

6. Schematic transorderings of information may effect the "mysterious leaps" between body and mind, mind and body, as well as the mysterious transmissions of mood between persons in families, group processes and crowds.

Schema theory is a point of convergence between psychodynamics and cognitive science and yet is the most speculative domain in either set of theories. Perhaps this very mov-

ing edge quality will be the best place for dialogue; perhaps it will turn out to be too ambiguous. In either instance, a dialogue can also focus on issues of the representation of ideas, memory, and serial associative elaborations of meanings as related to emotion.

Conclusions

Theory dictates how one observes as well as how one explains. Psychodynamic theory leads to a classification of phenomena in terms of deflections from volitional consciousness and rationally intended actions: as intrusions and omissions. The validity of this classification is itself subject to doubt, and further exposition of it will be given in Chapter 3. Even when there is agreement on the occurrence and description of a phenomenon, there are disagreements as to the processes that lead to its formation. The dynamic unconscious is a theoretical construct about formative processes, and there is much disagreement over the necessity of this construct. Its feature of inferred unconscious wishful motives and defensive opposing aims is not generally accepted in cognitive psychology. Alternative explanations can and will be given for the phenomena in question in subsequent chapters.

By looking at the same type of phenomena, a dialogue between diverse theories may lead to clearly defined hypotheses that can be subjected to validation or invalidation. Psychodynamic observations have located interesting phenomena; however, psychodynamic theory tends to have a clearer approach to issues of memory and representation and how information processing of conflictual motives may affect emotion. Its core theory of unconscious defense may itself have to be revised. At the level of sequencing ideas and feelings, psychodynamics would benefit from trying to infer how, rather than just why, unconscious defensive operations are carried out. At the same level, cognitive psychology might benefit from asking whether or not different processes operate in states of very high emotion and conflict from those that handle more neutral levels of information. Memory and associational networking might conceivably follow different rules in states of high excitation when the self organization is in a state of threat. Most studies of normal populations in situations of feigned emotion or externally induced mood would not elicit the relevant phenomena for finding such differences, were they indeed to exist.

Recurrent maladaptive alterations in self-esteem and interpersonal behavior patterns such as those seen in the personality disorders involve both intrusive instantiation of inappropriate schemas and omissions of realistic learning of new schemas from actual situations. An area of potential convergence of cognitive psychology upon psychodynamics would be on how to describe and explain such phenomena. Perhaps a theory of schemas could lead to improved ways of understanding the cycles of mood states of a single individual and how social triggers led to the repetition of a neurotic interpersonal pattern. For psychodynamics this would deepen theory about how identification, transference, and mourning of personal losses occur as exemplars of structural (schematic) change processes. For cognitive psychology this would mean a new look at top down organizations of lower-order schemas, for example how varied types of overall self schematization might affect lower-order schemas involved in such processes as those subsuming perception, memory, and emotion.

The construct of the dynamic unconscious is by its inferred nature a set of psychological meanings constantly undergoing symbolic transformations. Since the unconscious is by definition unavailable to the subject at the time of its supposed activity, this kind of science of meanings and information processing will have to rest on the people who observe the patterns of the subject. The rules for that type of scientific methodology have not been evolved, but they can be developed. What follows are strivings toward that goal.

Appendix: A Trial Lexicon of Terms for a Dialogue Between Psychodynamics and Cognitive Psychology

Each part of this book begins with a presentation that describes some phenomena from a psychodynamic perspective, phenomena that suggest explanations in terms of unconscious formative processes. These presentations are discussed from a variety of points of view, including those of cognitive psychology, which provide alternatives to the concept of unconscious wishes and defensive counter-aims. The goal is a dialogue between participants who usually talk within their own schools and in their own technical languages.

In order to have such a dialogue, a shared lexicon is desirable, and an approach to one is presented here. As a precursor to and as a result of the discussions of the authors of this book, a series of definitions of terms was developed and revised. Giving the revised version now will help the reader understand the vocabularies in this chapter and those that follow. Because the theories are not agreed upon, not all authors agree exactly upon the terms and definitions provided in this lexicon.

The terms that follow are loosely ordered, starting with motives, then going on to organizers of motives, representations of motives, and levels of formative processes leading to representation and expression.

Motives   A non-specific term referring to the forces, drives, needs, pressures, or reasons a mental process occurs. Motives include the intrinsic properties of a system of mental processes, which when exercised affect the processes of some other mental system. There may be motives to do as well as motives to not do an act or function.

Psychodynamic configuration   A constellation of motives defined at the psychological level in terms of meanings. These meaning forms may include wishes, fears, and defensive strategies. A psychodynamic configuration of conflict usually involves a *wishfully impulsive aim*, a *threat* along the way toward the initially desired goal, and a *defensive posture* compromising the wish to avoid its feared consequences.

Schemas (or schemata)   Usually unconscious meaning forms that can serve as organizers in the formation of thought. Schemas influence how motives reach awareness or action as well as how stimuli are constructed into awareness of perception. Schemas tend to endure and to change slowly as the integration of new understandings modifies earlier, basic forms. Small-order schemas can be nested into hierarchies acting as larger order or supraordinate schemas. Person schemas are such high-order, holistic views of individuals, either of self or others.

Instantiated schemas   Working models composed of elements from inner schematic repertoires and constructed views of perceived and current external situations.

Scripts   Schemas for sequences of representations, functions, or actions.

Role relationship models   Inner schemas and scripts blueprinting interpersonal transactions as well as views of self and others.

Codings   Prerepresentational retentions of information.

Representations   Iconic or symbolically encoded meanings that are capable of either conscious awareness or communicative expression. Representations occur in modes such as images, lexical (verbal) propositions, or enactive (motoric) propositions. The formative substrates for images may be organized into auditory, gustatory, kinesthetic, visual, olfactory, and tactile modes. Substrates for word representations may be organized in various languages such as English, German, and French. Substrates for motoric tensions may be subdivided into striated- and smooth-muscle systems.

Repression   The state of actively inhibiting codings that would otherwise be represented because of expressive motives.

Suppression   The state of consciously terminating the active representation of unwanted ideas and feelings.

Organizational and Computational Unconscious   The elements active at this level of mental function are parts of automatic processes and cannot become conscious except as the subject may make inferences about his own non-conscious computations.

Inhibited Dynamic Unconscious   The elements active at this level of mental function are not consciously represented but are coded in such a way that they could be conscious. There is sufficient motivation for these codings to become conscious representations were it not for avoidant operations set in the pathway to reflective awareness. The contents of the inhibited dynamic unconscious are in a state of repression because of these inhibitions.

Deep Dynamic Unconscious   The elements active at this level of mental function are needs or drives at the motivational and schematic core of the mind. These elements have no direct access to conscious contemplation and so are represented, if at all, only as secondary symbolic derivatives. Processing incoming information according to these elements can, however, lead to responses in emotional systems. The resulting bodily sensations can then be translated to other modes of conscious representation, such as words or images.

References

Anderson, J. R., and G. H. Bower. 1973. *Human Associative Memory.* New York: Winston.

Asch, S. 1946. Forming impressions of personality. *Journal of Abnormal and Social Psychology* 41:258–90.

Bandura, A. 1982. The self and mechanisms of agency. In J. Suls, ed., *Psychological Perspectives on the Self*, vol. 1. Hillsdale, N.J.: Erlbaum.

Bartlett, R. C. 1932. *Remembering: A Study in Experimental and Social Psychology.* Cambridge: Cambridge Press.

Bower, G. H. 1981. Mood and memory. *American Psychologist* 36:129–48.

Bowers, K. S., and D. Meichenbaum. 1984. *The Unconscious Reconsidered.* New York: Wiley.

Breuer, J., and S. Freud. [1895] 1958. Studies on hysteria. *Standard Edition vol. 2.* London: Hogarth Press.

Edelson, M. 1984. *Hypotheses and Evidence in Psychoanalysis.* Chicago: University of Chicago Press.

Ellenberger, H. F. 1964. *Discovery of the Unconscious.* New York: Basic Books.

Erdelyi, M. 1984. *Psychoanalysis: Freud's Cognitive Psychology.* New York: Freeman.

Fairbairn, W. 1954. *An Object Relations Theory of Personality.* New York: Basic Books.

Freud, S. [1900] 1953. The interpretation of dreams. *Standard Edition, vol. 4.* London: Hogarth Press.

———. [1923] 1961. The ego and the id. *Standard Edition, vol. 19.* London: Hogarth Press.

———. [1926] 1959. Inhibition, symptoms, and anxiety. *Standard Edition, vol. 20.* London: Hogarth Press.

Gedo, J., and A. Goldberg. 1973. *Models of the Mind.* Chicago: University of Chicago Press.

Greenberg, J. R., and S. A. Mitchell. 1983. *Object Relations in Psychoanalytic Theory.* Cambridge, Mass.: Harvard University Press.

Hastie, R. 1981. Schematic principles in human memory. In E. T. Higgins, C. P. Herman, and M. Zanna, eds., *Social Cognition: The Ontario Symposium.* Hillsdale, N.J.: Erlbaum.

Hilgard, E. R. 1977. *Divided Consciousness: Multiple Controls in Human Thought and Action.* New York: Wiley.

Horowitz, M. J. Forthcoming. *Introduction to Psychodynamics.* New York: Basic Books.

———. 1987. *States of Mind: Configurational Analysis of Individual Psychology.* 2d ed. New York: Plenum Press.

Horowitz, M. J., and N. Zilberg. 1983. Regressive alterations in the self-concept. *American Journal of Psychiatry* 140 (3):284–89.

Jacobson, E. 1964. *The Self and Object World.* New York: International Universities Press.

Jung, C. G. 1959. *The Archetypes and the Collective Unconscious.* New York: Pantheon.

Kernberg, O. 1976. *Object Relations Theory and Clinical Psychoanalysis.* New York: Aronson.

———. 1980. *Internal World and External Reality: Object Relations Theory Applied.* New York: Aronson.

Kihlstrom, J. F. 1984. Conscious, subconscious, unconscious: A cognitive perspective. In K. S. Bowers and D. Meichenbaum, eds., *The Unconscious Reconsidered.* New York: Wiley.

Klein, M. 1948. *Contribution to Psychoanalysis.* London: Hogarth Press.

Knapp, P. H. 1981. Core processes in the organization of emotions. *Journal of the American Psychoanalytic Association* 9:415–34.

Kohut, H. 1977. *The Restoration of the Self.* New York: International Universities Press.

Krumhansl, C., and M. Castellano. 1983. Dynamic processes in music perception. *Memory and Cognition* 11:325–34.

Luborsky, L. 1984. *Principles of Psychoanalytic Psychotherapy.* New York: Basic Books.

Marcel, A. J. 1983a. Conscious and unconscious perception: An approach to the relations between phenomenal experience and perceptual processes. *Cognitive Psychology* 15:238–300.

———. 1983b. Conscious and unconscious perception: Experiments on visual masking and word recognition. *Cognitive Psychology* 15:197–237.

Markus, H. 1977. Self-schemas and processing information about the self. *Journal of Personality and Social Psychology* 35:63–78.

Neisser, U. 1976. *Cognition and Reality.* San Francisco: Freedman.

Ostrom, T. M., J. B. Pryor, and D. D. Simpson. 1981. The organization of social information. In E. T. Higgins, C. P. Herman, and M. Zanna, eds., *Social Cognition: The Ontario Symposium.* Hillsdale, N.J.: Erlbaum.

Piaget, J. 1979. *Structuralism.* New York: Basic Books.

Rummelhart, D. E., et al. 1986. Schemata and sequential thought processes in PDP models. *Parallel Distributed Processors: Studies in the Microstructure of Cognition.* Cambridge, Mass.: MIT Press.

Taylor, S. E., and J. Crocker. 1981. Schematic bases of social information processing. In E. T. Higgins, C. P. Herman, and M. Zanna, eds., *Social Cognition: The Ontario Symposium.* Hillsdale, N.J.: Erlbaum.

Wegman, C. 1985. *Psychoanalysis and Cognitive Psychology.* New York: Academic Press.

2 Problems and Directions in the Study of Consciousness

George Mandler, Ph.D.

My comments are motivated by a tradition, recently rehabilitated, that is concerned with the functions and structures of consciousness. It has its antecedents in the early twentieth-century concerns in European psychology with *Bewusstseinspsychologie,* the psychology of consciousness. During the past twenty years there has been a revival of theoretical concern with the justification of consciousness and its uses and functions. Theoretical cognitive psychology of the past quarter century—in contrast to the psychologies of the nineteenth century—has assumed the dominance of unconscious processes in the explanation of thought and action. Locutions such as mental structures, representations, processes, and schemata imply a vast armamentarium of unconscious functions, few of which may be directly evident in consciousness. Once theoretical arguments assign major functions to unconscious mechanisms, questions about what the functions of consciousness might be arise naturally. What is the process whereby unconscious mechanisms affect conscious ones? How do we get from the unconscious to the conscious? Such questions certainly are a fundamental change from questions raised in the nineteenth century when Hartmann (1869) and Freud were vilified for even suggesting unconscious processes. It is not surprising that the discussions about the utility of consciousness are prevalent among the cognitive sciences, while conversely, discussions about the functions of the unconscious are dominant among clinical and personality theorists. In the tradition of psychodynamic theories, the latter are concerned with the fine structure of unconscious motivational mechanisms, just as the major concerns of the cognitive enterprise focus on the fine structure

This chapter incorporates passages and arguments from my *Cognitive Psychology: An Essay in Cognitive Science* (Hillsdale, N.J.: Erlbaum, 1985) and presents further developments of those ideas. This work has been supported by grants from the National Science Foundation and the Spencer Foundation.

of unconscious knowledge structures. However, it has been in the experimental and cognitive tradition, in part due to the behaviorist interlude, to question the transition from unconscious to conscious, to ask about the function of consciousness.

The quest for theories of consciousness—how unconscious processes generate or determine conscious states—exemplifies the major change in our view of consciousness since the nineteenth century. Whereas the then-dominant belief was in rational conscious humanity (and the notion of unconscious forces was an unlikely proposition), psychologists in the twentieth century have concentrated most, if not all, determinants of behavior in hypothetical or at least unconscious forces, and what needs to be explained is how those unconscious events interact with the subjective reality of consciousness.

Thus, not only are the unconscious forces and processes in need of theoretical exploration and inferences, but for purposes of investigation and understanding, we need to provide theoretical structures that give us some access to a systematic view of consciousness. The individual experiences feelings, attitudes, thoughts, images, ideas, beliefs, and other contents of consciousness, but these contents are not accessible to anyone else. Briefly stated, it is not possible to build a phenomenal psychology that is shared. Once private consciousness is expressed in words, gestures, or in any way externalized, it becomes necessarily a transformation of the private experience. No theory external to the individual (one that treats the organism as the object of observation, description, and explanation) can, at the same time, be a theory that uses private experiences, feelings, and attitudes as data (Gray 1971). Events and objects in consciousness are not available to the external observer without having been restructured, reinterpreted, and appropriately modified. The content of consciousness (or for that matter of unconsciousness) is not directly available as a datum in psychology. And there are additional vexations about consciousness.

First, the very nature of an interrogation affects the reported content of consciousness. More basically, the act of examination itself may affect the individually observable conscious contents, since the conscious act of interrogating one's conscious content must occupy some part of the limited capacity of consciousness. As a result, the available content is altered by the process of interrogation.

A second problem to be faced is the fact that the contents of consciousness are not simply reproducible by a one-to-one mapping onto verbal report. Even if these contents were always couched in language—and they are not—some theory of transmission would be required. As a result, we are faced, on the one hand, with individuals' knowledge of their conscious states and, on the other, with the psychologist's theoretical inference about those contents, on the basis of whatever data, including introspective reports, are available. Both sorts of knowledge may be used as relevant to the construction of a psychology of cognition, although it may in principle be impossible to determine, in any exact sense, the relation between these two interpretations of consciousness.

To the individual, experience *is* a datum, and, as a consequence, personal theories about one's own structures are, within limits, testable by direct experience. These individual, personal (and often cultural) theories of the self are both pervasive and significant in explaining human action, but they cannot—without peril—be generalized to others or to the species as a whole (Mandler and Mandler 1974).

Current Attitudes Toward Consciousness

Two attitudes toward consciousness have marked the extremes of its treatment in the recent history of psychology. One attitude considers consciousness ineffable and unapproachable as a scientific enterprise; the other sees it within the grasp of current technology. The former, a behaviorist formulation, made its escape from knotty problems by asserting that consciousness is epiphenomenal, an uninteresting and functionally impotent by-product of observable behaviors.[1] The other view, sometimes derived from current artificial intelligence endeavors and the theory of automata, asserts its domain over consciousness by suggesting possible relations between consciousness and computing machines.

Arguments against the epiphenomenal positions cannot be based merely on its outright rejection of the importance of consciousness nor on the assertion that modern approaches make

1. However, the assignment of consciousness to an epiphenomenal by-product of human mental life is not restricted to behaviorists; see for example such neuroscientists as Harnad (1982).

the study of consciousness possible. Rather, it should be shown, as it surely can, that consciousness does in fact have important functions in human thought and action. The behaviorist analysis of consciousness was more of an avoidance than a critique; a point made even by B. F. Skinner (1964), who bravely tackled the problem of these "private events." We should pay attention to his argument because it does not deny conscious events. Skinner finds them mostly unnecessary "way stations" between stimuli and behavior. And his assertion that some of our intentions and thoughts, rather than being initiators of actions, are often glosses on ongoing or incipient actions, needs to be taken seriously—if only because it is sometimes accurate. We must not merely show that the epiphenomenalists' analyses fail to do justice to human consciousness but demonstrate positively what it is that consciousness does, what it is needed for, what we cannot and would not do or think if there were no such mechanism.

Another psychological argument about conscious inefficacy has been made on the basis that "awareness often occurs *after* the events or the actions that Mind might be supposed to control" (Gregory 1981, 474, emphasis added). I shall argue that an important effect of consciousness is actually to be found in events *subsequent* to the occurrence of the aware state.

The issue of possible conscious states of computers or complex automata in general requires a different argument. Consider a comparison between two questions: first, whether computers can be conscious, and, second, whether they can be pregnant. The latter question is ridiculous because we know that in order to be pregnant one needs certain equipment and that certain prior conditions must be fulfilled. Computers do not have the equipment, and they cannot engage in the prior activities necessary for pregnancy. In the case of consciousness, we have little knowledge about the equipment or conditions necessary in order to reach that state. It is this absence of knowledge, this ignorance, that makes the question reasonable for some. However, if one were to consider first what it is that "being conscious" implies in terms of processes and equipment, one might be able to ask the question sensibly. At the present time, it is an empty question.

The proper question is *not* whether computers can be conscious, or whether certain automata might display consciouslike characteristics, but what theoretical account we can give for consciousness. If one were to assert that computers can be conscious, one would have to specify how that function is achieved or to imply that the equipment (as in pregnancy) is comparable to human constituents.

The renewed interest in consciousness has been informed in important ways by careful analyses of its occurrences and explorations of its implications. In addition, attempts to understand its role have played a part in practically all the various strands that have produced modern cognitive psychology.

Generally in the past, consciousness has been assigned an essentially passive role in the information flow. Thus, George Miller asserted that it is "the *result* of thinking . . . that appears spontaneously in consciousness" (Miller 1962; see also Lashley 1923).[2] Current positions generally subscribe to an active view of conscious states and processes (e.g., Marcel 1983b; Norman and Shallice 1980; Shallice 1972). Similarly, conscious processing as discussed by Posner and Snyder is "a mechanism of limited capacity which may be directed toward different types of activity" (1975, 64). Consciousness is "directed toward" an unconscious structure or process, which then becomes "conscious."

These various positions on consciousness can be divided into ones that follow the traditional view that conscious contents occur when a structure is pushed, pulled, or illuminated into consciousness (e.g., Freud [1900] 1975; Posner and Snyder 1975; Shallice 1972), and ones that state that only the results or consequences of mental processes are conscious (e.g., Lashley 1923; Miller 1962; Mandler 1975a). What all of them have in common is some implication of identity or overlap between consciousness and (focal) attention.

The Construction of Conscious Experience

The constructivist approach to the occurrence of consciousness (Marcel 1983b) presents a new development toward a model of active consciousness. This position asserts that most conscious states are constructed out of preconscious structures in response to the requirements of the moment. Consciousness is a constructivist process in which the phenomenal experience is a specific

2. Early information-processing models viewed consciousness as a central controlling system (e.g., Atkinson and Shiffrin 1968). Similar and more explicit suggestions have been made recently in the context of a central "information exchange" that services (unconscious) distributed special processors and produces a "stable and coherent global representation that provides information to the nervous system as a whole" (Baars 1983).

construction to which previously activated schemata have contributed.[3] We can be conscious only of experiences that are constructed out of activated unconscious structures.

From the viewpoint of schema theory (see my discussion in Mandler 1985), we are not conscious of the process of activation or the constituents of activated schemata. A conscious experience is constructed out of activated schemata that represent one or more of the constituent processes and features of the experience. The schemata that are available to constructive consciousness must be adequately activated and must not be inhibited. The resulting phenomenal experience is "an attempt to make sense of as much data as possible at the highest or most functionally useful level possible" (Marcel 1983b).

We are customarily conscious of the important aspects of the environs but never conscious of all the evidence that enters the sensory gateways or of all our potential knowledge of the event (see also Köhler 1929). A number of experiments have shown that people may be aware of what are usually considered higher-order aspects of an event without being aware of its constituents. Experimental subjects may be able to specify the category membership of a word without being aware of the specific meaning or even the occurrence of the word itself (Marcel 1983a; Fowler et al. 1981). A similar disjunction between the awareness of categorical and event-specific information has been reported for some clinical observations (e.g., Warrington 1975).

Conscious constructions represent the most general interpretation that is appropriate to the *current* needs and scene in keeping with both the intentions of the individual and the demands of the environment. In the absence of any specific requirements (internally or externally generated), the current construction will be the most general (or abstract) available. Thus, we are aware of looking at a landscape when viewing the land from a mountaintop, but become aware of a particular road when asked how we might get down, or of an approaching storm when some dark clouds "demand" inclusion in the current construction. In a problem-solving task, we will be conscious of those current mental products that are closest to the subjectively most likely solution to the problem.

---

3. See also Treisman and Gelade (1980) for a constructive view of focal attention that is very similar to Marcel's proposition.

When Are We Conscious and
What Are We Conscious of?

What are the most obvious occasions for conscious constructions? First, we are often conscious in the process of acquiring new knowledge and behavior. Even though not all new learning is conscious, the construction of complex action sequences and the acquisition or restructuring of knowledge require conscious participation. In the adult, thoughts and actions are typically conscious before they become well integrated and subsequently automatic. Learning to drive a car is a conscious process, whereas the skilled driver acts automatically and unconsciously. It follows that conscious evaluations of one's actions should more often reflect those mental and behavioral events that are in the process of being acquired or learned and less often the execution of automatic sequences.[4]

The sequence in learning from conscious to unconscious is not ubiquitous. It is reversed in the infant (J. M. Mandler 1984), and apparently is reversed in simple adult functions, such as in perceptual learning and in the acquisition of some simple motor skills, where skills learned unconsciously may only subsequently be represented in consciousness. The products of such acquisitions may also be divided into conscious and unconscious ones, a distinction that is found in the division between declarative and procedural knowledge. In addition, shifts from unconscious to conscious processing occur frequently. For example, the pianist will acquire skills in playing chords and trills and in reading music that are at first consciously represented but then become unconscious. However, the analytic (conscious) mode is used when the accomplished artist practices a particular piece for a concert, when conscious access becomes necessary to achieve the proper emphases, phrasings, and tempi. One wonders to what extent this process is similar to that seen in the psychoanalytic encounter where automatic (unadaptive?) ways of dealing with the world are the object of a conscious theory of their function and then become accessible for conscious repair and change.

Second, conscious processes are frequently active during the exercise of choices and judgments, particularly with respect to action requirements. These choices, often novel ones, require

4. For an early and a late statement of this conclusion, see Bain ([1859] 1875, 541) and Anderson (1982).

the consideration of possible outcomes and consequences. However, it seems to be unreasonable to postulate that a conscious state exists only when selections are required. How do we account for our continuous consciousness of the surround? I suggest, as a first approximation, that a state of consciousness exists that is constructed out of the most general structures currently being activated by current concerns and environmental requirements. It provides, in consciousness, a specification in rather abstract terms of where we are and what we are doing there. Choice and selectivity will then produce changes in that current "reflection" of the state of the world.

Third, conscious processes exercise an important function during "troubleshooting." Thus, relevant aspects of the world are brought into consciousness when automatic structures somehow fail in their functions, when a particular habitual way of acting fails or when a thought process cannot be brought to an appropriate conclusion. The experienced driver becomes "aware" of where she is and what she is doing when something new and different happens; when a near miss, a police car, or an unexpected traffic light is suddenly registered. The troubleshooting function of consciousness permits the repair of current troublesome or injudicious processing, and subsequent choice from among other alternatives. These arguments stress the role of consciousness in action, in contrast to a contemplative, reflective view of conscious states.

A current conscious state will be changed if it does not account for (make sense of) a situation in which the available alternatives fail to meet some criterion for action or problem solving. Our expectations may be violated when the environment keeps changing or when some external piece of evidence cannot be assimilated. Change is defined in terms of our current conscious state and the particular events that are acceptable and expected within that state. A jogger may not notice, or be conscious of, others along her path because they have always been encountered before, but she will become aware of an elephant. On the other hand, the jogger who revels in the loneliness of the long-distance runner may well become aware of intrusive others, whether elephants or not. When the environment is constant, we respond to internal demands and use those for conscious constructions. Daydreamers are unaware of their surrounds, until such time as a shout or a raindrop demands to be accounted for in the stream of consciousness.

One of the functions of the conscious construction is to bring two or more previously unconscious mental contents into direct juxtaposition. The phenomenal experience of choice seems to demand exactly such a function. We usually do not refer to a choice unless there is a "conscious" choice between two or more alternatives. The attribute of "choosing" is applied to a decision process regarding two items on a menu, several possible television programs, or two or more careers, but not to the decision process that decides whether to start walking across a street with the right or the left foot, whether to scratch one's ear with a finger or with the ball of the hand, or whether to take one or two sips from a cup of hot coffee. The former cases involved the necessity of deciding between two or more alternatives, whereas the latter involve only the situationally predominant action. However, given a cup of hot coffee, I may "choose" to take one very small sip, or I may "choose" to start with my right foot in a hundred-meter race, given certain information that it will improve my time for the distance. In other words, even for alternatives that are usually selected unconsciously, special conditions, such as possible consequences and social factors, may make it likely that conscious constructions will be involved and make those choices "conscious" too.

Choosing is carried out by complex unconscious mechanisms that have direct connections with and relations to action systems and other executive systems. Consciousness permits the redistribution of activations, so that the choice mechanism operates on the basis of new values of schemata and structures that have been activated in the conscious state. The mechanisms that select certain actions among alternatives are not themselves conscious, but the conditions for new choices are created consciously, thus giving the appearance of conscious free choices and operations of the will (see Norman and Shallice 1980). What consciousness does permit is the running through of potential actions and choices, the coexistence of alternative outcomes, the changing of weightings of currently active schemata in the direction of one that promises a greater likelihood of success, and so forth. The simultaneity of objects and events in consciousness makes possible the occurrence of new associations, of previously quiescent cognitive structures, now activated by the conscious structures. In problem-solving activities, our consciousness of various alternatives, of trying out solutions, is often taken for the process that determines the final outcome. Although these conscious activities are related to the unconscious activations and processing that they influence, they are not the only forces that directly determine actions. Their similarity, in many situations, to unconscious activities leads to the conclusion that thought determines actions directly. But thought, defined as conscious mental contents, is in one sense truly epiphenomenal and in another determinative of action. It determines further unconscious processes but is several steps removed from the actual processes that pervade our mental life. Conscious thoughts are good first approximations, in fact the best available, but they are no substitute for the representations and processes that need to be postulated for an eventual understanding of human action and thought.

The above discussion is intended primarily to account for changes in the contents of consciousness; it does not address itself to the other sense of consciousness, the distinction between being conscious and not being conscious as a continuing state. The state of "being conscious," as distinct from being unconscious and unreceptive to any internal or external evidence, implies some continuously activated mental structures that define the current state of our world and the expectations that such structures always generate.

Consciousness and Experiential Report

The fact that people develop representations not only *of* their perceptions, thoughts, and actions but also *about* these products is now well established. One of the important distinctions that need to be kept in mind in studying consciousness is between the underlying structures and schemata that construct thought and actions on the one hand, and the cognitive structures that are glosses on, describe, and sometimes access the determining structures. I have called these *secondary structures*. These secondary structures are particularly evident with respect to action systems, which often remain permanently inaccessible to conscious construction. Frequently it is such secondary schemata about our thoughts and actions, represented in personal theories and beliefs, that are available to consciousness. What is represented in consciousness and available for introspective reports is often not a reflection of the operating processes and structures at all.

The most extensive and detailed discussion of the relation between putative cognitive processes and conscious reports has been presented by Nisbett and Wilson (1977). In areas as diverse as attribution studies, perception, problem solving, choice, prediction, and emotional reactions, they found convincing evidence of a lack of correlation between what people report to have experienced and what objectively took place. Only when conditions are salient and are themselves plausible causes of the actions they produce are these reports likely to be accurate. Nisbett and Wilson concluded that experiential reports "are based on a priori, implicit causal theories, or judgments about . . . a plausible cause of a given response" (1977, 231). These implicit theories and judgments are what I have called secondary structures. They are frequently the folk theories about thought and action that inform the members of a culture about plausible socially acceptable causes.

Whenever a conscious content is constructed that seeks to recover an intrapsychic series of events that occurred some time in the past, it should be obvious that such constructions will be influenced by current as well as past activations. As a result, introspective reports will very often reflect not what "actually" happened but rather what is the most reasonable construction at the moment of introspection (Nisbett and Wilson 1977).

What determines the content that is constructed? After all, what makes sense in one situation may not in another. Furthermore, what is functionally useful may be very specific, such as knowing where the butter is usually kept in the refrigerator, or quite general, such as knowing that butter knives are not appropriate for slicing cucumbers. The major sources of a particular construction are current tasks and contexts, intentions, and needs. Just as current perceptions are, within schema theory, seen as the result of both external evidence and internal processes (top down and bottom up), so is consciousness in general determined by activated higher-order structures as well as by the evidence of the surrounds. Interactive, reverberative top-down and bottom-up processes are usually conceptualized as the instantiation of schemata that receive initial activation from external evidence and once activated become selective in the direction and inhibition of activation. In contrast, structures that represent intentions and interpretations of situational requirements are activated primarily "top down"; they depend on prior evaluations and activations of situational identifications and interpretations, of current needs and goals. They need not receive activation from the physical evidence of our surrounds. In the normal course of events, it is such more abstract and general structures that define what we are doing, what we want to do, and what we need to do. Their special role is to satisfy situational and intentional demands. It is only when task and intention are narrowed down to particulars that less general and more specific schemata determine conscious constructions.

There is some circularity in my suggestion that higher-order structures mold current consciousness but that constructed consciousness is not a reflection of or identical with existing unconscious structures. These higher-order structures are themselves "existing structures." To insist that these structures are highly abstract is one possible solution to this apparent paradox. By abstractness I mean that the instantiation of these structures may take on a large number of different variables and values of variables. Conversely, such structures maintain few default values as such. They are not active unless they take on specific evidence, specific information from the intra- or extrapsychic environment. In watching a play, one of the structures that constructs consciousness requires some information about plot features (who does what to whom?) and some identification of the dramatis personae. But there is no default value for the plot at this level—I do not assume that it is a murder mystery or a Shakespearean historical play if not enough information is available.

Since "intentions" are apparently one kind of structure that determines conscious contents, we must make a distinction between an intention as a theoretical, and as a subjective, state of affairs. As a theoretical state it embodies the notion of a goal, a future state of the world. However, subjective *awareness* of intentions may or may not parallel that theoretical state. Subjective intentions may frequently be more personal, often verbal, glosses on an ongoing sequence of action.

Consciousness is selective and responsive to both conscious and unconscious intentions. Its contents are obviously highly variable from time to time. One of the reasons for the rapid temporal change is that *only one conscious construction can be experienced at any one time*. The well-known ambiguous figures (whether ascending or descending staircases or young-and-old women) present one case where only one conscious construction for a given physical configuration is experienced, even though we know that two different ones are possible. A similar phenomenon occurs in the case of polysemous words. We know that the word *table* can refer to an object that occurs in rooms, or one that occurs in books, but we cannot think of the two meanings simultaneously. On the other hand when two separate objects are involved (as in the case of "A table of figures is on the dining room table") we have no difficulty in constructing a *single* conscious content.

Parenthetically I should note that consciousness necessarily is a serial system, if only as a consequence of the fact that only a single interpretation of an event is possible. The seriality of consciousness is one of the major solutions to a problem that has concerned contemporary theories of distributed parallel processing: how to produce serial out of parallel structures.

The Limitation of Conscious Experience

We are apparently never conscious of all the available evidence that surrounds us, but only of a small subset. What is the nature of that limitation? How much of our current surrounding or internal events can we represent in consciousness? Momentary consciousness is clearly limited. At the heart of historical concerns with conscious limitation is the notion that only a few (no more than six) "objects" can be apprehended by the mind at any one time.[5] Such a general characteristic of human functioning as limited attentional capacity should have a rather important role to play in thought and action. I assume in the first place that the limited capacity characteristic of consciousness serves to reduce further the "blooming confusion" that the physical world potentially presents to the organism. Just as sensory end organs and central transducers radically reduce and categorize the world of physical stimuli to the functional stimuli that are in fact registered, so the conscious process further reduces the available information to a small, manageable, and serial subset. The limitation of conscious capacity defines what is, in fact, cognitively manageable. Although we do not know why the reduction is of the magnitude that we observe, it is reasonable to assume that some reduction is necessary. Just consider a process of serial pairwise comparisons (in a choice situation) among n chunks in

5. William James firmly established the limited capacity concept as a cornerstone of our knowledge about consciousness/attention, and G. A. Miller (1956) made it a central thesis of modern approaches to human information processing.

consciousness; clearly the number n must be limited if the organism is to make a choice within some reasonable time.[6]

There are occasions and stimuli that demand conscious capacity and construction almost automatically. Among these are intense stimuli and internal physiological events such as autonomic nervous system activity. Whenever such events claim and preoccupy some part of the limited capacity system, other cognitive functions will suffer; they will be displaced from conscious processing, and problem-solving activities will be impaired. Particularly in the case of the interruption or failure of ongoing conscious and unconscious thought or action, the resultant visceral responses also require conscious representation and interfere even more severely with ongoing conscious activity (see Mandler 1979b for a review).

If we consider consciousness as an integrated construction of the available evidence—a construction that seems to be phenomenally "whole"—then it is likely that the limitation to a certain number of items, objects, events, or chunks refers to the limitation of these elements *within and by* the structures that determine the holistic conscious experience. The schema or schemata that are represented in the conscious construction are necessarily restricted to a certain number of features or relations. Cognitive "chunks" (organized clusters of knowledge) operate as units of such constructed experience. However, only a limited number of such chunks, themselves part of an organized whole, make up part of the current conscious experience. For example, as I look out my window I am aware of the presence of trees and roads and people, a limited number of individual organized schemata that make up "the view." I may switch my attention—reconstruct my conscious experience—to focus on one of these events and note that some of the people are on bicycles, others walk, some are male, some female. Switching attention (consciousness) again I see a friend and note that he is limping, carrying a briefcase, and talking with a person walking next to him. At that point, the trees, the people on bicycles, and so forth, are not part of my current consciousness any more. In each case

6. I have discussed elsewhere (Mandler, G. 1975b) the manner in which these momentary conscious states construct the phenomenal continuity and flow of consciousness. For other aspects of the limitation of conscious capacity, see Graesser and Mandler (1978), Mandler (1979a, 1980), Mandler and Graesser (1975), Miller (1956). On the phenomenon of subitizing, which provides extensive experimental evidence, see Kaufman et al. (1949) and Mandler and Shebo (1982).

a new experiential whole enters the conscious state and consists of new and different organized chunks.[7]

Consequences of Consciousness

I have mentioned earlier that one of the arguments against the causal efficacy of conscious states is that they usually occur *after* the event with which they are supposedly causally connected. The basis of that argument is found in the persisting speculations about mind-body relations, specifically about how it is that non-palpable conscious mental states could cause physical body events. I have discussed those implications elsewhere (Mandler 1985) and want to suggest here that conscious states can have effects on *subsequent* mental events and human, physical actions. In brief, I have developed the notion that events represented in consciousness activate relevant underlying structures.

Activation is necessary for structures to become incorporated into conscious states in the first place. We need to extend this notion to assert that the possible alternatives, choices, and competing hypotheses that have been represented in consciousness will receive additional activation and thus will be enhanced. This hypothesis of selective and limited activation of situationally relevant structures requires no homunculuslike function for consciousness in which some independent agency controls, selects, and directs thoughts and actions that have been made available in consciousness. The proposal can easily be expanded to account for some of the phenomena of human problem solving. Activation is necessary but not sufficient for conscious construction; it depends in part on prior conscious constructions. The search for problem solutions and the search for memorial targets (as in recall) typically have a conscious counterpart, frequently expressed in introspective protocols. What appears in consciousness in these tasks is exactly those points in the course of the search when steps toward the solution have been taken and a choice point has been reached at which the immediate next steps are not obvious. At that point the current state of the world is reflected in con-

---

7. The organized (and limited) nature of consciousness is illustrated by the fact that one is never conscious of some half-dozen totally unrelated things. In the local park I may be conscious of four children playing hopscotch, or of children and parents interacting, or of some people playing chess, but a conscious content of a child, a chess player, a father, and a carriage is unlikely (unless of course they form their own meaningful scenario).

sciousness. That state reflects the progress toward the goal as well as some of the possible steps that could be taken next. A conscious state is constructed that responds to those aspects of the current search that *do*, although partially and often inadequately, respond to the goal of search. Consciousness at these points truly depicts way stations toward solutions and serves to restrict and focus subsequent pathways by selectively activating those that are currently within the conscious construction.

This function of consciousness is generally conservative in that it underlines and reactivates those mental contents that are currently used in conscious constructions and are apparently the most immediately important and useful ones. It also encompasses the observation that under conditions of stress people tend to repeat previously unsuccessful attempts at problem solution. Despite this unadaptive consequence, a reasonable argument can be made that it is frequently quite useful for the organism to continue to do what is apparently successful and most appropriate. However, as a corollary of this mechanism, events that are totally disruptive and inappropriate to the current context should have a quite different function. There is no obvious conscious construction that can be adopted when both the currently dominant action tendencies and their possible alternatives are evidently inadequate. At this point new structures, some of which may have been previously at some relatively weakly activated level, will be called into service.

The Adaptiveness of Consciousness

There are many senses of the notion of adaptation; the most widely used is the adaptive consequence of evolutionary processes. However, the consequences of evolutionary processes are not necessarily adaptive, nor are adaptive functions of an organism necessarily the consequences of selective evolutionary processes focused on the structure or function in question. Utility and universality alone do not argue for evolutionary selection. Just consider that human beings who write universally use their hands; nobody would argue, however, that evolutionary processes have selected the human hand for its writing utility. Furthermore, the evolution of complex functions is typically the result of the evolution of a wide variety of functions and structures, sometimes entirely unrelated. Consciousness is probably one such complex function. No single event in our evolutionary history is likely to have resulted in all the aspects of consciousness discussed here.

Consciousness as a phenomenon emerges slowly and gradually as a characteristic of very complex organisms, with very complex minds. The conscious state occurs when a second-order serial representation of mental events becomes useful or necessary. Thus, bringing two or more previously unrelated mind-contents together or into juxtaposition, or characterizing the most important self-relevant aspects of the current state of the world, or trying to understand the reasons or causes of a current action (running off in parallel), requires a system of representation that can function independently of, and in parallel with, the other current processes that our mental apparatus engages. We are too often overwhelmed by the apparent palpability of consciousness, of its peculiar I-related status, of apparent things going on "in our heads." In contrast, such a secondary system, sometimes commenting, sometimes monitoring, sometimes just automatically occurring, happens to have the peculiar characteristic of consciousness or awareness. One might imagine that it could have had some other manifestations or characteristic, but it just happened to be constructed in this particular way in the course of human evolution.

As far as speculation about the evolution of consciousness is concerned, I suggest that the need for and the selection of some secondary monitoring system occurred at some time when the complexity of tasks to be accomplished and information to be monitored became sufficiently demanding. The secondary "conscious" system may have emerged with respect to only one of the functions of consciousness described here. Subsequently, and in a homologous fashion, the system was adopted for other functions and—over the millennia—developed into a complex system of its own. We still develop consciousness ontogenetically, as it is needed and made possible by the requisite underlying structures. The most striking representation in consciousness, of course, is the representation of the self, of the structures and schemata that represent knowledge of who we are, what constitutes our needs and wishes, fears and hopes. This ability to be aware of ourselves is not a separate characteristic developed or given at some blinding historical point. Rather it is the result of the ongoing development of consciousness.

This approach neither adopts nor rules out the possibility that the conscious system developed in the prehuman phase of evolution. Thus, complex animals may have limited secondary "conscious" systems as a result of common ancestry, or they may have developed it independently in response to the press of complex processing, or they may not have developed it at all.

This point of view does not regard consciousness as an all-or-none phenomenon, that is, either you have "it" or you do not. Rather it emerges in response to the demands of processing in special domains and in different domains at different times. Consciousness may or may not be a function exclusive to human beings, and more important, it did not suddenly or recently come into existence. Such a view is in direct contrast to philosophers and psychologists who give it a uniquely human flavor, circumscribed by language and human mentality. In particular it denies the claims of Julian Jaynes (1976) that consciousness emerged some few thousand years ago.

Current conscious contents are constructed by a higher-order schema or structure that accesses two or more lower structures and integrates them into a single conscious construction that responds to the requirements of the moment. This assumption is supported by the inability of amnesic patients to engage in such novel constructions, and by some of Marcel's work on the construction of perceptual phenomena. One of the consequences of such a position is that, rather than "consciousness" being a given characteristic of an individual person or animal, the individual has the potential of constructing a conscious content if and only if some higher-order structure is available that can construct a particular conscious content at any given moment. Thus, people are not and cannot be conscious of just anything in their environments or in their psychic armamentarium, but rather one may become conscious of specific kinds of events in one's internal or external environment. Which kinds of events are included depends on the prior experience one has had with the phenomena and experiences in question. This accounts for painters and musicians being able to perceive (consciously) aspects of art and music, for example, that the untrained eye and ear does not perceive. Prior experience with the constituents is necessary and some initial construction, need for, and knowledge about relevant higher-order structures is necessary. In other words, the development of consciousness about certain objects and events may be a slow and cumulative process.

This kind of approach may also be useful in understanding the development of consciousness in the young child. Thus, we would not expect that an infant suddenly becomes conscious of its entire world, but rather that the ability to construct conscious contents will depend on the child's developing experience with its surroundings. For example, one would expect the child to form early consciousness about its caretakers, about hunger management, and so forth. On the other hand, consciousness about language would take quite some time as specific initial structures are developed that then may become the constituents of higher-order structures that construct conscious knowledge about the use and structure of language. Thus, the metalinguistic abilities of children, that is, what it is that the child knows about language that the spider does not know about its web, will emerge with the development and mastery of language (Gleitman, Gleitman, and Shipley 1972).

One can take an additional speculative leap and consider the problem of animal consciousness. It may not be the case that mammals are either conscious or not, but rather that the ability to construct conscious contents has developed somewhere within the mammalian groups but the richness and extent of consciousness depends on the richness and extent of their underlying cognitive structures that encode and structure their ability to know and deal with the world. Cognitively relatively sophisticated animals, such as the primates, will have a more extensive conscious apparatus than less sophisticated animals such as rodents or canines. The question may be not whether the animal is conscious but rather what the limited number of events and objects are about which it can be conscious.

Discrepancies, Errors, and Mindlessness

I have been concerned with the emotional and, particularly, the autonomic consequences of interruptions and discrepancies for over twenty years (Mandler 1964, 1984). The relevance to emotion is that the violation of expectancies, the perception of discrepancies, and the blocking or interruption of action are all sufficient antecedents for autonomic (sympathetic) arousal. Briefly, my position has been that the constructed conscious experience is derived from representations of cognitive evaluations on the one hand and autonomic or visceral perception on the other. The resultant conscious content is unitary; it "feels" like a singular emotion and not like a composite, either of the underlying representations or of more basic fundamental emotions. This approach makes comprehensible the uniqueness of each emotional experience (no situation is the same or is evaluated in the same way as any other), and explains the similarities of different emotions (they all have as a part the visceral experiences and also the similarities among different situations and actions that generate the evaluative cognitions).

Thus, discrepancies and interruptions are one of the major sources for emotional experiences in that they provide one component for the emotional construction. We have found in our laboratory studies that even the most innocuous discrepancies, such as a banal but unexpected ending to a simple story, will produce increases in heart rate. When a discrepancy occurs, the mental system may easily find some way to assimilate it, but if not then a number of different consequences may follow. In particular, when current activations from the environment—the causes of the disruption—do not readily find an appropriate structure that accommodates their characteristics, then spreading activation will eventually find some alternative ones that provide support for the new evidence generated by the world. That sequence is what is usually involved in coping. In more extreme cases continuous interruptions and discrepancies may lead to panic and other emotional reactions.

The ability to create interruptions, new ways of seeing the world out of joint, seems to be necessary for scientific as well as aesthetic creations. An interesting example is found in the French psychoanalyst Lacan's use of the totally unexpected shortening and interruption of his sessions with clients. One participant reports his personal experience with one of Lacan's unexpected short sessions: "The ending of the session, unexpected and unwanted, was like a rude awakening, like being torn out of a dream by a loud alarm. (One patient likened it to *coitus interruptus*.)" These short sessions seem to facilitate access to the unconscious and "the combined pressure of the shortness of the sessions and the unpredictability of their stops creates a condition that greatly enhances one's tendencies to free-associate" (Schneiderman 1983).

I want to conclude with an agenda of issues to be faced by a contemporary psychology of consciousness. What are the goals of a satisfactory cognitive theory? What major problems are still in need of explanation and decomposition? One of the questions to be raised here concerns the conditions under which omissions from and intrusions into consciousness occur. It has been implied by some that such occurrences always involve the "operation of emotional motives and unconscious defensive operations." Let me start with the assertion that omissions and intrusions occur continuously as part of the normally functioning human mental system, that it may well be useful to study them in such normal circumstances, and that the study of the everyday functions of the human mind may well be a useful path toward understanding pathology, just as the investigation of pathology may be useful in understanding normal functioning.[8] In particular, it is useful to keep in mind that much of everyday human thought is constituted of "intrusions." We are continuously reminded nonvoluntarily and automatically of important and unimportant facts, of ways of solving a problem, of "irrelevant" associations—none of which can, by any stretch of the imagination, be said to be "dynamically" important. In fact, we can produce these intrusions of facts and memories in the laboratory without much effort. Current work on human errors has opened up the possibility of understanding the more mundane errors of commission and omission that people produce (e.g., Norman 1981, 1983), even though too little attention has been paid to emotional factors in these occurrences. The kind of theory that makes it possible for us to understand human error is presumably the same kind of theory that permits us, or will permit us, to understand the more dramatic and "dynamic" instances of omissions and intrusions in detail.

Specifically, I am describing activation and schema theory, the notion that previously activated schemata interact to facilitate and/or inhibit other structures and schemata. These schemata are similar if not identical with Freud's notion of the unconscious, preconscious, and conscious. In order for a structure to participate in a conscious construction, it needs to be "preconscious" or previously activated. Thus, when we find intrusions in everyday life or in the dynamic cases, we look for the schemata that have been activated and that now manifest themselves in new and often unexpected conscious contents. In the laboratory we can produce these activations experimentally and find automatic and

---

8. If we were to follow Freud and call these occurrences everyday psychopathologies, we would miss the goal of understanding the normal mind, nonpathological and adaptive as it presumably is.

involuntary errors and perceptions and memories that can be shown to be specifically a function of these prior activations. See for example the experiments on priming, on illusory conjunctions, and on blindsight (Neely 1977; Treisman and Schmidt 1982; Weiskrantz et al. 1974).

Many of these intrusions and omissions are nonmotivated in the usual sense of the term; they occur automatically and "mindlessly." One of the problems we have in showing the operation of "mindless" parallel systems in so-called rational thought is that we are still children of the nineteenth century and believe in the rationality of humankind. Rather, we should be more concerned how mindless mechanisms produce the appearance of rationality. The goal of theoretical psychology is to explain and explicate such commonsense notions as rationality, even to show how our phenomenal world is created. To assert human rationality (or intelligence or emotion) as the starting points of psychological explanation begs the question. It is proper to ask whether human thought is rational—assuming that we can agree on some precise definition of rationality. But commonsense appearances are and must be assumed to be the products of psychological mechanisms. We need to show how rational and irrational thought and action are constructed. Similar leftovers of the nineteenth century are notions such as will, purpose, and—as I have noted above—intentions. Even concepts like mental comparison and internal controls beg for a more explicit theoretical treatment. Recall my notion of secondary schemata—commentary and glosses on our thoughts and actions that are produced by unconscious processes. In many cases conscious intentions, purposes, and the sense of control are such commentaries, folk and idiosyncratic models and theories intended to make our behavior sensible to ourselves and others. They are not psychological mechanisms as such. Similarly, to say that a memorial content remains "active" because it is important to the individual requires some theoretical explication of the emergence of the commonsense notion of importance.

In short, we need to be aware of lurking homunculi, particularly when they are no more than metaphors and cultural interpretations rather than operative psychological mechanisms. How underlying representations construct specific mental conscious contents then emerges as the central theoretical enterprise that still confronts us.

References

Anderson, J. R. 1982. Acquisition of cognitive skill. *Psychological Review* 89:369–406.

Atkinson, R. C., and R. M. Shiffrin. 1968. Human memory: A proposed system and its control processes. In K. W. Spence and J. T. Spence, eds., *The Psychology of Learning and Motivation*, vol. 2. New York: Academic Press.

Baars, B. J. 1983. Conscious contents provide the nervous system with coherent global information. In R. J. Davidson, G. E. Schwartz, and D. Shapiro, eds., *Consciousness and Self-Regulation*, vol. 3. New York: Plenum Press.

Bain, A. [1859] 1875. *The Emotions and the Will*. London: Longmans, Green.

Fowler, C. A., G. Wolford, R. Slade and L. Tassinary. 1981. Lexical access with and without awareness. *Journal of Experimental Psychology: General* 110:341–62.

Freud, S. [1900] 1975. The interpretation of dreams. In Standard Edition, vols. 4 and 5. London: Hogarth Press.

Gleitman, L. R., H. Gleitman, and E. F. Shipley. 1972. The emergence of the child as grammarian. *Cognition* 1:137–64.

Graesser II, A. C., and G. Mandler. 1978. Limited processing capacity constrains the storage of unrelated sets of words and retrieval from natural categories. *Journal of Experimental Psychology: Human Learning and Memory* 4:86–100.

Gray, J. A. 1971. The mind-brain identity theory as a scientific hypothesis. *Philosophical Quarterly* 21:247–52.

Gregory, R. L. 1981. *Mind in Science*. New York: Cambridge University Press.

Harnad, S. 1982. Consciousness: An afterthought. *Cognition and Brain Theory* 5:29–47.

Hartmann, E. von. 1869. *Philosophie des Unbewussten*. Berlin.

Jaynes, J. 1976. *The Origin of Consciousness in the Breakdown of the Bicameral Mind*. Boston: Houghton Mifflin.

Kaufman, E. L., M. W. Lord, T. W. Reese and J. Volkmann. 1949. The discrimination of visual number. *American Journal of Psychology* 62:498–525.

Köhler, W. 1929. *Gestalt Psychology*. New York: Liveright.

Lashley, K. S. 1923. The behavioristic interpretation of consciousness. *Psychological Review* 30:237–72, 329–53.

Mandler, G. 1964. The interruption of behavior. In D. Levine, ed., *Nebraska Symposium on Motivation: 1964*. Lincoln, Nebr.: University of Nebraska Press.

————. 1975a. Consciousness: Respectable, useful, and probably necessary. In R. Solso, ed., *Information Processing and Cognition: The*

Loyola Symposium. Hillsdale, N.J.: Erlbaum. (Also in Technical Report no. 41 (1974), San Diego: University of California, Center for Human Information Processing.)

———. 1975b. *Mind and Emotion.* New York: Wiley.

———. 1979a. Organization and repetition: Organizational principles with special reference to rote learning. In L. G. Nilsson, ed., *Perspectives on Memory Research.* Hillsdale, N.J.: Erlbaum.

———. 1979b. Thought processes, consciousness, and stress. In V. Hamilton and D. M. Walburton, eds., *Human Stress and Cognition: An Information Processing Approach.* London: Wiley.

———. 1980. Recognizing: The judgment of previous occurrence. *Psychological Review* 87:252–71.

———. 1984. *Mind and Body: Psychology of Emotion and Stress.* New York: Norton.

———. 1985. *Cognitive Psychology: An Essay in Cognitive Science.* Hillsdale, N.J.: Erlbaum.

Mandler, G., and A. C. Graesser II. 1975. *Dimensional Analysis and the Locus of Organization.* Technical Report no. 48. San Diego: University of California, Center for Human Information Processing.

Mandler, G., and B. J. Shebo. 1982. Subitizing: An analysis of its component processes. *Journal of Experimental Psychology: General* 111:1–22.

Mandler, J. M. 1984. Representation and recall in infancy. In M. Moscovitch, ed., *Infant Memory.* New York: Plenum Press.

Mandler, J. M., and G. Mandler. 1974. Good guys vs. bad guys: The subject-object dichotomy. *Journal of Humanistic Psychology* 14:63–87.

Marcel, A. J. 1983a. Conscious and unconscious perception: Experiments on visual masking and word recognition. *Cognitive Psychology* 15:197–237.

———. 1983b. Conscious and unconscious perception: An approach to the relations between phenomenal experience and perceptual processes. *Cognitive Psychology* 15:238–300.

Miller, G. A. 1956. The magical number seven, plus or minus two: Some limits on our capacity for processing information. *Psychological Review* 63:81–97.

———. 1962. *Psychology: The Science of Mental Life.* New York: Harper and Row.

Neely, J. H. 1977. Semantic priming and retrieval from lexical memory: Roles of inhibitionless spreading activation and limited-capacity attention. *Journal of Experimental Psychology: General* 106:226–54.

Nisbett, R. E., and T. D. Wilson. 1977. Telling more than we can know: Verbal reports on mental processes. *Psychological Review* 84:231–59.

Norman, D. A. 1981. Categorization of action slips. *Psychological Review* 88:1–15.

———. 1983. Design rules based on analyses of human error. *Communications of the ACM* 4:254–58.

Norman, D. A., and T. Shallice. 1980. *Attention to Action: Willed and Automatic Control of Behavior.* Technical Report no. 99. San Diego: University of California Center for Human Information Processing.

Posner, M. I. and C. R. R. Snyder. 1975. Attention and cognitive control. In R. Solso, ed., *Information Processing and Cognition: The Loyola Symposium.* Potomac, MD: Erlbaum.

Schneiderman, S. 1983. *Jacques Lacan: The Death of an Intellectual Hero,* Cambridge, Mass.: Harvard University Press.

Shallice, T. 1972. Dual functions of consciousness. *Psychological Review* 79:383–93.

Skinner, B. F. 1964. Behaviorism at fifty. In T. W. Wann, ed., *Behaviorism and Phenomenology.* Chicago: University of Chicago Press.

Treisman, A. M., and G. Gelade. 1980. A feature-integration theory of attention. *Cognitive Psychology* 12:97–136.

Treisman, A. M., and H. Schmidt. 1982. Illusory conjunctions in the perception of objects. *Cognitive Psychology* 14:104–41.

Warrington, E. K. 1975. The selective impairment of semantic memory. *Quarterly Journal of Experimental Psychology* 27:635–57.

Weiskrantz, L., E. K. Warrington, M. D. Sanders and J. Marshall. 1974. Visual capacity in the hemianoptic field following a restricted occipital ablation. *Brain* 97:709–28.

2   A Clinical Psychodynamic Perspective

Part 1 ended with a debate over the issue of inferring unconscious intentions and purposes that might lead to siutations of conflicted motivation in the production of phenomena of intrusion and omission. In order to address this issue in more detail, the phenomena of intrusive episodes of thought after recent life stresses is examined in Chapter 3. After a brief summary that seeks to validate the phenomena of intrusions, a case vignette is used to model the issues of representation and schema seen as salient by both authors in Part 1. Chapter 4 discusses that presentation from a cognitive science perspective; Chapter 5 from a psychoanalytic one. All three chapters in this part are concerned with discussing a key issue emergent from Part 1, that of unconscious defensive processes, and ways to challenge the validity of that theoretical construct from an eventually empirical perspective. Part 3 will then advance that empirical perspective.

3   Unconsciously Determined Defensive Strategies

Mardi J. Horowitz, M.D.

A psychodynamic configuration is one in which there are at least three factors: wishes; fears, including the threat of consequences if wishes are expressed; and defenses. Conscious representation of the configuration may be hindered by unconscious efforts at inhibition. This theory about dynamic unconscious mental processes underlies psychotherapies aimed at modifying unconscious defensive regulations of thought and the schemas that organize different states of mind. Further specification of this theoretical model in terms of cognitive operations is necessary in order to test its validity, revise it, and improve an understanding of change processes.

One obstacle in the path of this effort is that the psychodynamic model is quite general. The specifics of defensive components are often left ambiguous in clinical reports. This chapter aims to model the unconscious defensive components in a more specific way. To do so, a particular sector of motivation is considered—the aim to understand and master stressful life events in order to protect the self. A particular sector of defense is also considered—the inhibition and facilitation of conscious representations and unconscious schemas of self and other that organize thought and affect mood. In this sector, the expressive forces are those directed toward a recollection of associations to a stressful event. The threat caused by such recollection is that highly intense and potentially overwhelming emotions might occur, with entry into a mood state that cannot be dispelled. Defensive avoidances are noted in such states of mind as those of denial after a traumatic event.

Introduction: Intrusive Repetition After Stressful Life Events

Intrusive ideas and feelings related to and often directly depicting memories of traumatic perceptions are a cardinal symptom of the Post-Traumatic Stress Disorders (PTSD) and were described by Breuer and Freud in 1895. Intrusive ideas about a stressful event were found in 77% of a group of 66 patients with PTSD (Horowitz, Wilner, Kaltreider, and Alvarez 1980).

To validate the proposition that stressful perceptions tend to be repeated as memories because of unconscious rather than conscious motives, a series of experiments were conducted using films as the media for presenting the same stimuli to different subjects in different contexts. Contexts and demand sets mediating against a repetition of film memories were provided. Intrusive images of the stressful films occurred even in these contexts. I will briefly summarize these experimental studies as a validation of intrusive phenomena that suggests an unconscious motive toward repetition. Then I will report a clinical case as a model of inferred defensive processes operating against motives toward the repetition of a stressful memory, processes that can lead to phenomena of both intrusion and omission such as those discussed in Chapter 1.

Experiments on Intrusive Thought Induced by Stressful Perceptions

The hypothesis for the experimental studies was that stressful representations would tend to be repeated in thought, even in situations where the repetition would be contrary to conscious intentions and social demands. This proposition involved an explanatory theory that stated, in part, that stress-inducing representations such as those of traumatic events were retained in an active memory store that tended toward repeated conscious representation as words or images until the processing of the inherent information reached completion. "Completion" was defined as the achievement of a good match between representations of the current "reality" (inner and outer) and inner, mental, enduring propositions in schematic form. The "motive force" was seen as a "completion tendency." Intentions to avoid recollection were seen as an analogue to defense; such avoidances would lead to the experience of any repetition as having a quality of intrusiveness. That quality was quantified by specification of it in content analysis manuals. These manuals were followed by independent judges in scoring subject narratives reporting consciously experienced thoughts during a given time frame.

Methods

Films were shown to subjects as the means of reproducing the same stressful stimulus in the laboratory. Lazarus and his colleagues had used fear-inducing films depicting bodily injury in a variety of cognitive paradigms in which the fundamental outcome measures were physiological response and self-reports of emotion (Lazarus and Opton 1966). Ekman and his colleagues (1984) had used the same films to heighten emotion. The hypothesis was that a subject's experience of intrusive thoughts, as an outcome measure, would be greater after viewing stressful films than it would be after neutral control films. Moreover, it was predicted that these intrusive thoughts would occur more frequently in subjects who reported higher affective arousal during films and in subjects who had previously had higher rates of life stressors.

Using methods equivalent to those employed by Antrobus, Singer, and Greenberg (1966) for sampling a subject's ongoing conscious thought, I constructed a tone-matching task that required the subject to hear a sound, repeat it in memory, wait a time, and match a subsequent sound with it. To eliminate errors, the subject was instructed to avoid thoughts that would interfere with good performance on this test, which required rehearsal memory of the just-previous tone. This task created the analogy of a psychological conflict. After each short segment of sound matching (1 or 2 minutes), subjects wrote narratives of all the episodes of consciousness during the segment. Independent judges, using content analysis manuals for one type of judgment at a time, analyzed these reports of thought experiences for intrusive and repetitive thinking. Spearman reliability correlations between judges ranged from .85 to .99.

A variety of films were used in order to elicit a variety of emotional states. Most of the experiments used films depicting bodily injury threats to evoke fear and anger. A specially edited version of *John*, a film made at the Tavistock Clinic by J. and J. Robertson, poignantly illustrated the early separation of a child from its parents; it powerfully elicited sadness, especially in subjects who reported earlier parental losses on a life events questionnaire. In a separate study, pleasurable effects were evoked with an erotic film. In addition, there was a neutral film, which had human characters in an active and mildly humorous setting

(Horowitz 1975; Wilner and Horowitz 1975; Horowitz and Becker 1972; Horowitz and Wilner 1976).

The social demand set was to do well by making a few tone-matching errors. The subjects were motivated to avoid recollecting the film in order to succeed. This motive was intended to conflict with the hypothetical tendency toward the repeated representation of incompletely processed stress-inducing perceptions and reactive ideas.

Subjects were given different instructions, which systematically varied the demand sets. Some subjects were just asked to report thoughts. Other subjects were told of a special research interest in intrusive thinking and visual images. Intrusive images, if specifically defined, were linked randomly for some subjects to the idea of being a normal response to stress or, for other subjects, to an abnormal response by mentioning that they were minor equivalents of a pathological process that could lead to hallucinations. The data from 133 subjects after baseline, neutral film, and stress film conditions were examined using Finn's Multivariate Analysis of Variance (see Horowitz 1975).

Experimental Results

The hypothesis that intrusive and repetitive thoughts would occur most frequently following the stress film condition was confirmed. Only the change in film conditions exerted a significant effect on the level of intrusions into conscious awareness ($MS = 57.5$, $df = 2$, $F = 20.69$, $p < .001$) and let to direct repetitions of film concepts while attempting to concentrate on the signal detection task that followed ($MS = 146.5$, $df = 2$, $F = 49.1$, $p < .001$). Population differences, film order, the sex of subjects, and instructional demand did not exert a significant effect. Intrusions and film repetitions correlated positively only in the stress condition ($r = .51$, $p < .001$). Intrusions in the post-stress film condition occurred at about three times the rate found in thought samples taken during the same kind of tone concentration task after the neutral film. The demand set suggesting intrusions were abnormal responses reduced the frequency of such reports after the neutral film but not after the stress film. Overall, 77% of the 133 subjects were scored by judges of verbal reports as having at least one episode of intrusion following the stress condition. A group of 77 subjects also rated themselves after the stress film on a 1–100 "thermometer"-type scale for felt experiences of emotion and physical stress during the film. Felt emotion and physical stress were rated for the period of watching the film and correlated significantly and positively with intrusion levels during the subsequent perceptual task.

The experimental work indicated that intrusive thinking does increase after stressful perceptions despite situations and demands that would motivate subjects to avoid repetitions of memories of the films. One possible explanation is that the conscious intention not to think of the film is counteracted by some form of unconscious motive pressing toward conscious representation. Such experiments are only analogues of real-life stressors. And in these instances the defense against repetitive film memory was only a conscious intention to do well on a task that required attention if one was not to make errors and so appear less competent at it than others. This is not the same situation that is believed to be operative when unconscious defensive operations are inferred. To model this further required clinical studies of real-life stressors and conflictual emotional responses.

Clinical Investigation of Responses to Stress

In the study of responses to such real-life stressors as loss and injury or severe threat, it was clear that intrusive thinking, unbidden images, and bad dreams repeating aspects of the trauma persisted for some time. It is of great relevance that these intrusive experiences occur in phases. A phase characterized by intrusiveness may follow a relatively long period of denial in which significant omissions of memory and emotional reaction occur (Horowitz [1976] 1986).

I will summarize a contemporary psychodynamic theory to explain the interaction of motives toward repetition and toward the inhibition of repetition, which leads to intrusive thinking or significant omissions of thoughts about stress-related themes. Then I will give a more specific model, related to a case example.

Serious life events such as a loss or injury present news that will eventually change inner models, such as the schemas described in Chapters 1 and 2. But time is essential to review the implications of the stressful news and construct available options for response. The mind unconsciously continues to process important new information until there is a change in either the external stressful situation or the inner schemas so that the new reality and the inner models of reality reach accord. This important tendency to integrate reality and schemas can be called a *completion tendency.* Until completion occurs, the new information and reactions to it are stored in active memory.

According to this theory, active memory contents will be transformed into conscious representations whenever the process is not actively inhibited. The tendency for repeated representations will end only when these memories and memories of their associations are no longer stored in active memory. The reason for conscious representation is to gain use of the special properties of conscious thinking for resolving incongruities and discrepancies and deciding how to deal with problems and conflictual alternatives.

In the instance of very important contents, termination in active memory will not occur with decay of codings, but only when the processing of the stored information is complete. Memories of stressor life events will be especially encoded or rehearsed in unconscious but active memory banks. When information processing is complete, the bad news that was coded in active memory has, in effect, been transformed to schemas. Until then, there will be a comparison of the new event with preevent schemas. Because a stress event is, by definition, a significant change, there will be a discrepancy. That discrepancy evokes emotional responses that are also represented, thereby becoming part of the associated elements in the constellation stored in active memory. As emotional responses surge in intensity, the person may unconsciously anticipate entry into an uncontrolled, distraught, and overwhelmed state of mind. The dread of this threat is the motive for defensive controls.

When other tasks are more immediately relevant or when dreaded emotional states of mind are a threat, controls are initiated. This feedback modulates the flow of information and reduces emotional response. Optimal controls slow down recognition processes and so provide tolerable doses of new information and emotional responses. Excessive controls interrupt the process, change the state of the person to some form that restricts experience, as in the omissive phenomena of ideational denial and emotional numbing. Continued excessive controls may prevent a complete processing of the stressful event. On the other hand, failures of control may lead to excessive levels of emotion, flooding, and retraumatization, causing intrusive types of phenomena.

Inner schemas of self and others will eventually conform to the new reality, as in the process of completion of mourning.

When this happens, information storage in active memory will terminate. Until then, at any given time, different sets of meanings of a stress event will exist as codings or instantiated schemas in different stages of processing. Words such as *instantiated schemas* are defined in the lexicon which appears as the appendix to Chapter 1, pp. 16–18. At a given time, for example, fear of the repetition of an event might be a recurrent intrusive theme, while an incipient survivor-guilt theme might be completely repressed from conscious experience. Later, in situations of greater safety, the survivor-guilt theme might intrusively enter awareness. Still later it might be contemplated less intrusively as it had been integrated in a template of life history and personal meanings.

Treatment can be conceptualized as an effort to assist patients in their own natural completion process. This will usually involve efforts to work through conflicts that have stymied the patient's own attempts toward this goal. It will also involve an examination of latent conflicts and schemas of defectiveness of self that have been activated by association to a stressful event and its implications. This process involves the alteration of unconscious regulatory stances. Because psychotherapy provides a context in which the person is likely to express what he or she has been warding off, careful reviews of video-recorded brief therapies became a part of a research effort described elsewhere (Horowitz, Wilner, Marmar, and Krupnick 1980; Horowitz et al. 1984; Horowitz [1976] 1986; Horowitz, [1979] 1987). The case that follows is drawn from a review of such therapies following a systematic method called configurational analysis.

My colleagues and I expected to analyze the videotapes and transcripts in the following manner. The recent traumatic event would be a clear anchoring focus: one could review and reorder the patient's emotional expressions, ideas, and intrusive memories as they related to this event and emerged in sequences over time. When warded-off themes of various kinds were eventually expressed in the therapy, one would draw inferences about the processes by which these new elements had been repressed or dealt with by other unconscious defensive maneuvers until that time. When we reviewed the data, warded-off themes were found to occur, but we were surprised by what seemed at first to be a "disorderly" sequence. A complex of ideas and feelings seemed to be consciously available to the patient in some states of mind, intrusive at others, and omitted or completely disavowed during still another state.

In a given state, an idea might be too much to bear, while in another state it could be contemplated. Such observations required us to move from a linear, temporal theory of organizing responses to a recent trauma, to a system that recognized differences within an individual in terms of his or her states of mind. The clinical facts of bereavement reactions, where an important relationship was lost in reality and yet continued "alive" in the mind, also forced us to focus on issues of varied schemas for self and roles of relationship with the same deceased person. That, in turn, led to a reconsideration of the repertoires of schemas in an individual and how different elements from that repertoire might organize different states of mind.

Configurational Analysis

The configurational analysis system for segmentalizing and ordering multivariate qualitative data was developed following principles of Erikson (1954), Jacobson (1964), Knapp (1969, 1974, 1981), Knapp and Teele (1981), Luborsky (1977, 1984), and Kernberg (1976), among others. Like the Symptom Context Method presented by Luborsky in Chapter 10, state transition analysis is a procedure for finding a clinically meaningful shift (Horowitz [1979] 1987). The aggregation of recorded information by specific states of mind allows the detection of features salient to each state, features whose changes indicate a state transition. From these features self concepts, role-relationship models, and other organizing schemas for each state are inferred. Role-relationship models contain self and object concepts as well as scripts for the expression of personal wishes and responses to feared or desired responses of others. Such schemas may be activated or inhibited as a consequence of unconscious motives. The regulatory maneuvers that shift themes and organizing schemas can be inferred from patterns of state transition and their triggers.

It is important to note that this view of dynamic unconscious processes does not map completely with the theoretical constructs of preconscious processing (Dixon 1981) or the unconsciously coded procedural knowledge (Anderson 1983) referred to in cognitive science theories described by Mandler in the previous chapter or what Jackendoff will call the computational mind in Chapter 9. The difference lies in the concepts of *drives, signal anxiety,* and *defense* as discussed in Chapter 1 and as Shevrin will discuss again in Chapter 6.

Although there is a debate over the fundamentals of *drive*, the basic concept is a motive force arising within the organism that can then empower the use of certain schemas associated with the gratification of a particular appetite. The concept of *signal anxiety* is also debatable in terms of how it works, but the fundamental concept is an unconsciously appraised threat of the consequences of expression leading to avoidances of expression. *Defenses* are impedances and distortions placed in the path of such conscious or behavioral expressions, motivated by unconsciously calculated aims at safety in the face of such threats.

The dynamic unconscious concept involves thinking unconsciously about self and others in a way that is affected by drive-activated schemas of how the self wants to relate to them, what the self wants to obtain from them or give to them, as well as wishes and fears about the aims of others toward the self. To be "dynamic" in this sense, the unconscious mental processes must involve a conflict between wishes and threats so that some ideas and feelings are warded off from conscious representation and some are expressed, and so that some schemas are used as organizing forms and some otherwise salient ones are not.

I will now describe a case fragment and some formulations to illustrate some aspects of states and schemas of self and other as unconscious organizers, as well as some aspects of unconsciously warding off certain person schemas to serve defensive purposes. The inferences are a composite derived from the consensus of six clinicians. These observers were first divided into two teams of three each. They reviewed the case materials of Ann, using the videotapes and process notes from her psychotherapy. They independently followed the configurational analysis formats, and each team produced a written document. These were compared and gaps or areas of disagreement were checked by reviewing the videotapes and transcripts until a consensus was reached. The reports were then condensed into a fuller report that is presented elsewhere (Horowitz et al. 1984).

Ann: A Case Illustration

Ann was a twenty-four- year-old married woman who sought help seven months after her father's death. She was aware that she was exhibiting a marked denial of the reality of the loss and of its implications. Despite this sense of numbing and avoidance, Ann had intrusive thoughts of her father, his death, her own death, and an associated shattering, painful sense of despair. Among troublesome intrusive thoughts that she hoped to dispel was the guilty idea that she could have saved her father from death by taking better care of him, and the opposite idea that his death was just another example of how he frequently abandoned her when she needed him.

Since the death of her father, Ann had repeatedly suggested to friends that he was alive. She became frightened by her "irrationality," and a state of panic broke through her sense of numbness as she envisioned the potential humiliation she would feel when friends learned of his death. Ann also worried about the increased constriction in her activities as she forced herself to avoid any external reminder of her father. This phobic avoidance included a particular street. On this street was a house in which Ann's father had attended a party for her on the day of his death. She reacted with profound anxiety to passing the area, even in a car.

Ann was the youngest of five siblings. Her father worked in an institutional setting where he felt that his potential for productive work had been destroyed by inane bureaucratic requirements. He counterbalanced his job dissatisfaction with an intense dedication to long-distance running. His wife designed her life around her children and husband and assumed a role of "weakness" in order to emphasize the strong compensatory role of her husband as head of the family.

Ann was a good student, but she juggled her career choice between ambivalently held alternatives. She attended several colleges and frequently changed her mind about two possible vocations. She married a man who was very involved in his own work, and she had episodic doubts about whether she had been ready to marry.

During the course of her father's increasing incapacitation, Ann and he had difficulty acknowledging the terminal nature of his chronic obstructive lung disease. He felt assaulted unfairly by his illness and was therefore sometimes sarcastic and hostile. At such times he demanded more attention from her than she could give.

Her father was hospitalized with his second attack of pneumonia in three months, but he improved and was eventually discharged from the hospital one week before his death. She described going to visit him in the hospital, thinking that she could share with him her growing acceptance of his condition.

When she got there, he was so actively denying his problems that she avoided the discussion. As mentioned earlier, shortly before he died he attended a luncheon party in Ann's honor. That very night he succumbed to his illness.

The suddenness of his death left Ann stunned and reluctant to give up a residual sense that her father was somewhere else, still alive. Ann went to the mortuary the night before the funeral to view her father. She was suddenly shocked that he did not move. Having a sudden, out-of- control urge, she angrily shouted at him that he was unfair to have left her.

After the funeral Ann kept herself extremely busy. She worked at two jobs and regimented her time so that she almost always had an essential "duty" to perform. This method of avoiding ideas and feelings that were pressing toward conscious representation broke down when she drove to work. By the time she pulled out of the driveway, she began to cry angrily. She felt that these outbursts were shamefully uncontrolled expressions of raw emotion, to be stricly avoided when she was with companions.

When her mother had first informed Ann of her father's medical difficulties, Ann's response was that she wanted him to live long enough to support her in completing her education and to proudly see the result. When he died, she felt that he had lived just long enough to provide financial support without being able to enjoy her success. She therefore felt that she had exploited him.

When Ann was an adolescent, her father was often withdrawn, except for caustic criticism or angry outbursts. In efforts to please him, she described herself as seeking but never finding perfection. She also had to insulate herself from him to pursue her own goals without the deflations in self-esteem he could easily induce in her. She felt she had to pursue her own course, which she did most emphatically, even during the period of his terminal illness. This led to guilty self-criticism that she was being neglectful of him when he was most in need.

Ann's States of Mind

Intrusive and omissive phenomena such as Ann's eruptive ideas and feelings about her father's death and her irrational and pronounced denial of the reality of the event were not evenly spaced throughout her conscious experience. They occurred episodically and variably. Configurational analysis approaches this observation by organizing such features as intrusive and omissive phenomena into different states of mind. This allows one to examine concurrent features in a given state of mind and to draw inferences about its possible causes.

Intrusive phenomena were most prominent in a state of mind in which Ann experienced waves of sadness, a sense of personal incompetence to withstand loneliness, shame over defectiveness, and intrusive crying, with the fear that she would not stop or would have such sobbing episodes in public. In the configurational analysis we gave a short label to this state of mind: *frightened yearning*. Such pining states are common during the mourning process. During her version of this state, Ann felt out of control; she felt that her coping capacity and psychological defenses were inadequate to master her grief.

Omissive phenomena were most prominent in a state of mind that was labeled *numb immobilization*. During this state of mind Ann was not experiencing many thoughts and emotions about her father's recent death, but she was also unproductive. If she was with people when in this state, as could be seen on the videotapes of her interviews, she looked inattentive, held her eyes downcast, spoke slowly and tersely, and seemed by facial expression to be feeling deflated and vaguely hurt, with self-criticism for not being able to rouse herself.

The frightened yearning and the numb immobilization states contained her chief complaints; in a sense they were the problem states that she wanted reduced as an outcome of her psychotherapy. Both were also undermodulated states in the sense that she felt out of control of them, wanting other states of mind but being unable to achieve them by dispelling the current views that organized these unwanted states of mind. Thus, while we infer high levels of inhibitory defenses operating during the numb immobilization state, she experienced it as undermodulated because of her inability to change into another state.

There were two other undermodulated states, even more uncontrolled, reported later in the therapy. These occurred rarely, but she dreaded entry into either one of them. Both states were characterized by high frequencies of intrusive phenomena. One was a state we labeled *explosive rage*, the other *searing guilt*. In the rare moments of entry into explosive rage she felt dangerously impulsive and "crazy," that she might shout irrational accusatory complaints about how badly others were treating her. When in her state of searing guilt, she would excoriate herself as if she were an assailant who had harmed others, or a caregiving person who failed to provide them with responsible care. In this state she had intrusive fantasies of receiving devastating criticism.

These four unpleasant, unwanted, undermodulated states are summarized at the top of Table 3.1, and contrasted with well-modulated and overmodulated states of mind important during this period of her life. The well-modulated state that Ann wanted, and planned to be in, was a state of *assured productivity*, in which she could work calmly while feeling wise and strong. She was unable to achieve this wish during her response to her father's death. Indeed, she had problems entering and remaining in this positive state of mind before this stressful event. Unconscious factors prevented the gratification of this conscious plan.

Ann could often stabilize herself in a state that was close to assured productivity, one in which she was able to be thoughtful, with tolerable levels of anxious tension. In these states during therapy, she looked worried or hurt, had abrupt or jerky bodily movements, but was able to express her ideas and feelings in a progressive and useful manner. The configurational analysts called this her *vulnerable working* state.

TABLE 3.1 List of Ann's States

Label	Description
Undermodulated States	
Frightened yearning	Waves of sadness, weakness, and shame. Feels alone; fears that if she starts to cry, she may not be able to stop. Sometimes intrusive crying occurs.
Numb immobilization	Deflated, vaguely hurt, inattentive to others, unproductive. Eyes downcast.
Explosive rage (warded off)	Accusatory complaints. Feels dangerously impulsive and "crazy."
Searing guilt (warded off)	Sees herself as a hurtful assailant or failed caretaker; fantasies devastating criticism.
Well-Modulated States	
Vulnerable working	Has tolerable anxiety; looks thoughtful, worried, or hurt. Abrupt, jerky movements.
Assured productivity (ideal)	Calm problem-solving, productive; feels wise and strong.
Overmodulated State	
Artificially engaging	Coyly ingratiating, playacting, blustery.

In contrast to the relatively well-modulated states of *assured productivity* and *vulnerable working,* Ann exhibited a state that seemed to observers to be very defensive in quality. This over-modulated behavior was called her *artificially engaging* state, because she seemed to be pretending or playacting some wished-for version of the unachievable state of *assured productivity.* She would be coyly ingratiating to the interviewer, playacting emotions she was not really feeling at the time or behaving with a blustery, contrived animation. This *artificially engaging* state seemed to approach *assured productivity* and served to ward off entry into the state of *numb immobilization.* It was a defensive compromise that lay somewhere between *assured productivity* and *numb immobilization.*

In a more detailed report of this case elsewhere, other states of mind were reported, but they are too complex for the illustration of contemporary psychodynamics intended here to demonstrate issues of defense against motive forces at various levels of mental process.

I have just described wishes, threats, and compromise defensive positions in terms of states that might or might not contain these phenomena. At this relatively superficial level of analysis, the wish was to accomplish work within a state of *assured productivity.* The fear was of entry into states of *searing guilt* and *explosive rage,* with the loss of self-control associated with such episodes. The defensive compromises ranged from the *artificially engaging* state to the less successful but still inhibited state of *numb immobilization.*

The concept of wishes, fears, and defenses that forms "a psychodynamic configuration" can now be examined at a less superficial level. Each state of mind may be organized by its own particular set of schemas; the properties of the schemas would lead to the features characterizing that state.

Person Schemas

One form of person schemas is a role-relationship model (Horowitz [1979] 1987). These units contain a view of self; a view of others; and scripts for actions of self, responses anticipated from the other, and subsequent reactions of self. Aspects of such schemas will now be inferred for each state.

During the *frightened yearning* state Ann had a sense of herself as a despairing or bitterly resentful, weak, and abandoned child, as shown in Table 3.2. She wished to regain a relationship with a caregiver and supplicated for one to obtain attention. But, in this model, she schematized her caregiver as neglectful and expected disappearance rather than succor as a response. Her reaction was fear, frustration, and intense yearning. When in this state, she was intensely aware of the loss of her father and refused to accept his death as real. She worried about the unbidden entry of these ideas and feelings into her thoughts and was frightened by the possibility that when she began to cry, she would lose control and be unable to stop. Ann fought against *frightened yearning*, because in this state she felt alone in the world and overwhelmed by waves of sadness, weakness, and shame.

Ann could enter another, even more dreaded and undermodulated state, that of *explosive rage*. In this state she often condemned others for neglecting her, and her self concept seemed like that of a self-righteous assailant carrying out revengful aims, also as shown in Table 3.2. The destructive accusations directed toward a willful abandoner who had failed her as a caregiver then set in motion an unconscious fantasy sequence or schematic script. Her father was perceived early in the "script" of this state as a strong, willful abandoner of his caregiving role; he would be seen later in the unfolding script sequence as a weak victim of her retaliatory hostility. Anyone, including herself, in a critic role would then shift from blaming her father (for neglect) to blaming Ann (for too intense and inappropriate revengeful rage). As the father had been unjustly harmed by Ann's rage in this fantasy, the script involved a transition to feelings of guilt if and when the first steps were enacted, even when enacted in thought rather than action. Ann would then be vulnerable to entry into another dreaded and generally warded-off state, one of *searing guilt*. The *searing guilt* state was based on a schematic view of herself as bad and harmful to her father, who was viewed first as a victim and then as a righteous assailant, retaliating upon her. Now she was a failed caregiver who warranted criticism and punishment. The transition in state from *explosive rage* to *searing guilt* involved the instantiation of different schemas with the roles of self and other reversed.

The *explosive rage* and *searing guilt* states were painful but rare, being usually warded off by unconscious defensive operations, Ann's most frequent problematic state was *numb immobilization;* in this state she felt constricted, vaguely hurt, and deflated. Although she felt driven to do her work, she made no

TABLE 3.2 Motivational Organization of Ann's States and Inferred Role-Relationship Models

State	Self	Aims	Other
Problematic Role Relationships			
Frightened yearning	Abandoned child	Supplicate → / ← Disappear	Neglectful caregiver
Numb immobilization	Weak and defective	Conceal self → / ← Scorn	Superior critic
Dreaded and Warded-off Role Relationships			
Explosive rage	Righteous assailant	Harm → / ← Avoid	Failed caregiver
Searing guilt	Failed caregiver	Harm → / ← Avoid	Righteous Assailant
Desired Role Relationships			
Assured productivity	Wise and strong	Benefit and approve → / ← Do and show	Wise and strong
Compromise Relationships			
Artificially engaging	Ingenue	Perform → / ← Encourage	Mentor

progress and was withdrawn and dulled. We inferred that her mood was organized by a role relationship model of herself as a weak and defective woman trying to conceal herself from a strong and scornful (rather than sustaining) critic.

In contrast to her state of *numb immobilization* Ann could enter her desired state of *assured productivity* if and when she felt safe from criticism. She was able to sit erectly and speak firmly to the therapist. She became more reflective and bold and could present her thoughts and feelings without disavowal. We inferred that she organized this state according to a self schema as competent, strong, calm, "wise" (this word indicated a highly prized "trait" in her family), productive, and admirable, and in relationship to another person, schematically viewed as an appreciative, equally wise and strong companion.

In the *artificially engaging* state we inferred that Ann acted according to a schema of self as an ingenue, coyly performing for an approving mentor. Constant monitoring of her own and others' responses, with the subsequent shifting of ideas and subjects, contributed to Ann's sense of emotional distance. In this *artificially engaging* state, she told stories that were greatly detailed but were not emotional or moving toward any resolution or decision. She did this in a singsong voice, using sweeping hand gestures.

The role-relationship models for each of the states just redescribed in terms of schemas of self and other are presented in Table 3.2. This table follows a motivational organization that includes the psychodynamic concept of wish, threat, and defense. In this instance each of the three components is stated in terms of person schemas. The wish is to infuse into organizational dominance the role-relationship model containing a self schema as wise and strong. In this desired role-relationship model she would perform outstanding work, showing it to a wise and strong companion (such as her father) who would respond with pride, happiness, and approval. The major threats are of entry into states in which the self is seen as a strong but dangerous assailant who would hurt another person by showing off independent work that would deflate the other as well as indicate that the self has pulled away from him. This role-relationship model is placed in the "Dreaded and Warded-Off" position of the motivational format used in Table 3.2. Her *defensive purpose* is to avoid use of the schemas organizing dreaded states. Her *defensive process* is to inhibit these schemas and to facilitate the use of alternative role-relationship models. A *defensive outcome* is to enter the *artificially engaging state*. This state is organized by the view of self as a performing ingenue, as shown in the "Compromise Relationships" position of Table 3.2. The relative dominance of various available schemas in organizing mood states would partially determine whether Ann felt good, bad, or silly about her wish to be competent in pursuing her career.

Defensive Regulation

Ann's states, and a prominent organizing schema for each state, have just been summarized. In a preliminary way, at the level of schemas, a distinction was made between defensive purposes, processes, and outcomes. By adding a bit more detail on the clinical findings, more aspects of defensively motivated regulation of mental processes can now be considered.

Ann had a conflictual relationship with her father. Early in life she idealized him, but over time she became disappointed by his aloofness and concerned over his too-ready criticism. Blame shifted among family members as to responsibility for evoking her father's hostile outbursts. Ann conceptualized her mother both as a quietly strong preserver of the family security and as too weakly submissive to her father. She was not clear about whether her mother's failure to confront her father regarding his faults was due to her unempathic obliviousness or to a resolute, even heroic determination to make the best of a difficult situation. Her father appeared strong, productive, and assertive, but much of his presentation had a quality of bluster to compensate for inferiority. He was self-enhancing, but often at the price of the well-being and esteem of others.

Ann wanted to become independent of her father, and because of her warded-off contempt for him, she also wanted to become better than he in her profession. She too could be strongly assertive, yet when she saw herself as strong, she then became worried that she had harmed her father by leaving, neglecting, and surpassing him (the threats if her wishes were acted upon). As a defense against her fear of the danger of enacting the scripts organized by strong, assertive self schemas, she could then switch to one of several weaker self concepts. Scripts organized by these weak self schemas would be safe for a time but would then run the danger of making her contemptible.

There was potential self-criticism with regard to both the dominant and submissive stances organized by the strong and weak self schemas. For example, as Ann entered a dominant role in describing her work successes and career ambitions to her husband, she immediately became worried that she was too aggressively controlling for a woman and that he would be first hurt and then critical of her. To undo that threat, she would then rapidly reverse roles, praising her husband's work and regarding her work as second class, just as her mother had "supported" Ann's father. However, the submissive role reminded her of her father's criticism of her mother and of her own fears of incompetence, and she had to switch to dominance once again. She seemed locked into an undoing process since both strong and weak self concepts led to some threat.

Fear and sadness were the most prominent themes in Ann's conscious experiences just before seeking psychotherapy for her pathological grief reaction. These themes occurred most prominently during her *frightened yearning* state of mind. Yet, as is often the case in pathological grief reactions, there were important unconsciously processed themes such as anger and guilt that surfaced rarely but intrusively as conscious ideas and feelings.

This situation is not surprising; it occurs to an extent in normal grief reactions as well as pathological intensifications. Sadness is socially expected during mourning, and fear is also not unexpectable, since the person is bereft of a supportive relationship and must now face life without that relationship. Fear of sadness, and the ability to master the loss is also well understood and not opposed by social demands and personal values. Unconsciously motivated defensive avoidances of fear and sadness are less likely, although conscious efforts to suppress the level of these emotions are common.

Anger at the deceased, however, is more taboo in a social value system. It tends to lead toward shame or guilt as responses to thinking or expressing unacceptable ideas that blame a person who has suffered death, about whom only good ought to be thought or spoken. Yet the mind continues the relationship after the death has occurred, and anger surfaces during normal mourning responses and is then mitigated by other realizations. Similarly, guilty feelings of not having done enough for the deceased are common, but others seldom wish to hear about them, although they will give sympathy for sorrow. Thus defensive avoidances of anger and guilt themes are more likely.

Because of social taboos and internalized moral values, the

individual may not only consciously suppress anger and guilt themes during a mourning process, but may unconsciously aim to avoid conscious representations of such themes. These themes may be less contemplated for that reason and thus impeded in terms of the working-through process that can lead to completion of the mourning process.

In persons with a previously ambivalent, unresolved relationship with the deceased, anger and guilt themes are more likely to be intense, complex, and conflicted. Unconscious defensive aims and processes may be heightened in such instances. Thus these preexisting themes, as noted in studies of mourning, may be predispositions for extended, excessively intense, or distorted mourning processes. This was the case with Ann, and in her psychotherapy the anger and guilt themes were an important topic, which I will focus on in the following paragraphs.

A Conflictual Theme Predisposing Ann to Pathological Grief

Ann's experience of her father's death dashed her hopes that she could resolve conflicts in her relationship with him. She had especially hoped that he would eventually acknowledge in a proud, loving way her growing competence and independence. That would have relieved her fears of leaving and surpassing him. Instead, his death intensified three major conflicts: between her wish for dependent closeness and her wish for developmental independence; between her wish for identification with her father and her fear of being like him; and between her wish to express her anger toward her father for not taking care of her and her fear and guilt over thinking that it was she who had harmed him by her bitterness. The grief process included guilt over "independence" because she had done her work as her father died, remorse over insufficient closeness, and fear that she "should" die herself to join into a union with him. We shall focus here on the harm theme as it emerged during her mourning process, because it embodied the elements that led to intrusive episodes during the states of explosive rage and searing guilt.

For Ann, the harm theme included prominent role reversals. In different states of mind she saw herself as aggressor or victim, the critic who blamed others or the one at fault. One of her immediate responses to her father's death was intrusive ideas of anger with him for harming her by abandoning her, both by his death and in her aroused memories of inadequacies in her past life with him. As part of her mourning process of recollection, she had images of his many instances of previous emotional unavailability or frustration of her wishes to spend time with him.

In life, the father had been sniping and judgmental, and Ann now feared his magical retaliation for her intrusive angry criticism of him. She also felt that his death signaled a failure of her own caregiving actions. This concept was associated with memories of her leaving him alone during the period of his terminal illness in order to concentrate on her work. Further, Ann knew that physical weakness and vulnerability to death would be intolerable for her father, even as they were frightening for herself, and that would make him "nasty" and likely to lash out at caregivers, especially failed caregivers, after he died. Such irrational, magical ideas of his continued reactivity after death are organized by unconscious primary-process thinking, and these ideas surface as conscious moods and ideas of anxious foreboding, as well as the occasional intrusive ideas of guilt.

An aspect of the harm theme was Ann's concern over the power of her previous angry thoughts to cause real harm to her father, and her compensatory need to maintain perfectionistic standards of altruism. Ann feared that she had hurt her father by pursuing her own interests when he was terminally ill; that is one reason she disavowed the terminal nature of his illness and, later, his death. On the other hand, at a dissociated level, as is frequent when a parent has a chronic illness, Ann found herself occasionally wishing that her father would die soon in order to end his suffering and relieve the constant tension of anticipating his death. She remembered these episodes remorsefully during the review process instigated by his death and her mourning responses.

Ann knew that her father would experience death as a deprivation, and she felt guilty that she had not always "wished him the best." She quickly displaced the target of her anger from her father to "inept doctors." She disavowed her memories of her momentary, conscious wishes for her father to die. The rapidity with which she clamped control over her thoughts did not give her sufficient time to process, revise, or accept the memories of her "death wish" thoughts as ordinary, not the cause of real harm to her father, and more than compensated by her overall loving feelings toward him and wishes for his health.

Ann also felt guilty that she had been selfish for wanting to complete her career training and some of her work before her father died, and for not paying a complete farewell tribute to him. Her guilt was related to the enduring belief, propagated within the family (usually implicitly) that *taking care of yourself depletes others*. The occurrence of her father's death soon after a party for Ann was an unfortunate coincidence that reinforced her attitude that her own achievements were a dangerous triumph at her father's expense.

Ann habitually coped with threats of intense emotional arousal by a strategy of *heightened intellectuality* and a focus on *detailed planning* of her next efforts. Meanwhile, she *dampened emotional excitement* by deflecting from the affective heart of conflictual themes to peripheral thematic issues. She discussed conflicts abstractly, as if they were general human conditions and not her specific personal concerns. The location was not within herself; the time was not specifically now. Her use of rapid *switching* of ideational and emotional meanings within a theme was an especially prominent aspect of this defensive style of generalization, affect flattening, and rationalization.

During Ann's psychotherapy, the early focus on fear and sadness themes led to a later focus on the more warded-off and difficult topics related to anger and guilt. The signal for this focus was her disclosure of the momentary but dreaded states of *explosive rage* and *searing guilt* that she experienced as sets of intrusive representations of memories and feelings. The therapeutic communication then examined the ideas, memories, and fantasies around emotions of anger and guilt as related to her father or as expected from her father as responses to her actions. The defensive avoidance of these themes manifested itself in therapy, as usual, as resistances to these communicative expressions. The form of such resistances is always of central interest in dynamic therapy.

In Ann there were a variety of regulatory processes that used not only the *inhibition* of conscious representation of memories and associated ideas to avoid emotions but also a *switching to counter-ideas* to kindle some other emotion and to reciprocally inhibit the too-intense feeling that was anticipated. These switching maneuvers involved the facilitation of one set of memories for conscious representation and the inhibition of another set of memories from conscious representation. At the same time, there was a *facilitation and an inhibition of schemas* for organizing recollection and representations of ideas and feelings.

The emotion of anger was activated by memories of times when her father deprived her of his support and by the associated idea that he was selfishly neglecting her. The memories and ideas and the emotional responses were organized by a schema in which she was an assailant who could righteously be hostile toward him, because he was a caregiver who unfairly and irresponsibly neglected her. His presumed response in this schema would be to avoid being harmed by her hostility, perhaps avoiding her anger by being good to her.

The emotion of remorse or guilt involved a different set of memories and ideas and a reversal of the role of self and other in the involved schema. The memories associated with a nodal feeling of guilt were of the times when she neglected her father, pursuing her own work during his terminal illness, and these memories were associated with the idea that she had been selfish. As with the anger theme, an enduring script, a serial schematic attitude, was that taking care of yourself will then deplete another person dependent on your care. According to this view, her acts of performing desirable career work depleted and harmed her father. These associations and emotional responses were organized into a state of mind by the schema of herself as a failed caregiver. In this use of the role-relationship model, her father could be righteously hostile toward her and she would want to avoid his wrath.

By oscillating between schemas, she could recall different memories and ideas, use anger to undo guilt, and guilt to undo anger. Rapid switching back and forth led to some confusion but reduced the intensity of both emotions. The controls that accomplished this *reversed the role designated as self* in role-relationship models and inhibited or facilitated memories and ideas selectively. These operations were not part of Ann's conscious awareness. They involved unconsciously motivated and conducted regulations. The overall model of this oscillation between two warded-off states on the harm theme is presented in Table 3.3.

The inferences presented above and modeled in Table 3.3 are not presented as necessarily valid or as proofs of a given type of psychodynamic configuration. Rather, the purpose has been to present a model of a psychodynamic approach to theory about

Table 3.3 Oscillation Between Two Warded-off States on the Harm Theme

States	Explosive Rage ⟵⟶ Searing Guilt	
Organizing Person Concepts		
Self	RIGHTEOUS ASSAILANT	FAILED CAREGIVER
Aim	harm→ ←avoid	→avoid ←harm
Other	FAILED CAREGIVER	RIGHTEOUS ASSAILANT
Enduring Attitude	Taking care of yourself depletes others	
Active memories, emotions, and ideas	Times when father deprived her (anger)	Times when she neglected her father during his terminal illness (remorse)
	"He selfishly neglected me."	"I have been selfish."
Controls	Reverse roles designated as *self* in the role-relationship model of righteous assailant to failed caregiver	
	Inhibit memories evocative of the current most threatening emotion	

unconscious defensive operations as they might involve not only conscious representation of memories, thoughts, and emotions but also the schemas in use for forming states of mind: periods of protracted subjective experience, mood, and extensive behavioral patterns. Specific memories and ideas for conscious representation in diverse states around a current important life theme are presented in Table 3.3, as are specific schemas of self and other for generating that mood and organizing its information processing. The model assumes the use of varied schemas from an available repertoire in different states of mind.

Recapitulation

Expressive tendencies characteristic of the grief process and the tendency to complete the mental processing of stressful life events led Ann to review various themes in the current and past relationship with her deceased father. Yet for unconscious reasons, she interrupted this grief work in order to avoid intense, negative, and uncontrollable states of mind. The concept of unconscious defensive regulations could be illustrated in her behavior pattern of trying to do meaningful work, to stabilize a desired state of mind labeled *assured productivity,* and to avoid *searing guilt* or *explosive rage* states. This coping effort of high work involvement failed.

She used another habitual state, *artificially engaging,* to prevent the exposure of her feelings. If she could not enter this defensive state because of impending sorrow and loneliness, she tended to enter the state of *numb immobilization. Numb immobilization* was a defensive compromise that was a problem to her, because it interfered with her work. In spite of this maladaptive consequence, it was at times a useful avoidance of the more dreaded and warded-off states of *explosive rage* and *searing guilt.*

When the harm theme was approached during the expressive enterprise of psychotherapy, Ann undid anger with guilt, and guilt with anger, by rapid shifts in her repertoire of schemas and by the facilitation of some memories (and reactive ideas) and the inhibition of others, as modeled in Table 3.3. These shifts were manifested in the grammatical structure of her verbal communication, where she would juggle the subject and object of verbs, adverbs, and adjectives from self to other. "Defense," then, could be conceptualized at various levels in terms of states, person

TABLE 3.4 A Conflictual-Relationship Schematization for Ann

Aim:[1]	I want to be independent from my father.

But I have these impediments:	
Personal deficiencies:	I feel weak and defective.
Environmental deficiencies:	My father is dead, leaving me no further opportunity to get him to agree to (permit) my independence.

If I get what I want, then:[1]	
Internal positive responses:[1]	I will feel competent.
External positive responses:[1]	Others will respect and admire me as a model of how to be assertive.

If I get what I want, then:[1]	
Internal negative responses:[1]	I will lose the hope of a close relationship with my father and will feel selfish and guilty for hurting him.
External negative responses:[1]	Others, including my father, will see me as a selfish abandoner of him.

So I will use these coping strategies:	
Interpersonal behavior patterns:	When I experience too much submission, as in being a caregiver, I will strike out independently. When I feel that that is too aggressive, I will emphasize my caregiver (submissive) roles.
Intrapsychic beliefs:	If I keep my accomplishments minimal and am insufficiently caring, I can prevent the danger of being either too caring or too accomplished.
Intrapsychic styles of regulating thinking and feeling:	Dampen emotion by switching attitudes back and forth to avoid the threat of any one position.
Intrapsychic styles of viewing self and others:	Oscillation between strong and weak self schemas; reverse roles.

And the results will be:	
Problems or symptoms:	Avoidance of closeness, anxiety attacks, depression, or mood.
Recurrent states of mind:	Overcontrolled states such as *artificial and engaging* ruptured by breakthroughs of frightened yearning or of irritation at others.
Patterns of state transition:	Stabilizes overcontrolled states for a long time. Experiences any emotional states of mind as dangerous or embarrassingly out-of-control.

TABLE 3.4 (continued)

Likely life course (accomplishments in working, relating, experiencing):	
Short-range:	Inability to progress in work or in relationship with husband.
Long-range:	Absence of career development or close interpersonal attachments, leading to embitterment or depression.

Source: Horowitz et al. 1984.
¹These rows contain the Luborsky (1984) Core Conflictual Relationship Theme.

schemas as organizers of states, and ideational-affective process layerings within a state, all governed by regulatory processes and anticipations largely out of conscious awareness. Defense can also be seen in a longer order pattern about what is expected in expressing an aim such as a wish for independence in a conflictual relationship. Table 3.4 rearranges some of the inferences about Ann's longer-range views about this conflictual relationship. Some of the propositions stated in Table 3.4 in "I" as subject form were consciously represented. Others were obscure or unconscious, and the inferences translated into how they might become "I"-based statements.

This case fragment merely illustrates the possible structure of conflicts between aims toward conscious representation and defenses against conscious representation or communicative expression. The death set in motion a train of experience: the grief process. During Ann's bereavement she was internally but unconsciously motivated to review memories of her relationship with her father. This review reactivated earlier conflicts. The expressive tendency, moving in some way toward conscious representations, was sometimes opposed by inhibitions of information processing as a feedback loop to avoid excessive emotional tension. Ann's intrusive experiences of unbidden images and feelings occurred as a result of periods of relative defensive failure. Her omissions of expectable experiences resulted, we inferred, from high defense. These intrusions and avoidances (for instance, Ann's phobia of locations associated with her father and his death) were reduced during a mourning process facilitated by psychotherapy.

Methodology: The Validity of Such Inferences

The consensual validity of inferences, such as those partly illustrated in the case of Ann, can be checked by several means. The first would be to have different clinicians independently review the same material (exact transcripts and videotapes), recording results on systematic formats and then comparing their judgments. Discrepancies could be resolved by repeated joint reviews of the original data, looking for the evidence to support or invalidate the diverse inferences. Improved terminology and formats and an examination of individual data from varied exploratory situations would sharpen that kind of pattern recognition and explanatory description.

Once the states of mind of a given subject were assessed, it would be possible to have content analysts review the material and reliably segmentalize it by state transition points and types of state (as reported by Horowitz, Marmar, and Wilner 1979; and Marmar, Wilner, and Horowitz 1984). This mode of segmentation could be used to yield material that might be scored by content analysis methods using as inferred schema classification systems the interpersonal diagnostic protocols developed by Kiesler (1983), Wiggens (1982), Benjamin (1979), and Rosenberg (1979). Other methods related to self-concept and role-relationship models include Luborsky (1984) on Core Conflictual Theme Analysis (used for part of Table 3.4); Loevinger on ego development level (1976, 1979); and Ryle (1975), Kelly (1955), and others on personal constructs. These different methods could be applied to the same video-recorded material, and the results examined for a convergence of the theories of classification of interpersonal phenomena and an explanation of them.

Another method of testing inferences would involve the presentation of experimental stimuli to a person such as Ann after an inference of important conflictual themes, especially propositions presumed to be warded off from conscious representation in contrast with control themes (not inferred as dynamically salient for a given subject). Hypotheses about differential subjective, physiological, and social responses to the sets of stimuli could be checked by the actual outcomes in laboratory tests using such procedures as subliminal stimulation and electrophysiological outcome assessment. This type of method will be discussed especially in the next part of this book, led by Shevrin in Chapter 6, and also in sections by Erdelyi (Chapter 4), Marcel (Chapter 7), Spence (Chapter 11), and Baars (Chapter 13).

Conclusion

The unconscious mental processes of most interest to psychodynamics are those involved in conflict, with aims toward representation and defensive strategies operating against expression. When there are both motives toward representation and motives for regulatory efforts opposing it, episodes of consciousness may occur that are experienced as unusually intrusive or omissive.

Whether intrusions or omissions occur is the result of a play of forces and their relative strengths at a given time. Thus the concept of defense is central to the psychodynamic theory of motivation. This chapter conceptualizes defensive processes as operative on several levels. Defensive regulations may be directed at choices of themes for potential conscious thought. Defensive processes may be directed at regulating the schemas used to organize thought. In addition, defensive processes can be examined as regulations of the conscious representation of specific contents. In each instance, more detailed theory of how unconscious defense might be accomplished would be useful in order to validate or invalidate this hypothetical concept. That theory might be developed in articulation with theoretical constructs from cognitive psychology and should be consistent with whatever is known about human information processing.

References

Anderson, J. R. 1983. *The Architecture of Cognition.* Cambridge, Mass.: Harvard University Press.

Antrobus, J. S., J. L. Singer, and S. Greenberg. 1966. Studies in the stream of consciousness. *Perceptual and Motor Skills* 23:399–417.

Benjamin, L. S. 1979. Use of structural analysis of social behavior (SASB) and Markov chains to dyadic interactions. *Journal of Abnormal Psychology* 88, no. 3:303–19.

Breuer, J. and S. Freud. [1895] 1954. Studies on hysteria. *Standard Edition,* vol. 2. London: Hogarth Press.

Dixon, N. F. 1981. *Preconscious Processing.* New York: Wiley.

Ekman, P. 1984. Expression and the nature of emotion. In P. Ekman and K. Sherer, eds., *Approaches to Emotion.* Hillsdale, N.J.: Erlbaum.

Erikson, E. H. 1954. The dream specimen of psychoanalysis. *Journal of the American Psychoanalytic Association* 2:5–56.

Horowitz, M. J. 1975. Intrusive and repetitive thoughts after experimental stress: A summary. *Archives of General Psychiatry* 32:1457–63.

————.[1976] 1986. *Stress Response Syndromes*. 2d ed. New York: Aronson.

————.[1979] 1987. *States of Mind*. 2d ed. New York: Plenum Press.

Horowitz, M. J., and S. Becker. 1972. Cognitive response to stress: Experimental studies of a compulsion to repeat trauma. In R. Holt and E. Peterfreund, eds., *Psychoanalytic and Contemporary Science*, vol. 1. New York: Macmillan.

Horowitz, M. J., C. Marmar, J. Krupnick, N. Wilner, N. Kaltreider, and R. Wallerstein. 1984. *Personality Styles and Brief Psychotherapy*. New York: Basic Books.

Horowitz, M. J., C. Marmar, and N. Wilner. 1979. Analysis of patient states and state transitions. *Journal of Nervous and Mental Diseases* 167:91–99.

Horowitz, M. J. and N. Wilner. 1976. Stress films, emotion, and cognitive response. *Archives of General Psychiatry* 30:1339–44.

Horowitz, M. J., N. Wilner, N. Kaltreider, W. Alvarez. 1980. Signs and symptoms of post traumatic stress disorder. *Archives of General Psychiatry* 37:85–92.

Horowitz, M. J., N. Wilner, C. Marmar, J. Krupnick. 1980. Pathological grief and the activation of latent self images. *American Journal of Psychiatry* 137:1157–62.

Jacobson, E. 1964. *The Self and Object World*. New York: International Universities Press.

Kelly, G. A. 1955. *The Psychology of Personal Constructs*. New York: Norton.

Kernberg, O. 1976. *Object Relations Theory and Clinical Psychoanalysis*. New York: Aronson.

Kiesler, D. J. 1983. The 1982 interpersonal circle: A taxonomy for complementarity in human transactions. *Psychological Review* 90:185–214.

Knapp, P. H. 1969. Image, symbol, and person. *Archives of General Psychiatry* 21:392–406.

————. 1974. Segmentation and structure in psychoanalysis. *Journal of the American Psychoanalytic Association* 22:14–36.

————. 1981. Core processes in the organization of emotions. *Journal of American Academy of Psychoanalysis* 9:415–34.

Knapp, P. H., and A. S. Teele. 1981. Self, other, and free association: Some experimental observations. In S. Tuttman, C. Kaye, and M. Zimmerman, eds., *Object and Self: A Developmental Approach*. New York: International Universities Press.

Lazarus, R. S., and E. M. Opton. 1966. The use of motion picture films in the study of psychological stress: A summary of experimental studies and theoretical formulations. In C. Spielberger, ed. *Anxiety and Behavior*. New York: Academic Press.

Loevinger, J. 1976. *Ego Development*. San Francisco: Jossey-Bass.

————. 1979. Construct validity of the sentence completion test of ego development. *Applied Psychological Measurement* 3:281–311.

Luborsky, L. 1977. Measuring pervasive psychic structure in psychotherapy: The core conflictual relationship. In N. Freedman and S. Grand, eds., *Communicative Structures and Psychic Structures*. New York: Plenum Press.

————. 1984. *Principles of Psychoanalytic Psychotherapy: A Manual for Supportive-Expressive Treatment*. New York: Basic Books.

Marmar, C., N. Wilner, and M. J. Horowitz. 1984. Recurrent patient states in psychotherapy: Segmentation and quantification. In L. Rice and L. Greenberg eds., *Process Measures in Psychotherapy Research*. New York: Guilford Press.

Rosenberg, M. 1979. *Conceiving the Self*. New York: Basic Books.

Ryle, A. 1975. *Frames and Cages*. New York: International Universities Press.

Wiggens, J. S. 1982. Circumplex models of interpersonal behavior in clinical psychology. In P. C. Kendall and J. N. Butcher, eds., *Handbook of Research Methods in Clinical Psychology*. New York: Wiley.

Wilner, N., and M. J. Horowitz. 1975. Intrusive and repetitive thought after a depressing film: A pilot study. *Psychological Reports* 37:135–38.

4   Issues in the Study of Unconscious and Defense Processes: Discussion of Horowitz's Comments, with Some Elaborations

Matthew Hugh Erdelyi, Ph.D

The Unconscious

I shall begin at the beginning, with some observations on the concept of the unconscious. As Freud clearly saw, the existence of unconscious mentation was not only an empirical proposition but a scientific necessity. For, without the assumption of unconscious processes, the phenomena of conscious experience, to which Wilhelm Wundt had consigned scientific psychology by definition, present themselves in an unresolvable haphazardness. William James spoke of "the stream of consciousness," but that is only one metaphor and—according to Eastern wisdom—a delusional one. The Buddhist's image, based on a vast and sophisticated tradition of empirical introspection, is a rather different one: untrained consciousness is not a flowing stream; it is, instead, a crazed monkey jumping in its cage.

If consciousness or, for that matter, behavior is a stream, then it is a most peculiar one in any case: it ends abruptly; it becomes an ocean; it shrinks into a drop of water; it becomes separate streams; it flows forward, suddenly backward; it dries up, disappears altogether; it suddenly flows again but is another stream. In Horowitz's terms, it is characterized by omissions and intrusions. On such a chaotic stream no science of mind can be launched; or if launched, not without an early shipwreck. This was Freud's seminal insight. There is no coherent stream of consciousness; there is a stream of mind, and it flows mostly underground. At this general level Freud's view has prevailed. The notion of unconscious process, in the sense of psychological processes unfolding outside consciousness, is about as uncontro-

This work was supported in part by Grant No. 6-64345 from the City University of New York PSC-CUNY Research Award Program and by Grant No. 19156 of the National Institute of Mental Health, U.S. Public Health Service.

versial in experimental psychology today as it is in psychoanalysis. It is at the finer-grained levels that problems arise.

Terminological Problems

One source of perennial difficulty is that psychologists mean
different things by the unconscious. Freud himself held to at
least three acknowledged "senses" of the unconscious (Erdelyi
1985) and these senses are endemically confused in the psychological literature—and in the psychoanalytic one. For example,
the term *preconscious* is used in a significantly different way by
many contemporary writers than Freud, who introduced the term
into psychology. There is particularly widespread confusion about
Freud's "systemic" sense of the unconscious (Freud [1915] 1957,
[1923] 1961, [1933] 1964), which denotes not a gradation of
awareness but a *system* of the mind characterized by its primitive
cognitive style (*primary-process thinking*) and its peremptory
hedonism (it "obeys" the *pleasure-unpleasure principle*). In part,
to undo the endless semantic confusions surrounding it, the systemic Unconscious—or "system Ucs."—was renamed the *id* and
contraposed to the *ego* (formerly the "system Cs."). Thus, when
Freud states that the laws of the unconscious are different from
the laws of the conscious, he does not mean that conscious processes obey different laws from unconscious ones but that the
laws of the id differ from the laws of the ego (primary vs. secondary process thinking; the pleasure-unpleasure principle vs.
the reality principle). These are just a few examples of the ter-
minological problems that extend, of course, beyond the ambit
of merely psychoanalytic psychology.

Philosophical and Conceptual Problems

As long as the notion of unconscious processes retains its current
vogue, philosophical issues touching on it are likely to be ignored
or shrugged off. These philosophical concerns have only become
latent, however, and will no doubt reassert themselves with any
change in the current consensus on the unconscious—or with
more searching conceptualizations of it. Even today the Wundtian
equation of the psychological with the conscious and, therefore,
the exclusion by definition of unconscious psychological processes surfaces on occasion (White 1980).

A more subtle issue, which inevitably impinges on methodology, is the question of whether a true dichotomy—defined by

a threshold, or limen—actually exists between the conscious and unconscious. Mainstream variants of mathematical decision theory hold that there is no such threshold (Macmillan 1986; Swets 1964), and thus it is hardly a settled issue whether we are dealing with a continuum or two categories of mind.

Methodological Problems

If the history of past efforts by experimental psychology to come to terms with unconscious processes is any guide (see Dixon 1971, 1981; Erdelyi 1974, 1985; Eriksen 1962), the great counterattack against the concept will be methodological, centering on the question of whether purported subliminal effects are actually subliminal in a strict or absolute sense (i.e., $d' = 0$). Such questions are already surfacing in reaction to Marcel's influential work (Holender 1986; Merikle 1982; Purcell, Stewart, and Stanovich 1983). It is hard to suggest the depth and complexity of the problem, which gives the impression, the more one confronts it, of being methodologically impenetrable (Erdelyi 1986). For example, how can it be shown that a stimulus is strictly subliminal (in the sense of $d' = 0$) when accessibility of information, d', can either increase or decrease with time and effort (Erdelyi 1984, 1986) and, therefore, depends on the time and effort expended by the subject prior to measurement? Or, worse still, what can be made of any particular d', including $d' = 0$, given the fact that under identical psychophysical conditions, different modes of questioning produce different values of accessibility (Eriksen 1962; Graf, Squire, and Mandler 1983).

If even within the narrow confines of the laboratory setting the demonstration of strict subliminal effects is this problematic, how much more so does the problem become in a clinical context? How is one to know—in a scientific rather than a clinically intuitive way—that a particular "state" or process—a defense maneuver, for example—is indeed unconscious?

Defense

Although the concept of unconscious processes has suddenly entered the mainstream of experimental psychology, the same cannot be said for defense processes. It is hard to know what experimental cognitive psychologists actually think about defense processes since the topic receives no treatment in the typical textbook. Modern texts on memory, which readily address matters of the most exotic nature, fail as a rule even to mention the term *repression*. The state of the literature brings to mind Horowitz's "omissions." It is almost as if the literature, imitating a Zen master, were conveying the profound essence of the repression process through inexplicable acts (and omissions of acts) rather than through formal verbal exposition.

As has been shown by Erdelyi and Goldberg (1979), there exists a fundamental dissociation in the empirical literature on repression: the laboratory evidence has failed to provide viable proof for the existence of repression, while the clinical literature provides overwhelming corroboration. The trade-offs between the two methods are sadly familiar. The laboratory provides rigor but is often artificial. It is doubtful, for example, that the types of "emotional" stimuli explored in the laboratory have any business even to be considered in the context of defense processes. They are probably the emotional counterparts of Hermann Ebbinghaus's nonsense syllables. However, clinical materials such as those provided by the research of Horowitz as well as that of Luborsky and Shevrin, include precisely the stimuli that produce overwhelming threats and call for the deployment of defensive coping devices.

An interesting feature of Horowitz's clinical observations, which impinges simultaneously on the problems of the unconscious and of defense, needs to be underscored. Note that the identified defensive maneuvers are characterized usually (though not always, e.g., p. 8) as unconscious, but that the clinical data presented do not necessarily demand such an assumption. Omissions do often suggest the operation of an inhibitory process, but why an *unconscious* inhibitory process (pp. 7–8)? Although the unconscious nature of defense mechanisms is taken as a truism by psychoanalysts—even if it was not by Sigmund Freud, notwithstanding the regnant belief to this effect (see Erdelyi and Goldberg 1979)—the scientific basis of this assumption has not been carefully buttressed. Subjects widely report using the full range of standard defense mechanisms in a conscious manner (Erdelyi and Goldberg 1979). This point is emphasized not only because of its empirical interest but also because of a significant methodological ramification. As a result of the methodological intractability of the unconscious, any experimental program attempting to demonstrate simultaneously the operation of (1) defense processes that (2) are unconscious is bound to strain beyond the perimeters of current experimental methodology (Erdelyi and Goldberg 1979).

The point here is not to deny that defense processes are often unconscious but to emphasize that they are not exclusively unconscious and can, therefore, be readily addressed in their conscious manifestations by current experimental techniques. Thus, there is no necessity to foist a discontinuity on the laws that govern conscious as against unconscious defense processes (note Jerome Singer's similar emphasis of the continuity between nightdreams and daydreams). Indeed, methodological convenience apart, there is no justification for the theoretical imposition of such a discontinuity in the absence of empirical evidence. As already noted, Freud's remark that the laws of the conscious differ from those of the unconscious referred to the *systems* Ucs. and Cs. (the id and the ego, respectively), not to the laws that govern conscious and unconscious processing. It was precisely Freud's intent to show the continuity or coherence of mental life by extending the realm of the mental to the unconscious. The fundamental thrust of his project was to reveal unsuspected continuities, not discontinuities, not only in regard to conscious versus unconscious processes but also in regard to a multitude of superficially discontinuous phenomena such as dreams, daydreams, fantasy, symptoms, and religion (Erdelyi 1985).

The ultimate problem with defense, as with so many other constructs in pyschology, is that it is anchored to the notion of intention or purpose and is thus problematic on both philosophic and methodological grounds. As emphasized by Erdelyi and Goldberg (1979), we have as yet no explicit methodology of purpose. Consider the controversial phenomenon of *perceptual defense*, the purported elevation of perceptual thresholds to threatening stimuli. Let us assume that the methodological objections to the phenomenon have been resolved and that it is (for at least certain classes of subjects) veridical. Is such a phenomenon—lowered sensitivity to threatening stimuli—necessarily a *defense* phenomenon, as its name suggests? Not necessarily. Such a phenomenon could also be accounted for by the nondefensive disruption of perception and memory by emotion or by any other attention-disrupting event (Erdelyi and Appelbaum 1973; Erdelyi and Blumenthal 1973; Loftus and Burns 1981). This is precisely the objection advanced by Holmes (1974) and others in connection with supposed experimental demonstrations of memory defense, that is, repression. Thus, memory failures associated with anxiety or any other cognitive disturbance, such as Luborsky has beautifully instantiated in real clinical protocols, need not be construed as evidence for repression; somehow—and here is where current methodological (or epistemological) techniques leave off—it must be demonstrated that the memory loss is intentional. A methodology needs to be developed capable of corroborating—or falsifying—clinical conceptualizations such as "intrusions were breakthroughs of themes defensively warded off . . . from conscious representation."

The problem might not be as intractable as I have tended to make it out; experimental psychologists do seem comfortable in assuming intentionality in many other research situations, and perhaps with more justification than I have been willing to concede them. Some variant of context analysis (e.g., Erdelyi 1985; Luborsky, Sackeim, and Christoph 1979) probably holds the key, for ultimately it is the context of an event that yields information about intent—indeed, about meaning. The scientific underpinning of such a method, whatever form it takes, will be, as Horowitz suggests, consensual validation by independent observers.

The Language Problem

An important theme for Horowitz is the need for some "lexicon" or appropriate set of "descriptive" or "explanatory terms." Here, Horowitz is identifying a fundamental problem, although I would prefer to think of it not as a problem of lexicon (words, terms, etc.) but as an outright problem of language (cf. Erdelyi 1985), by which I mean, in psychology, the implicit or explicit analog systems through which concepts are articulated. (Their counterparts in physics would be different mathematical systems.) My review of the perceptual defense and vigilance literature a decade ago convinced me that many, perhaps most, controversies within experimental psychology are linguistic problems masquerading as experimental problems. In the New Look area, for example, the standard conceptualization of "perception" was based on an implicit reflex arc analogy, of the following form (e.g., Eriksen 1958):

$$\text{stimulus} \rightarrow \text{perception} \rightarrow \text{response}$$

Such an analogic premise virtually dooms the concept from the outset since it suggest that "perception" is a single, "either-or" event rather than a multiprocess phenomenon. How could a perceptual process that either happens or fails to happen yield perceptual defense, since for perceptual defense to take place it is first necessary to perceive the threatening stimulus, the very perception that defense supposedly prevents? Such paradoxes, as I showed in my review article (Erdelyi 1974), disappear when the term *perception*—note, the same term—is reformulated in a different analogic system, such as the computer.

In the more immediate context of Horowitz's chapters, let us consider a key term associated with defense and, more generally, psychodynamics, the notion of "force." Suppose we conducted a "gedanken survey" of mainstream experimental psychologists in which we ask the question, "Do you believe in the existence of 'living forces' in the mind, of cathexes, anticathexes, and so forth?" Now compare the likely percentages of Yes and No responses to those of another hypothetical survey question: "Do you believe in 'mental interactions,' of thought interacting with thought, emotion with thought, memories with schemata, and so forth?" It would be hard it imagine a Yes response rate significantly below 100 percent to the second question, and one substantially above zero percent to the first.

Now this is strange since in a formal sense the two questions may be identical. A physicist may speak of "strong forces" or "strong interactions" and mean exactly the same thing. "Dynamics" in physics may or may not be couched in the metaphor of "force," although the choice of using a mathematical system to articulate the concept may not be trivial. The point, of course, is that the difference, if any, does not formally reside in the term used to designate the concept but in the *operationalization* of the concept. There are "forces" in the mind but these are not operationalized as F = mass × acceleration.

The problem of terminology in psychology is that, typically, the adopted vocabulary subliminally co-opts an implicit analogic system (and vice versa). What needs to be explored, perhaps more than the choice of terms, is the analogic premise that is implied by the terms and the extent to which the theorist actually wishes to subscribe to the implicit analog. Thus, if *psychodynamics* is taken to mean "the play of forces in the mind" (Freud 1917, 60) in a literal sense—of either "force" or "play"—we would be saddled with an absurdist formulation. Freud himself frequently warned against such literalizations. On the other hand, if we defined psychodynamics as the phenomena of mental "interactions and counteractions" (Fenichel 1945, 11), it would be hard to understand in what sense any "cognitive" process is not inherently "psychodynamic," and, thus, how one could even loosely contrapose "psychodynamic approaches" to "cognitive approaches" (Erdelyi 1985).

These concerns apply directly to some theoretical alternatives that Horowitz is interested in exploring, which may actually turn out to be indistinguishable in a *formal* sense. Several years ago (before Lakoff and Johnson's [1980] influential monograph) I posed the following matching question to some students: Which (see Fig. 4.1) represents *repression* and which represents *dissociation?*

With no exception, (a) was chosen as representing dissociation and (b) as representing repression. Of course, there is no formal basis for such a choice; the up-down or left-right dimension is simply not relevant to either. Indeed, Freud at times used "dissociation" or "splitting" to conceptualize repression, and his models of mind were expressed in both horizontal (e.g., Freud [1900] 1953) and vertical orientation (e.g., Freud [1923] 1961), with the orientation having no theoretical status. Nevertheless, very much in line with my students' responses, the literature (of hypnosis, for example) reflects a propensity to treat repression and dissociation phenomena as distinct. We note, then, a tendency to distinguish between terms not on formal grounds but on the basis of analog nuance. For this reason, I would urge great caution about contrasting different explanatory "principles" of psychodynamics such as "Signal Anxiety Theory" versus "Special States Theory" until it is established that they actually constitute, vocabulary aside, different principles. All of these theories may in fact be (although they need not be) the same theory.

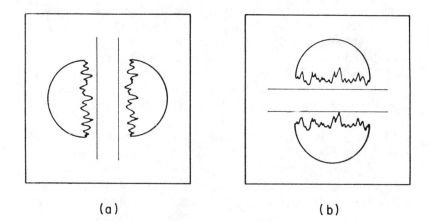

(a)   (b)

FIGURE 4.1 Which is *repression* and which is *dissociation?*

Jungian "Complexes" and "States of Mind"

It is interesting to note Horowitz's tendency toward a variant of Jungian "complex" theory—which actually is a dissociationist theory that does go beyond Freud's conceptualization of repression. Horowitz states:

When we reviewed the data, warded-off themes were found to occur, but we were surprised by what seemed at first to be a "disorderly" sequence. A complex of ideas and feelings seemed to be consciously available to the patient in some states of mind, intrusive at others, omitted or completely disavowed during still another state.

In a given state an idea might be too much to bear, while in another state it could be considered. Such observations required us to move from a linear, temporal theory of organizing responses to a recent trauma, to a system that recognized differences within an individual in terms of his or her states of mind.

There is here, as in Jung, a polypsychist flavor. Consciousness (the "ego" in Jung's system) is simply the dominant complex at a particular moment. In the Jungian system, too, there is "switching" and "oscillation" of the complexes, so that the dominant one at a particular time is superseded by another one at another time. When these configurations or complexes are abnormally developed, we encounter the phenomenon of multiple personality. Horowitz's paper suggests, as Jung would, that all of us to some extent are multiple personalities. Some of these notions—especially the evolution of a Freudian structural scheme into a Jungian complex one—have been brilliantly rendered, in novelistic form, by Herman Hesse in *Steppenwolf*.

Oscillation and the "Concentric Stratification"
of Emotional Memories

Quite apart from the theoretical advantages or disadvantages of such a "complex" psychology, Horowitz's systematic clinical observations provide an interesting empirical find—and provoke an important empirical question. The technique of systematic desensitization, which is conventionally regarded as antithetical to psychoanalytic approaches, can be shown actually to bear formal similarities to early psychoanalytic procedures, especially Breuer's cathartic technique (Erdelyi 1985; Wachtel 1977).

One of these similarities involves the notion of "hierarchy." However, in the cathartic technique and its variants, the hierarchy is not formally constructed but is conceived of as inherent in the patient's mental organization. The patient is thought to bring to the therapy a built-in hierarchy—a "concentric stratification"—of emotional memories:

"We must not expect to meet with a *single* traumatic memory and a *single* pathogenic idea as its nucleus; we must be prepared for *successions of partial* traumas and *concatenations* of pathogenic trains of thought. . . . The psychic material . . . presents itself as a structure in several dimensions. . . . To begin with there is a nucleus consisting in memories of events or trains of thought in which the traumatic factor has culminated or the pathogenic idea has found its purest manifestation. Round this nucleus we find what is often an incredibly profuse amount of other mnemic material which has to be worked through in the analysis. . . . It was as though we were examining a dossier that had been kept in good order. . . . Each [theme] is—I cannot express it any other way—stratified concentrically around the psychological nucleus. . . . Resistance . . . increases in proportion as the strata are nearer to the nucleus. . . . The most peripheral strata contain the memories (or files) which . . . are easily remembered and have always been clearly conscious. The deeper we go the more difficult it becomes for the emerging memories to be recognized, till near the nucleus we come upon memories which the patient disavows even in reproducing them. It is the peculiarity of the concentric stratification of the pathogenic material which . . . lends to the course of these analyses their characteristic features. (Breuer and Freud [1895] 1955, 287–89)

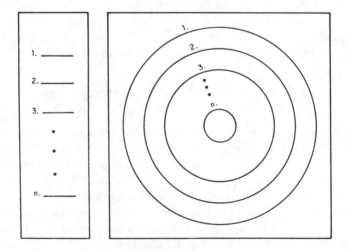

FIGURE 4.2 Organization of emotional material: Wolpe's explicit linear "hierarchy" (left) and Freud's implicit "concentric stratification" (right). (Erdelyi 1985)

As I have noted elsewhere (Erdelyi 1985), Wolpe's hierarchy is an *ordered list*, Freud's a *concentric stratification*. (See Fig. 4.2). Horowitz does not, to his surprise, find such an arrangement. This now raises the question whether Freud's original formulation was incorrect (or simplistic), a question that Horowitz's systematic clinical technique has the power of answering: Is there in fact no dynamic ordering of memories, or is there a stratification but with variability? Thus, would a clinician find that *on the average* the memories/themes dealt with get progressively more troublesome, or is there actually no clear pattern—or perhaps another pattern or a different pattern for different personality types?

Methodological Notes on the Clinical-Experimental Approach

In the paper I wrote with Goldberg on repression (1979), we called for a "hybrid" methodology that would combine the vigor of the clinic and the rigor of the experimental laboratory. We argued that only by such a hybrid approach is progress in the study of psychodynamic phenomena likely to be made. I note with satisfaction that the paper by Horowitz and, indeed, the work of several of the contributors to this volume are in this emerging tradition. Note, for example, that in this approach there is no question about the effectiveness of the stimuli, that is, the emotional valence of the memories or themes dealt with. Moreover, individual differences are taken into account in the clinical-experimental approach; the threatening materials—the effective stimuli—are quite different for different patients/subjects.

There are methodological advantages, but there are methodological problems as well. One critical issue is the presentation, in some manageable form, of the specific data base on which inferences are made—a clinical analog, perhaps, of tables and figures. The critical reader has to be brought into the inference process somehow and the evidence—pro and con—made available for conclusions such as "Ann wanted to become independent of her father, and because of her warded-off contempt for him, she also wanted to become better than he in her profession." I believe that some kind of systematic appendix (e.g., Luborsky, Sackeim, and Christoph 1979) or context summary and table (e.g., Erdelyi 1985) would be critical, listing some of the strongest evidence for and against a particular interpretation. The documentation prob-

lem in the clinical-experimental approach is all the more important in view of Horowitz's emphasis on consensual validity. I completely agree with him; it is only when consensual agreement is
demonstrated that interpretations will take on scientific value. For
this reason especially, it is necessary to present the evidence (context) for interpretations in a form that can be publicly examined.
Not all readers will agree about an interpretation; precisely for
this reason the material must be made available. Moreover, some
kind of concordance coefficient should be reported, based on the
inferences of independent judges. The idea of "control themes"
is an excellent one as a check on the validity of judges' interpretations. The overall topic of documented interpretation is far too
complex to be dealt with in a summary fashion, and I raise it here
mostly to underscore its importance and to place it on the methodological agenda for future psychodynamic research involving
the clinical-experimental approach.

I would add two final suggestions, both rather inconvenient.
I would like to see variants of the clinical-experimental method
extended to long-term therapy, where some of the interpretations
and extracted configurations might receive clearer and more
extensive undergirding. Second, in line with a tradition in experimental psychology of the experimenter serving as his own
subject, I would like to see volunteer subject-patients serve as
"co-experimenters" in the analysis and interpretation of their
own protocols. They would, after all, be in a special position to
evaluate their own materials—and to react to the analyses of the
therapist-experimenter. Their "special" position may not be a
privileged one, but the time may have arrived for the therapist
not to be the only one to have the last word. I, for one, would
be interested in the comments of the Annas of the clinical laboratory—from Breuer's Anna to Horowitz's Ann.

References

Breuer, J., and S. Freud. [1895] 1955. Studies on hysteria. *Standard
    Edition*, vol. 2. London: Hogarth Press.
Dixon, N. F. 1971. *Subliminal Perception: The Nature of a Controversy.*
    London: McGraw-Hill.
———. 1981. *Preconscious Processing.* New York: Wiley.
Erdelyi, M. H. 1974. A new look at the New Look: Perceptual defense
    and vigilance. *Psychological Review* 81:1–25.

————. 1984. The recovery of unconscious (inaccessible) memories: Laboratory studies of hypermnesia. In G. Bower, ed., *The Psychology of Learning and Motivation: Advances in Research and Theory*, vol. 18. New York: Academic Press.

————. 1985. *Psychoanalysis: Freud's Cognitive Psychology*. New York: Freeman.

————. 1986. Experimental indeterminacies in the dissociation paradigm of subliminal perception (Commentary). *The Behavioral and Brain Sciences* 9:30–31.

Erdelyi, M. H., and G. A. Appelbaum. 1973. Cognitive masking: The disruptive effect of an emotional stimulus upon the perception of contiguous neutral items. *Bulletin of the Psychonomic Society* 1:59–61.

Erdelyi, M. H., and D. Blumenthal. 1973. Cognitive masking in rapid sequential processing: The effect of an emotional picture on preceding and succeeding pictures. *Memory and Cognition* 1:201–4.

Erdelyi, M. H., and B. Goldberg. 1979. Let's not sweep repression under the rug: Toward a cognitive psychology of repression. In J. F. Kihlstrom and F. J. Evans, eds., *Functional Disorders of Memory*. Hillsdale, N.J.: Erlbaum.

Eriksen. C. W. 1958. Unconscious processes. In M. R. Jones, ed., *Nebraska Symposium on Motivation*. Lincoln: University of Nebraska Press.

————, ed. 1962. *Behavior and Awareness*. Durham, N.C.: Duke University Press.

Fenichel, O. 1945. *The Psychoanalytic Theory of Neurosis*. New York: Norton.

Freud, S. [1900] 1953. The interpretation of dreams. *Standard Edition*, vols. 4 and 5. London: Hogarth Press.

————. [1915] 1957. The unconscious. *Standard Edition*, vol. 14. London: Hogarth Press.

——. 1917. *A General Introduction to Psychoanalysis*. New York: Liveright.

————. [1923] 1961. The ego and the id. *Standard Edition*, vol. 19. London: Hogarth Press.

————. [1933] 1964. New introductory lectures in psychoanalysis. *Standard Edition*, vol. 20. London: Hogarth Press.

Graf, P., L. R. Squire, and G. Mandler. 1983. The information that amnesic patients do not forget. *Journal of Experimental Psychology: Learning, Memory, and Cognition* 10:164–78.

Holender, D. 1986. Semantic activation without conscious identification in dichotic listening, parafoveal vision, and visual masking: A survey and appraisal. *The Behavioral and Brain Sciences* 9:1–66.

Holmes, D. S. 1974. Investigations of repression: Differential recall of material experimentally or naturally associated with ego threat. *Psychological Bulletin* 81:632–53.

Lakoff, G., and M. Johnson. 1980. *Metaphors We Live By*. Chicago: University of Chicago Press.

Loftus, E. F., and T. E. Burns. 1981. Paper read at the annual meeting of the Psychonomic Society, November, Philadelphia, Pennsylvania.

Luborsky, L., H. Sackeim, and P. Christoph. 1979. The state conducive to momentary forgetting. In J. F. Kihlstrom and F. J. Evans, eds., *Functional Disorders of Memory*. Hillsdale, N.J.: Erlbaum.

Macmillan, N. A. 1986. The psychophysics of subliminal perception (Commentary). *The Behavioral and Brain Sciences* 9:38–39.

Merikle, P. M. 1982. Unconscious perception revisited. *Perception and Psychophysics* 31:298–301.

Purcell, D. G., A. L. Stewart, and K. E. Stanovich. 1983. Another look at semantic priming without awareness. *Perception and Psychophysics* 34:65–71.

Swets, J. A., ed., 1964. *Signal Detection and Recognition in Human Observers*. New York: Wiley.

Wachtel, P. 1977. *Psychoanalysis and Behavior Therapy*. New York: Basic Books.

White, P. 1980. Limitations on verbal reports of internal events: A refutation of Nisbett and Wilson and of Bem. *Psychological Review* 87:105–12.

5 Steps Toward a Lexicon: Discussion of "Unconsciously Determined Defensive Strategies"

Peter H. Knapp, M.D.

This enterprise brings together differing scientific traditions, two in particular. The first, cognitive psychology, opens fresh avenues to the study of mental processes; the second, psychoanalysis, approaches the same task after nearly a century of naturalistic case studies. A convergence of these streams is in the contemporary air, in the linguistic, cognitive, social, historical, literary, and clinical atmosphere. Horowitz has sensed the fitful contact between these traditions and seen an exciting prospect. To help such divergent currents truly mingle, we must be clear about their respective sources—theoretical, methodological, and empirical.

Cognitive psychology has been shaped by the creative paradigms of cybernetics, information processing, and artificial intelligence; it has relied heavily on the computer sciences. Moreover, it has seen the computer not as a black box, forever inscrutable, but as a box with circuitry and programming, both of which can be understood. So viewed, cognitive psychology presents an exciting mixture of approaches to understanding conscious and nonconscious processes.

Methodologically, the psychological laboratory has pursued experimental attempts to control and observe behavior and to plan quantitative tests of cognitive models; for example, the elegant, if controversial, experiments about the nature of imagery by R. N. Shepard and Z. Pylyshyn, both contributors to another symposium (Block 1982.)

Psychoanalysis emerged much earlier, from the nineteenth-century traditions of romantic philosophy and mechanistic biology—the two strands identified by Ellenberger (1970). Guided (at times dominated) by the genius of its founder, psychoanalysis followed Freud in constantly revising many of its concepts, some according to clinical dictates, some by borrowing from other disciplines, at times indiscriminately, at times shrewdly.

The primary data of psychoanalysis have come from the clinic, supported and elaborated by developmental, anthropological, and linguistic observations. Forays into experiment, as Erdelyi points out (1985), have often achieved precision at the expense of weakening or losing sight altogether of the crucial phenomena they seek to study. The most illuminating psychodynamic experiments have incorporated features of the clinical setting, such as those tracing the effects of subliminal perception in dreaming and waking imagery, carried out originally by Poetzl (1917) and later by Fisher (1954). Quasi-clinical experiments have also used hypnosis (Hilgard 1952) and systematic exposure to stressful stimuli (Lazarus 1966; Horowitz 1976). An ingenious experiment reported by Keet in 1948 made use of a miniature counseling situation: Keet reported the induction of amnesia for emotionally painful words, selected on individual grounds for individual subjects; then he intervened, psychotherapeutically, using either a passive associative Rogerian approach or an active interpretative approach. He claimed the latter but not the former approach was successful in overcoming the artifically induced memory block (Keet 1948). This quasi-clinical approach is intrinsically interesting, although attempts to replicate Keet's work have foundered, encountering difficulties in inducing his presumed conflict state and resultant amnesia.

The main bulk of psychoanalytic data has come from the study of patients undergoing treatment, starting with the early case reports of Freud, some written with Joseph Breuer, followed by those written by other early collaborators. We should not diminish the dramatic impact of those early observations: the jointly authored "Studies on Hysteria"; Freud's first child-analytic study of Little Hans; his study of the obsessional "Rat Man"; and his tour de force, the "analysis" of a patient he never saw, the floridly paranoid Magistrate Schreber. Such case reports provided brilliant insights, although they left questions: how to replicate, generalize, and validate.

An increase in rigor has characterized scientific effort in psychoanalysis and has particularly marked the surge of activity within the past two decades in psychotherapy research. The definition of theoretical views and of technical approaches, the accurate characterization of subject populations, the control of relevant variables, the measurement of outcome and the assessment of the processes involved—all of these features have marked the maturation of this field. Two major contributors to it are Luborsky and Horowitz.

A psychiatrist, psychoanalyst, and research scientist, Horo-witz's early research began with observations about psychophy-siologic changes and variations in imagery in response to stress. More recently he has become an acknowledged leader in psy-chotherapy research. He has shown an eagerness to assimilate new concepts to psychoanalytic thinking, and he has attacked difficult problems of measurement. He has resisted two opposing vices of many previous psychoanalytic scholars: to downgrade the importance of measurement because of the alleged private, ineffable nature of clinical data, and to become lost in a search for methodological perfection so as largely to avoid factual questions.

My substantive response to Horowitz's chapter will center on his call for a lexicon—specifically on four terms: Unconscious, Defenses, Emotions, Stress. I will add some terms of my own and will suggest the need for organizing all of these terms into models that specify their interrelationships and that may facilitate studying them empirically.

First, and perhaps foremost, the term *unconscious*. Factors operating out of awareness were posited long before Freud, as Erdelyi (1985), Whyte (1960), and others have noted. They are inherent in many cognitive psychological theories. Yet their na-ture is far from simple, no matter how hard our theorists strive for simplification. Freud's initial formulations pictured a rational, conscious mind separated by a clear barrier—somehow actively maintained—from a nether world pictured as hedonistic, self-seeking, disorderly, and violent. In casual parlance "The Un-conscious" was personified, as if it were a replica of the conscious self but a bit of a ragamuffin.

This original theoretical separation into two distinct realms soon required qualification. The puzzling zone of preconscious processes, not conscious but capable of becoming so, was an early, essential addition. Freud moved on toward a view of struc-tural agencies in the mind and conceptualized the ego and the superego, one responsible for adaptation to outer reality, the other for moral regulation. Both were in some ways pitted against the unconscious id, but it soon became apparent that many of the functions ascribed to ego and superego, originally seen as con-scious agencies, in fact operated outside of awareness.

Mankind clings to simplicity. What Margolin (1949) termed in the psychosomatic sphere a fantasy of function—what R. Jackendoff called in the discussion of these papers, the mythology of consciousness—has persisted. Conscious thought is often seen as simple and obvious activity, resulting from a state of full awareness and full self-control: this activity emerges somehow *de novo* in the human species; it is a self-evident given. The limitations of this view have been pointed out by numerous observers, some of whom are at this conference. Marcel (1983), for example, has stressed that perception—a crucial function of consciousness— is an active process of making as much sense as possible, for intentional ends, of a welter of stimuli that impinge on an organism. Perception matches input to a model of reality and involves a continual testing of hypotheses. This view can be seen as a focused, sophisticated version of that of Schilder (1935), who spoke of the body image—a crucial product of consciousness— as a continual re-creation by the individual from the flux of his experience.

Selection implies exclusion. Obviously some potential experience is excluded and remains or becomes nonconscious. However, unconscious aspects of mental life are more complex than simply unattended or discarded perceptions. Certainly they are not a mere replica or a mere image of conscious experience. Unconscious activities probably constitute far more of mentation than could ever be caught in the spotlight of consciousness. Not only may they resemble, in Freud's simile, the submerged bulk of the iceberg, but they are far from monolithic. Differing processes must be distinguished. These can be seen as forming a crude hierarchical array. Provisionally we may divide them as follows.

1. "Pure" cognitive operations, having to do with the processing of perceptual and other information. Probably wired into the organism, these are efficient, automatic mechanisms concerned with incoming and outgoing communication: an example is the perception and production of speech. In psychoanalytic theory these are ego activities, autonomous and for the most part conflict-free.

2. Other unconscious processes that we may call protocognitive operations. These consist of mechanisms for regulating satisfaction and dissatisfaction, using a minimax principle, minimizing pain and maximizing pleasure. They comprise ways of restricting, transforming, and selecting among affective-

instinctive-motivational elements in experience. From an "ego-centric" point of view, we call them ego defense mechanisms. They are not conflict-free, in the sense that they have ambivalently valued consequences; we cling to them. They promote adaptation but can also be hampering in their effects. They, too, are genuinely unconscious; they themselves cannot be directly seen but only inferred. Possibly in some instances they may be traced to very early behavioral levels; for instance, as Freud noted ([1925] 1961), "spitting out" and turning away may be a prototype of what later emerges as the defense of denial.

3. All of this implies that there are also unconscious affective-instinctive-motivational processes. These are full bodily-and-mental core components, shared by man with other members of the animal kingdom. They, too, are genuinely unconscious. Components of them can be experienced as feelings, largely because these carry with them bodily effects. However, they cannot be directly experienced in their total range, and they can only be approximately translated into words. They activate various levels of phantasy (a term to which we will return). Phantasies, in turn, are linked to bodily processes, although many of the "defensive" operations mentioned in the preceding paragraph are aimed at diminishing these bodily aspects or withdrawing attention from them.

The last group of unconscious processes mentioned was the first to be noted by Freud; it constitutes the crux of what has been called the "dynamic" unconscious. These are quite different from perceptual regulatory features, tacit cognitive assumptions, or other nonconscious aspects of information exchange between the subject and his world. These affective-instinctive-motivational factors, common to our animal forebears, lead ineluctably to clashes with society and to conflicts within each individual. The defensive regulatory factors already mentioned, with the aid of societal pressures, partially control these primitive urges, although never completely. Such dynamic unconscious elements deal with more than information processing, easily modeled after a computer; we may say they deal with the computers' power supply or, to use a different metaphor, with the animal, filled with desires and fears, who directs the computer.

Somewhat like Marx in his different conceptual domain, Freud advanced a radical view of man-as-animal. This had been adumbrated, although less radically, by many predecessors, ironists from Aristophanes to Molière, tragedians from Sophocles to

Shakespeare. Freud's extreme view of man's basic motivational matrix gave a distinctive philosophic cast to him and, allowing for wide variations, to his followers. The theoretical stance was complicated by Freud's biological background and also by his authoritarian temperament. Not only was his view of man in many ways disturbing; it was also ideological and rigid. The scientific task ahead is to test his views, discarding the ideological blinders while not watering down the force of his theory.

The task is challenging. It is easier to assess overt formal features of mental life than (putative) hidden content. An example comes from a study of errors in linguistic performance. Fromkin's introduction to a recent symposium devoted to that topic (1980) pays tribute to both R. Meringer and Freud, who were respectively philological and psychoanalytic pioneers. Many of the contributors to that book acknowledge the appeal of "Freudian" formulations but remark that linguists as a whole have been content to assume that "the mechanics of slips can be studied linguistically without reference to their motivation" (A. W. Ellis, in Fromkin, 1980, 123, quoting D. S. Boomer and J. Laver); or if slips of the tongue are seen as a "part of Freudian theory . . . [they are] . . . out of the mainstream of modern cognitive theory" (G. S. Dell and P. A. Reich, in Fromkin, 1980, 273).

This emphasis is understandable. Knowledge has accumulated rapidly about many levels of information processing involved in the perception and production of speech. Such knowledge has disclosed linguistic regularities in the formal properties of errors. M. Motley (in Fromkin, 1980) and Baars (Chapter 13 of this volume) have reported experimental efforts validating the original claims that global motivational sets are important determinants of these errors, even if they may not have the exclusive role claimed by Freud.

Dynamic unconscious factors are predictably difficult to demonstrate because of the circumstances surrounding them: they are actively warded off; in Freud's terms they are held in a state of repression. The converse term is *resistance* to their emergence. Horowitz discusses, and Erdelyi elaborates, two types of evidence for the existence of such unconscious factors: gaps and intrusions, errors of omission and commission. Actually both, as errors, imply some disruption of the smooth surface of repression, a degree of strain. By their nature, they are exceptions to the rule—using that word in a dual sense—of an untroubled consciousness.

A third, more pervasive phenomenon is profoundly important for defenses; it applies to most of what is dynamically unconscious, although the evidence surrounding it is even more difficult to unravel. That is the phenomenon of symbolic transformation. A threatening mental element—a phallic image, a murderous wish—is not simply abolished from the stream of awareness, perhaps leaving an obvious discontinuity, possibly reintruding itself abruptly. Such an element often remains but in symbolic disguise: a cigar may *not* be just a cigar; abstract musings about death may represent a concrete death wish. Thus, in manifest content we read latent meanings. The detection of unconscious aspects of communication becomes a matter of symbolic decoding, of interpretation.

Symbolic transformation takes many forms. A speaker, a self, may use a term metaphorically, that is, use it in a sense that stands for another, more "literal" sense. This may be a difficult matter to ascertain, for literal use itself may be shrouded in a metaphorical past. Metaphor, defined in this traditional, restricted way, poses a challenge to linguists, psychoanalysts, and cognitive psychologists. The precise constraints of congruence between terms, custom, and context, which make a metaphor apt and also understandable, remain elusive (as indicated by Ortony and others in still another symposium [1979]; see also MacCormac 1985). The metaphoric nature of language is one of the perennial shoals on which machine translation has foundered.

There are other, related kinds of symbolic transformation. Not only may an aspect of the environment, or its image, be used quasi-metaphorically (again, the cigar), but individuals of whom or to whom a speaker refers may represent still other individuals. They may represent the speaker himself, as a whole or in part. At various levels he may confuse subject and object or part and whole.

In the intimate associative discourse of psychoanalytic therapy, a speaker brings a wealth of schemata representing self and others. Thus, Ann, in Horowitz's material, displayed a number of states of mind, for instance, *explosive rage* or *frightened yearning*. Proceeding carefully from less to more inferential levels, Horowitz sees these essentially emotional states as embedded in different, subjectively experienced interpersonal contexts: a child raging at a dominating, hurtful parent; a child yearning for an absent, abandoning parent. It is worth noting the use of active gerunds to describe these states. Let us set aside for a moment the question of how the particular verbs and agents are selected from the recorded interview and with what degree of reliability and validity. The central point is that Ann's communication can be seen as revealing schematic patterns. These are crudely symbolic, allusive, elusive, but persistent; in Suzanne Langer's terms (1951) they are presentational rather than discursive.

Moreover, such patterns do not characterize a constant, unchanging speaker addressing an equally constant audience. In Ann's case, the speaker herself oscillated. At one moment she was the subject, at another the object of angry attacking impulses, not only in what she reported but—Horowitz hints—in what she experienced with the therapist. She could become *artificially engaging*, sometimes with "sniping" overtones, presumably to be more actively in control of the encounter and to ward off guilt or retaliation as a consequence of her rage, or to defend against a sense of helplessness from her longing. Horowitz implies that role reversal was a major feature in these defensive operations: He further suggests an important line of evidence pertaining to the structure of these reversals, saying that "she would juggle the subject and object of verbs, adverbs, and adjectives from self to other."

A further feature of symbolic transformation constitutes another clinical cornerstone. It is the compulsion of an individual to use present relationships to reenact relationships from the past: this is the phenomenon of transference. A central discovery of Freud's, its centrality is underlined by Luborsky, among others, in his concept of the core conflictual-relationship theme (1984). Indeed, Luborsky feels that a nucleus of reenactment transferred from the past can be demonstrated in virtually every psychotherapeutic interview.

The argument has landed us in the theoretical heartland of psychoanalysis—not its abstract, metapsychological theory but its concrete clinical theory. This theory has largely to do with symbolic relationships; it deals with meanings and thus confronts us with the problems of validating them.

Meaning has been called "a harlot among words" (Cherry 1966). The many "meanings of meaning" (Ogden and Richards 1923) convey a host of relations between phenomena and terms. The relations differ in the degree of invariance they specify, as Goodman reminds us (1968): a chemical equation and a painting follow different dictates. Human discourse, lying somewhere in between those two, inevitably has multiple determinants and suffers from ambiguity. In dealing with psychotherapeutic or psychoanalytic discourse, a preliminary simplification is to distinguish two broad classes: semantic and pragmatic meaning. Semantic meaning refers to the denotations and connotations of words, and to the analogous symbolic referents of images and motor acts. Pragmatic meaning refers to the intended import and purport of communication (Knapp 1983).

Using guidelines stemming from that broad division, one can select specific segments of discourse. Horowitz's effort to identify states of mind, as well as the points of shift between them, addresses this problem of segmentation. Once segments have been determined, one can ask targeted questions about them. Questions may be open-ended, making the assessment of agreement difficult but allowing ambiguity to spawn imaginative richness; or forced choice may be used, which constricts but tests more rigorously the nature of observer judgments. Context may be controlled: contextual background information may be supplied in minimal accounts, then progressively enlarged.

If present, interobserver agreement may be heavily influenced by shared bias. It is necessary to find other validating criteria. Here we encounter further difficulties, for the determination of meaning is essentially a judgment, although, as we have noted, it can be guided by rules of varying specificity. Repeated instances of a phenomenon in the text may permit the extraction of common contextual features. At times these can be compared to features found in comparison contexts, as in the method outlined by Luborsky (Chapter 9 of this book). At times the simple accretion of regularities lends conviction to observer judgments.

Often, however, we must interpret a relatively isolated occurrence, as must the historian. For the most part we have to rely on something best called goodness of fit. Fit is a persuasive and potentially powerful matter. To discover meaning, in the sense of finding that an element from one domain fits into another, implies numerous points of congruence. As more and more aspects fit into conceptual place, the level of sureness grows. In a crossword puzzle a word—and its semantic meaning—fit a definition, as well as fitting into the required spaces (say, the horizontal ones). But it is possible that another word also fits. When one's choice gets added validation from matching a letter with a second word that fits into other spaces (say, the vertical), the alternative possibility that success was spurious becomes negligible. If validation comes from a match of several letters, the possibility of "error" becomes infinitesimal. (Anyone can confirm this by trying to compose a crossword corner made up entirely of two sets of such "correct" alternatives, even using simple three letter words.) Similar certainty of fit is seen in a jigsaw puzzle.

Yet for neither of these two examples do we have a clear statistical metric to buttress what is intuitively obvious. And intuition becomes a treacherous guide when we are dealing with the subjectively tinged meanings attached to words or images, not to mention translation between them. Alice of Lewis Carroll's *Wonderland* warned us that "anything can mean anything." One way of enhancing confidence is by prediction, by stating in advance the anticipated further aspects or consequences of a meaning that have been suggested by goodness of fit. We must still heed Alice's warning and spell out precisely what will constitute the confirmation or—at times even more useful—the disconfirmation of a given prediction (Knapp 1963; L. Horwitz 1974).

Some of these approaches may be combined. For example, in an experiment with free association, we used a small associative sample, part of a memory that a subject had recalled with vivid, imagelike intensity. He had told about an episode of horseback riding, in which he had ridden up a slight slope. He described it as dirty with a grassy border and said that he could see it clearly. His horse had slipped back down the slope—ignominiously, he felt. This bare fragment of imagelike memory was given to a number of persons, ranging from trained psychoanalytic clinicians to naive judges. We asked them to speculate about the semantic meaning of the image. A set of questions in multiple choice format then followed, including what we felt was the "correct" one. Next, we gave a broader context for the fragment and again asked a series of semantically targeted questions. All questions, up to this point, asked what the image "meant" in terms of its referent. Finally we gave a still broader context and asked for judgment about pragmatic meaning, by way of a set of questions referring to the intent of the free-associating subject in his quasi-clinical situation. The result of this pilot study suggested that psychoanalysts indeed had a different view of the material than that of lay persons. We used some data from the associative session and subsequent ones, as partially confirmatory evidence for the psychoanalytic view. The question of which view was ultimately more "correct" or "sound" would take us too far into details of the experiment. Here we are concerned with Horowitz's study. These fragmentary observations are mentioned only to illustrate the many possibilities for approaching crucial problems in the area of validating judgments about meaning.

A similar, although looser, sequence is often seen in clinical psychoanalysis. The analyst forms a hypothesis about the semantic or pragmatic meaning of a production by the patient and offers it as a tentative explanation. The patient may produce further confirming or disconfirming evidence. The best confirmation is material that amplifies, that improves the fit, that essentially shows when a prediction had validity. Clearly even that type of confirmation leaves room for debate. Other types, such as the subjective "Aha!" feeling in either patient or analyst are still weaker evidences, as remarked by Paul and the authors he gathered together in a volume discussing psychoanalytic clinical interpretation (1963). The therapeutic dyad may represent yet another embodiment of Chomsky's celebrated John: the patient too eager to please, the analyst too easy to please.

A combination of molar assessments guided by clinical judgment and molecular analysis of the structure of discourse will be necessary to further our understanding of the many aspects of unconscious meaning.

Defenses are really another aspect of the problem of unconscious mentation. The term refers to postulated mechanisms by which particularly distressing unconscious aspects of mental life are warded off or kept from awareness. Defensive maneuvers are part of the process rather than the context of mental activity; that is, they are unconscious in the first sense described in the preceding pages. They are not directly experienced but are inferred from aspects of the text, like some strain that stands out or distorts communication or some contextual element left hanging; they suggest a gap, a dog that failed to bark in the night.

Horowitz speaks of defensive strategies. Strategy implies tactics. It was in tactical, moment-to-moment interaction in the psychoanalytic encounter that the notion of defenses took root. Such activity is also part of a complex ongoing stream of behavior; it is not surprising that there has been little agreement in efforts to define the many postulated "mechanisms of defense."

Classification will undoubtedly prove possible, and it will likely depend on elucidating general principles and developing, as Horowitz and his colleagues are undertaking to do, new models of the mind. Here I offer a few preliminary suggestions, stimulated by Horowitz's presentation. The purpose of defense is to protect conscious awareness from disturbing urges, attitudes, or emotions. We may consider two aspects of this task. First, the extent of mental activity that appears to be required: is it minimal, a mere focusing of attention on "safe" features; or is it extensive, involving much in the way of auxiliary activity and elaborate structure, so as to evade disturbing elements or to mobilize safe substitutes? A second, somewhat different aspect is the overall efficiency of a given defensive mechanism or set of mechanisms. Is defensive activity smooth and effective or does it show signs of strain, as if it were barely containing the material it is defending against? (This notion of efficiency does not contravene C. Marmar's suggestion at this workshop that the "healthiest" style of coping may at times be to admit disturbing material into awareness and take realistic measures to manage the consequences.)

Let me amplify briefly, indicating a number of ways in which a subject may avoid a disturbing topic (using that word as shorthand for urge/attitude/feeling—which, of course may partly stem from the particular object or person who is stimulus or target of the urges, etc.).

1. A subject may exclude a disturbing topic by focusing elsewhere. If such a maneuver exists in pure form, it constitutes repression. We should note that in some sense repression is primary among defenses; all other maneuvers in one or another way support repression. Repressive activity moreover may be efficient and total, or it may be inefficient and show strain, as in blatant denial, on the verge of breaking down.

2. A subject may admit the disturbing topic but in a symbolically disguised form. He may represent an angry, attacking urge by the image of a thunderstorm or by the symbolic substitution of an essentially safe target. Again, this defense may be efficient, as in sublimation (earthly passion replaced by religious passion). Defensive activity may be inefficient, as in massive states of dissociation, in which an essentially undisguised topic is placed in a split-off context and disavowed (a variety of defensive maneuvering that comes close to a distorted self-other field, the final category listed here).

3. A subject may admit a disturbing topic but in an abstract intellectual fashion, so as to detach it from real affective involvement. Again, this may be efficient, as in well rationalized, dispassionate analysis of upsetting material. Or it may be inefficient, resulting in states of paralyzing doubt and indecision.

4. A subject—in a potentially disturbing context—may mobilize strong attitudes, feelings, or affects, but of a sort that serves to, or seems designed to, replace disturbing feelings with "safe" ones. Here, too, such activity may be efficient, as in states of strong, sustained reaction formation, or inefficient, oscillating back and forth (doing and undoing) or attacking the self (as in depressive, self-destructive states).

5. The subject may distort or confuse his perception of self or other. Such a maneuver implies a basic reorganization of one's whole habitual grasp of inner and outer reality. It still may be relatively efficient, as in states in which the outer world of persons is split into good or bad to spare the subject the pain of intense ambivalence. It may be inefficient, as in gross distortions or frank projective delusions in which the subject ascribes urges, attitudes, or feelings in himself to others in the outside world.

Clearly these mechanisms, which are summarized in Table 5.1, are not mutually exclusive. The major problem in the study of "defenses" is that defensive activity is continuous and variegated; it uses the many components of cognitive and affective life and pursues the purposes of self-protection and adaptation. Others would divide the realm of defenses differently or, to put it more accurately, construct different models of mental activity, including defensive organization.

A further distinction is that between moment-to-moment tactics and long-range strategic defense. By *strategies,* Horowitz means larger organizations of key elements that govern smaller tactical units (see also Knapp 1969; Knapp et al. 1975). Such strategies involve systems of hierarchical ordering of inner (cog-

TABLE 5.1 Defenses

Mechanism[1]	Efficiency	Strain
Selective inattention	Repression	Denial Avoidance
Symbolic disguise	Sublimation	Dissociation
Intellectual mastery	Intellectualization	Obsessive doubt
Emotional countermobilization	Reaction formation	Undoing Depression Self-attack
Distortion of self-other field	Splitting	Projecting

[1]In order of increasingly extensive mental activity.

nitively structured and emotionally colored) representations or schemata; these refer primarily to the self and to the world of key others. In his use of defensive strategy, a term that harmonizes with my own use of it (Knapp 1969; Knapp et al. 1975), the issue of *fantasy* becomes crucial. Horowitz considers unconscious fantasy a key term for his lexicon. Fantasy, as a plan or guiding schema is, indeed, a crucial concept. We are governed by such plans; but since they are symbolic and are complex representations of ourselves and others, it is difficult to assess them precisely. They occur in layers, one serving to defend against another, as illustrated by Horowitz's case material. I would be interested to hear more about whether he found any overarching organization in his patients' states of mind. As the case material is presented, without contextual information about the unfolding sequences of interaction in the therapeutic encounter, it is not clear whether Ann's states, which include important self-other fantasies, tended to have a favored "safe" organization that was adaptive but also difficult to change. Such a "safe equilibrium" has characterized patients in long-term psychoanalytic treatment (Knapp 1969; Knapp et al. 1975). It would be interesting to see whether similar equilibria can be detected in the more fluid, acute stress syndromes and the active short-term interventions used with them.

It is worth pausing for a moment to consider the concept of fantasy in more detail, including unconscious forms of fantasy. As already noted, fantasy is central to the more clinically focused concept of transference. Fantasies vary widely, from high articulated narrative or pictorial representations to archaic urges having an indistinct cognitive structure. It may be useful, as a starting point, to make a broad division into more sharply and less sharply articulated fantasies. The latter, deeper fantasy processes differ from ordinary conscious thought in many ways, in their lack of form and in their instinctive imperiousness. Isaacs (1952), speaking from within the original British psychoanalytic tradition, suggested that these inaccessible but powerful elements be called phantasies—spelled with *ph*—in contrast to the more usual largely or totally conscious daydreams that are part of everyday waking experience, fantasies in the usual sense and spelling.

Table 5.2 lists some features that differentiate these two conceptual poles: on the left are features of (conscious or preconscious) fantasy; on the right are those of (unconscious) phantasy. Fantasy refers to contents of thought or speech extracted from

TABLE 5.2 Emotive-Cognitive Organization of Fantasy and Phantasy

Fantasy	Phantasy
Contents	Process
Script	Motivator
Manifest and reportable	Latent and inferred
Detached from core emotions	Linked to core emotions
Specific, flexible, novel	General, rigid, repetitive
Roots in preoperational and separation-individuation stage	Roots in symbiotic and sensorimotor stage

direct observation or from a factual summary of a record, for example, of a therapeutic encounter. Phantasy refers to a postulated process enacted by a thinking or speaking subject.

Fantasy is manifest or reportable, even though not always reported. Phantasy is latent, essentially unreportable; it can only be inferred.

Fantasy has the characteristics of a script; it usually describes some sort of act, scene, agent or agents, agency, and purpose—the characteristics of reported events that Burke has described (1962). Phantasy has inferred motivational force; it reflects the impact of key others on a self, and the intent of the self toward key others.

Fantasy is variably detached from core emotions. It may be colorful and affectively vivid; it may on the other hand be bland and seem designed to protect against strong emotions. Phantasy is, by definition, part of the deepest core of affective-instinctive-motivational behavior. Elsewhere I have used the term "schemactive" in referring to phantasies, to indicate both their schematic nature as they organize urges and their pragmatically active role.

Fantasies are specific, flexible, often novel, potentially limitless in number; they may embody many variations on a theme. Phantasies are generalized, stereotyped, repetitive; each individual has a limited repertoire of them.

Fantasies have their roots in Piaget's preoperational stage and the later phases of separation-individuation; they are the product of early magical thinking and the world of fairy tales. Phantasies have their roots in Piaget's sensorimotor stage and in the earliest phase of symbiosis, before symbolic thought and language begin to free the individual from his bondage to the immediate surrounding world and to his body.

Dichotomies, like beauty, are often in the eye of the observer. This tentative subdivision refers to extremes. We may well be dealing with varying continua, as Kris (1950) pointed out in discussing preconscious mental processes. At the least, it is important to underline the widely differing phenomena included under the broad umbrella of unconscious fantasy.

Let me turn to *emotion*. I have referred so far to affective-instinctive-motivational systems. What are they? It is curious that psychoanalysis, which deals with emotions, still lacks a coherent theory of emotion, although there are numerous other theories now extant. My view, elaborated elsewhere (1981, 1983) centers on certain core components. These have to do with: (a) pleasure and pain; (b) generalized activation, in equilibrium with generalized inhibition; (c) expressive emotional systems that, on the one hand, are part of erotic and eliminative transactions with the world and, on the other hand, are part of a mobilization for dealing with threat by either fight or flight. For the future it will be necessary to find how such a model, or another one, interdigitates with our growing understanding in the area of cognition. Material like that provided by Horowitz offers many opportunities to build bridges between these two artificially separated realms.

His notion of states of mind is rich and stimulating. Such states are mixtures of fantasy and feeling. In proposing them Horowitz conceptualizes emotions as prolonging themselves into moods. His conceptualization is similar to that of Lewin (1950) in his analysis of the manic depressive state, who says that a mood is not a mere vapor—it has cognitive content. Horowitz brings evidence of how pure affect becomes supplemented by and organized by fantasy (cognitive) structure. He thereby advances beyond familiar, oversimplified descriptions of mood and also beyond abstract metapsychological descriptions, such as "punishment by a harsh superego." He opens the way, too, for a rich description of transference reactions.

The notion of states of mind is similar to Luborsky's concept (1984) of a core theme, although in ways more complex. In describing the rapidly shifting states of mind, the case material about Ann as well as other reports from the same research suggest that multiple themes—not simply a wish, a fear, and an ensuing reaction—interact during a session. Various reactions echo one another and are linked to coping strategies and symptom formation.

The accurate measurement of such states presents methodological problems. Some of these concern the validation of meaning judgments, as already mentioned. The main reliance in Horowitz's studies has been on interobserver agreement, certainly an important first step. Given careful preparatory definition and training, judges can make a reliable assessment of extremely complex mood, fantasy, and defensive states (Knapp et al. 1975). However, investigation remains at the level of ipsative scales, derived from one individual's material and applied to further material from the same individual. Dangers of circularity arise, as well as risks of imposing on the material idiosyncratic views of the judging group or at times of its leader. At the least, one is faced with the difficulties of generalizing across cases. Horowitz and his colleagues have been ingenious in searching for additional methods of cross-validating such judgments and testing specific hypotheses about the process and outcome of psychotherapy. Some of their approaches involve segmentation. As noted already, this is a difficult task; it has plagued the analysis of content and of discourse (Knapp 1974). Humans speak in units, sentences, paragraphs; they deal with themes and topics; they obey rules and take turns. All of these features can be discerned in the discourse of patients, punctuated by interventions from a therapist. But segments have ways of overlapping or flowing together. Precise systems of selecting units tend to become more and more microscopic, so that they obscure rather than illuminate important clinical events. Most often one must settle for a somewhat arbitrary set of units. The more they conform to the natural shape of interactions—rather than being mere counts of words or mere time units—the more fruitful such segmentation tends to be.

Horowitz points to the ability of judges to reach high levels of agreement about the boundaries of different states of mind. That observation confirms the findings of others (Knapp 1974) that "change of topic" may be the best indicator of natural segmentation as well as a fruitful place to search for evidence of unconscious activity. Horowitz has also suggested some further uses to which units, however selected, may be put. Multiple judges or groups of judges may assess, for instance, material prior to and following interventions. Exact linguistic measures may be applied in similar fashion. He further mentions the possibility of "control" segmentation: a device similar to Luborsky's use of comparison samples in his symptom context method. Horowitz also speaks of the possible examination of material by judges using different frames of reference. Ideally, one might hope for predictions based on competing hypotheses that might be supported or disconfirmed by the impartial examination of a single text. The possibilities are substantial, once the step has been made of seeing psychotherapy or psychoanalysis not as a tool for ascertaining truth but as a clinical encounter that provides unique data, which may then be subjected to research scrutiny.

A final postscript about *stress*. It is a seductively simple term that conveys a kind of pseudo-respectability. "Stress" encompasses a wide range of events in the world (for humans, the world of meanings). These evoke an equally wide range of psychophysiological reactions mediated by f/phantasies (with both spellings). We have much to learn about the reciprocal roles of outer and inner happenings, noxious or reparative. We do not know what ingredients of therapy are crucial to restoring integration and promoting growth. Is there a kind of involuntary learning from tacit reexperience with a trusted caring person (should we say an ally)? And is there a more active learning from exploring the past and, more important, testing the immediate therapeutic present with that person? The answers to such questions will come from the type of work being carried forward by Horowitz and his colleagues.

In summary, my position is that of a psychoanalyst, interested in psychosomatic phenomena and emotion. As a psychoanalytic lexicographer, I suggest the following key terms for a lexicon: dynamic unconscious; self-other schemata and fantasies; transference; resistance; defensive tactics and strategies; emotions, including hedonic, activational, and expressive aspects; and symbolic organization.

We must not only list and define these terms but also formulate their interrelationships in a series of models. These stem from broader, theoretical, ultimately philosophic positions. Models allow us to accumulate and organize data, thus exposing the fruitfulness or weakness of broader theoretical positions and slowly increasing our understanding of cognitive and emotional processes.

References

Block, N., ed. 1982. *Imagery.* Cambridge, Mass. MIT Press.
Burke, K. 1962. *A Grammar of Motives and a Rhetoric of Motives.* Cleveland: World Publishing Co.

Cherry, C. 1966. *On Human Communication.* 2d ed. Cambridge, Mass.: MIT Press.

Ellenberger, H. 1970. *The Discovery of the Unconscious.* New York: Basic Books.

Erdelyi, M. 1985. *Psychoanalysis: Freud's Cognitive Psychology,* Baltimore: W. H. Freeman.

Fisher, C. 1954. Dreams and perception: The role of pre-conscious and primary modes of perception in dream formation. *Journal of the American Psychoanalytic Association* 2:389–445.

Freud, S. [1925] 1961. Negation. *Standard Edition, vol. 19.* London: Hogarth Press.

Fromkin, V. F. 1980. *Errors in Linguistic Performance: Slips of the Tongue, Ear, Pen, and Hand.* New York: Academic Press.

Goodman, N. 1968. *Languages of Art.* New York: Bobbs Merrill.

Hilgard, E. R. 1952. Experimental approaches in psychoanalysis. In E. R. Hilgard, L. S. Kubie, and E. Pumpian Mindlin, eds., *Psychoanalysis as Science.* New York: Basic Books.

Horowitz, M. J. 1976. *Stress Response Syndromes.* New York: Aronson.

———. [1979] 1987. *States of Mind: Analysis of Change in Psychotherapy.* 2d ed. New York: Plenum Press.

Horwitz, L. 1974. *Clinical Prediction in Psychotherapy.* New York: Aronson.

Isaacs, S. 1952. The nature and function of phantasy. In J. Riviere, ed., *Developments in Psychoanalysis.* London: Hogarth Press.

Keet, C. D. 1948. Two verbal techniques in a miniature counseling situation. *Psychological Monographs* 62:294.

Knapp, P. H. 1963. Short term psychoanalytic and psychosomatic predictions. *Journal of the American Psychoanalytic Association* 11:245–80.

———. 1969. Image, symbol, and person: The strategy of psychological defense. *Archives of General Psychiatry* 21:392–406.

———. 1974. Segmentation and structure in psychoanalysis. *Journal of the American Psychoanalytic Association* 22:13–36.

———. 1981. Core processes in the organization of emotion. *Journal of the American Academy of Psychoanalysis* 9:415–34.

———. 1983. Emotions and bodily changes: A reassessment. In L. Temeshok, C. Van Dyke, and L. S. Zegans, eds., *Emotions, Health, and Illness: Theoretical and Research Formations.* New York: Grune and Stratton.

Knapp, P. H., R. Greenberg, C. Pearlman, M. Cohen, J. Kantrowitz, and J. Sashin. 1975. Clinical measurement in psychoanalysis: An approach. *Psychoanalytic Quarterly* 44:404–30.

Kris, E. 1950. On preconscious mental processes. *Psychoanalytic Quarterly* 19:540–60.

Langer, S. 1951. *Philosophy in a New Key.* New York: Mentor Press.

Lazarus, R. 1966. *Psychological Stress and the Coping Process.* New York: McGraw-Hill.

Lewin, B. D. 1950. *The Psychoanalysis of Elation*. New York: W. W. Norton.

Luborsky, L. 1984. *The Principles of Dynamic Psychotherapy: A Manual*. New York: Basic Books.

MacCormac, E. R. 1985. *A Cognitive Theory of Metaphor*. Cambridge, Mass.: MIT Press.

Marcel, A. J. 1983. Conscious and unconscious perception: An approach to the relation between phenomenal experience and perceptual proceedings. *Cognitive Psychology* 15:238–300.

Margolin, S. G. 1949. Psychoanalysis and the dynamics of psychosomatic medicine. *Psychoanalytic Quarterly* 18:277–78.

Motley, M. 1980. Verification of "Freudian slips" and semantic prearticulatory editing via laboratory-induced spoonerisms. In V. A. Franklin, ed., *Errors in Linguistic Performance*. New York: Academic Press.

Ogden, C. K., and I. A. Richard. 1923. *The Meaning of Meaning*. New York: Harcourt Brace.

Ortony, A., ed. 1979. *Metaphor and Thought*. London: Cambridge University Press.

Paul, L., ed. 1963. *Psychoanalytic Clinical Interpretation*. New York: MacMillan (Free Press of Glencoe).

Poetzl, O. 1917. Experimental erregte Traumbilder in ihren Beziechungen zum indirekten Sehen. *Zeitschrift fur Neurologie und Psychologie* 37:278–349.

Schilder, P. 1935. *The Image and Appearance of the Human Body: Studies in the Constructive Energies of the Psyche*. London: Kegan Paul.

Whyte, L. L. 1960. *The Unconscious Before Freud*. New York: Basic Books.

Zetzel, E. R. 1970. The so-called good hysteric. *The Capacity for Emotional Growth*. New York: International Universities Press.

3　An Experimental Psychodynamic Perspective

The previous three chapters considered theories of how to formulate unconscious dynamic conflicts and how these factors might influence information processing and conscious representation. A call for empirical tests of such inferred processes was raised. This section describes a three-part methodology that might provide such an empirical approach, one that might eventually invalidate or validate the hypotheses of warded-off themes and unconscious processing of them. Chapter 6 by Shevrin presents an experimental approach that considers how to infer warded-off contents, deliver stimuli related to these themes by subliminal perception so that consciousness of the subject is not involved, and examine the neurophysiological response to such stimuli in contrast to responses to various sets of control stimuli. Chapter 7 by Marcel challenges some of Shevrin's basic assumptions and is followed by a spirited reply from Shevrin in Chapter 8. The result is a presentation of both a psychodynamic perspective on the difference between conscious and unconscious mental processes and a different cognitive psychology view on the same issues.

Jackendoff adds a fascinating third view in Chapter 9, where he approaches these topics from the theoretical stance of linguistic studies of syntax and phonology. He goes on to reconsider salient issues raised in Part 2, drawing these two parts together. He takes up issues of unconscious defenses and describes how these processes might operate in terms of combinatory rules and processes of regularization. He concludes that the outlook of linguistic theory not only confirms and refines the psychodynamic view of the unconscious but provides an important precedent for a more finely grained empirical analysis of the states and processes involved. This provides a needed bridge to formal information-processing theory and adds to the dynamic and cognitive perspectives already elaborated.

6 Unconscious Conflict: A Convergent Psychodynamic and Electrophysiological Approach

Howard Shevrin, Ph.D.

A new method for investigating the relationship between conscious and unconscious processes in psychopathology is offered in this paper. The method is based on a convergent psychodynamic and electrophysiological approach. Brain responses in the form of event-related potentials (ERPs) are obtained to two groups of pathology-related words presented subliminally and supraliminally; these two groups of words, selected from assessment interviews and test protocols, are intended to capture saliently the patient's conscious experience of his symptom (phobias or

The initial version of this paper was presented at the workshop Emotional and Cognitive Factors in Unconscious Processes, an invitational meeting at the Center for Advanced Study in the Behavioral Sciences, Palo Alto, Calif., July 5–9, 1984, sponsored by the John D. and Catherine T. MacArthur Foundation.

The research it describes was broadly interdisciplinary in nature, involving people in psychoanalysis, psychiatry, clinical psychology, electrical engineering, medical engineering, and computer science. William J. Williams, Ph.D., has been a major collaborator, bringing to the research his expertise in computer science and information theory. He has been mainly responsible for developing the trans-information method. Robert E. Marshall, M.E.E., as a medical engineer with expertise in ERP research and computer hardware, has contributed substantially to all aspects of our laboratory procedures, as well as developing the procedures for systematizing the word selection method. Prominently contributing to the clinical assessment have been Richard K. Hertel, Ph.D., a psychoanalyst who interviewed some of the subjects; Dwarakanath G. Rao, M.D., who conducted the medical-psychiatric interviews; and Susan Beth Miller, Ph. D., who tested the patients described in the study. The clinical group was augmented from time to time by John Hartman, Ph.D., psychoanalyst; Robert Hatcher, Ph.D., psychoanalyst; and James Bond, Ph.D., clinical psychologist. The laboratory team headed by Williams included Dorothy Holinger and Scott Dickman, clinical psychology students; Leo Iasemidis and Hitten Zaveri, electrical engineering and computer science graduate students; and Anna Tornow, EEG technologist. Beverly Knickerbocker expertly transcribed all patient tapes.

Appendix 6.A was prepared by Robert E. Marshall, and Appendix 6.B by William J. Williams.

pathological grief reactions) and the hypothesized unconscious conflict underlying the symptom. The method seeks to combine the richness of clinical intuition and experience with objective brain responses based on operations quite independent of clinical judgments and on the technique of subliminal stimulation, which makes it possible to study unconscious processes experimentally. By the use of these convergent approaches, it becomes feasible to investigate objectively unconscious processes related to psychopathology.

To give the reader a flavor of what our clinical data are like, a transcribed segment of an interview is presented with a phobic patient describing his symptom, followed by a discussion of different conceptions of the nature of unconscious processes. The research method, findings, and implications will then be described in greater detail.

A Clinical Vignette: AM's Blood Phobia

Let us imagine a bright, quick-witted, intensely proud young man of twenty-two troubled by a restless, uneasy sense of inner tension and turbulence, who suffers from a blood phobia he finds shameful and humiliating. In the course of his first psychiatric interview, he describes his problem in these words:

It's been something that's been on and off ever since I remember. I can remember maybe I was nine, no, maybe it was younger than that, seven is the youngest I can remember, and it seems to come and go. It's worse at times than others, and I feel weak when I see—it's also a more hypothetical type of situation. . . . If I cut my finger or cut myself shaving, that's not really a problem, but when I see it in a movie or something, it's . . . how it's shown, or how it's talked about, you know, in class or something, I have to leave class sometimes, I almost faint. I've run out of movies 'cause I had to faint. I don't faint, I almost faint, and I get very light-headed and weak, and, pictures and things like that, you know, gory pictures bother me and . . . I feel very weak in my feet and my hands . . . and my chest too. I think that's been going, the chest thing, has been going on for maybe five years, I feel pretty strange in my chest and have to get everything off my chest and I feel, I'm sure that's . . . some sort of symbol, symbolic of getting something off my chest, like something I have to talk about or something. . . . I was calmed down for a while and then I saw *One Flew over the Cuckoo's Nest* about a couple weeks ago, three weeks ago, and that was one of the worst times. I had to just get out, run out of there, in the scene where Billy either slits his throat or his wrists or something, I don't know what, but I wasn't ready for it and it just, like squirting blood is really bad. I'm feeling, right now, even talking about it, it's bothering me, something with the veins, like slitting wrists, that's real bad, that's probably the worse thing, you know. . . . The idea of giving blood is just, terrible to me. . . . I saw blood on the nurse, oh jeeze, and, and, and she screamed, and, that's all I saw, it was obvious what happened. . . . Shocked, I knew I was in trouble, right then, I knew I was going to have a reaction because I wasn't even ready for it, I should have closed my eyes if I'd have known it was coming, I guess. Still, the idea is pretty bad though. . . . How embarrassed I was. I was with a girl, I had to run out. . . . I can't be normal and just watch the movie and just realize it's not real blood. Even if it is I shouldn't, you know, you treat it like something, that's what it is, blood is just in somebody, in everybody, and, you know, that's the way it goes. Somehow I get almost angry that I have to do that. . . . Female problems bother me, like, that's why I think it may be castration anxiety, because, psychology is my major so I might know some terminology or something so I'm just warning you. . . . Female problems, menstruation, sometimes when they talk about it it bothers me, which would seem to support that notion, you know, female problems like that, bother me, just some horrifying instance maybe, you know, may bother me.

In this self-description, the phobia is not simply a fearful re-action to a concrete, circumscribed stimulus; in fact, the sight of blood itself need not arouse fear. Rather, there are certain specific anticipations of scenes and situations that trigger the most un-settling reactions; they are depictions or representations, as in films or stories, and not actual occurrences. One can say that, paradoxically, it is not blood he is fearful of but its representation in certain contexts. Nor is it correct to describe this phobia simply as a fear in the usual meaning of the word, when we consider that he actually describes a compelling variety of feelings that are not usually intrinsic to fear, such as the feeling of "getting things off his chest." In addition to these puzzling and not nec-essarily fearful affects, he clearly describes a variety of autonomic reactions such as weakness and fainting. Finally, the patient does not simply *describe* his symptom, he reacts to it and has his own ideas as to what might be causing it; for example, he suggests that "castration anxiety" might be involved.

Model of a Psychoanalytic Explanation

To refer to a phobia as an irrational fear is only the beginning of the inquiry. Of importance are the nature of the empirical method and the theoretical frame of reference within which the phobia is considered. For example, in the excerpt just cited, the particular clinical method at work permitted the patient to describe as fully as possible the nature of his experience and his ideas about it. Were he to have been restricted to a questionnaire and his responses limited to designating a point on a scale, we might have learned about the severity of his symptom, of some interest to be sure, but the associated phenomena would have been totally strained out of the measure. Behavior modification, a prevalent approach to the treatment and understanding of phobias, relies on this structured approach. As a result, as Fodor has noted, behaviorism "can't construct the notion mental process . . . [or of] causal sequences of mental episodes" (1981, 6). It is evident that even in the brief excerpt cited there are complex sequences of mental episodes involved in the patient's description and account of his phobia that cannot be captured by a rating of severity alone.

What method can assure access to these necessary sequences of mental episodes? Immediately, we run into a problem inherent in the nature of the symptom: the very experience of it contains a mysterious hiatus—the patient is moved to feel, act, and think with powerful urgency, yet without a rational basis. He can attempt to account for his urgent action afterward and thus to offer his own explanation, but he is in no more privileged position to understand these actions than a naive bystander. Indeed, the psychoanalyst would argue that there are mental forces within the patient that will steer him away from the true explanation. What is so humiliating to the patient is not solely the childishness of his action but his inability to present it as based on a rational decision. As Rapaport has defined it, there is a *discontinuity* in his experience and behavior that must be explained (Rapaport 1967; see also Shevrin 1984).

The model of a psychoanalytic explanation makes several central assumptions. First, the apparent discontinuity in experience in, for example, the blood phobia, is really continuous, that is, there are *knowable psychological* causes; second, these knowable psychological causes are *inaccessible* to the patient. What follows from these two assumptions is one important corollary: the psychological unconscious is the locus of those inaccessible psychological causes. Thus, the psychoanalyst must assume the existence of the psychological unconscious, which is then relied on repeatedly in the exploration of experience constituting the treatment process. The main advantage of this method is that it casts a wide net that is able to sink deep into the troubled waters of an individual's inner life and thus to multiply the opportunities for identifying the many possible inaccessible psychological causes. The main limitation of the method is its knack for eliciting an embarrassment of riches; even though it can enliven the search for hypotheses, it is an awkward and clumsy means for selecting and testing them. Other methods must be created for that purpose. Before going on to discuss in detail one such method that was briefly described in the introduction, I would like to explore different views of unconscious processes, because of the vital role the concept plays in much contemporary thinking in cognitive science and psychoanalysis as well as in the research to be described.

Conceptions of Unconscious Processes

There are several pairs of opposite characteristics that have been used to define different conceptions of unconscious processes: (1) psychological-neurophysiological, (2) spontaneous-automatic, (3) active-latent, (4) cognitive-dynamic, (5) motivational-attitudinal (or dispositional), (6) content-process, (7) different from consciousness–similar to consciousness.

These different pairs are not mutually exclusive; in fact, the different models of unconscious processes can be defined in terms of several members from different pairs joined together. Thus, the psychoanalytic view of unconscious processes can be defined as psychological, spontaneous, active, dynamic, and motivational. Some nonpsychoanalytic models can be defined as neurophysiological, automatic, latent, cognitive, and dispositional.

Let me briefly define the terms making up the pairs.

1a. *Psychological*
All the terms ordinarily used to describe conscious events, such as thought, affect, judgment, and motivation, can also be applied to unconscious processes.

1b. *Neurophysiological*
Only conscious experience can be defined in psychological terms; all unconscious processes can only be considered as neurophysiological in nature.

2a. *Spontaneous.*
Unconscious processes can participate in complex, variable adaptive behavior such as problem solving and creativity, as well as in complex, ad hoc psychopathology such as slips, symptom formation, and unconscious conflict.

2b. *Automatic.*

Unconscious processes are organized on the basis of tightly knit structures that once triggered will proceed along the same lines each time unless interrupted or overridden by conscious considerations. This automatization is best illustrated by any habitual complex action, such as driving a car or reciting a poem already well learned and rehearsed.

3a. *Active.*

Unconscious processes are only relevant when interacting with and influencing the course of consciousness and behavior.

3b. *Latent.*

Unconscious processes are potential in the sense of existing, for example, as programs that organize experience and behavior. Once the program is operative, it is an inherent part of the particular state of consciousness and behavior. Thus the unconscious can be defined as a file of temporarily unused programs.

4a. *Cognitive.*

Unconscious processes are inherently cognitive in nature in the sense that they are early aspects of information processing operating prior to consciousness itself. The best instance of this is probably to be found in the way selective attention works.

4b. *Dynamic.*

Unconscious processes are not simply cognitive but are made up of drive structures (sexual and aggressive), affects and motives.

5a. *Attitudinal (dispositional).*

This is similar to the latent characterization but more closely linked to the concept of schemata in psychology or social role in sociology. The unconscious is the repository of certain attitudes, dispositions, or schemata that organize consciousness and behavior.

5b. *Ad hoc motivational.*

This is similar to the dynamic and active characteristics but stressing the immediacy and variability of individual motives at work in the unconscious.

6a. *Content.*

Consciousness is defined as the awareness of contents or representations; no contents or representations exist unconsciously.

6b. *Process.*

The unconscious is defined as all those processes going on prior to the conscious experience of a representation or content. Unconscious processes cannot be accessible to consciousness directly. Usually those who maintain this view also assume that these processes are neurophysiological in nature or, by analogy with the computer, that the unconscious refers to all the computational processes and consciousness to the readout.

7a. *Different from consciousness.*
Unconscious processes are either *organized* in some way uniquely different from consciousness or the *content* of unconscious processes are different, for example, more "primitive," than is true for conscious content.

7b. *Similar to consciousness.*
In all respects unconscious processes are similar to conscious processes in organization and content except that they lack the attribute of consciousness.

Based on the terms just defined we can raise several questions bearing on the role and nature of unconscious processes.

1. Are unconscious processes to be defined solely as automatic, neurophysiological events that are essentially preparatory or complementary to conscious events and behavior?

2. Are unconscious processes to be defined as essentially a file or repository of programs, dispositions, or attitudes that, once active, organize conscious experience and behavior?

3. Are unconscious processes to be defined as psychological in nature (so that we can speak of unconscious fantasy), spontaneous, active, and ad hoc motivational?

4. Finally, are unconscious processes, no matter how organized and defined, different from or similar to conscious processes?

In the research to be discussed next, I will draw on several of these models, which, as already noted, are not necessarily mutually contradictory but rather have emerged out of different kinds of research and represent attempts to explain different phenomena. Thus the investigation of overlearned, habitual behavior leads to a conception of the unconscious as automatic. The heavy emphasis in cognitive psychology on learning and discrimination paradigms has led to a purely cognitive, nonaffective, nonmotivational conception of the unconscious. Psychoanalytic clinical experience, on the other hand, deals with powerful affective, conflictual, and drive-implicated experience and behavior and thus favors a dynamic, motivational, spontaneous conception of unconscious processes. There is also in psychoanalysis a locus for something closer to the cognitive view of the unconscious, the so-called preconscious as distinct from the dynamic unconscious.

The Research

The original impetus for developing the method came from certain problems in psychotherapy research. A growing number of psychotherapy researchers have been calling for a shift in emphasis away from investigations focused on treatment outcome; in such studies several different treatments are compared for effectiveness. Future research needs to explore the change process itself as it is affected by the nature of the particular treatment, type of patient, and therapist. Outcome research has shown that most treatments are effective at about the same rate (Andrews and Harvey 1981). Is this same rate of cure determined by factors common to all treatments, as Frank (1961) has proposed, or do the similar rates obscure significant differences in what changes, for whom, and in whose hands? Understanding of the change process itself is little advanced when studies focus only on outcome. It is interesting that criticism of current methods has come both from researchers who are convinced that outcome studies have established that all forms of treatment work equally well (e.g., Luborsky, Singer, and Luborsky 1975) and from researchers who feel that these studies have demonstrated little of value (e.g., Rachman and Wilson 1980). The felt need in both research camps is for a strategy aimed at clarifying the nature of the change process as a function of type of treatment, patient, and therapist. Rachman and Wilson (1980) have also called for studies benefiting from the specificity of hypotheses bearing on the nature of treatment change, as has Parloff (1980).

Those who propose new approaches to psychotherapy research in some cases suggest that this new type of study would need to depart from the model of the purely clinical investigation based entirely on clinical data and measurements. With our convergent psychodynamic and electrophysiological method, the effects of different treatments on homogeneous groups of patients could be investigated through an assessment of different change variables, evaluated clinically and experimentally. These change variables could contribute to establishing the validity of one or another theory of change.

The crucial difference between the behaviorist and the psychodynamic conception of therapeutic change is the role of putative unconscious conflict and so-called structural change. The behavior modifier asserts that the behavior anomaly to be treated (e.g., a phobia) can be changed by the extinction of the anxiety associated with it. Various means such as flooding or desensitization are used to extinguish anxiety. Behaviorists Rachman and Wilson have argued forcefully against the disease model as applied to psychological disorders that posits an underlying disturbance resulting in the behavioral disorder, or "symptom." They believe that the behavioral disorder is primary and that it creates secondary disturbances in living that can be alleviated by eliminating the behavioral disorder itself. Although behaviorism has no explicit use for a concept of the unconscious, in the terms outlined earlier one could define the behaviorist unconscious as implicitly a dispositional, "hard-wired" set of automatic processes established either genetically or through learning; it is likely neurophysiological in nature.

In contrast, psychodynamically oriented clinicians assume that the behavioral disorder or symptom is part of a widespread disorder of which the symptom is a secondary effect rather than a cause. The symptom is secondary insofar as it is itself a *consequence* of certain presumed psychological processes in conflict at the time but inaccessible to the patient. According to Brenner, the "components of conflict are 1) wishful striving, 2) anticipated danger, 3) defense and 4) compromise among these" (1976, 9). The symptom as the compromise itself is the only step that achieves consciousness. In order for a lasting and substantial change to take place, these underlying, inaccessible unconscious psychological processes must be changed, or in clinical terms, the conflict among them must be resolved. The major scientific problem posed by the psychodynamic model of emotional disorder is that it has proven thus far difficult to establish the nature or reality of such a change in any objective and replicable manner. The convergent psychodynamic and electrophysiological method has features that may remedy this deficiency.

A significant difference exists in the conception of change between behavioral and psychodynamic points of view. Behavioral approaches benefit from the greater accessibility of the presumed behavioral change process, although some question has been raised as to whether the changes brought about are mainly due to heightened expectations of improvement rather than to the particular behavioral technique (Kazdin and Wilcoxon 1976). In psychodynamic approaches it has proven difficult to identify the nature of the treatment and the nature of the structural change intended to be achieved. We are thus confronted with a situation in which one major therapeutic approach is operationally definable and its outcome can be readily determined, although it is not clear that its effectiveness is achieved by the defined means, while another major therapeutic approach suffers from a difficulty in specifying the treatment modality and its expected effects, although it remains widely practiced and supported by a weight of clinical evidence made up largely of therapist and patient judgments. Aside from purely clinical considerations, what is also at stake in this confrontation of behavioral and psychodynamic approaches is dramatically different conceptions of human nature and how the mind works. The clinical arena, important in its own right, assumes an enhanced importance because it may provide the place in which significantly different theories of mind can be tested. This theoretical issue assumes special importance because in recent years developments in cognitive psychology have begun to cast doubt on the purely behavioral assumptions of behavior therapy and to provide support for the psychodynamic assumption of unconscious psychological processes (Shevrin and Dickman 1980).

The increasing use of information processing as a frame of reference has permitted cognitive psychologists to take a close look at cognition in the forms of attention, perception, judgment, and memory. Perhaps the most thorough work has been done with respect to attention. Although there are various theories of attention, all conclude that to some degree psychological processes *preceding* attention play a vital role. Neisser (1967) and Posner (1982) have perhaps taken the clearest position: they hypothesize that unconscious processes play a vital role in "preattentive" processing. Posner has suggested that these unconscious processes appear to follow a rule of parallel processing, as compared to alert waking consciousness, which appears to follow a rule of single-channel processing. These "preattentive" unconscious processes involve contact with memory stores and decision making on the basis of a given set of instructions. Shevrin and Dickman (1980) have drawn together evidence from several areas in cognitive psychology including attention and subliminal perception. The evidence supports an assumption that unconscious processes play an important role in all cognitive activity. Subliminal perception, originally introduced by psychoanalytic researchers (Fisher 1954; Shevrin and Luborsky 1958), is seen by a growing number of cognitive psychologists as consistent with selective attention (Posner 1982; Nisbett and Wilson 1977; Erdelyi and Goldberg 1979). Marcel (1983) and Kunst-Wilson and

Zajonc (1980) have used subliminal stimulation successfully in studies of the relationship of subliminal activation to consciousness and in the study of the relationship between affect and cognition, respectively. Thus, the concept of unconscious psychological processes has been receiving increasing support from laboratory investigations in cognitive psychology, and the technique of subliminal perception as a way of investigating unconscious psychological processes has aroused increasing interest among nonpsychodynamically oriented investigators.

Hand in hand with recent developments in cognitive psychology have been comparable developments in the electrophysiological investigation of event-related potential (ERP) correlates of cognitive processes, especially attention, decision making, and the recognition of meaning. The ERP is a brain response derived from the electroencephalographic record. Whenever a stimulus in any sensory modality is presented a sufficient number of times, it is possible to extract from the ongoing EEG record the regularities in the brain response to the particular stimulus. The resulting curve measures the changes in electrical potential between a given active electrode and a reference electrode selected to be electrically neutral. The work of several investigators is of particular relevance to this research. Begleiter, Porjesz, and Garozzo (1979) have shown that the ERP can discriminate between pleasant and unpleasant words. Chapman and his colleagues (Chapman 1979; Chapman et al. 1977, 1978, 1980) have demonstrated that ERPs can be obtained that discriminate among groups of words differing in their connotative meanings as established by the Osgood Semantic Differential (Osgood, May, and Miron 1975). Thus, a cluster of pleasant words (E + in the Osgood studies) will be associated with a different ERP from the one associated with a cluster of unpleasant words (E −). Even though the individual words forming the cluster will vary in denotative meaning, length, and letter organization, the ERP remains sensitive to the *affective category* membership (E + or E −) of the words. In addition to the Chapman studies there have been others demonstrating that the ERP can index semantically relevant information such as verb-noun differences (Brown and Lehmann 1979) and antonym-homonym differences (Kutas, Lindawood, and Hillyard 1983). The Chapman studies are the first, however, to show that the ERP can be used to index connotative or affective significance for groups of words. The method might thus be applicable to brain indices of stimuli having affective significance to patients. The ERP would have the further advantage of providing measures that are independent of clinical judgment and are adaptable to experimental manipulation.

In a series of earlier studies I demonstrated the existence of ERP correlates of subliminal stimulation (Shevrin and Rennick 1967; Shevrin and Fritzler 1968a; Shevrin, Smith, and Fritzler 1971) and the relationship of ERP correlates of subliminal stimulation to repression (Shevrin, Smith, and Fritzler 1969, 1970). Confirmatory studies reporting ERP correlates of subliminal stimulation have been contributed by Libet, Alberts, Wright, and Feinstein (1967), Kostandov and Arzumanov (1977), Barkoczi, Sera, and Komlosi (1983), and Brandeis and Lehmann (in press). I have reviewed elsewhere ERP evidence for unconscious processes (Shevrin 1978).

Research Design

The design required that patients be selected who had clear-cut complaints that could become the focus of the research. For this reason we decided to work with patients suffering from phobias and pathological grief reactions. Other patients might also prove suitable: for example, anorexics, panic disorders, or conversion reactions. A further requirement of the design was that patients be agreeable to participate in an intensive diagnostic evaluation and thereafter participate in the ERP laboratory part of the research. The diagnostic evaluation consisted of three or four (determined by diagnostic and/or dispositional requirements) unstructured, psychodynamic interviews, one unstructured psychiatric interview aimed at identifying any medical disorder or biological psychiatric disorder, and a battery of psychodiagnostic tests (WAIS, Rorschach, TAT, and Early Memories). All interviews and testing sessions were sound-recorded and transcribed. Patients who were known to suffer from neurological complaints or psychoses were screened out in advance. On the basis of this assessment, five clinical judges (two in addition to the two interviewers and tester) made a DSM-III multiaxial diagnosis, described the patient's experience and understanding of the complaint and inferred from the data the nature of the unconscious conflict related to the complaint. After performing these tasks, the judges selected two categories of the patient's own words from the interview and test protocols: (1) words consciously related to the complaint (conscious words) and (2) words related to the inferred unconscious conflict (unconscious words). A final selection of eight words in each category was arrived at by consensus. Prior to the laboratory session, two additional categories of eight words each were added for control purposes, drawn from the Osgood lists (Osgood, May, and Miron 1975): (3) E+ words and (4) E− words. The E+ words served as a control for unpleasantness because the other three categories were made up of unpleasant words. The E− words served as a control for the two pathologically related unpleasant word categories. The thirty-two words were flashed in a tachistoscope, first subliminally (unaware condition) and then supraliminally (aware condition). ERP responses were recorded and then analyzed according to the transinformation (TI) method to be described below. We hoped to answer one main question: would the ERP responses categorize the words in the same way as the clinicians?

The Clinical Method

Our clinical task was to see if we could arrive at a convincing psychodynamic understanding, which in turn would form the basis for the selection of relevant words. The ERP method would permit us to see if the word selections formed self-contained categories having special properties on the basis of totally different and independent operations, thus providing convergent evidence for the clinical word selections. We conducted the clinical assessment of patients on the basis of unstructured open-ended interviews concentrating on the interactive process between patient and interviewer as a major source of diagnostic information. At the first of two Clinical Evaluation Team (CET) meetings, the independent judgments of the patient's experience and understanding of the complaint and the inferred unconscious conflict related to the complaint were read and discussed; a tentative consensus was arrived at and questions were formulated for the interviewer to pursue in subsequent interview(s). After the last interview(s), the same procedure was followed and a final consensus reached. Only words that had been selected by at least two judges were considered in the pool of final selection. At this preliminary stage of the research, no effort was made to evaluate reliability formally. We are currently developing a more systematic approach to word choice combining an estimate of "belongingness" to a word category based on the modeling of the decision process described by Shortliffe (1976) with the Delphi procedure for revising word weightings on the basis of judge interaction (Dalkey 1975; see appendix 6.A).

In the case of AM, the young man whose blood phobia was presented earlier, the clinical team decided that there was ample evidence in the interview and tests to support the hypothesis that the patient had longstanding problems with sadomasochistic impulses directed mainly at women. In our formulations we concluded that the blood phobia was the consciously experienced compromise arising from the conflict over sadistic wishes aimed in particular at pregnant women, the need to defend against such wishes because of the danger they posed to those he loved and the threat they posed to his own moral standards. The wished-for bloody attack was thus externalized and the patient could literally flee the representation of these impulses. Indeed, the outcome of the phobic experience was for him to become the weak, attacked victim, who must himself flee in terror. AM's phobic symptom was largely an effort to deal with his cruel, sadomasochistic impulses directed at a sadistically attacking and depriving mother he yearned for nevertheless. Especially salient in this respect was a masturbatory fantasy he dated back to early adolescence in which Cat Woman would lash him down and beat him with a whip, during which there would be, in his words, an "intense atmosphere of love and hate between them." It is of further interest to note that when the patient's parents divorced, the patient, then eleven, persuaded his siblings to stay with the father rather than go with the mother. The words we selected for the conscious, unconscious, E − and E + categories are listed in Table 6.1.

The Transinformation Method

The findings of Begleiter and Chapman previously cited suggested that it might be possible for the ERP to distinguish pathologically unpleasant words from pleasant words. We faced a methodological problem, however, insofar as we could not repeat the words as many times as Chapman had or for as many sessions. Many of the words were emotionally disturbing, and we wished to minimize our patients' discomfort. Also, many repetitions of psychologically complex stimuli run the risk of changing the meaning of these stimuli, as noted by Vidal (1977). There was the further important consideration that the straight averaging method followed in most ERP research might obscure the phenomenon we were interested in. A preliminary analysis as performed by Chapman was not promising. A special method was

TABLE 6.1 Words Selected for ERP Response (Subject AM)

Patient's Own Words

Conscious	Unconscious
weak	beating up
childbirth	Cat Woman
horrifying	tormented
suffer	rambunctious
queasy	tiger
spurting	screaming
gory	deprived
pictures	impale
veins	

Control Words

E −	E +
lying	friendship
air pollution	cleanliness
sickness	spring
cancer	fresh
sin	quality
criminal	peace
cheating	space travel
poor people	right hand

devised based on a transinformation model (Williams, Shevrin, and Marshall 1987). Transinformation refers to the information transmitted over an information channel from an information source to an information output on the receiving end. For example, the person talking into the telephone is the information source; what the person on the other end actually hears is the information output. Since information is usually lost in transmission, the amount of transinformation conveyed is always less than the total amount of information at the source.

It is important to note that information as such must be distinguished from the means by which the information is actually transmitted. The same information may be transmitted by a variety of different means, varying greatly in their operational characteristics. The same information or meaning may be conveyed by telephone, letter, or face-to-face communication. In each instance the means are different but the nature of the information may be the same. I stress this point because the application of an information-theoretic approach to ERPs has the main advantage of permitting the identification of shared or mutual information between any source and receiver but does not in and of itself permit the identification of the particular electrophysiological means by which the information is transmitted. Identification of these ERP characteristics is a second step, which one is readier to take once one is first assured that information is in fact getting through. The further advantage of the information-theoretic approach follows from its separate level of analysis independent of the means of transmission: it need not be tied to any a priori set of channel parameters such as various ERP components defined by latency and voltage (e.g., P_{300}, N_{100}), or to mean differences among these components; the transinformation method will "pick up" the transmitted message by whatever parameters it is conveyed. Another example may further clarify this point: we have no doubt that much information is conveyed from one English speaker to another: we can, in fact, measure the amount of information. But we still do not know the rules by which this information is transmitted. Early efforts to apply the rules of Latin grammar to English did not work, and currently there is much controversy among psycholinguists as to the true nature of these rules: how, for example, can an English speaker understand a variety of sentence forms as conveying the same information when it has proven difficult to identify the rules governing these variations? Some psycholinguists refer to this problem as following from the distinction between "surface" and "deep" structures. Similarly, the transinformation method as applied to ERPs will measure in information units (bits) the amount of information transmitted from word presentation to ERP responses but will not directly reveal the information-carrying characteristics of the ERPs. The transinformation method will, however, establish that information is being conveyed, the amount of this information, and at approximately what latency, and thus one would be helped by knowing *where* to look in the ERPs for the information-carrying parameters. If conventional ERP components are carrying the information, these would emerge in the second step of the analysis; on the other hand, the ERP characteristics may be quite different and may prove to be as elusive as the rules of English. For our present purposes, it is of paramount importance to determine if category information is being conveyed at all from word presentations to ERP. A finding of this nature would stand on its own, quite apart from the ERP parameters.

Recently, Sayre (1986) and Pribram (1986) have independently proposed the use of an information-theoretic approach in investigating the problem of intentionality (or reference) in cognitive science and in bridging the mind-body gap. Both authors argue that the value of the information-theoretic approach is precisely its capacity to identify shared information quite apart from the parameters of the systems involved. In the case of cognitive science, Sayre suggests that the amount of mutual information between the object of perception and perception can be studied quite apart from the particular perceptual system and that this mutual information defines what we mean by intentionality, or the referential character of perception. In the case of psychosomatic issues, Pribram suggests that it is again the amount of mutual information between mental and somatic systems that provides a useful mind-body bridge, quite apart from the different characteristics of these two systems.

In our case, as already noted, the information source is the word as presented in a tachistoscope and the information output is the ERP. We asked this question: How much of the information present in the word having to do with its category membership (e.g., conscious, unconscious, E+, E−) is present in the ERPs? Obviously there is much more information present at the source than this particular parameter of information. We are, however, free to choose an aspect of the information relevant to some task, just as we might choose to select only the lexical meaning of words transmitted in a telephone message and ignore accent, loudness, sex typing, etc. (see appendix 6.A for mathematical derivation of the transinformation method).

The Subliminal Procedure

The psychodynamically oriented clinician relies on a method, as described previously, that *assumes* the existence of unconscious factors. The assumption can be defended as useful, but it cannot be supported solely on clinical findings gathered by applying the method itself. Other, independent evidence must be obtained based on different methods so that the findings converge to point in the same direction and thus strengthen the likelihood that the assumption is tenable. Shevrin and Dickman (1980) have summarized a wide range of nonclinical experimental research that provides this kind of convergent evidence in research on attention, the stopped retinal image, binocular rivalry, and subliminal perception. There is also research on laboratory-induced slips of the tongue, which demonstrates that personality and motivational factors influence the production of slips by effecting preconscious editing processes (Baars and Motley 1976; Motley 1980).

The use of subliminal stimuli has a special value because it makes possible the experimental manipulation of awareness itself. The experimenter knows what stimuli have been presented outside the subject's awareness. Thus, the fate of stimuli in and out of awareness can be compared quite independently of any clinical judgment or inference based on the assumption of unconscious factors. The null hypothesis is easily stipulated: no effects will be found for subliminal stimuli beyond control levels. In addition to the studies cited above, a number of reviews have appeared on research on subliminal stimulation. One of the earliest concluded that the phenomenon existed although the evidence did not support the view that subliminal processing was different in kind from supraliminal processing (Bevan 1964). One of the most recent reviews and evaluations of the literature, based on hundreds of additional studies, concluded that the phenomenon not only existed but that subliminal processes under certain conditions are different in nature from supraliminal processes (Dixon 1981). The present author has contributed a number of such studies (Shevrin 1973, 1978, 1986). The research literature strongly suggests that subliminal stimulation can provide a laboratory-based experimental method for studying unconscious processes and that the ERP method can be linked successfully with subliminal stimulation.

Subjects

Seven subjects have participated thus far in the study, six patients and one normal control. Of the six patients, the first patient was tested before the clinical and laboratory procedures were fully developed; for this subject (SE) only the aware condition was administered, and the word categories were different from those of subsequent patient subjects. The normal control was given the same words as had been given to one of the patient subjects (AM). Results of these two subjects will be presented separately. In the group of five subjects constituting the experimental group, two were phobic and three were suffering from pathological grief reactions. AM was the twenty-two-year-old male college student suffering from a blood phobia of at least fifteen years' duration, and BP was a thirty-nine-year-old woman suffering from agoraphobia and panic attacks. The remaining three patients were suffering from pathological grief reactions: DA, a twenty-year-old woman, whose grandmother, responsible for having raised the patient, had died two years before; the patient reported never having been the same since, complaining of serious depression, headaches, inability to concentrate, and much continued grieving over her grandmother's death. SH, a thirty-five-year-old woman, whose three-week-old baby daughter died of SDS some two years before, described herself as not having been the same since the baby's death and having attempted suicide twice as well as suffering from a severe depression. DT, a thirty-year-old businessman whose mother had committed suicide when he was nineteen and whose life was marred since then by unhappy relationships with women and great fears of success that involved the necessity to destroy whatever success he achieved. In this case, the evaluation revealed, as originally suspected from the referral material, an occult pathological grief reaction to the mother's suicide. Each patient was offered a suitable disposition following his or her participation in the research.

Experimental Procedure

Following the completion of the clinical evaluation, the subjects were seen in the laboratory. They were told that they would be shown a series of words, some of which were related to their complaints; for some of the time they might not be able to see anything at all. For detecting ERPs one main electrode placement was used, the same placement used by Chapman, one-third of the distance from Cz to Pz ($CzPz$), along the front-back midline of the head. The electrode was referred to linked ears. For four subjects the words were presented in a modified randomized order within each block of thirty-two words six times. For one subject (DT) and the normal control (WL), words were presented in a series of six successive repetitions for each word. This word order was tried in order to see if the procedure could be speeded up. The unaware condition was administered first, followed by the aware condition. This sequence was used to ensure that any evidence of unaware processing would not be affected by a previous awareness of the stimuli selected, a consideration of greater importance to the basic research hypothesis at this preliminary stage than to the determination of the influence of order on awareness. Subjects were instructed to fixate a dot in the middle of a blank field, to be alert and attentive, and not to blink or move their eyes from the time the experimenter said "ready" until the experimenter said "blink," a time duration varying from 2 to 8 seconds. The experimental procedure lasted approximately three hours (including electrode placement and removal).

Words were presented to the subjects in a Gerbrand Model T3-8 three-field tachistoscope with an internal mirror removed to obtain slightly higher brightness. Field brightness was 3.0 foot-lamberts and tested for steady state and pulse brightness to verify the equivalence of the fixation and stimulus fields. Words were flashed for 1 msec. in the unaware condition. For the aware condition, prior to the presentation of stimuli, several neutral words were presented, starting at 30 msec., to determine if the subject could clearly identify the words. The time varied from 30 to 40 msec. for subjects to identify words. This speed was then used for the aware condition. Each word was printed on a 3 × 5 card in Helvetica light 18 point type. The white background had approximately four times the reflectance of the black-lettered words. A discrimination series at the end of the experiment demonstrated that subjects could not report seeing any words (or anything other than the fixation point) during the 1 msec. condition.

Data Analysis

Data were collected using a 120-msec. pre-stimulus sample and continued for approximately one second. Electrode signals were amplified and monitored, using a 24-channel Grass Model 8 EEG. Signals contaminated with ocular artifacts or large alpha waves were rejected either manually or automatically by the computer. Gain and band width were set at 7 microvolts/mm and from 1-70Hz. Data were sampled at 250 per second using an HP 1000 computer system, including a 2131G printer-plotter, a Model 2648 graphics terminal, and a 20 MB disc and 800 bpi 9-track tape. All individual ERPs were preserved in disc files for subsequent processing.

As a first step, each ERP was mapped for each time bin (4 msec.) into a transinformation profile based on a comparison with all of the other categories. These transinformation profiles were averaged across trials within categories to produce a category profile. The features of the transinformation profile consist of a series of sharp peaks or amplitudes measured in bits, distributed over the post-stimulus interval. Each peak represents a point of differentiation between the given category and the other three categories. By "point of differentiation" I mean the information present in the ERPs for the particular category that distinguishes it from the other three categories. The information related to a specific word category conveyed by the tachistoscopic word presentations was transmitted to the ERPs so that they now contain information related to distinguishing word categories. As Sayre (1986) has noted, this mutual information (transinformation) shared by source and receiver (word presentation and ERP) can be understood to reflect the intentionality or referential function of cognition: the category information present in the ERPs is therefore related to what we ordinarily refer to as the "meaning" of the category. I say "related to" the meaning rather than "being" the meaning itself because the concept of meaning is broader than any one particular manifestation or correlate of it. When a person says "I know what that means," the experience is more comprehensive than any particular brain process going on at the time, which may contain only one aspect of that total "meaning experience." This should not be surprising since we know, for example, how short language itself falls in conveying all of what we mean, yet it does capture an important part of our meaning, that is, *some* information of what we mean is in fact transmitted by language. The ERPs are a silent concomitant of the process by which some portion of meaning is transmitted.

Assuming independence of adjacent time bins, the total transinformation across all time bins should add up to unity, or one bit. (The relative failure to meet this condition and efforts to deal with it are described later.) The relationship between the ERPs and the transinformation profile can be intuitively grasped by first examining two such ERP average curves, one for the supraliminal conscious category and the other for the E + category, both from AM's records (Fig. 6.1). (For purposes of illustration, the comparisons to be presented are based on a two-way analysis: the conscious, unconscious, and E − categories are compared with the E + category. The four-way comparisons turn out to be essentially the same.) Inspection of the ERP curves reveals that sizable differences exist at about 500–600 msec. The transinformation (TI) profile will highlight the points at which differences exist between the average ERP curves and bring out differences that may not otherwise be apparent. These voltage differences

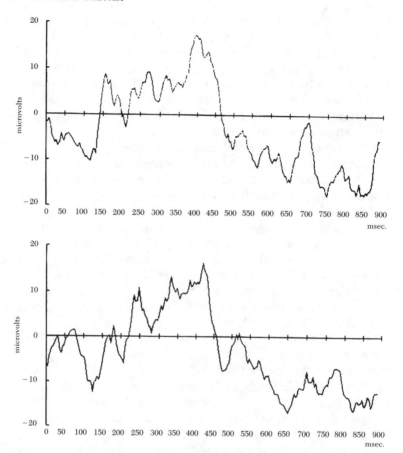

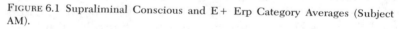

FIGURE 6.1 Supraliminal Conscious and E+ Erp Category Averages (Subject AM).

between the category ERP averages convey information distinguishing the categories. However, the reader should be cautioned on this score: the TI method will also pick up information when differences are not so apparent in the ERP averages because the TI method is also sensitive to other information-bearing characteristics such as variances, which are not easily caught by the eye or by tests of mean differences.

A visual inspection of the TI profiles of our first two subjects (AM, DA) suggested an interesting hypothesis: an interaction appeared to exist between word category and the presence or absence of awareness. For the supraliminal condition the TI profiles for the two pathological word categories were characterized by late-appearing information (404–704 msec. range), while for the subliminal condition the pathological TI profiles were characterized by *early*-appearing information (100–400 msec. range). No such interaction was found for the nonpathological E − category. We can see this relationship when we compare AM's subliminal and supraliminal TI profiles for the conscious and unconscious categories (Figs. 6.2, 6.3). The TI profiles for E − do not show this interaction; early information was present both for the supra- and subliminal conditions (Fig. 6.4). The same pattern was present for a second subject, DA, who suffered not from a phobia but from a pathological grief reaction. The inspection of the TI profiles again reveals that information appears early subliminally for the pathological words and later for the supraliminal TI profiles, and no difference between subliminal and supraliminal conditions exists for the nonpathological E − words (Figs. 6.5, 6.6, 6.7). There are also striking similarities between the TI profiles for AM and DA, suggesting the possibility that there are similar information properties for pathological word categories despite differences in the particular content of the pathology. An examination of the supraliminal TI profiles shows that the profiles for DA and AM are quite similar in the 500–600 msec. range.

As an initial approach to a measure that might capture this interaction effect and test the interaction for level of statistical probability, we went through the following steps.

1. Each evoked potential was mapped into a transinformation profile (by each ERP, I mean an ERP collected for each word presentation, of which there would be six for each word in the subliminal and six for each word in the supraliminal condition).

2. After each ERP was mapped into an individual transinformation profile, the largest or *peak* transinformation amplitude between 100 and 400 msec. and the largest or *peak* transinformation amplitude between 404 and 704 msec. were selected; these two TI peaks in effect constituted a considerable data reduction because a great deal of each transinformation profile was not included in this measure.

3. These two peaks, referred to as *early* and *late*, were the scores entered into a univariate repeated measures ANOVA (BMDP2V for the three test subjects: BP, SH, DT).

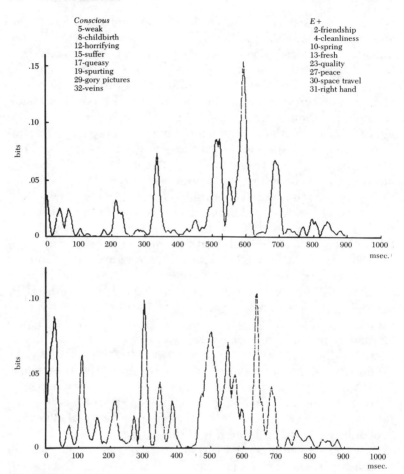

FIGURE 6.2 Supraliminal and Subliminal Conscious TI Category Averages (Subject AM).

4. In addition to subjects, there were the following sources of variance: (a) category (conscious, unconscious, E +, E −); (b) duration (aware/unaware); (c) peak (early and late); and (d) presentation (one through six). The ANOVA yielded a number of interactions, the most important of which was the three-way interaction for category, duration, and peak. We had hypothesized that this three-way interaction would exist and that it would be in the following direction: the two pathological categories (conscious and

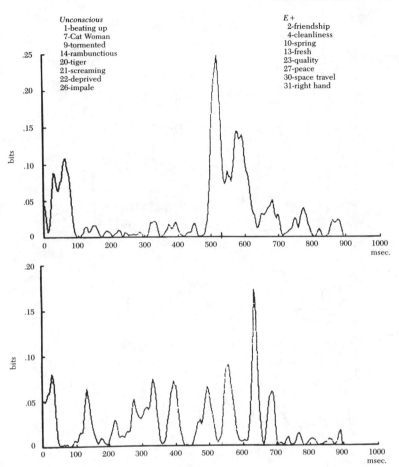

Unconscious
1-beating up
7-Cat Woman
9-tormented
14-rambunctious
20-tiger
21-screaming
22-deprived
26-impale

E+
2-friendship
4-cleanliness
10-spring
13-fresh
23-quality
27-peace
30-space travel
31-right hand

FIGURE 6.3 Supraliminal and Subliminal Unconscious TI Category Averages (Subject AM).

unconscious) would show a significantly greater *early* peak *subliminally* and a significantly *later* peak *supraliminally,* while the E − category would have a significant *early* transinformation amplitude both *supra-* and *subliminally.* We did not have any hypotheses developed for the E + category.

Because words were confounded with subject (most words differed from subject to subject), it was not possible to treat words as a separate, within subject source of variance; instead the TI

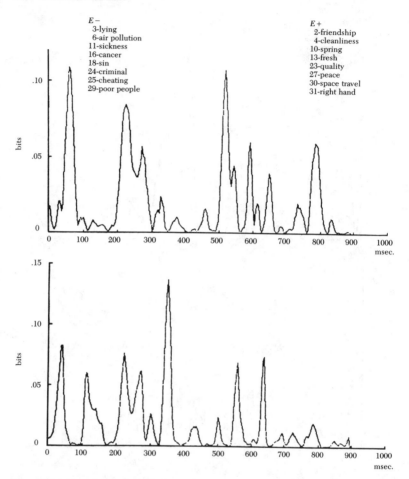

FIGURE 6.4 Supraliminal and Subliminal E− TI Category Averages (Subject AM).

peaks were averaged across all eight words in the category for each
of the six presentations so that there were six early peaks and six
late peaks per subject per category per duration for a total of 288
degrees of freedom.

The results were encouraging. For the three test subjects the
interaction was significant: $F = 5.87$, 3/6 df, $p = .0471$, Green-
house-Geisser correction. We would still need to know if this significant interaction was in the expected direction. A further analysis of contrasts in which all contrasts other than the one
hypothesized were averaged out revealed that when the two pathological categories were contrasted with the two nonpathological

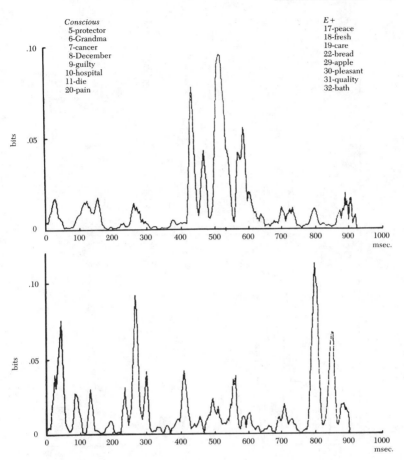

FIGURE 6.5 Supraliminal and Subliminal Conscious TI Category Averages (Subject DA).

categories for the hypothesized interaction a significant difference was found ($t = 5.651$, 2 df, $p = .0299$). Were there any differences between the two pathological categories (conscious vs. unconscious)? A separate ANOVA was computed solely for the pathological categories. (In future work, we are planning to do pairwise transinformation comparisons; although the four-way analysis in which each category is compared with the other three is useful in order to establish unique differences, it does not lend itself as readily to identifying the nature of differences between any two categories.) For the two pathological categories an interaction was found between the two categories for *early* and *late*

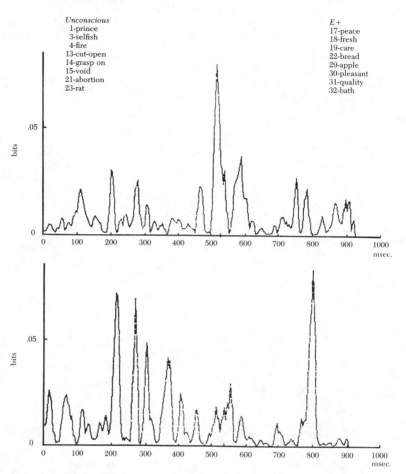

Unconscious
1-prince
3-selfish
4-fire
13-cut-open
14-grasp on
15-void
21-abortion
23-rat

E +
17-peace
18-fresh
19-care
22-bread
29-apple
30-pleasant
31-quality
32-bath

FIGURE 6.6 Supraliminal and Subliminal Unconscious TI Category Averages (Subject DA).

peaks regardless of duration. The conscious category had relatively greater TI amplitudes for the *early* peaks, while the unconscious category had relatively greater TI amplitudes for the *late* peaks ($F = 12.50$, $1/2\ df$, $p = .07$). It should be borne in mind that this interaction is independent of duration: the same category-related differences for *early* and *late* peaks are present *both* subliminally and supraliminally. We would interpret this finding to mean that there is a tendency for the unconscious late peaks carrying the most information to be later than the conscious late peaks, and the reverse with respect to the early peaks. This would

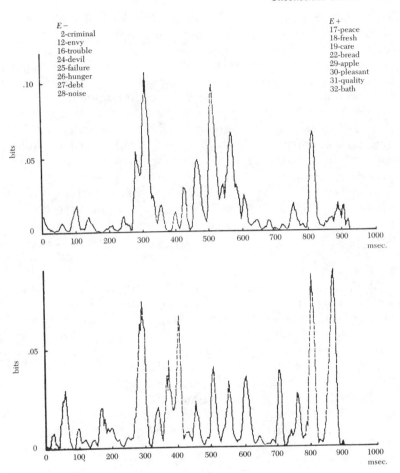

FIGURE 6.7· Supraliminal and Subliminal E − TI Category Averages (Subject DA).

fit with the general hypothesis (to be explored in the discussion) suggesting that there is more inhibition supraliminally (later appearance of information) for the pathological words (conscious and unconscious) than for the nonpathological words (E − and E +), and generally more inhibition for the unconscious than for the conscious category, regardless of duration.

The findings from the two analyses can be put together as follows: the two pathological categories can be differentiated from the two nonpathological categories on the basis of the interaction between duration and the TI peaks. The relationship between the early and late peaks changes as a function of duration for the pathological categories, while the relationship between the peaks remains the same regardless of duration for the nonpathological categories. Within the two pathological categories there is a tendency for the late peaks to convey more information for the unconscious category and for the early peaks to do so for the consciously related category. A good analogy might again be taken from language: all English speakers use the *th* sound, no French speaker does (pathological vs. nonpathological), but *among* English speakers, some use the sound less often (i.e., people from Brooklyn; conscious vs. unconscious).

What is the strength of these analysis-of-variance findings? Their main strength is that *regardless of differences* among subjects there are differential relationships between the pathological categories and the nonpathological categories and differences between pathological categories. These transinformation findings stand on their own regardless of what the particular characteristics of the evoked potentials themselves may turn out to be. What are the weaknesses of these findings? There are two. First, the data have been substantially reduced by selecting just two transinformation amplitudes from each ERP. In future work we plan to overcome this limitation by computing noise-generated distributions against which to compare the entire transinformation profile with all of its peaks, not simply the early and late peaks. Second, as already mentioned, the four-way transinformation comparisons may obscure pairwise differences that are of particular interest to us, such as the comparison of the unconscious to the conscious category.

In addition to the ANOVA, we also tried other approaches available in the literature. We applied the principal component approach for classifying ERPs to our data. Although this approach was used with success by Chapman (1980), we were unable to duplicate his results. This may well be due to the fact that Chapman used an order-of-magnitude greater number of presentations. It is probable that the principal component approach is not reliable with the small number of presentations possible in our setting. We have also tried a quadratic classifier approach suggested by Westerkamp, Aunon, and McGillem (1983). In this approach a Bayesian model is derived based on sample values of ERP at several time points. After applying this approach to our data in an attempt to classify the word classes by pairs, we concluded that it can produce inflated classification accuracy because of the dependence of the feature selection process. Perhaps a modification of the approach can relieve this problem. The Bayesian classifier picked the best time point near the peak of the transinformation profile. The second best time point was often near another peak of the transinformation profile. Beyond that, however, time points selected by the procedure seemed to be randomly scattered about.

We also made use of a bootstrapping approach suggested by Diaconis and Efron (1983) in which the original ERP data were shuffled on the basis of two different shuffling principles: ERPs for a given word were either distributed systematically across four dummy categories so that any effect present would vanish or distributed entirely randomly so that it was possible by chance for more than one ERP belonging to a true category to appear in one of the dummy categories. If there was any category effect, the shuffles made on the basis of the second principle should show it when compared to the shuffles made on the basis of the first principle. The two sets of data were shuffled 350 times each. A Hotelling T^2 was computed on the resultant transinformation profiles (Rao 1952). This statistic permits us to take into account the lack of independence among adjacent time bins by providing a vector score. We found that the Hotelling T^2 for each of the subjects, supra- and subliminally, was significantly greater than the Hotelling T^2 obtained for a set of artificially generated noise data treated by the same shuffling procedures. These results strongly support the hypothesis that a category effect is present once the covariance among adjacent time points is taken into account. A more refined application of this procedure is currently in progress, which should provide us with more precise findings bearing on the category interaction previously cited.

Controlling for Extraneous Variables

Successful efforts were made to control for a number of extraneous variables: horizontal visual angle subtended by words, frequency of usage, and parts of speech, all of which were not significantly different across categories. In the initial selection of words, categories were balanced as closely as possible for these variables. The measurement of frequency of usage posed special difficulties because we were dealing with *spoken* words in the case of the pathological categories and with *written* words in the case of the E + and E − categories. We used a catalogue made up of words used by patients in psychotherapy and psychoanalysis that seemed to be the closest to our own data (Dahl 1979). Some were compound words that did not appear in the catalogue. In these instances we averaged the frequencies for the individual words in the compound term.

There are additional findings of interest. Several emerged when the data from our first pilot subject and the control subject were analyzed. Our first subject, SE, was phobic for thunderstorms. Because of an error in the experimental procedure, the subliminal condition was not recorded properly. In addition, the two control categories were drawn from the patient's Fear Questionnaire (Marks and Matthews 1979) made out by her at an earlier time. One control category was made up of words that she had checked off as frightening but nonphobic; the other control category was made up of words that were neither phobic nor frightening. The latter category was used as equivalent to the E + category for the other subjects, and the nonphobic frightening words were used as the equivalent of the E − category. The resulting transinformation profiles for the three categories (conscious, unconscious, E −, all compared with the E + category) were similar in configuration to those found for the other subjects. The conscious and unconscious words showed the delayed latency for category information, and the nonphobic frightening words showed early category information similar to what we obtained for the E − words (Figs. 6.8, 6.9, 6.10). These findings from SE suggest that phobia-related words can be distinguished from merely frightening words

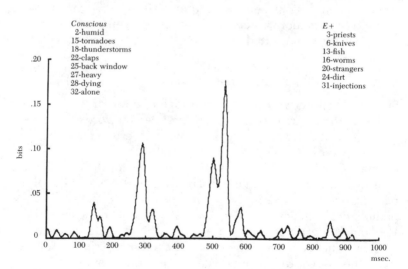

FIGURE 6.8 Supraliminal Conscious TI Category Average (Subject SE).

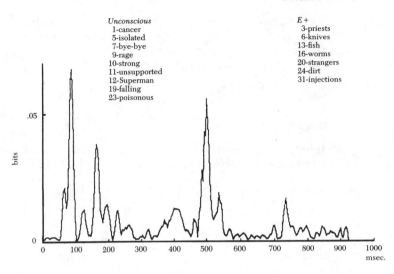

FIGURE 6.9 Supraliminal Unconscious TI Category Average (Subject SE).

on the basis of delayed latency of ERP category information in the aware condition and that words bearing on the unconscious conflict related to the phobia can also be differentiated from nonphobic, nonfrightening words.

The normal control subject, a twenty-year-old woman (WL), was given the same words as one of the experimental subjects (AM). Interestingly, the control subject's transinformation profiles showed

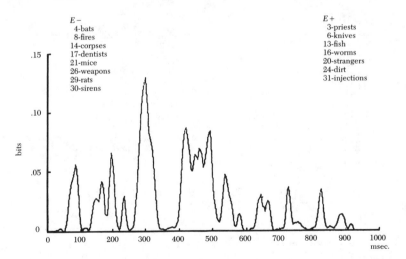

FIGURE 6.10 Supraliminal E− TI Category Average (Subject SE).

the reverse TI patterns from those of the experimental subject. Indeed, the pattern for the pathological affect words was similar to the one for the E − words, suggesting that for the control subject the words that were pathological for the experimental subject were simply unpleasant (Figs. 6.11, 6.12, 6.13).

Discussion

The research findings supported the view that it may be possible to explore the nature of unconscious conflict on the basis of con-

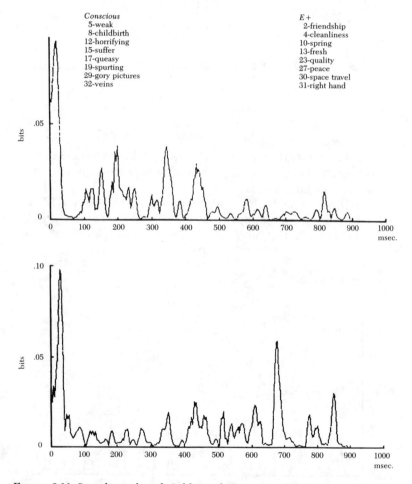

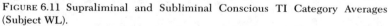

FIGURE 6.11 Supraliminal and Subliminal Conscious TI Category Averages (Subject WL).

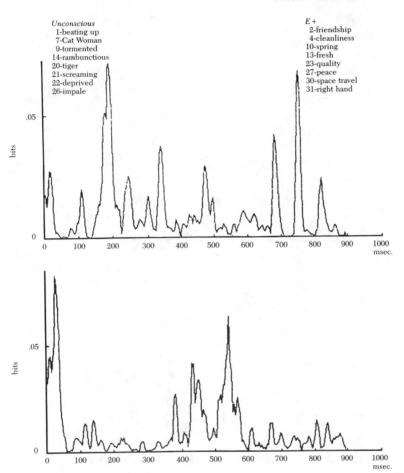

FIGURE 6.12 Supraliminal and Subliminal Unconscious TI Category Averages (Subject WL).

vergent clinical, subliminal, and electrophysiological methods. As recent ERP research has shown, the ERP is remarkably sensitive to meaning, both denotative and connotative, and to other aspects of language, such as noun-verbal differences and antonym-homonym differences. Our work extends these findings to the realm of psychopathology and the highly idiosyncratic meanings involved in symptoms and unconscious conflict. Furthermore, the presence of subliminal ERP information effects makes it possible to explore aspects of unconscious processes not avail-

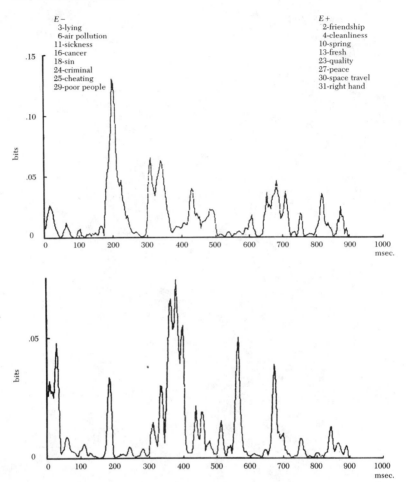

FIGURE 6.13 Supraliminal and Subliminal E − TI Category Averages (Subject WL).

able directly to the clinician. Both general and highly individual aspects of language can be explored with the approach described.

Three further points will be taken up in the discussion: (1) the relatively stable transinformation patterns found across subjects despite the individuality of the particular pathology and the uniqueness of the words used in each instance; (2) the relationship between supraliminal and subliminal transinformation patterns; and (3) the relationship between the conscious and unconscious transinformation profiles.

THE STABLE TRANSINFORMATION PATTERNS
ACROSS SUBJECTS

Although the individual words within the pathological categories differed from subject to subject, the *functional* significance of the words remained the same. If they were consciously or unconsciously related to the complaint, they showed a different pattern of information properties from nonpathological affect words. Although the particulars of each subject's experience differed, once properly categorized these particular words played the same role in each individual's pathology and the pattern of ERP information properties was similar. Thus, it can be concluded that the salient aspects of the conscious experience of the complaint and the unconscious conflict related to the complaint are organized along distinctive lines in the information content of the brain processes, despite wide differences in the particular elements comprising the pathology. Subjects AM and DA have different complaints (blood phobia vs. pathological grief reaction), different ways of experiencing their complaints so that different words were used, and different unconscious conflicts, yet their patterns of transinformation were quite similar. One could say that unconscious processes related to conflict can be characterized as spontaneous and ad hoc (given the unique character of the words used) and at the same time organized on the basis of some overriding principle, perhaps related to inhibitory processes.

THE RELATIONSHIP BETWEEN SUPRALIMINAL AND
SUBLIMINAL TRANSINFORMATION PATTERNS

Although it is necessary to be cautious in interpreting this interaction in view of the fact that only one duration order was used (subliminal followed by supraliminal), the finding that category information is present earlier subliminally than supraliminally is of some interest. Let us assume for the sake of argument that the subliminal condition is sampling the status of preconscious activity and that the supraliminal condition is sampling brain activity during consciousness. It would then appear that for the pathologically related words the *later* appearance of category information supraliminally suggests some kind of highly selective and inhibitory process. Indeed, the earlier subliminal appearance of category information suggests something cognitive psychologists have hypothesized concerning the preconscious occurrence of parallel processing. Subliminally, multiple simul-

taneous coding may be occurring. Among these activated codes
for the pathological words will be a number that are related to
the person's conscious complaint and unconscious conflict.
Avoiding these codes will take longer when selective attention
operates to bring to consciousness a neutral meaning. On the
other hand, for the E− category no such additional codes will
be activated and thus selective attention will take a shorter time
to bring to consciousness an appropriate code.

THE RELATIONSHIP BETWEEN CONSCIOUS AND UNCONSCIOUS WORD CATEGORIES

From our findings there does not appear to be any substantial
difference in pattern between the consciously related and unconsciously related words, although one finding suggested a
somewhat greater delay in category information for the unconscious words than for the conscious words, perhaps some greater
inhibition. This finding is consistent with the structural hypothesis in psychoanalysis advanced by Brenner (1976). On the basis
of the structural hypothesis, symptoms such as phobias are the
outcome of complex compromises among wishes, defenses, and
moral standards. Each symptom therefore has within it a disguised expression of a rejected impulse, its punishment, and
some effort at adaptation. We can apply this to AM's blood phobia
as follows: The presumed wish to find pleasure in harming powerful and depriving women becomes intensely active in circumstances that are likely to elicit this wish (films such as *One Flew
over the Cuckoo's Nest*). However, this unacceptable wish cannot
be permitted direct access to consciousness and, at the same time,
its activation must be punished in some way. The patient appears
to reverse the relationship between the sadist and the masochist,
himself becoming the victim of his phobia and thus suffering the
punishment that would be predicted by the structural theory. By
the same token, the symptomatic experience itself is related to
the unconscious conflict and, indeed, represents a partial break-
through of it within the symptomatic compromise. Thus, from
this point of view the consciously related words, which are such
a salient part of the patient's *experience* of the phobia, are distant
cousins of the unconsciously related words. The two sets of words
should not then give rise to drastically different transinformation
profiles. They may, however, undergo a different fate as a function
of treatment change. For example, if AM were to undergo behavior modification treatment successfully, we might find that

the pathological pattern for the conscious words was attenuated as his avoidant behavior and perhaps his conscious experience of fear disappeared; on the other hand, the unconscious words might still show the pathological pattern if the behavior modification approach did not change this level of the patient's difficulties. If a dynamically oriented psychotherapy were undertaken, which had as its aim the resolution of the underlying conflict, we might find a successful treatment would result in a change in the pathological pattern for *both* conscious and unconscious words. At least in principle, on the basis of the method described, this test becomes possible to conduct.

The combined electrophysiological and subliminal procedures used in the research permit us access to unconscious processes as they are occurring. When we add to these procedures the psychodynamically based selection of symptom- and conflict-related words, it is probable that the unconscious processes measured by the subliminal and ERP procedures are dealing with complex issues of meaning, affect, and conflict, all cognized without benefit of consciousness. Thus, the unconscious would appear to be capable of highly complex, highly spontaneous, affective, motivational, and cognitive processing. If the interaction between pathology and duration of exposure stands up in subsequent research, it would appear that, at least with respect to conflict-related issues, there are differences between unconscious and conscious processing.

The method we have used can be adapted to investigate a variety of clinical and experimental research problems. For example, key terms in individual states of mind related to pathology described by Horowitz (1987) can be explored in the ERP laboratory and after brief or intensive treatment. Similarly, the symptom context method developed by Luborsky (1967) can be combined with the method. Beyond these clinical research applications, issues of language organization and meaning, the nature of categorization itself, and the relationship between affect and cognition might be usefully investigated with the help of the method.

Appendix 6.A: Techniques for Word Selection

An essential part of the methodology of ERP word-response testing is the selection of words used as stimuli. In this process it is important to be able to select words that "belong" in some sense to the four categories of interest, that is, words related to the conscious or unconscious pathology and words possessing pleasant and unpleasant connotations. It is also important to provide a framework for the process itself, to afford the team of clinicians a readily interpretable set of metrics to indicate the convergence or divergence of opinion and, at the same time, allow the assessment of relative degrees of belonging and nonbelonging to the categories of interest. It is also desirable to indicate the joint properties of words—for example, a word may be considered "unpleasant" and also highly revelant to "conscious" pathology.

These considerations have led to a technique of quantifying the various aspects of this process. "Belonging" is quantified for each word in terms of each of four categories on a scale ranging from $+10 - 10$. This constitutes a multivariate metric space in which the orthogonal axes are the measures of "belonging" for each category. In this manner the joint properties, as well as the individual properties, of the words may be analyzed. These rankings may also be thought of as measures of "belief" and "disbelief" in the sense of Shortliffe (1976), enabling the modeling of the decision process in production rules as in MYCIN.

The process of reviewing the word weightings is an interaction among the members of the team of clinicians. Such a process has been formalized as a Delphi procedure (Dalkey 1975; Scheibe, Skutsch, and Schafer 1975), in which some or all of the developing opinions are made available to the team as the process continues through several iterations. Problems that may arise and premises for such procedures are discussed. Presently the raw scores for all iterations are employed by the team to obtain rankings and discover inconsistencies. However, a metric appears desirable for this.

The development of a single metric to express all relevant properties of the selection process is desirable but may not be realistic. Properties of interest in word selections are several but not easily confined in a single meaningful metric. An important property is closeness to an ideal category. This implies a distance metric and is readily expressed as a Euclidian distance of the multivariate word ranking to the ideal ranking, that is, a ranking of $+10$, -10, -10, -10 for a four-category space. Coupled to this property is a distance from other categories. Combining these two distances in a single function serves to provide a meaningful measure of "closeness" to the ideal ranking and "distance" from other categories. In other words, it is a combined measure or simultaneous measure of "belonging" and lack of ambiguity. The most promising measure among many available (Sneath and Sokal 1973) seems to be the mean square distance for the distance metric and a form of likelihood ratio for the function. A promising function is a product of distance to ideal category and the sum of inverse distances to other categories.

Another property of interest is the convergence or divergence of opinion during the selection process. This may best be expressed as the sequence of variances for each iteration of the ranking process. This is employed in Delphi procedures (Dalkey 1975; Scheibe, Skutsch, and

Schafer 1975). Should a variance sequence prove divergent, for example, the word should probably be rejected as ambiguous or poorly defined.

Another property relates to the intercategory distance structure. It may be desirable to include an explicit evolution of the compactness of the set of category words and the separation of the several category sets. Measures for these properties include the Hotelling T^2 functions of the Mahalonobis distance and various likelihood functions (Scheibe et al. 1975).

There is a certain amount of overlap among the above described functions but each serves to quantify properties meaningful to the selection process and may be difficult to combine. However, it is evident that this approach, employing a multivariate metric space quantifying opinions, is well suited to the process and makes available a well-developed statistical methodology for its analysis.

Appendix 6.B: The Transinformation Method

Signal Analysis: Transinformational Analysis

After briefly presenting the basis in information theory transinformation method, I will discuss its application to ERP signal processing.

Basis in Information Theory

Shannon (1948) has suggested the following measure of uncertainty or entropy associated with the sample space of a complete finite mean:

$$H(x) = \sum_k - P_k \log_2 P_k,$$

where P_k is the probability of occurrence of the event E_k. $H(x)$ is an indicator of the amount of information contained in the events E_k (which are mutually exclusive).

This formulation can be justified intuitively. If P_k is the probability of the event E_k, the self information of the event is $I[E_k] = -\log_2(P_k)$.

The unit of information is called the bit, where one bit is the amount of information associated with the selection of one of two equally likely events ($P_k = 1/2$). Four equally likely events would yield 2 bits of self information ($P_k = 1/4$). The four outcomes can be indicated by two bits in the binary system ($0_{10} = 00_2$, $1_{10} = 01_2$, $2_{10} = 10_2$, $3_{10} = 11_2$), where the subscript 10 indicates the number to base 10 and the subscript 2 indicates the number to base 2.

The expected amount of information in the scheme can be found by taking the expectation of $I[E_k]$:

$$E\{I[E_k]\} = \sum_k P_k(-\log_2(P_k)) = H(X)$$

Thus entropy, $H(x)$, can be considered to be the average amount of self information in the scheme.

The H function has the following properties:

1. Continuity. If the probabilities of the events change slightly, the measure of uncertainty H should vary in a continuous manner.
2. Symmetry. The measure should be invariant with respect to the order of the events.
3. Extremal Property. When all events are equally likely, the largest entropy is obtained. For example, for two events E_1 and E_2

$$\text{if} \quad P_1 = 1/2 \quad \text{and} \quad P_2 = 1/2,$$
$$H(x) = -\log_2(1/2) \cdot 1/2 - \log_2(1/2) \cdot 1/2 = 1 \text{ bit};$$
$$\text{if} \quad P_1 = 0 \quad \text{and} \quad P_2 = 1,$$
$$H(x) = -\log_2(0) \cdot 0 - \log_2(1) \cdot 1 = 0.$$

If one event is certain and the other is impossible, there is no information conveyed by being told that the certain event has occurred or that the impossible event has not occurred.

If the probability of both events is 1/2, then 1 bit of information is conveyed by being told that one or the other of the events has occurred.

4. Additivity. This property relates to the additivity of entropy obtained from subsets of events.

Suppose a 2-bit digital display is available. The display can convey 00, 01, 10, 11. The entropy associated with the first digit ($P(0) = 1/2$, $P(1) = 1/2$) is 1 bit. The entropy associated with the second digit ($P(0) = 1/2, P(1) = 1/2$) is 1 bit also. The total entropy is $1 + 1 = 2$. If taken as a whole and $P(00) = 1/4, P(01) = 1/4, P(10) = 1/4, P(11) = 1/4$, the entropy is 2 bits, the same as obtained by adding the entropies of the first and second digits. If both digits change together and we view either 00 or 11, then the entropy is only 1 bit. Additivity can not be used because the first and second digits results are not independent.

These brief observations do not do justice to the concept involved, but space and purpose do not permit a fuller presentation.

Transinformation

Transinformation is a further elaboration of the idea of information. Transinformation is a measure of the amount of information that is transmitted over an information channel (Reza 1961). If the set of stimulus symbols is called x and the set response symbols is called y, then transinformation may be defined to be

$$I(X;Y) = H(X) - H(X/Y),$$

where $H(X)$ is as before and $H(X/Y)$, termed the equivocation entropy is

$$H(X/Y) = -\sum_i\sum_j P(x_i/y_j)\,[\log_2 P(x_i/y_j)]P(y_j).$$

As an example, suppose there are two input stimuli x_1 and x_2 and two output responses y_1 and y_2.

$$P(x_1) = 1/2, \; P(x_1/y_1) = 1, \; P(x_2/y_2) = 0;$$
$$P(x_2) = 1/2, \; P(x_2/y_2) = 1, \; P(x_1/y_2) = 0;$$
$$P(y_1) = 1/2, \; P(y_2) = 1/2;$$

Then

$$
\begin{aligned}
I(x;y) = & -1/2 \, \log_2(1/2) - 1/2 \, \log_2(1/2); \\
& -[1 \cdot \log_2(1)] \cdot 1/2 - [0 \cdot \log_2(0)] \cdot 1/2; \\
& -[0 \cdot \log_2(0)] \cdot 1/2 - [1 \cdot \log_2(1)] \cdot 1/2 \\
= & \; 1 \text{ bit.}
\end{aligned}
$$

All of the input information is transmitted through the channel. If the equivocation entropy is zero, given the output responses there is no equivocation about the input. If, however,

$$P(x_1/y_1) = 1/2, \; P(x_2/y_1) = 1/2;$$
$$P(x_1/y_2) = 1/2, \; P(x_2/y_2) = 1/2;$$
$$P(y_1) = 1/2, \; P(1/2) = 1/2;$$

with $P(x_1) = P(x_2) = 1/2$ as before, then the equivocation entropy is $-[1/2 \, \log(1/2)] \cdot 2 = 1$ bit. Thus the equivocation is total, and no information is transmitted through the channel since $H(X) - H(X/Y) = 1 - 1 = 0$. This is true even though the input and output probabilities are the same as before.

Application of the Transinformation Analysis to ERPs

It is proposed that transinformation can be developed into an ideal measure of the information about a set of stimuli in terms of evoked potentials. Vidal (1977) has proposed the idea of an information wave derived from evoked potentials.

The development will proceed along a different pathway from that suggested by Vidal. The inputs X_1, X_2, etc., are the word categories. The outputs Y_1, Y_2, etc., are the ERP voltage levels.

The transinformation is derived for N categories of stimuli and M evoked potentials. This is

$$I[x;y(n)] = -\sum_{i=1}^{N} P(x_i) \log_2 P(x_i) + \sum_{j=1}^{M} \sum_{i=1}^{N} (P(x_i/y_j(n))) \log_2 [P(x_i/y_j(n))] \cdot P(y_j(n))$$

where the x_i are the word categories and the $y_j(n)$ are the evoked potentials, n is the nth bin or time sample and j is the jth word presented. N is the total number of categories and M the total number of words presented. If the probabilities were known, the amount of information about the categories transmitted or available via the ERPs could be computed for every value n or every 4-msec. post-stimulus time. Four categories could yield a maximum of 2 bits of transinformation.

Unfortunately, it is quite difficult to determine the required probabilities from the small data sets we have available. A number of attempts to develop good estimates of the probabilities produced disappointing results. The "jacknife" method suggested by Tukey (1976) was tried. Preliminary results were disappointing but were sufficiently interesting to stimulate further attempts to compute useful transinformation measures. The initial goal was to find out if certain time bins were potentially more promising in carrying information concerning the stimulus categories and which bins were of little use. Then, presumably, conventional analysis techniques could be concentrated on effective bins, while ineffective bins would be discarded. However, it was soon realized that the transinformation profiles had distinctive features that were consistent from subject to subject. This led to an intensive search for stable and reliable statistical estimators of the transinformation profiles. The present approach is the result of that effort and is reasoned as follows: If the probabilities required could not be estimated from the data, the transinformation profiles could be estimated in another way. The $y_j(n)$ were assumed to be drawn from normal distributions. This model was well confirmed by the data. Then the $P(x_i/y_j(n))$ could be estimated by the following means. By Bayes's theorem

$$P(x_k/y_j(n)) = \frac{f_{Y/X_k}(y_j(n)/x_k)\Delta y \cdot P(x_k)}{\sum_{i=1}^{N} f_{Y/X_i}(y_i(n)/x_i) \cdot \Delta y \cdot P(x_i)}$$

where the $f_{Y/X}$ are the conditional probability density functions of the voltage y given the stimulus category x_i. The quantity $f_{Y/X_i}(y_j(n)/x_i) \cdot \Delta y$ is the probability of the voltage of the jth ERP being in a tiny zone Δy around y given stimulus category x_i. All of the stimulus categories are chosen to be equal; therefore

$$P(x_k/y_j(n)) = \frac{f_{Y/X_k}(y_j(n)/x_k)}{\sum_{i=1}^{N} f_{Y/X_i}(y_i(n)/x_i)}$$

The probability density functions are assumed to be gaussian or normal where the $\mu_i(n)$ and the $\sigma_i(n)$ are estimated at each time bin for the ith category

$$f_{X/Y_i}(y(n)/x_i) = \frac{1}{\sqrt{2\pi}} \sigma_i(n) \exp\left\{-\frac{(y(n) - \mu_i(n))^2}{2\sigma^2(n)}\right\}$$

from the ERPs evoked by stimuli in that category. This completes the requirements for estimating the part of the equivocation entropy due to the jth ERP, that is,

$$h(X/y_j(n)) = \sum_{k=1}^{N} \left\{ \frac{f_{Y_j/X_k}}{\sum\limits_{i=1}^{N} f_{Y_j/X_i}} \log_2 \left[\frac{f_{Y_j/X_k}}{\sum\limits_{i=1}^{N} f_{Y_j/X_i}} \right] \right\}$$

Then,

$$H(X/Y(n)) = \sum_{j=1}^{M} h(X/y_j(n)) \cdot P(y_j(n))$$

if $Y_j(n)$ is considered to be discrete. However, $H(X/Y)$ can be estimated by

$$H(X/Y(n)) = \frac{1}{M} \sum_{j=1}^{M} h(X/y_j(n)).$$

The $h(X/y_j(n))$ can be considered to be the equivocation entropy of the jth ERP. The transinformation of the jth ERP can be expressed for four categories as

$$t(X/y_j(n)) = 2 - h(X/y_j(n))$$

since the stimulus entropy is 2 bits for four equally likely categories, and for two equally likely categories

$$t(X/y_j(n)) = 1 - h(X/y_j(n))$$

since the stimulus entropy is 1 bit for two equally likely input stimuli.

The $t(X/y_j(n))$ can be considered to be the transinformation for the *single* ERP. If all $t(X/y_j(n))$ are averaged over all ERPs evoked from stimuli within a given category, the result can be considered to be the transinformation for a given category.

The transinformation profiles for different subjects are quite similar for the same category of stimuli. The individual transinformations for the same word presented several times are often remarkably similar. Typically there is consistently a series of sharp peaks between 100 and 400 msec. post-stimulus with the concentration of peaks in the midrange. There is another series of peaks concentrated in the range between 404 and 704 msec.

A given peak may move from bin to bin over a range of perhaps 20 msec. even when the same word is presented each time. Sometimes the peak is missing altogether, but the general pattern of peaks is often quite stable. Averaging the individual transinformation profiles to produce the category transinformation estimates provides results that are satisfying because one can clearly see the category difference when viewing the plots. For purposes of statistical analysis we have found it to be useful to identify the maximum peak in the 100–400 msec. range (early) and the maximum peak in the 404–704 msec. range (late). Thus the maximum peak is captured even if it moves about a bit from presentation to presentation. Early/late peak data distinguish between unpleasant and pathological categories at a highly significant level. However, it is clear that there are a number of other submaximal peaks that may be exploited to discriminate between word groupings and perhaps even individual words within categories as well as aid in category discrimination.

The transinformation formulation presented assumes mutually exclusive input categories and a system without memory. Both of these considerations are probably violated to some degree. The assignment of words to categories is not perfect. A given word may intersect with two or more categories. The category boundries may be different than supposed or the category differences may be due to other than the attributes that we assign to them. As previously mentioned, a number of extraneous category factors such as visual angle, number of syllables, parts of speech, and frequency of usage have been taken into account.

The previously presented word may influence the ERP evoked by the present word. This would violate the no-memory consideration. An examination of experimental results for several subjects indicates that this is not a problem, but it needs further scrutiny. Violation of the mutual exclusion and memory considerations would tend to degrade the transinformation results, not produce falsely inflated results.

Memory from bin to bin during the ERP can be accounted for under stationarity consideratons by formulating the transinformation in terms of a vector of successive time points. Multiple electrodes can also be accounted for by extending along the electrode dimension as well, so that a matrix of points is used as the output. There is no barrier to accomplishing this at present except for available computer memory if the matrix is too large. A multiple electrode formulation has been tested for one subject. The results are encouraging since they seem to support the single electrode results even more strongly.

The computations required are computationally and memory-use intensive. In practice, the ERP transinformation profile for each ERP is computed by formulating the statistical model with the ERP excluded. Then the ERP is used with the model to compute the transinformation profile. The mean and variance for each category has to be recomputed for each time point with the particular ERP excluded. This produces a more conservative estimate than would be the case if the ERP were included. Such computer-intensive techniques often produce results unobtainable by conventional statistical methods (Diaconis and Efron 1983). Such methods have considerable promise with the use of modern high-speed computers. As pointed out by these authors, present statistical techniques arose in the early part of this century when the ability to perform computations was severely limited. New techniques are just beginning to emerge that are free of many of the restrictions imposed by these earlier approaches and depend on intensive computation.

Questions can be raised about the bias, variance, and stationarity of the transinformation estimator. These properties have not been explored thoroughly. The estimator's use can be justified purely on an empirical basis since it appears to function well as a high-order differencing algorithm that reveals differentures between category ERPs while reducing or eliminating redundant features and noise.

Work will continue to place the estimator on a firm statistical basis. The probability distribution of the transinformation values is distinctly nonnormal, as might be expected. A logarithmic transformation of these values satisfactorily normalizes them, as was done when the data were used for the ANOVA.

The time jitter or bin movement of the peaks from presentation to presentation is due to a basis nonstationarity in ERPs that has been recognized. An excellent recent review (McGillem, Aunon, and Childers 1981) touches on many issues of importance to the project. Methods for handling single ERPs are discussed. The alignment of ERPs to reduce the effects of time jitter has been carried out by McGillem and Aunon (1977). Also a method of filtering was discussed.

Cleaning up the ERPs by filtering and aligning them before averaging may improve the transinformation results. The transinformation profiles might also be aligned at peaks. If the mean and variance vary systematically with word presentation habituation or other longer time changes in the system, it might be helpful to track mean and variance as functions of time by use of regression equations. The transinformation profile could then be computed, based on the regression estimated mean and variance at the time of the individual ERP.

Once the transinformation profiles are optimized, sophisticated pattern-recognition techniques will be applied to classify ERPs via their transinformation profiles. We believe that much can be learned about cognition by examining transinformation profiles. If pattern-recognition techniques are applied without a concomitant understanding of the brain events contributing to the classification, simple classification may be performed very well, but underlying brain phenomena may be missed.

References

Andrews, G., and R. Harvey. 1981. Does psychotherapy benefit neurotic patients? *Archives of General Psychiatry* 38:1203–8.

Baars, B. J., and M. T. Motley. 1976. Spoonerisms as sequencer conflicts: Evidence from artificially elicited errors. *American Journal of Psychology* 38:467–84.

Barkoczi, I., L. Sera, and A. Komlosi. 1983. Relationships between functional asymmetry of the hemispheres, subliminal perception, and some defense mechanisms in various experimental settings. *Psychologia* 26:1–20.

Begleiter, H., B. Porjesz, and R. Garozzo. 1979. Visual evoked potentials and affective ratings of semantic stimuli. In H. Begleiter, ed., *Evoked Brain Potentials and Behavior.* New York: Plenum Press.

Bevan, W. 1964. Subliminal stimulation: A pervasive problem for psychology. *Psychological Bulletin* 61:81–99.

Brandeis, D., and D. Lehmann. In press. Event-related potentials of the brain and cognitive processes: Approaches and applications. *Neuropsychologia.*

Brenner, C. 1976. *Psychoanalytic Technique and Psychic Conflict.* New York: International Universities Press.

Brown, W. S., and D. Lehmann. 1979. Linguistic meaning-related differences in ERP scalp topography. In D. Lehmann and E. Callaway, eds., *Human Evoked Potentials.* New York: Plenum Press.

Chapman, R. M. 1979. Connotative meaning and average evoked potentials. In H. Begleiter, ed., *Evoked Brain Potentials and Behavior.* New York: Plenum Press.

Chapman, R. M., H. R. Bragdon, J. A. Chapman, and J. W. McCrary. 1977. Semantic meaning of words and average evoked potentials. In J. D. Desmedt, ed., *Language and Hemispheric Specialization in Man: Cerebral Event-Related Potentials.* Basel: Karger.

———. 1978. Brain responses related to semantic meaning. *Brain and Language* 5:195–205.

Chapman, R. M., J. W. McCrary, J. A. Chapman, and J. K. Martin. 1980. Behavior and neural analysis of connotative meaning: Word classes and rating scales. *Behavior and Language* 11:319–39.

Dahl, H. 1979. *Word Frequencies of Spoken American English.* Detroit: Verbatim Books, Gate Research Company.

Dalkey, N. C. 1975. Toward a theory of group estimation. In H. A. Linstone and M. Turoff, eds., *The Delphi Method: Techniques and Applications.* Reading, Mass.: Addison Wesley.

Diaconis, P., and B. Efron. 1983. Computer intensive methods in statistics. *Scientific American* 248, no. 5:116–29.

Dixon, N. F. 1981. *Preconscious Processing.* New York: Wiley.

Erdelyi, M. H. 1974. A new look at the new look: Perceptual defense and vigilance. *Psychological Review* 81:1–24.

Erdelyi, M. H., and B. Goldberg. 1979. Let's not sweep repression under the rug: Toward a cognitive psychology of repression. In J. F. Kihlstrom and F. J. Evans, eds., *Functional Disorders of Memory.* Hillsdale, N.J.: Earlbaum.

Fisher, C. 1954. Dreams and perceptions: The role of preconscious and primary modes of perception in dream formation. *Journal of the American Psychoanalytic Association* 2, no. 3:389–445.

Fodor, J. A. 1981. *Representations: Philosophical Essays on the Foundations of Cognitive Science.* Cambridge, Mass.: MIT Press.

Frank, J. D. 1961. *Persuasion and Healing.* Baltimore: Johns Hopkins University Press.

Horowitz, M. J. 1987. *States of Mind: Analysis of Change in Psychotherapy.* 2d ed. New York: Plenum Press.

Kazdin, A. E., and L. A. Wilcoxon. 1976. Systematic desensitization and non-specific treatment effects: A methodological evaluation. *Psychological Bulletin* 83:729–58.

Kostandov, E., and Y. Arzumanov. 1977. Average cortical evoked potentials to recognized and non-recognized verbal stimuli. *Acta Neurobiologica Experimentalis* 37:311–24.

Kunst-Wilson, W. R., and R. D. Zajonc. 1980. Affective discrimination of stimuli that cannot be recognized. *Science* 7:557–58.

Kutas, M., T. E. Lindawood, and S. E. Hillyard. 1983. Word expectancy and event-related brain potentials during sentence processing. In S. Kornblum and J. Requin, eds., *Preparatory Processes*. Hillsdale, N.J.: Erlbaum.

Libet, B., W. W. Alberts, E. W. Wright, and E. Feinstein. 1967. Responses of human somato-sensory cortex to stimuli below the threshold of conscious sensation. *Science* 518:1597–1600.

Luborksy, L. 1967. Momentary forgetting during psychotherapy and psychoanalysis: A theory and research method. In R. R. Holt, ed., "Motives and Thought: Contributions to a Psychoanalytic Theory of Behavior." *Psychological Issues* 18–19:175–217.

Luborsky, L., B. Singer, and L. Luborsky. 1975. Comparative studies of psychotherapists: Is it true that everyone has won and all must have prizes? *Archives of General Psychiatry* 32:995–1008.

McGillem, C. D., and J. I. Aunon. 1977. Measurements of signal components in single visually evoked brain potentials. *IEEE Transactions on Biomedical Engineering* 24, no. 3:232–41.

McGillem, C. D., J. I. Aunon, and D. G. Childers. 1981. Signal processing in evoked potential research: Applications of filtering and pattern recognition. *CRC Critical Reviews in Bioengineering* 6:225–64.

Marcel, A. J. 1983. Conscious and unconscious perception: An approach to the relations between phenomenal experience and perceptual processes. *Cognitive Psychology* 15, no. 2:218–300.

Marks, I. M., and A. M. Matthews. 1979. Brief standard self-rating for phobic patients. *Behavior Research and Therapy* 17:263–67.

Mosteller, F., and J. W. Tukey. 1976. *Data Analysis and Regression.* Reading, Mass.: Addison-Wesley.

Motley, M. M. 1980. Verification of "Freudian slips" and semantic prearticulatory editing via laboratory-induced spoonerisms. In V. A. Fromkin, ed., *Errors in Linguistic Performance*. New York: Academic Press.

Neisser, U. 1967. *Cognitive Psychology.* New York: Appleton-Century-Crofts.

Nisbett, R. E., and D. D. Wilson. 1977. Telling more than we can know: Verbal reports on mental processes. *Psychological Review* 84:231–59.

Osgood, C. E., and W. H. May, and M. S. Miron. 1975. *Cross-Cultural Universals of Affective Meaning*. Urbana, Ill.: University of Illinois Press.

Parloff, M. B. 1980. Psychotherapy and research: An anaclitic depression. *Psychiatry* 43:279–93.

Posner, M. I. 1982. Cumulative development of attentional theory. *American Psychologist* 37:168–79.

Pribram, K. H. 1986. The cognitive revolution and mind/brain issues. *American Psychologist* 41, no. 5:507–20.

Rachman, S., and G. T. Wilson. 1980. *The Effects of Psychological Therapy*. New York: Pergamon Press.

Rao, C. R. 1952. *Advanced Statistical Methods in Biometric Research*. New York: Wiley.

Rapaport, D. 1967. The scientific methodology of psychoanalysis. In M. M. Gill, ed., *The Collected Papers of David Rapaport*. New York: Basic Books.

Reza, F. M. 1961. *An Introduction to Information Theory*. New York: McGraw Hill.

Sayre, K. M. 1986. Intentionality and information processing. An alternative model for cognitive science. *Behavioral and Brain Sciences* 9:121–66.

Scheibe, M., N. Skutsch, and J. Schafer. 1975. Experiments in Delphi methodology. In H. A. Linstone and M. Turoff, eds., *The Delphi Method: Techniques and Applications*. Reading, Mass.: Addison Wesley.

Shannon, C. E. 1948. A Mathematical Theory of Communication. *Bell System Technical Journal* 27:379–423 and 623–56.

Shevrin, H. 1973. Brain wave correlates of subliminal stimulation, unconscious attention, primary and secondary process thinking, and repressiveness. *Psychological Issues* 8, no. 2:56–87.

———. 1978. Evoked potential evidence for unconscious mental processes: A review of the literature. In A. S. Prangishvili, A. E. Sherozia, and F. V. Bassin, eds., *The Unconscious: Nature, Functions, Methods of Study*. Tbilisi: Metsnierebe 52:610–25.

———. 1984. The fate of the five metapsychological principles. *Psychoanalytic Inquiry* 4, no. 1:33–58.

———. 1986. Subliminal perception and dreaming. *Journal of Mind and Behavior* 7:379–96.

Shevrin, H., and S. Dickman. 1980. The psychological unconscious: A necessary assumption for all psychological theory? *American Psychologist* 34:421–34.

Shevrin, H., and D. Fritzler. 1968a. Visual evoked response correlates of unconscious mental processes. *Science* 161:295–98.

———. 1968b. Brain response correlates of repressiveness. *Psychological Reports* 23:887–92.

Shevrin, H., and L. Luborsky. 1958. The measurement of perception in dreams and images: An investigation of the Poetzl phenomenon. *Journal of Abnormal Psychology* 72, no. 4:362–68.

Shevrin, H., and P. Rennick. 1967. Cortical response to a tactile stimulus during attention, mental arithmetic, and free associations. *Psychophysiology* 3:381–88.

Shevrin, H., W. H. Smith, and D. Fritzler. 1969. Repressiveness as a factor in the subliminal activation of brain and verbal responses. *Journal of Nervous and Mental Disease* 149:261–69.

———. 1970. Subliminally stimulated brain and verbal responses of twins differing in repressiveness. *Journal of Abnormal Psychology* 76:39–46.

———. 1971. Average evoked response and verbal correlates of unconscious mental processes. *Psychophysiology* 8, no. 2:149–62.

Shortliffe, E. H. 1976. *Computer-Based Medical Consultations: MYCIN.* New York: Elseview.

Sneath, P. H. A. and R. R. Sokal. 1973. *Numerical Taxonomy.* San Francisco: Freeman.

Vidal, J. J. 1977. Real time detection of brain events. *Procedures of IEEE* 65, no. 5:633–41.

Westerkamp, J. J., J. I. Aunon, and C. D. McGillem. 1983. Classification of event-related brain potentials. *IEEE Frontiers of Engineering and Computing in Health Care* 209.

Williams, W. J., H. Shevrin, and R. E. Marshall. 1987. Information modeling and analysis of event related potentials. *IEEE Transactions on Biomedical Engineering.* BME-34:12, 928–37.

7   Electrophysiology and Meaning in Cognitive
         Science and Dynamic Psychology—Comments on
         "Unconscious Conflict: A Convergent
         Psychodynamic and Electrophysiological
         Approach"

Anthony J. Marcel, Ph.D.

Nonconscious and Unconscious in Cognitive
Psychology and Dynamic Psychology

This essay is a commentary upon several aspects of Shevrin's
contribution in this volume. His investigation is concerned with
the relationship between electrophysiological measures of perception and psychodynamic characterizations of the subjects. More
specifically it focuses, in psychiatric patients, on event-related
potentials (ERPs) to single-word stimuli, presented both when
the perceiver is aware and when unaware of them, where such
stimuli relate to concepts that are either consciously or unconsciously significant in terms of the patient's neurosis, as clinically
interpreted. The investigation attempts to combine dynamic psychology, electrophysiology, and the experimental psychology of
cognition into a convergent approach. An important problem for
such an enterprise is that the focuses and statuses of these three
disciplines are quite different. The general nature of these differences will be returned to later, but let us start with a specific
point.

In Shevrin's article, extensive use is made of the recent experimental literature on nonconscious perception, and most of
the techniques and inferences are based on a parallel between
what is nonconscious in perception and the systemic (psychodynamic) unconscious. This parallel needs closer examination,
since these two concepts differ not only in the aims and paradigms of the disciplines from which they arise but also in their
location in an information-processing characterization of a purely
functionalist nature. To clarify this, it is appropriate to start by
summarizing some relevant work in experimental cognitive psychology. In the study of visual perception, reading, and effects
of neurological damage, several authors (especially myself) have
been concerned with the relationship between (a) perceptual

and other processes, and (b) phenomenal experience related to such processes (Marcel and Patterson 1978; Marcel 1979; Marcel and Wilkins 1982; Marcel 1983a, 1983b). The basic point is that perceptual processes and representations are not themselves identical to phenomenal experience. This can be understood with the following example. Suppose the output of a video camera is fed to programs for image processing and scene analysis as envisaged by recent artificial intelligence (e.g., Marr 1976; Marr and Nishihara 1978). One will supposedly end up with perceptual processes functionally equivalent to human visual processes, which result in representations varying from spatial-frequency descriptions to both viewer-centered and object-centered descriptions of the scene and the objects in it. There would be little reason, however, to ascribe consciousness (phenomenal experience, sentience, subjectivity) to such programs when they run on the computer or at any other point. (Mind you, many psychologists are unwilling even to make this distinction.)

A potential human example of this distinction may turn out to be provided by certain patients with cortical blindness showing "blindsight" (Weiskrantz et al. 1974). Where there is extensive postgeniculate damage to the visual pathways projecting to the occipital cortex or to the cortex itself (usually on one side), but where visual projections to the tectum are left intact, the person is rendered phenomenally blind in one visual half-field. The exciting thing about this is that, following from Weiskrantz's work, we have shown that virtually all visual functions in the blind hemifield of two such people seem to be intact and functional (Marcel and Wilkins 1982, and Marcel in preparation). If forced to attempt to grasp an object in the blind field, the preparatory adjustments of fingers, arm, and wrist are appropriately suited to the shape, size, orientation, and 3-D location of the object. Further, we can reliably bias the interpretation of an auditorily presented polysemous word (e.g., BANK) by a preceding visual presentation to the blind field of an uppercase word related to one of its meanings (RIVER/MONEY). These findings (among others) imply that sophisticated descriptions of 3-dimensional shape and location and of the structure and order of strokes composing letters and words have been achieved. Apparently the major deficit of such people is a lack of visual phenomenal experience in that hemifield—they do not "know" that they can see! The same logical distinction is illustrated in normal people by experiments using visual masking techniques where subjects are rendered unaware of the presence of a stimulus but where both structural and semantic aspects of that stimulus reliably affect the processing of a subsequent stimulus (Marcel 1983a; Evett and Humphreys 1981). The barest account of such perceptual processes has been attempted, as has an approach to the relations between them and phenomenal experience: how a subset of the representations computed by such processes get translated into what we consciously experience (Marcel 1983b).

What is referred to as the unconscious (or the dynamic unconscious) in the present context is quite different from that of which we are not aware in perception. Especially when the term is used as a noun with the definite article, it presumably refers to the systemic unconscious. An individual's dynamic unconscious (in that sense) does not refer merely to his knowledge of the world but includes tacit beliefs, a set of interpretations of his experiences in terms of their "significance," and a set of relationships and dispositions (desires, fears, beliefs) to prototypical actors, entities, and situations that give the actors, entities, and experiences their significance. These concepts and dispositions are mentally represented in symbolic terms that underlie the language and semiology of our psychodynamic lives. Whereas the concepts and attitudes constituting the dynamic unconscious are long-standing and enduring, the representations produced in the course of nonconscious perceptual processing are momentary. Further, much of what constitutes the dynamic unconscious has presumably been originally conscious, while most if not all perceptual processes and the representations they produce have not been and will not be conscious. In my own approach, as in Polanyi's (1966), no nonconscious representation ever becomes conscious as such: it is qualitatively translated if it is to be represented consciously (see Marcel 1983b).

Recently, people concerned with the unconscious from psychoanalytic perspectives have considered relevant the current work and ideas in cognitive psychology such as that mentioned above (see Chapter 6 of this volume; Erdelyi 1985). To identify the aspects of perception or action that are not equivalent to phenomenal experience with the dynamic unconscious or even to treat them as on a par with it seems unjustified, if not an error. Thus unconscious representations and effects of stimuli (whether we are aware of the stimuli themselves or not) do not necessarily have anything to do with the domain of unconscious mentality that supposedly affects our social and emotional life and experience. The one point of contact between the cognitive non-conscious and the dynamic unconscious is that what is consciously experienced (in perception, memory and emotion) and how it is experienced is probably determined in part by the enduring attitudes and beliefs that constitute the dynamic unconscious.

What has been said above is clearly a reservation about some of the assumptions and interpretations in Shevrin's paper. In the rationale, in the methodology, and in the interpretations of his paper, it appears that nonconscious perceptual processes and effects are equated with the dynamic unconscious. This is not legitimate. In addition, it appears that the presentation of a subliminal stimulus is equated with accessing its dynamic unconscious significance. This is a logical and a semantic error. Why should giving a subliminal stimulus access the dynamic unconscious any more than giving a supraliminal stimulus? Masking a stimulus appropriately does not make it any more nonconscious than leaving it unmasked; it merely prevents a conscious percept. But of more general importance, I hope that what has been said above explains why it should not be assumed that cognitive scientists concerned with the conscious and nonconscious in perception, action, or even memory should necessarily have anything to say about the dynamic unconscious and its relation to consciousness.

Let us return, however, to the "one point of contact" mentioned above, between cognitive and psychodynamic interests in the relationship between consciousness and nonconscious processes: the nature of the process by which a conscious percept is achieved. In the vast majority of accounts of the relationship between perceptual processes and consciousness, what one is conscious of at any moment is conceived of as either identical to, or a direct reflection of, what has been computed by perceptual processes (though for most psychologists this remains a tacit assumption). The subset of computed descriptions that becomes conscious is taken to be a function of strength of activation (Dixon 1981; Shallice 1978) or attention (Treisman and Gelade 1980). The contents of consciousness and their nonconscious counterparts are taken to be identical, and accordingly the process of "becoming conscious" is seen as the opening of a door to one or more of the aspiring entrants, or something becoming activated beyond a threshold, or the shining of a beam on an otherwise unlit landscape. In my own deliberations I have felt there is good reason for a different conception. Several different types of theoretical points and empirical phenomena have impelled me to suggest (with Helmholtz) that the process of becoming conscious of percepts at each moment is conceptually mediated in several ways. The reasons for this conception are diverse: evidence suggesting that the conscious and nonconscious representations of the same aspect of perceptual input may be radically and qualitatively different; evidence that conceptual categories are necessary for and shape our phenomenal experience, in the perception of speech and visual space, and in the experience of pharmacological effects; evidence suggesting that our belief systems affect our phenomenal experience, in cultural effects on visual illusions and on pain perception. I have suggested (Marcel 1983b) that what we consciously experience and the way we experience it (systemic awareness and its phenomenology) are subject to the existence of conceptual categories and to tacit beliefs we hold about the world and about our perception, such categories and beliefs being themselves nonconscious.

This viewpoint is aggressively cognitive, in its emphasis on conceptual mediation and on the interpretive nature of phenomenal experience and in contradistinction to energy-based or information-flow-based conceptions (Shallice 1978; Allport 1977). There are several reasons for conveying this cognitive viewpoint in the present context. First, it provides a theoretical justification and vehicle for thinking about how the enduring dynamic unconscious affects and shapes our consciousness of perceptual events. It not only allows for nonconscious dispositional evaluative attitudes to determine attention and give a mechanism for "perceptual defence," it gives a role to the dynamic unconscious in determining the nature of our experience. Second, it thereby invites a most welcome incursion from the dynamic unconscious: affect. Traditional approaches in psychology have separated cognition, conation, and affect. So-called cognitive psychology mostly treats our cognition as cold or affectively neutral. Yet one thing I know about my day-to-day consciousness is that it is almost never neutral. Everything I do, think, perceive has an affective tone, positive or negative and of a particular kind; furthermore, I have an attitude to everything I do, think, and perceive. Not all of these affective colorings come from the dynamic unconscious. But in the case of conceptually based perception, the dynamic unconscious is preeminently the source of affect and attitude, which concepts bring with them when they take conscious form. Third, a conceptual and interpretive formulation of the process of becoming conscious legitimizes the symbolic transformations and defense mechanisms appealed to by psychodynamically oriented theorists. Indeed, the importance of interpretation and symbolization in a cognitive view of consciousness is something that is peculiarly absent from so-called cognitive psychology yet central to a truly cognitive psychology and to psychodynamic psychology; it is something to which we shall return below. Fourth, it is the rejection of the identity assumption (the assertion of the nonidentity of equivalent conscious and nonconscious entities) that entails conceptual mediation between nonconscious and conscious. This conflicts with Freud's account of repression and of symptoms or slips of action, where an idea or wish that is banished from or appears in consciousness retains the identical form of its prior counterpart. But this rejection and its entailment do accord with the distinction between primary and secondary process and with Rapaport's (1951) conception of drive versus conceptual organization of thought. Further, the conceptual mediation means that what is unconscious is never *directly* recoverable to consciousness. The relevance of this last point to ideas of personal significance will be indicated in the last section.

Event-Related Potentials, The Transinformation Method, and Convergent Approaches

Shevrin's paper is, in one aspect, an attempt to dispel such reservations as have been expressed above by showing that the two domains—the perceptually nonconscious and the dynamic unconscious—are indeed related. This is done by examining reactions to words related to dynamic accounts of neurotic behavior. His paper is also an attempt, by means of ERP data, to validate the psychodynamic account, which is in terms of the unconscious.

At first it appeared that Shevrin's use of the ERP was one more sophistication within a long tradition in psychology, that of the use of physiological indices of psychological states, including hand pressure, the Galvanic Skin Response, the Hoffman Reflex, heart rate, pupil dilation. The differences claimed for the ERP are that (a) it reflects cognitive processes, and (b) it reflects online the temporal microstructure of those interpretive processes and their conscious or unconscious status. However, Shevrin and Williams's use of the transinformation method potentially takes the ERP much further than it has previously been taken. In fact they appear to have made a qualitative leap. The simple ERP averages a large number of presentations of a single stimulus in order to get rid of the variations due to particular stimuli, so that its peaks and troughs will reflect what is *common* to all stimuli processed in a certain way. That is, it supposedly shows the electrophysiological manifestation of information-processing stages. By contrast, the transinformation method attempts to examine what the simple ERP throws away as "noise," in order to see just what is significant about specific events. The transinformation method takes ERPs to classes of events with different significance to the individual perceiver and compares the ERPs to such classes in order to find reliable and meaningful *differences* between different classes of signifiers. Thus it attempts to find the neurophysiological manifestation of people's particular symbolic and affective reactions. This is a large and welcome step for cognitive science, since the transinformation method focuses on content, and cognitive science has consistently tried to filter out "content" in order to be able to grasp "process" (Fodor 1980).

Does the method work? The first difficulty in answering this question is in understanding the data and procedures reported by Shevrin and Williams. The technicalities, in both the mathematics of the transinformation method and the electrophysiology of ERPs, are quite complicated for the novice. However, the data certainly seem to dispel some of the reservations expressed in the preceding section. For instance, there were differential effects in the ERPs of word–awareness/unawareness and of phobia-related versus neutral words. But, in view of discussions in the early part of Shevrin and Williams' paper, it is curious that there were no substantial differences between the effects of consciously related and unconsciously related words. On the other hand, in view of the logical points made in the section above, one would not expect such differences, since what is significant for the dynamic unconscious is not differentially tapped by the techniques used. This is further explicated below.

Both the methodology and the theoretical assumptions of the proposed approach raise several problems. Even the validity of the transinformation method has not really been shown. All the comparisons are carried out against two reference sets: Osgood's emotionally pleasant and unpleasant words ($E+$ and $E-$). The reason for using these as reference sets was to maintain the emotionality of the stimuli, since the critical stimuli themselves are emotional to the subject. However, we do not know what peculiarities these classes of words or their members have. First, the reference set ought to be a set of neutral words or even a row of asterisks. Second, the method depends *asymmetrically* on comparison with a reference set. What would happen if the procedure was reversed and, instead of comparing, for example, each of the conscious category to the E + words, we compared each of the E + words to the conscious category? The point of this question is that it asks to what extent the pattern of data is a product of the peculiarities of the method. A third and related issue is that since the E + and E − sets are used as reference sets, it is assumed that they have internal consistency. In order to establish that this is the case, an averaged transinformation curve ought to be computed, which is derived from each E + word compared with the remaining seven E + words, and the same ought to be carried out for the E − words. So long as this measure or its equivalent is not taken, the method remains prey to the fallacious assumptions of stimulus homogeneity pointed out by Clark (1973) in his seminal paper. These points suggest that the transinformation data provided in the study in order to validate the method and to map the subject's mind may be spurious. We may be dancing in the dark!

In addition to basic methodological issues, there is a most curious and needless omission in the procedure as presented. The crucial part of the procedure yielding a transinformation profile is the obtaining of differences (in time bins) between the ERPs for different stimulus-by-condition categories. The transinformation profile highlights the points at which differences exist. Yet in obtaining each profile, the sign of the difference is ignored. This seems to be throwing away valuable information. The theoretical reason for the transinformation method is the supposition that the divergences in evoked potentials to significant stimuli, from those to control stimuli, tell us about the particular significance of those stimuli for the individual. Underlying this supposition is the belief that the relative magnitude of positive potentials and of negative potentials reflects the particular affective influence of individual stimuli on information-processing components. Presumably, then, we can only examine the relative magnitudes of the effects of two different classes of events if the arithmetical sign of the difference in any time bin is preserved. Without such information, not only is our ability to interpret the effects of particular events reduced, but also our ability to assess the validity of the procedure is impaired. Suppose that in a particular time bin, compared with the ERP to control words, the individual members of another class of words produce more variance, in both directions. The obtained transinformation difference will signify nothing consistent but will be indistinguishable from cases where the direction of difference is consistent.

There are several more fundamental problems, concerning the rationale of the study. ERPs probably can and do reflect nonconscious perceptual processes and their conscious and nonconscious significance for the individual. In Shevrin's earlier review paper (1978) a range of data and a critical discussion were presented that are compelling. Yet I still have certain reservations. Although it seems plausible and probable, I am not fully convinced that ERP data are an index of the dynamic unconscious, or at least of *when* they are. This is really a reiteration of the doubts expressed at the start of this commentary about the relevance of work in cognitive psychology on nonconscious processing. One is quite unaware of the presence of visual flow fields and of their effects on one's posture. Yet no one would identify that sort of unawareness with the dynamic unconscious. Not only are such effects momentary and stimulus-dependent, they have nothing to do with symbolism or with permanent affective or evaluative predispositions. In fact Shevrin himself has acknowledged this reservation in a previous review paper (Shevrin and Dickman 1980). He concluded that the ERP research he reviewed in support of the unconscious was exclusively concerned with external stimuli, whereas clinicians are concerned with internal dispositions—wishes, needs, and symbolic structures, for example. What I would want to see as ERP evidence of the dynamic unconscious would be a direct reflection of nonconscious dispositional conceptions and representations of significant people, objects, and situations, and that is what I doubt will be obtained. Of course, it is a problem in psychology as well as in other sciences to obtain direct evidence of permanent dispositions and structures; the usual method is indeed to infer them from responses given to stimuli. There is a set of procedures taken to reflect such enduring dispositional representations. It consists of projective techniques. And the most reliable of such projective techniques, because it uses the widest sampling procedure and focuses on the most ecologically valid situations (including transference), is the lengthy process of psychoanalysis itself.

Shevrin suggests that the ERP could be very useful in the course of therapy, to see changes in the ways significant events are responded to consciously and unconsciously. This sounds very appealing. But to what extent is it possible? We would indeed be able to see if the electrophysiological manifestation of reactions to significant events, compared to neutral events, changes over therapy. But it is not the case that we would have any better grasp of how such events are responded to. First, what the therapist means by "how significant events are responded to" is how they are responded to psychologically, what they mean to the perceiver. Any difference or lack of difference between ERPs to different classes of events will still have to be interpreted psychologically or functionally. This is an obvious but important point. Second, a significant event will still remain significant, even if therapy changes its particular meaning or implication for the goal structures of the individual. Differences or the lack of them in ERPs just cannot capture this. Electrophysiological measures, however sophisticated, cannot capture the semiology of events. To clarify a little, there are two aspects to the significance of an event for an individual. First, there is what it signifies or represents in the sense of referential symbols. Thus a cat may signify the concept of mother, for reasons of both cultural symbolization and individual experience. Second, there is what the cat-mother concept signifies to the individual in terms of the goal structures of that individual. Thus, the mother, and her conceptual properties in relation to other conceptual agents, may represent a threat or a goal to be obtained or a reminder of some aspect of the individual's self-model, for example, impotence anxiety or the need for a caretaker. Suppose that either the first or the second aspect of signification, or the goal structure, or the self-model of an individual changed over therapy. Electrophysiological measures may well indicate a change but they would not indicate where that change had been and especially what its nature was.

The last of what seem to be fundamental problems is a logical problem in Shevrin's enterprise. It appears that there is at the same time (a) an attempt to validate the psychodynamic unconscious by ERP data, (b) an attempt to validate ERP data by the psychodynamic accounts, and (c) a desire to claim a convergent approach. The enterprise has a feel of circularity. Most important, the psychodynamic and electrophysiological approaches are *not* convergent. Convergent approaches require independent and independently valid measures. Neither of the approaches in question has the status of psychological evidence. The psychodynamic approach is an interpretive account of psychological data. The electrophysiological approach consists of data, but data which are not themselves psychological. The stimuli it uses are derived from and depend on the psychodynamic data and interpretation, and the obtained electrophysiological data require interpretation, that of the dynamic account. Thus neither approach stands alone. Interestingly, if one believes in the validity of the expert psychoanalytic interpreter, one may ask, why bother with the ERP? To sharpen the focus of this question, we might ask what one would infer if the ERP data submitted to the transinformation technique did not agree with the clinical account (i.e., if the clinically derived categories showed no consistent or interpretable ERP differences). If it is not considered inadmissible evidence, Shevrin has admitted that in such a case he would rely on the expert interpreter and worry about the validity of his ERP techniques. I think I would do the same.

It has just been noted that neither approach stands alone. In fact, this is only true of the psychodynamic approach insofar as one wishes it to yield objective data that is commensurate with the data in experimental psychology. As an *interpretive* paradigm, the psychodynamic approach does stand alone. This will be returned to in the next section, but the crucial point here is that when you try to use psychodynamic accounts and electrophysiological data convergently, you violently distort the theoretical and philosophical status of one or both. The very stuff of psychodynamic descriptions is meaning; it is concerned with intentionality and symbolism. The physiological domain of discourse has no intentionality, no meaning, no symbolism. The two domains are not commensurate and therefore cannot be used to converge.

Significance and Meaning in Cognitive Science and Dynamic Psychology

At one point our purpose was phrased as an attempt at a "rapprochement" between cognitive science and dynamic psychology. Often I have the feeling that such rapprochements are asymmetric: the psychoanalytic psychologists more often look to cognitive psychology (e.g., for validation of their theories or for formalisms for their concepts) than the other way round. I would like to redress this subjective imbalance by suggesting an area where it is cognitive psychology that is more lacking and that can gain from dynamic psychology.

Consider the following two extracts from Shevrin's paper:

As recent ERP research has shown, the ERP is remarkably sensitive to meaning, both denotative and connotative, and to other aspects of language, such as noun-verbal differences and antonym-homonym differences. Our work extends these findings to the realm of psychopathology and the highly idiosyncratic meanings involved in symptoms and unconscious conflict.

On the basis of the structural hypothesis, symptoms such as phobias are the outcome of complex compromises among wishes, defenses, and moral standards. Each symptom therefore has within it a disguised expression of a rejected impulse, its punishment, and some effort at adaptation. We can apply this to AM's blood phobia as follows: The presumed wish to find pleasure in harming powerful and depriving women becomes intensely active in circumstances that are likely to elicit this wish (films such as *One Flew over the Cuckoo's Nest*). However, this unacceptable wish cannot be permitted direct access to consciousness and, at the same time, its activation must be punished in some way. The patient appears to reverse the relationship between the sadist and masochist, himself becoming the victim of his phobia and thus suffering the punishment that would be predicted by the structural theory.

There is something of a disparity between these two passages. Obviously, the description of mental life implicit in the second extract is much richer than what the first extract refers to as the domain of sensitivity of ERPs. Yet the difference goes further than merely different levels or the scope of the semantics invoked. And it goes much further than merely concern with different levels of description of mental life. The point of the second extract, and indeed of psychodynamic accounts in general, is that they characterize an individual's whole social, emotional, conative, and existential life and concerns, how he or she construes them, and the significance of the actors, objects, and situations in that drama. In the papers of both Shevrin and Horowitz we are confronted by words, concepts, situations, and relationships that have personal significance for the individual concerned. Indeed, these are the starting points and the primary data for the investigations that follow.

What do we mean by significance when used in this sense? We seem to be referring to at least two things. First, we mean that what is significant symbolizes and is assimilated to something other than the literal object or situation, some construct that is more basic in the individual's construal of the world and himself (i.e., that it has a latent as well as a manifest content). Second, we mean that either the literal object or what it symbolizes has important consequences for the goals of that individual. What sort of approaches can offer us something in dealing with this? The behaviorist treatment would be in terms of classical and instrumental conditioning, but significance would emerge only in the theorist's analysis—it would not exist for the individual. A more elaborate response would be given by modern cognitive psychology, which would deal in terms of interpretation according to some "schema," "frame," or "script." However, it does not seem that these approaches offer anything that deals with either (a) symbolization and why certain things symbolize particular other things, or (b) the importance of the signifier with respect to goals. Psychodynamic accounts emphasize both of these things: (a) symbolic relationships and the constraints on them, and (b) that these symbolic relationships have motivational consequences from which emotional effects derive. By contrast, cognitive science continues to treat cognition, conation, and affect as separate. Let us explore what cognitive science *could* offer by first considering the viewpoint of structural anthropology and hermeneutics and then mentioning cybernetics.

Particular (cultural) divisions of both the natural and the social worlds yield categories most of which *in their relationships* have significance for all members of the culture (Lévi-Strauss 1962). Thus employer-employee has significance, just as father-son has significance. Almost all of these categories, which imply relationships within a system (of kinship, of work and economics), also have symbolic significance that is universal in the culture. Thus, not only do certain exchanges have particular significance (the paying of wages signifies the employer-employee relationship), but certain categories and their implied relationships have higher-order symbolic significances. For example, the father-son relationship stands for a whole set of relationships (involving, among other things, power, dependence, taboos, and duties) in different domains of discourse. That is, certain categories are paradigmatic. They are equivalent to and stand for categories in other domains: "father" is equal to and yet not equal to "teacher," "employer," and so forth. In addition to these basic senses of significance, certain categories acquire particular significance for particular individuals. But such categories could not acquire their particular significance unless they already had the signifier properties donated by their existing in the categorical system of signs implied in the culture. Thus, in the case of AM discussed by Shevrin, the terms "childbirth," "spurting," "Cat Woman," and "impale" have particular significance for the patient by virtue of his construal of the relationships between men and women, and mothers and sons; his construal of his relationship to pregnant women; and his construal of his own kinship relationships and duties, and of his moral position.

Yet the particular significances for each individual could not exist without the symbolic potential donated to the relevant categories by their being embedded in the structural system of the culture. Childbirth and cats have conceptual locations and therefore conceptual relationships, which differ between cultures. Whether or not cats can symbolize food, predators, male or female power depends on the culture (Leach 1964). Indeed, Horowitz (chapter 3 of this volume) provides an excellent exemplification of this point. Each of the affective states through which the patient passes, as listed in Table 3.4, has underlying semantics of a particular role-relationship model. The relationships of child-caretaker, assailant-critic, ingenue-mentor imply attitudes and behaviors. The various placings by the patient of herself and her father into these roles relate congruently or conflictually to received, culturally given relationships. But crucially, the meaning and significance of each of these derives from the total system of potential roles and relationships in the culture. That is, child-parent and ingenue-mentor are not only proper relational categories in the kinship and nonkinship domains but are prototypically substitutable in our culture, while neither maps onto the friend-friend relationship and both are incongruent with an assailant relationship. The meaning of each role relationship lies in the propositional syntax linking the terms (children depend on, learn from, owe respect to parents); the significance derives from other category pairs that share or are debarred from the same syntactic linkage. What Horowitz does beautifully but tacitly is to give a *structuralist* analysis. Why is this important? It is only with this type of analysis that one can begin to define the nature of the entity that is "significant" and why it is (although this is only a beginning). That is, the significant concept or situation can only be defined or characterized in terms of how it fits into a system of concepts or situations and the structural equivalences it has to concepts or situations in other domains.

This is not easily offered by current cognitive science for two related reasons. For the most part, so-called cognitive psychology and its cognate disciplines in Britain and the United States concentrate on process descriptions of mind, having left the analysis of content to anthropologists, sociologists, psychoanalysts, and structuralists in various disciplines, and, of course, literary critics and artists. This is necessarily the case since cognitive psychology has chosen the positivist, functionalist road. What behavior and experience "mean" and what is signified to an individual are almost only treatable within a framework of interpretation (hermeneutics) and a framework that can deal with the social roles of prototypical actors and objects and their relationships. Within the positivist tradition, entities and individual concepts can exist apart from other such entities and concepts. There are no constraints other than empirical and biological ones on what can be related. By contrast the structuralist approach specifies relationships and significances and constrains them by virtue of the conceptual structure of the categories within any one domain of discourse (Lévi-Strauss 1962; Leach 1964).

Cognitive science will be far richer if it takes account of how one object or situation relates to another paradigmatically, rather than only syntagmatically. Only then it will be able to deal fully with metaphor and attitude. This abstract statement can be illustratd in terms of Schank and Abelson's concept of scripts (Schank and Abelson 1977). They have proposed that we have representations of familiar, prototypical situations, representations that guide our actions and allow us to predict and infer. Yet, as far as one can see, each script is quite separate from other scripts. Thus, what happens in a restaurant and the role relationships involved are treated as unrelated to what happens in a shop, in a school, or during a family meal. These scenarios are related only hierarchically, that is, via the superordinate categories describing each script, such as "food ingestion" or "social exchange," but not analogically via the parallel structural relationships within each script (see Schank 1982). If the equivalences and differences between the scenarios were examined, we would probably begin to have an explanation not just of the skilled behavior but of the attitudes of the actors involved. When the wife of a college professor says to her husband, "Don't talk to me like that; you're not in the lecture room now!" she is not merely being figurative, she is making a statement about mental structures and how they generate behavior that is not as yet dealt with by cognitive psychology. She is implying that her husband's internal representation of his relationship to his wife, which gets translated into behavior, is assimilated to his representation of his formal (power) relationship to students in a lecture. How an internal representation generates behavior by symbolic assimilation to another representation is an important but neglected issue.

Both the disparity between the two passages quoted from Shevrin's chapter and my misgivings about the validity of seeking a convergent approach from psychodynamics and electrophysiology raise another question about the relation of psychodynamic psychology to cognitive science. To seek mutual validation from psychodynamics and electrophysiology or to appeal to support from experimental psychology for psychodynamic constructs is potentially to misunderstand or distort the nature of the differences between the enterprises. Experimental cognitive psychology and electrophysiology in their current state are firmly within the natural sciences. Indeed such adherence in cognitive psychology may be one of its shortcomings. Nevertheless, in cognitive psychology as in natural science, the concern with mental life and behavior is to explain it and predict it in terms of its causes or at a lower level of analysis, usually both. In so doing, even though professional psychologists may acknowledge some problems, most of them adhere to the principle of psychic determinism.

Even though psychoanalytic psychologists may adhere to the doctrine of psychic determinism, this is not necessarily the whole of their enterprise, nor even its main feature. Freud (who can be taken as paradigmatic for the sake of argument) never claimed to predict behavior, choices, or experience. His principal contribution was not to explain behavior, choices, or experience causally but to understand them and give them meaning. One of the great contributions of the nineteenth century was the idea that behavior and experience is meaningful, that it has coherence and significance. Although it is true that Freud wanted to attempt a materialist explanation of the mind in terms of causes and models (cf. Project for a Scientific Psychology [1895] 1966), he was principally engaged in the semantic and hermeneutic procedure of making sense of behavior. One example of this is the revelation in the case of the "Rat Man" that the patient's senseless slimming program potentially represented an attempt to get rid of a rival called Richard (the German for *fat* is *dick*). A clearer example, which antedates Freud, is to be found in Charles Dickens's novel *Great Expectations*, where we can make sense of Miss Havisham's behavior in terms of the trauma of being jilted on her wedding day. She wears a wedding dress and one white shoe "because" that is what she had been wearing when she heard of her fiancé's desertion on her wedding day. Note that the satisfactoriness of the understanding does not depend on the original clothing having a causal status, only a representational status. The premise on which this sense making is based, that the manifestations of mind are meaningful, is just not encompassed by the positivist tradition in the natural sciences and is even somewhat antithetical to it (Harré 1983). The natural science tradition explains only by reference to underlying processes or to causal mechanisms and precursors. The meaning of the content of the phenomena it deals with is of no great moment. The apparent exceptions to this rule, which are to be found in functional approaches or ethological biology (e.g., the "significance" of the red spot on a herring gull's beak), are not really exceptions since significance is dealt with only as the role something plays in a total system at a level above that of the individual. The biologist does not assume that, for the chick, the red spot on the parent gulls' beak "stands for" food, only that it causes the chick to open its mouth.

Shevrin refers early in his paper to what Rapaport (1967) has defined as a discontinuity in the patient's (and everyone's) experience and behavior, which must be solved. Shevrin focuses on a solution in terms of knowable (but inaccessible to the subject) psychological *causes*. This emphasis clearly places the enterprise in the domain of natural science. But one can equally solve the discontinuity problem by giving an account of the structure and significance of behavior and experience, much as one would do to a text (Ricoeur 1970). If one postulates what the cause of something is, then others are entitled to ask for empirical validation or an empirical test of the truth of the relationship. If one gives an account of the structure and meaning of something, it is bizarre to ask for such tests. An account of *Lord Jim*, of Sonnet 34, or of the meaning of what somebody says or does is neither true nor false in empirical terms, nor can you validate the account except in its own terms (e.g., in terms of consistency, the scope of the account, or its implications). Of course, in psychoanalysis the therapist and client have to find the appropriate interpretation or significance. But the interpretive solution to the discontinuity problem is not itself a causal account, it is one that makes sense, a hermeneutic solution.

This argument has been presented by Szasz (1962) and by Home (1966), as well as by the French school of psychoanalysts. However, it has also been rejected by many other analysts and theorists (cf. Grünbaum 1984). Nonetheless, the main point is that neither cognitive science nor empirical natural science can deal comprehensively with meaning. Insofar as they cannot, it is inappropriate at the moment for psychodynamic theorists to look in those directions for help or even for useful exchange if they want to explore the concepts necessary to their accounts when such accounts are essentially interpretive. This of course is not to deny that cognitive science can offer useful accounts of mechanisms.

As long as experimental psychology keeps itself penned into the natural science mold, it will have little or nothing to say about our actions and experiences in the real phenomenological world of our lives as lived. It is not good enough for psychology to say that the phenomenological and social world is not its concern and that its concern is only with the functional characterization of mechanisms in the head. Much of experimental psychology's primary data consists of phenomenal experience (what one perceives and remembers in experiments on such topics) and actions. And our phenomenal experience and actions are at least partly determined by how we construe the world and how we conceive of our perceptions and actions (see Marcel 1983b).

The second aspect of significance noted above is what something represents in terms of an individual's goal structures. This seems to be the crucial link between representation and behavior on the one hand, and between cognition and affect on the other. Without reference to goals, it is hard to see how any representation can lead to action, except by intention and reason. Without such reference, it is also hard to see why perception should lead to emotions and how evaluative attitudes are evoked. Some psychologists (Miller, Galanter, and Pribram 1960; Neisser 1976) have already indicated that perception should be thought of in terms of the ongoing task or the goals of the perceiver. It would be no great leap to embed this further within the longer-term or permanent goals of the individual. When you want to put a nail in a wall, your shoe can be conceived of as a hammer; if you need to avoid feelings of powerlessness, a teacher can be seen as a threat rather than a helper. In this sense, something is significant to the extent that it or what it represents either contributes to or impedes one's goals. This amounts to couching our representational theories in cybernetic terms. A current example of this is provided by Oatley and Bolton's (1985) attempt to deal with the effect of life events on depression. It should be remembered that the relevant goal structures of an individual to which we are referring, or the terms in which they are represented, may well be, and probably are, unconscious.

This section has proposed that the discontinuity problem can be solved in terms of unconscious significances rather than unconscious causes. It has also suggested that significance needs to be conceived in structuralist and cybernetic terms. It is not clear that we need a hierarchic concept of the systemic unconscious to deal with this solution to discontinuity. The hierarchic concept refers to the common view of the dynamic unconscious as a second, hidden consciousness or personality, coexisting with the one that is on view, in some sense "beneath" it. Consider the domain of everyday conversational pragmatics as seen in indirect speech acts or rhetorical devices such as irony or sarcasm. In such cases it seems quite appropriate to characterize the reference versus the sense of such utterances as their manifest versus their latent meanings. This characterization is equally appropriately applied to the surface forms versus the interpretations of literary works and jokes (see Erdelyi 1985). Yet we would not claim an unconscious in the utterance or text to be the source of such interpretations. The dispositions that underlie our pragmatic interpretations are tacit. They can be made manifest to us by perceptual restructuring, just as the phonemic structure of speech can be made manifest to the beginning reader for whom such structure has so far remained tacit, or as the medical student learns to see meaningful structures in the previously incoherent scene under a microscope. It seems plausible that the lengthy process in psychoanalysis whereby the patient is helped to become conscious of his/her own unconscious wishes, fears, attitudes, and concepts can be viewed in exactly the same way. That is, during psychoanalysis the patient gains an understanding of a hitherto-unconceived relation between expression and immanent meaning (see the discussion of Politzer's and Sartre's views in Lapointe 1971).

In discussing normal perceptual processes, it was recently proposed (Marcel 1983b) that what we are conscious of can be viewed as the result of Gestalt structuring processes. Psychoanalysis can be viewed similarly. In the case of perceptual effects and illusions, sometimes verbally conveyed information will change the percept or enable us to apprehend a hidden figure; in many cases it will not have such effects. In the case of ambiguous figures, one structure seems to be stronger than another even though the latter is represented "potentially." (Irvin Rock has recently shown that an embedded figure will prime an associate even though the former has not been consciously seen). The paper referred to above (Marcel 1983b) also provides a way of looking at Shevrin's concern, the manifestations of unconscious significance in components of the ERP, according to the present conception of latent and manifest meaning. The signified meaning of a stimulus, in terms of tacit conceptual structures, will be computed automatically, but if the perceiver does not have a conceptual structure by which that significance can be explicitly represented, it will remain nonconscious and different from the conscious percept and understanding. This seems to be an alternative model to the usual one of the dynamic unconscious. If cognitive science can make any contributions to dynamic psychology, this may be one of them.

References

Allport, D. A. 1977. On knowing the meaning of words we are unable to report: The effects of visual masking. In S. Dornie, ed., *Attention and Performance, vol. 6*. London: Academic Press.

Clark, H. H. 1973. The language-as-fixed-effect fallacy. *Journal of Verbal Learning and Verbal Behavior* 12:335–59.

Dixon, N. 1981. *Preconscious Processing*. New York: Wiley.

Erdelyi, M. H. 1985. *Psychoanalysis: Freud's Cognitive Psychology*. New York: Freeman.

Evett, L. J., and G. W. Humphreys. 1981. The use of abstract graphemic information in lexical access. *Quarterly Journal of Experimental Psychology* 33A:325–50.

Fodor, J. A. 1980. Methodological solepsism considered as a research strategy in cognitive psychology. *The Behavioral and Brain Sciences* 3:63–73.

Freud, S. [(1895)] 1966. Project for a scientific psychology. In *Standard Edition*, vol. 1. London: Hogarth Press.

Grünbaum, A. 1984. *The Foundations of Psychoanalysis: A Philosophical Critique*. Berkeley and Los Angeles: University of California Press.

Harré, R. 1983. *Personal Being*. Oxford: Blackwell.

Home, H. J. 1966. The concept of mind. *International Journal of Psycho-Analysis* 47:42–49.

Lapointe, F. H. 1971. Phenomenology, psychoanalysis, and the unconscious. *Journal of Phenomenology* 3:5–25.

Leach, E. 1964. Anthropological aspects of language: Animal categories and verbal abuse. In E. H. Lenneberg, ed., *New Directions in the Study of Language*. Cambridge, Mass.: MIT Press.

Lévi-Strauss, C. 1962. *La pensée sauvage*. Paris: Plon.

Marcel, A. J. 1979. Phonological awareness and phonological representation—investigation of a specific spelling problem. In U. Frith, ed., *Cognitive Processes in Spelling*. London: Academic Press.

———. 1983a. Conscious and unconscious perception: Experiments on visual masking and word recognition. *Cognitive Psychology* 15:197–237.

———. 1983b. Conscious and unconscious perception: An approach to the relations between phenomenal experience and perceptual processes. *Cognitive Psychology* 15:238–300.

————. In preparation. Blindsight: A Deficit of Vision or of Visual Consciousness?

Marcel, A. J., and E. K. Patterson. 1978. Word recognition and production: Reciprocity in clinical and normal studies. In J. Requin, ed., *Attention and Performance, vol. 7.* Hillsdale, N.J.: Erlbaum.

Marcel, A. J., and A. J. Wilkins. 1982. Is cortical blindness a problem of visual function or visual consciousness? Paper presented at the Fifth International Neuropsychology Society European Conference, Deauville, France, June.

Marr, D. 1976. Early processing of visual information. *Philosophical Transactions of the Royal Society B* 275:483–534.

Marr, D., and H. K. Nishihara. 1978. Representation and recognition of the spatial organisation of three-dimensional shapes. *Proceedings of the Royal Society of London B* 200:269–94.

Miller, G. A., E. Galanter, and K. H. Pribram. 1960. *Plans and the Structure of Behavior.* New York: Holt.

Neisser, U. 1976. *Cognition and Reality.* San Francisco: Freeman.

Oatley, K., and W. Bolton. 1985. A social-cognitive theory of depression in reaction to life events. *Psychological Review,* 92:372–88.

Polanyi, M. 1966. *The Tacit Dimension.* Garden City, N.Y.: Doubleday.

Rapaport, D. 1951. *Organization and Pathology of Thought.* New York: Columbia University Press.

————. 1967. The scientific methodology of psychoanalysis. In M. M. Gill, ed., *The Collected Papers of David Rapaport.* New York: Basic Books.

Ricoeur, P. 1970. *Freud and Philosophy: An Essay in Interpretation.* Trans. D. Savage. London: Yale University Press.

Schank, R. 1982. *Dynamic Memory.* Cambridge: Cambridge University Press.

Schank, R., and R. Abelson. 1977. *Scripts, Plans, Goals, and Understanding.* Hillsdale, N.J.: Erlbaum.

Shallice, T. 1978. The dominant action system: An information-processing approach to consciousness. In K. S. Pope and J. L. Singer, eds., *The Stream of Consciousness.* New York: Plenum Press.

Shevrin, H. 1978. Evoked potential evidence for unconscious mental processes: A review of the literature. In A. S. Prangishvili, A. E. Sherozia and F. V. Bassin, eds., *The Unconscious: Nature, Functions, Methods of Study.* Tbilisi: Metsniereba.

Shevrin, H., and S. Dickman. 1980. The psychological unconscious: A necessary assumption for all psychological theory? *American Psychologist* 34:421–34.

Szasz, T. S. 1962. *The Myth of Mental Illness.* London: Secker and Warburg.

Treisman, A. M., and G. Gelade. 1980. A feature-integration theory of attention. *Cognitive Psychology* 12:197–236.

Weiskrantz, L., et al. 1974. Visual capacity of the hemianoptic field following a restricted occipital ablation. *Brain* 97:709–28.

8   A Response to Marcel's Discussion

Howard Shevrin, Ph.D.

Anthony Marcel's discussion of my paper bears the marks of a painful struggle to come to terms as a cognitive psychologist not only with my methods and findings but with the fundamental problems involved in exactly how psychoanalysis and cognitive science can mutually clarify each other. His startling conclusion appears to be that cognitive science could benefit by becoming, in his judgment, more of an "interpretive" science of human significance on the model of psychoanalysis. In so concluding, he appears to deny psychoanalysis any standing as an empirical science, while believing that cognitive science could but advance by going beyond its own empirical, positivist foundations. Otherwise, he seriously doubts that any significant collaboration can exist between psychoanalysis and cognitive science. This interesting conclusion rests on the belief that the unconscious in contemporary cognitive science is a computational process, while the psychoanalytic dynamic unconscious is defined in dispositional and content terms, formed by concepts and the significance attributed to objects. Moreover, these concepts and their significance are embedded in a cultural matrix within which they assume their essential meaning. Meaning itself is given a special significance beyond that of a cause or effect in ordinary terms; it emerges as a new category requiring a different kind of science. Marcel endorses the hermeneutic critique of psychoanalysis in its attempts to be an empirical, natural science and, as already noted, he takes the critique a step further by asserting that cognitive science as well might be better served if it moved in a hermeneutic direction.

It is within this conceptual context that Marcel undertakes to evaluate my method and its findings. Mainly his reservations have to do with whether or not "ERP data are an index of the dynamic unconscious, or at least *when* they are." He would be more fully convinced if the "ERP evidence of the dynamic unconscious would be a direct reflection of nonconscious dispositional conceptions and representations of significant people, objects, and situations, and that is what I doubt will be obtained." He then suggests that methods other than laboratory investigations such as projective techniques and psychoanalysis itself may be better suited to establish these "nonconscious dispositional conceptions and representations."

First, it is worth noting that we, in fact, used projective techniques along with in-depth interviews to provide the data for our clinical inferences and word choices. Second, Dr. Marcel is not entirely clear on the category comparisons we made for the statistical analyses of the transinformation peak amplitudes: each category was compared *against every other* category (four-way analysis). Moreover, Dr. Marcel is concerned about the homogeneity of categories without a specific test to determine whether in fact categories exist. All the $E+$ and $E-$ words were drawn from the end points of the evaluative dimension validated extensively by Osgood (1975) and thus would be expected to form homogeneous categories. In addition, we dealt statistically with this problem as described in the text (see page 147), where we describe two word-shuffling procedures, one of which violates category boundaries and the other of which retains them, and then show through a Hotelling T^2 statistic that the basic structure of the transinformation profiles is retained for the second shuffle and not for the first. These shuffled data were also compared with noise-generated signals drawn from a single random source having the same variances and power spectra as the raw ERPs which were then converted into transinformation profiles. These noise-based transinformation profiles did not have the same structure as the real category transinformation profiles, thus providing support for the existence of categories. (These procedures are described in greater detail in Williams, Shevrin and Marshall [1987].)

I will not in this response take up the issue of whether or not psychoanalysis is a natural or hermeneutic science. As Marcel points out, not all psychoanalysts would agree with his characterization and, furthermore, the issue is being hotly debated in and out of the psychoanalytic literature (Eagle 1984; Edelson 1984; Grünbaum 1984; Wallerstein 1986). Rather, I will concentrate on the specific criticisms of my approach offered by Marcel. As I understood it they are the following.

1. ERPs cannot *validate* the psychoanalytic clinician's judgments because they are qualitatively different phenomena.

2. ERPs must be *interpreted* in order to become psychologically or functionally relevant; they do not provide direct access to meaning, nor do psychoanalytic accounts, which are also based not on observation but on an interpretive account of psychological data.

3. The transinformation method itself ignores a vital dimension of ERP data—the direction of differences—and thus it confounds the case in which nothing consistent is present from the case in which the direction of difference is consistent.

"ERPs cannot validate. . . ."

The claim is not made that the ERP *validates* the clinician's judgments, but that it provides a possible avenue of convergent evidence. Marcel is entirely correct when he states that were there no congruent evidence to be found in the ERPs I would still stand by the clinician's judgments, perhaps with a bit more skepticism. I say that because it seems to me that any scientific enterprise is built on the premise that the more evidence we accumulate in favor of a hypothesis, the more likely it is to be correct. If, therefore, one attempt after another were to fail, our belief in that hypothesis would be weakened; but there are very few instances in science in which *one* finding invalidates a hypothesis. That would require a rigorous theory from which one and only one inference could be drawn, in which the nonsubstantiation of that inference would call the entire theory into question or invalidate it. There may be such instances in physics (e.g., the confirmation of Einstein's prediction that light bends around heavenly bodies). Certainly, there are no such ironclad theories in psychology or psychoanalysis. It is for this reason that I use the term *convergent* in order to stress the contingent nature of the independent operations brought together in the method. But as I will discuss below, convergent and contingent do not mean circular.

"The ERPs must be interpreted. . . ."

I see this criticism as fundamental to Marcel's position, for the contrast between "interpretation" and "observation" is at the heart of his doubts about the method proposed in the paper. It would go well beyond the limits of this response to enter into a consideration of the controversy in psychoanalysis between those who advocate a hermeneutic approach and those who insist that psychoanalysis is a natural science. The reader is referred to Grünbaum's excellent discussion in response to Ricoeur, another hermeneuticist, for the present author's views on the subject (Grünbaum 1984). For present purposes I will only ask, "Do *any* facts exist *independent* of interpretation?" Is there such a clear opposition between "interpretation" and "observation"? Let me quote from a historian of physics, the paradigmatic natural science:

Theory and experiment constantly interact with, and mutually support, each other, and the question of which came first is of no relevance. It should, however, be emphasized that the synthesis cannot be described as a fusion of two "pure" components, namely of "pure facts" and "pure concepts." What actually happened in the course of the long process of merging "factual" and "conceptual" elements into a higher unity was that the former gradually came to be seen less as "pure facts," immediately dependent on sense perception, and more as "higher order facts," the understanding of which tacitly presupposed the knowledge of simpler facts as well as an increasing theoretical element. The conceptual components, on the other hand, became more and more remote from the elementary abstractions of the world of commonly accepted concepts and changed into scientific constructs which combined the results of purely theoretical considerations with a knowledge of facts of a higher order. In brief: the synthesis of the factual and conceptual components of scientific knowledge emerged as the result of a long and gradual evolution, during which each of these components itself turned out to be the product of a synthesis of factual and theoretical elements. [Sambursky, 1975]

Sambursky (1975) says that a scientific fact, an observation, is significant in a given scientific theoretical context, hence its significance is based on an "interpretation" in the light of that context. The necessity for interpretation does not change the scientific status of the phenomenon from a natural science to an interpretive, hermeneutic science. As Marcel concedes, our method yields heretofore unanticipated findings on the relationship between ERP information characteristics and clinically selected categories of words presented subliminally and supraliminally. Morever, the operations used to obtain the ERPs and the operations used to present the words subliminally and supraliminally are *independent* of the operations used to select the words. They are totally different operations. It is this reason—the independence of operations—that saves the method from circularity and supports the claim of convergence. How we interpret the independently reached findings depends on our theoretical frame of reference. Others are welcome to apply their frame of reference, which would give rise to alternate hypotheses to explain the results. If Marcel has alternate hypotheses, then we should be ready to consider them. But to dismiss the findings as circular because they are due to interpretation gravely misses the point; or to insist that ERPs are of a different order of phenomena and cannot be "interpreted" divides the subject matter of science into artificially separate domains. As Sambursky points out, scientific facts are *all* products of interpretations in all sciences from physics to psychoanalysis—what differs is the power of their methods and the reliability of their measures.

> "The transinformation method ignores a vital
> dimension. . . ."

The information-theoretic approach applied to our data is not easy to grasp because it runs counter to our customary approach to data. We desire mainly to identify variables measurable in dimensional terms that are intrinsic to the phenomena—thus, in the case of ERPs we desire to measure voltage fluctuations, latency bands, frequency distributions, and so forth, and then to apply the model of mean differences to these scores. The information-theoretic approach is not limited to any one ERP parameter or method of measuring it. Whatever characteristic—known or unknown—that is conveying the information will be reflected in the transinformation profiles. If there are mean voltage differences at certain latencies, or bidirectional patterns of such voltages resulting in variance differences, or particular frequency patterns, the TI profile will reflect these patterns. In fact, we have been able to demonstrate with noise-generated, dummy ERPs divided into four categories, into which known directional and bidirectional voltages have been introduced at a fixed latency, that the transinformation method can map these variables. In Figure 8.1 a three-dimensional representation of transinformation (z axis), time (x axis) and "word" presentation by category (y axis) is depicted. In dummy category 4 a unidirectional pulse has been introduced at an early latency, and a bidirectional pulse has been introduced into dummy category 3 at a later latency. These three-dimensional dummy TI profiles reveal a great deal of information at these particular latencies for categories 4 and 3. But Marcel is correct in noting that the transinformation profile itself does not tell us whether the differences are unidirectional or bidirectional. For this we would need to take the next step of

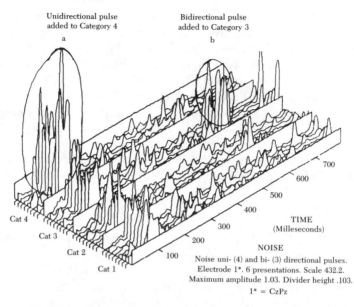

Unidirectional pulse
added to Category 4

a

Bidirectional pulse
added to Category 3

b

700

600

500

400

Cat 4

300

TIME
(Milleseconds)

Cat 3

200

Cat 2

100

NOISE

Cat 1

Noise uni- (4) and bi- (3) directional pulses.
Electrode 1*. 6 presentations. Scale 432.2.
Maximum amplitude 1.03. Divider height .103.
1* = CzPz

FIGURE 8.1 Uni- and Bidirectional Electrical Pulses Added to Noise ERPS.

examining the ERPs directly at the key latencies. However, the initial transinformation analysis not only helps us to know where to look but establishes a finding in its own right—that information, in whatever ERP form, is being conveyed that bears on category membership, which is what we set out to find. It need not have worked out; there was nothing in our method that biased the outcome in our favor.

Marcel quite correctly appreciates the goal of our method: "The transinformation method takes ERPs to classes of events with different significance to the individual perceiver and compares the ERPs to such classes in order to find reliable and meaningful *differences* between different classes of signifiers. Thus it attempts to find a neurophysiological manifestation of people's particular symbolic and affective reactions. This is a large and welcome step for cognitive science, since the transinformation method focuses on content, and cognitive science has consistently tried to filter out 'content' in order to be able to grasp 'process.' " He has a number of reservations about whether the method achieves this goal, which I have attempted to answer in this response. Clearly the dialogue must go on.

Appendix 8.A: Comments on
Dr. Shevrin's Response

Anthony Marcel

While it is unusual for a discussant to reply to an author's response, it appears that a lack of clarity in my discussion of Howard Shevrin's paper has led to some misunderstandings. But, as in conversations, misunderstandings often help to sharpen both ideas and their expression.

First, I did not intend to deny psychoanalysis *any* empirical standing; I was merely pointing out that it could deal with much broader aspects of meaning and significance in its hermeneutic aspects than current cognitive science. Second, I did not mean to suggest that a collaboration between psychoanalysis and cognitive science could be achieved *only* if cognitive science goes beyond its empirical positivist foundations. I was merely suggesting that there are other collaborations, from which cognitive science would benefit. After all, Artificial Intelligence is not strictly empirical in its criteria; and Winograd and Flores (1986) have provided a perfectly respectable precedent for urging a broader approach on cognitive science.

However, the main misunderstanding seems to be that I was criticizing Dr. Shevrin's enterprise in general and that the criticism was based on subsuming natural science to hermeneutic science. First it should be clear that I was not denigrating the enterprise, though I did see my job as discussant as one of indicating areas of theoretical and methodological doubt as well as affirmation. Second, the main critical comments on Dr. Shevrin's paper are contained in the first two sections of my discussion and are made quite outside the context of my speculations about hermeneutics and structuralism in the third section, which had little direct bearing on Dr. Shevrin's paper.

Dr. Shevrin's response makes it clear where the misunderstanding arose. He states that he sees the criticism that "the ERPs must be interpreted . . ." as fundamental to my position, and he sees this as stemming from my later discussion of the hermeneutic approach. Perhaps this confusion arises from my use of the term "interpretation" in two distinct senses. In one case I was saying that for psychological purposes physiological measures need interpretation in terms of psychological variables that they are presumed to reflect. Here Dr. Shevrin is quite correct to say that all scientific facts exist only as interpretations. In the other case I was discussing the meaning of texts, how symbols have signification, and the exercise of ascribing such meanings. Dr. Shevrin says of scientific facts that "the necessity for interpretation does not change the scientific status of the phenomenon from a natural science to an interpretive, hermeneutic science." I agree with that. Indeed my questioning of the convergent approach was partly that while interpretation of physiological data *is* natural science, psychoanalytic interpretation may not be entirely so.

The main thrust of Dr. Shevrin's response seems to be that since all science is a matter of interpretation, there is therefore no difference in kind between the supposed hermeneutic aspect of psychoanalysis and its natural science aspect: accounts in terms of meaning and in terms of causes are the same enterprise, since meanings are instantiated as material structures. To show how I both agree and disagree, it is necessary to consider the two senses of interpretation. The meaning of a text is quite separate from what the text or its meaning reflects about the mind of its author (which can be said to have produced the text). Claims about the former need not be empirical; claims about the latter are. Claims about the former are not causal; claims about the latter are. A text, an utterance, or a piece of behavior may have multiple meanings, such meanings may change with cultural context, and further, they may have entailments which were not in the mind of the author. I can come to know about aspects of my behavior which have nothing to do with what produced that behavior, consciously or unconsciously.

From the foregoing, it would seem reasonable to suggest that psychoanalytic interpretations of behavior and psychological accounts of physiological data may both be perfectly valid, while the two may be quite different in kind and may not converge for that reason. Psychoanalytic interpretations of behavior or experience view their objects as semantically symbolic representations of underlying beliefs and desires. Interpretations of physiological data however, are not usually taken as representations of such intensional states. Except for conversion hysteria, psychological accounts of physiological data are claims about equivalence at another level or about causality, where symbolism is not involved; that is, they view the interpreted relationship as one of symptomatic manifestation, rather like medical diagnosis.

Of course, hermeneutic claims *can* sometimes be converted into empirical claims. For example, if I confront the author of a behavior with a series of its possible meanings and s/he reacts differently to one of them (e.g., physiologically), then I have circumstantial evidence that that meaning has differential status (e.g., it was "behind" the behavior). This is the sense in which I agree with Dr. Shevrin and endorse his enterprise.

Curiously, the sense in which I disagree with him is also an endorsement. One of the points I was trying to make in my discussion of hermeneutics and structuralism was that one can only arrive at what Dr. Shevrin is doing if one engages in the exercise of asking what a person's behavior and experience means. This is not normal practice in cognitive science. The concepts which are critical for Shevrin's patient *stand for* other concepts (e.g., Cat Woman stands for Mother). When one thing symbolically stands for something else, there is not usually a causal relationship. While I see this as an endorsement of his enterprise, from which cognitive science can learn, Dr. Shevrin may not. He may feel that *Geisteswissenschaft* and *Naturwissenschaft* can be assimilated; I cannot see how that is possible. Symbolic relationships are in the mental domain. While some aspects of them are clearly instantiated in the nervous system, they are not reducible to statements about the nervous system, since such discourse does not deal with symbolism and I am not aware of any successful attempts as yet to show how nervous systems can represent or have intensional states. This is what sets limits on inferences from physiological data. So, yes, both physiological and psychoanalytic evidence alike require interpretation; but, no, the nature of the interpretive activity in the two cases is not usually the same.

Appendix 8.B: A Final Word?

Howard Shevrin

The question mark after the title is meant to suggest that there can be no final word on the issues Dr. Marcel has raised about my research, but only a continuing quest and fruitful dialogue as reflected in this exchange of views. I am gratified by Dr. Marcel's clarification in his response, in which he clearly endorses our research method, while attempting to qualify and make more specific the limits of its applicability. In this further clarification he distinguishes two different uses of meaning, (*a*) meaning in the sense of something 'standing for' something else (e.g., Cat Woman "standing for" Mother), (*b*) meaning as the *intent* of the author of a text. According to Dr. Marcel, the latter is subject to empirical investigation, the former is not; the latter is a matter of cause and effect, the former is not.

Let me briefly take up each of these meanings. If for author of a text we substitute *patient*, it is not hard to see that the psychoanalyst's task is in fact to infer the patient's intentions (conscious and unconscious) from his "text" (e.g., free associations, dream reports, symptoms, behavior, etc.). Our clinical team concluded that Cat Woman "stood for" Mother by inferring from the patient's "text" (interviews and test responses) that Cat Woman was a substitute for Mother and that it was more acceptable and less threatening for the patient to ascribe to Cat Woman attributes he would shrink from consciously attributing to his mother. Thus, the "beliefs and attitudes" associated with mother are *displaced* onto Cat Woman; in this sense the beliefs and attitudes serve as intentions expressed and in part gratified through the conscious fantasy about Cat Woman. Dr. Marcel agrees that as a result of this "meaning," the presentation of Cat Woman might elicit a differential electrophysiological response, which in fact we found to be the case. But he would deny that the electrophysiological response was elicited by the *signification* of the word Cat Woman. Rather, the electrophysiological response is akin to an emotional reaction which a particular meaning might arouse and would thus be subsequent to the meaning.

I would also like to argue against this conception of meaning as independent of any physiological response and as existing on a different, hermeneutic plane. It is, I would submit, the meaning *as signification* that is instantiated in the electrophysiological response. What is the evidence for this? First, as cited in my chapter, there is much ERP research to show that significations have ERP correlates. I refer to the work of Brown and Lehmann (1979) who show that verbs and nouns, which are different classes of signifiers—a noun standing for an object, a verb for an action—have different ERP patterns which cut across language groups. Further, Chapman and his colleagues (1977, '78, '79, '80) have found that clusters of words differing in connotative meaning (unpleasant versus pleasant) have different ERPs. And in our own work, the transinformation method permits us to index electrophysiological properties of *categories of meaning* related to the conscious significance of a symptom and its unconscious conflictual significance. Moreover, these brain responses occur within 250 msec., well before any affective response, and there is much evidence to suggest that the processing that goes on during that time has to do with meanings in both of Marcel's senses.

References

Brown, W. S. and Lehman, D. 1979. Linguistic meaning-related differences in ERP scalp topography. In D. Lehmann, and E. Callaway, eds., *Human Evoked Potentials*. New York: Plenum Press, 31–42.

Chapman, R. M. 1978. Brain responses related to semantic meaning. *Brain and Language*, 5:195–205.

———. 1979. Connotative meaning and average evoked potentials. In H. Begleiter, ed., *Evoked Brain Potentials and Behavior*. New York: Plenum Press.

———. 1980. Behavior and neural analysis of connotative meaning: Word classes and rating scales. *Behavior and Language*, 11:319–39.

Chapman, R. M., et al. 1977. Semantic meaning of words and average evoked potentials. In *Language and Hemispheric Specialization in Man: Cerebral Event-Related Potentials*.

Eagle, M. 1984. *Recent Developments in Psychoanalysis: A Continued Evaluation*. New York: McGraw-Hill.

Edelson, M. 1984. *Hypothesis and Evidence in Psychoanalysis*. Chicago: University of Chicago Press.

Grünbaum, A. 1984. *The Foundations of Psychoanalysis: A Philosophical Critique*. Berkeley and Los Angeles: University of California Press.

Osgood, C. E., W. H. May, and M. S. Miron. 1975. *Cross-Cultural Universals of Affective Meaning*. Urbana, Ill.: University of Illinois Press.

Sambursky, S. 1975. *Physical Thought: From the Presocratics to the Quantum Physicists*. New York: Rice Press.

Wallerstein, R. 1986. *Forty-two Lives in Therapy*. New York: Guilford.

Williams, W. J., H. Shevrin, and R. E. Marshall. 1987. Information modeling and analysis of event related potentials. *IEEE Transactions on Biomedical Engineering*. BME-34:12, 928–37.

Winograd, T., and Flores, F. 1986. *Understanding Computers and Cognition*. Norwood, N.J.: Ablex Publishing Corporation.

9   Exploring the Form of Information in the Dynamic Unconscious

Ray Jackendoff, Ph.D.

This chapter will necessarily be somewhat roundabout, in that I must begin by briefly describing my theoretical biases and the view of the unconscious that they imply. I will then relate this view to Shevrin's seven pairs of terms defining different conceptions of unconscious processes, showing how my approach compares with his. Finally, I will suggest an approach to studying phenomena in the dynamic unconscious that grows out of my general methodology.

I

As a theoretical linguist, I am primarily concerned with the form of linguistic information as it occurs in the natural languages of the world. My particular interest is in the form of semantic information—the meanings of words and sentences, how meaning is related to overt grammatical form, and how meaning reveals the organization of thought (Jackendoff 1978, 1983, 1987).

One of the most important lessons to emerge from the last three decades of work in generative grammar, stemming from the work of such linguists as Noam Chomsky, Roman Jakobson, and Morris Halle, is that language does not wear its organization on its sleeve. Rather, knowledge of one's native language—the ability to undersand and utter an indefinite number of sentences that one has never heard before—is governed by complex principles of which one is not and cannot be consciously aware. Moreover, since adults are not consciously aware of these principles, they cannot pass them down to the next generation of speakers by explicit instruction. Thus language learning—the acquisition of the principles of one's native language—is itself a process of great complexity and subtlety (see Chomsky [1965, 1972, 1975] and Lightfoot [1982] for discussion).

Let me give three examples of the sorts of complexities found in English, one each from phonology (the sound system), syntax (the structure of phrases), and semantics (meaning). First, consider the following ten words chosen from different languages, including English.

(1)   ptak thole hlad plast sram mgla vlas flitch dnom rtut

I quote Halle (1978), from which these examples are drawn:

If one were to ask which of the ten words in this list are to be found in the unabridged Webster's, it is likely that readers of these lines would guess that *thole, plast,* and *flitch* are English words, whereas the rest are not English. This evidently gives rise to the question: How does a reader who has never seen any of the words on the list know that some are English and others are not? The answer is that the words judged not English have letter sequences not found in English. This implies that in learning the words of English the normal speaker acquires knowledge about the structure of the words. The curious thing about this knowledge is that it is acquired although it is never taught, for English-speaking parents do not normally draw their children's attention to the fact that consonant sequences that begin English words are subject to certain restrictions that exclude such words such as *ptak, sram,* and *rtut,* but allow *thole, flitch,* and *plast.* Nonetheless, in the absence of any overt teaching, speakers somehow acquire this knowledge. (1978, 294)

A second example comes from Chomsky (1972). Sentences (2a) and (2b) differ only in the main verb. Yet the difference in sense is striking: in (2a), the boys are to like one another, while in (2b), John seems to like the boys.

(2)   a. John appealed to each of the boys to like the others.
      b. John appeared to each of the boys to like the others.

Now, consider the sentences in (3):

(3)   a. John appealed to the boys to like each other.
      b. John appeared to the boys to like each other.

Notice that (3a) is synonymous with (2a). By analogy, we would expect (3b) to be synonymous with (2b). In fact, however, it is ungrammatical; in some curious way, it is sensed by speakers not to be a sentence of English at all.

Thus the same question arises as with (1): on what grounds do speakers of English judge that (3b) is ungrammatical? It is not its *meaning* that is at fault. It *should* mean the same as (2b). Evidently something is amiss in the use of the reciprocal expression *each other* in this context—something that none of us ever was taught.

The third example comes from Jackendoff (1972). Sentences (4a) and (4b) contain exactly the same words and the same intonation pattern, with one exception: the pitch rises slightly at the end of (4a) and falls slightly at the end of (4b). (Capitals indicate stress; the intonation is indicated by the curved line below the sentence.)

(4) a. Both John $\underset{\smile}{\text{AND}}$ Bill didn't go.

  b. Both John $\underset{\smile}{\text{AND}}$ Bill didn't go.

The meanings are quite different, though. Sentence (4a) means that either John or Bill went; (4b) means that neither went. How does the slight change in intonation at the end of the sentence communicate this difference? Again, this is a fact about English that native speakers will intuitively recognize if it is pointed out to them, but it is clear that it was never taught to us. Like the observations above, it was not even *noticed* until less than twenty years ago. Nevertheless, by virtue of having acquired English by whatever means we did, we have unwittingly acquired the ability to make these judgments.

What we have not acquired, however, is a conscious ability to explain the reasons for these judgments. Instead, we must resort to empirical methods of research to discover the principles behind them. Each of the observations above has played a role in extensive discussion in the literature, involving dozens of other phenomena, in some cases in many languages. Whatever the explanation (or whatever putative explanation the reader may come up with on his or her own), the point is that it is after the fact—it does not play a role in making one's judgments about (1)–(4), which, from a conscious point of view, are quite direct and immediate.

There is no space here to even begin an analysis of these phenomena, but the overall form of the analysis is a theme song of contemporary linguistics. These particular words and sentences are themselves not part of one's knowledge of language. Rather, one's knowledge of language is internalized as a *rule system* or *grammar*, of which any particular word or sentence is a special case. These rule systems can be applied creatively in understanding and uttering sentences one has never heard before. The content of the rules and the way they apply—and in fact their very existence—are almost entirely hidden to intro-spection. Only the *results* of their application appear in aware-ness, as conscious judgments of grammaticality, comprehensi-bility, similarity or difference of meaning, appropriateness to the situation, and so forth.

Research in linguistics thus seeks to discover the rule systems that make up knowledge of a language. The linguist's exploration is guided not by direct introspection of the rule systems them-selves—which is in principle impossible—but by examination of the conscious by-products of the rule systems, in particular the patterns of grammatical judgments arrived at by speakers of the language. Further evidence often arises from other languages, which insofar as possible we would like to describe by means of rule systems of a similar character, from the history of languages, from children's acquisition of language, from experiments on language processing, and from language deficits due to brain damage.

This mode of linguistic explanation displays an interesting parallel to the model of psychoanalytic explanation to which Shevrin aspires in his paper. To paraphrase him, there is an "ap-parent discontinuity in experience" in the fact that speakers make secure and consistent judgments about examples like (1)–(4) without having any conscious basis for making such judgments, and even though in some cases (such as the disanalogy between (2) and (3)) the judgments seem bizarre from a rational point of view. The linguist, however, assumes that there are *knowable psychological causes* for these judgments, namely the rule sys-tems underlying the organization of language—but that these causes are *inaccessible* to the language user.

This approach is subject to the very limitation that Shevrin envisages, a "knack for eliciting an embarrassment of riches," and one of the principal concerns of linguistic theory is how to appropriately constrain the rule system so as to explain why the observable phenomena come out the way they do and not some other conceivable way. In order to develop appropriate con-straints, the linguist often draws on the full arsenal of evidence from other languages, history, acquisition, psycholinguistic ex-periments, and brain damage, in an effort to triangulate on a maximally precise and general hypothesis. Although we can hardly claim full success as yet, I have the sense that considerable prog-ress has been made in understanding the principles underlying language in the past twenty years. In particular, whatever arguments still rage, there has come to be substantial agreement about the way numerous well-studied phenomena must be integrated into the system as a whole.

II

Let us take a more detailed look at the implications of this approach to language for the general problem of conscious and unconscious processes. It is significant that a theory of the sort that linguists seek to develop—a description of the rule systems governing linguistic behavior—does not fit comfortably into either of the traditional categories for explaining the mind. On the one hand, the form of linguistic information and the rules that govern it are not conscious phenomena; on the other hand, they are not assumed to be in any especially close relationship to what is known about neurophysiology, either. We haven't the slightest idea, for instance, of how something as simple as the speech sound p is encoded in the neurons, not to mention the organization of more complex linguistic entities such as this sentence.

So what is the psychological status of the rules of language, if they are neither conscious nor physiological? The metatheory assumed by linguists is that they play a role in the *organization of information* in the brain. Just as one can speak of the organization of information in a computer—its programs and database structures—without knowing much at all about the physical and electrical structure in which this information is realized, the assumption is that one can describe the principles governing the structure and processing of mental information, independently of their neurological instantiation. This view of mental information in the "computational mind" is fairly standard in modern-day cognitive science, although there are major ideological splits on how literally to take the computer analogy. (Dennett [1978], Fodor [1975], and Pylyshyn [1984] are among the more important contributions to the foundations of the computational theory of mind.)

While the relationship of the computational mind to the neurophysiology finds a strong analogy in the relation of programs and data structures to computer hardware, the relationship of the computational mind to consciousness is far less well understood. In fact, cognitive science has more or less appropriated the term "mind" for "computational mind," leaving no term available for the more traditional phenomenological sense. A reasonable first assumption, however, seems to be the following condition (which I treat in more detail in Jackendoff 1987):

Correspondence Condition
Every distinction present in consciousness is supported by a corresponding computational distinction.

This condition essentially says that consciousness is not magic—that its content proceeds in a principled way from underlying information structures and the processes that operate on them. Note however that the implication is one-way only, in that there must be computational distinctions that do not appear directly in consciousness, for example the rules of language.

In thinking of the brain as an information-processing device, it is useful to distinguish between the *structure* or *form* of the information and the *processes* that give rise to mental information. A great deal of contemporary cognitive psychology has focused on information flow through different kinds of memory and different kinds of processors, on the role of attention in processing information, on constraints on retrieval from memory, and so forth—all considerations of processing. By contrast, there has been relatively little discussion by psychologists of the precise *form* of the information being processed—what the basic elements of mental information are and how they are built up into complex cognitive constructs. However, this seems precisely the right way to construe the principles of linguistic theory: the rule systems underlying language govern the possible forms of linguistic information, without necessarily addressing the processes in time by which these forms are developed and used in communication. In the computer analogy, they are descriptions of the data structures on which programs operate.

Other areas of psychology have begun to display a more explicit interest in form. In particular, the theory of vision has taken on new dimensions through research on visual information structure by such people as Marr (1982), Shepard and Cooper (1983), and Kosslyn (1980). In the psychology of music, my work with Fred Lerdahl on the forms of information underlying musical cognition (Lerdahl and Jackendoff 1983) seems to clarify the relationship between issues of traditional music theory and those of experimental work on music perception.

I stress the distinction between form and process because it is crucial to the issue of consciousness. In a widely quoted passage, Lashley (1956) points out that information *processing* per se is always unconscious. For example, one's visual awareness consists of the arrangement of elements in a scene, not of the internal mental processes that give rise to this perceived arrangement. In other words, the most direct support for conscious awareness comes from the information *structures* or *forms* in the computational mind, not from the processes. (Note that one may have dynamic mental representations of external processes, say of an object in motion, but one still has no conscious access to the *mental* process by which one constructs such representations.) Thus the correspondence condition can be refined as follows:

Correspondence Condition (revised)
Every distinction present in consciousness is supported by a corresponding distinction in the information structures present in the computational mind.

If I wished to be iconoclastic, I might point out that Lashley's observation undercuts the commonly assumed distinction between "conscious processes" and "unconscious processes": if Lashley is right, there *are* no conscious processes. Rather, strictly speaking, one should be asking questions about conscious and unconscious *information structures*. The term "conscious process" might serve, however, as a useful shorthand for "unconscious process that applies to conscious information structure," and when I use it here, I will always mean it in that sense.

Even the term "conscious information structure" is somewhat suspect, in that one is not conscious of the structure but rather of the aspect of the world that the structure represents. So I will use the term here as shorthand for "information structure that directly supports the form of awareness." In other words, the view is that the computational mind is all unconscious (and may be all there is to the unconscious) but that a certain selected set of the information structures in the computational mind are most directly responsible for the form of our conscious experience. The question I deliberately leave open is *how* these selected structures support awareness. Within my approach, this issue is the locus where the venerable mysteries of the mind-body problem come into play (see Jackendoff [1987] for discussion).

III

Let us now see how the notion of the computational mind, as elucidated by our few brief examples of linguistic phenomena, bear on Shevrin's list of possible conceptions of the conscious/unconscious distinction.

Psychological/neurophysiological. The terms appropriate for conscious events, such as thought, affect, and judgment, have computational counterparts, which also apply to information structures that do not appear in consciousness. That is, it is appropriate to speak of unconscious assumptions, goals, and so forth. On the other hand, there may be computational terms that have no conscious counterpart, for example many of the notions appropriate for grammatical description.

Neurophysiological description is, of course, not ruled out. Neurophysiological events underlie all conscious and unconscious processing, and the relation of these events to psychological events must be worked out. This is crucial, for instance, in order to describe the effect of chemical changes due to drugs or hormone imbalances on the operation of the computational mind, and thereby on awareness.

Spontaneous/automatic. Unconscious processes must participate in complex, variable adaptive behavior such as everyday language use. On the other hand, they are organized by tightly knit structures that proceed automatically unless overridden by conscious considerations: one automatically speaks in sentences that conform to the dictates of English unless one is in some pathological state or deliberately playing with the language. Speaking is by all means automatized—one does not consciously consider every grammatical and phonological detail unless writing poetry or pursuing linguistic research. (Incidentally, the common notion that driving a car is rigidly automatized bears rethinking, in that driving requires a constantly creative reaction to traffic and road conditions. One does not memorize a set of motor responses and repeat them every time one drives the same road.) The conclusion is that spontaneity and automaticity are not mutually exclusive.

Active/latent. Computational processes are active during conscious awareness, supporting the form and individuation of entities in awareness by means of correspondingly differentiated information structures. However, many aspects of these information structures and of the processes that maintain them are not present to awareness. Hence unconscious structures and processes are active in influencing consciousness and behavior. At the same time, many unconscious information structures (e.g., any sort of long-term memories) may be thought of as latent.

Cognitive/dynamic. Language use as such has no bearing on the question of whether sexual and aggressive drive structures are present in unconscious processes. However, let us consider the question in the broader context of the computational theory of mind. Insofar as these drive structures are directed toward some person or object, this implies an internal mental representation of the person or object. In turn this requires the participation of the computational mind in the realization of these drives as behavior or imagery.

Turning to the cognitive side of the dichotomy, Shevrin repeats a common assumption that unconscious process are *"early"* aspects of information processing operating prior to consciousness itself. Again looking at language, since we find that unconscious processes are involved continually in language use, both prior to and during conscious phases, "early" is inaccurate for this case.

Attitudinal/ad hoc motivational. The conclusions above suggest that unconscious processes deal with both enduring attitudes and their application in dynamic situations, as well as with the development of new attitudes and motivations in response to novel encounters.

Content/process. This is an important distinction, and I find it necessary to do a pedantic exegesis of Shevrin's text:

1. "Consciousness is defined as the awareness of contents or representations." "Defined as" is strained here; I would be happier with "involves," because I don't know how to *define* consciousness.

2. "No contents or representations exist unconsciously." This is false in the case of language, in that there is a great deal of organized content that surfaces only symptomatically by virtue of generalizations over conscious judgments.

3. "The unconscious is defined as all those processes going on prior to the conscious experience of a representation or content." I would prefer: "The unconscious *consists of* all those processes *and representations* existing prior to *and during* the conscious experience of a representation or content," for reasons that should be clear from the previous section.

4. "Unconscious processes cannot be accessible to consciousness directly." Lashley's observation supports this assertion as it stands. However, Shevrin does not distinguish information structures from information processes as strictly as I have here, so it is worth adding that many unconscious *structures* cannot be accessible to consciousness directly either.

5. "Usually those who maintain this view also assume that these processes are neurophysiological in nature." Again, one ultimately *has* to assume this unless the mind works by magic.

However, the computational description is for many psychological purposes more perspicuous than a neurophysiological description.

6. "Or, by analogy with the computer, that the unconscious refers to all the computational procedures and consciousness to the readout." Following what was said in the previous section, the computer analogy to the unconscious would include the programs, the organization of the data base, the input information in hearing speech (one is not aware of the form of the acoustic signal), the course of computation, and most of the results of the computation. The closest computer analogy to consciousness would be some small selected portion of the output of computation. However, Shevrin's term "the readout" suggests that there is a "mind's eye" reading the results, and this is patently impossible as an account of consciousness. Coming up with an alternative, however, is not so easy.

Different from/similar to consciousness. If anything, unconscious representations must be more highly articulated than those that appear in consciousness, not more "primitive." They cannot be less highly articulated because of the Correspondence Condition. (This is a major point of disagreement with Marcel [1983].) In addition, as many have observed, it is likely that unconscious processes involve some degree of parallel computation of multiple representations, only one of which (per modality) appears in consciousness under usual circumstances.

To sum up, the conception of the unconscious as a computational system that supports the form of awareness and behavior leads to a quite precise position on the issues raised by Shevrin, one that is moreover essentially in tune with the psychoanalytic position. In turn, this conception is supported by empirical study of hundreds of linguistic phenomena like those illustrated in the previous section.

But why should one's position on the unconscious processes and representations involved in language be germane to psychodynamic issues? The reason, I think, is that language gives one a secure sense both of the rich structure possible in the unconscious and of the precision with which one can study it. It therefore might encourage one to consider psychodynamic theories of comparable abstractness and depth—one is less daunted by complexity known to exist elsewhere—and at the same time to aspire to the higher standards of explanation that can be achieved in a formalized theory.

IV

Let me give a rough idea of what I have in mind. From my acquaintance with the psychodynamic literature, it appears to me that a wide range of symptoms can be described as underlying conceptual organizations that are the product of *erroneous displacement* followed by *regularization*.

To explicate these terms, let me start with a phonological analogy: the production of speech errors, or "slips of the tongue." In studying speech errors, linguists have concentrated on what they reveal about linguistic structure, not on what unconscious motivations may have led to their production, and that is what I am going to examine here, very briefly.

Consider the class of speech errors in which a speaker misplaces or exchanges consonants. It has been observed by Fromkin (1971) that the possible positions to which a consonant can be erroneously moved are highly restricted. For example, one might say "tips of the slung" for "slips of the tongue," exchanging the *sl* and *t* at the beginnings of their respective words. But speakers never say something like "slits of the pung," exchanging the initial *t* of "tongue" and penultimate *p* of "slips." That is, sound exchanges invariably involve parallel positions in different words.

Furthermore, when a sound is moved to an incorrect position, it never creates a consonant cluster that violates constraints on possible sound combinations for the language in question. For instance, "slips of the tongue" might be erroneously spoken as "lips of the stung," by movement of the *s*; but it would never become "sips of the tlung," by movement of the *l*, because *tl* combinations are prohibited word-initially in English. (Notice that *tl* is not unpronounceable; it is for instance a permissible combination in the language Tlingit.) In other words, speech errors confirm the existence of those unconscious and untaught principles of English sound structure that we were led to posit in order to account for one's judgments about the putative words in the beginning section of this chapter.

Thus speech errors are not completely wild phonologically; there are strong constraints on possible displacements, describable in terms of the phonological structure of words. Such evidence of what occurs and what *never* occurs, drawn from corpora of several thousand speech errors recorded in ordinary conversation, is of great importance in developing theories of speech production (e.g., Garrett 1975).

A second, altogether predictable effect in speech errors, noted by Fromkin (1971), is that such a displacement is invariably compensated by a regularization if necessary. For example, suppose that the *m* in "a monkey's uncle" is erroneously transposed to the second word. The result is always "an unkey's muncle," not "a unkey's muncle." That is, the alteration of *a* and *an,* which depends on whether the following word begins with a consonant or vowel, is sensitive to the removal of the *m;* the article takes the form that is phonologically appropriate for the following non-word "unkey." The upshot of these constraints and regularizations is that an utterance containing a speech error, even if meaningless, is phonologically perfect English.

The principles governing psychodynamic displacement, of course, do not involve phonological structure. Rather, the appropriate form of mental information appears to be conceptual structure, which encodes one's understanding of entities in the world, the categories into which they fall, and the relationships among them. Well-known approaches to conceptual structure include the production systems of Anderson (1983), the "scripts" of Schank and Abelson (1975), and the prototypes of Rosch (1977). Conceptual Semantics, the approach I develop in Jackendoff (1983, 1987), is, I believe, more attentive than others to the microproblems of finding primitive elements and combinatorial principles and to the necessity of mapping perspicuously onto the grammatical structure of language.

Among the important functions of conceptual structure is the ascription of identity to objects and especially to persons in the environment. As is well-known, the identity of an object can be independent of changes in its physical appearance over time— a person (or car) can change radically over the years or even in a brief time and still remain the same individual. My book, *Semantics and Cognition* (1983, chapters 3 and 5) shows that conceptual structure contains the mental representations that keep track of identity over time and coordinate it with physical appearance and location.

As a first example of psychodynamic displacement, then, consider the not uncommon phenomenon in dreams where a person appears with the face of some acquaintance X but somehow the dreamer "knows" it is really someone else Y—without any necessary sense of incongruity. Let us not for the moment inquire into the causes for such a displacement, which may vary from case to case; rather let us ask how such an anomalous experience could occur at all. In terms of the computational theory, the question is, is it possible to find an information structure that underlies the experience? Given the little that has already been said about conceptual structure, the beginning of an answer is already at hand: the information specifying the appearance of X has been erroneously linked in short-term memory with the identity Y, temporarily displacing Y's proper link to an appearance. Thus, what one knows as Y comes to look like X. Just as in speech errors, then, an anomalous occurrence is caused by the shift of information from its proper place in a structure to somewhere else, a simple formal transfer.

Another characteristic of conceptual structure is that it is the form of information over which processes of reasoning and inference take place. Such processes are conceived of as formal operations that take one or more conceptual structures ("propositions" or possibly other forms) as input and produce new conceptual structures as output. For instance, the familiar rules of syllogism ("All men are mortal; Socrates is a man; therefore, Socrates is mortal") are to be treated as relationships not among the overt linguistic forms of sentences but rather among the conceptual structures of sentences, in which the commonalities of syllogistic form are explicit. (Note, though, that the conceptual structures are not themselves directly accessible to consciousness—only the judgments based on them.)

Similarly, another rule of inference might be stated informally as "If X has changed to state Z at time T, X was not in state Z immediately before time T." This principle is in part responsible for the effect of the sentence "Have you stopped beating your wife? " in which a question about the occurrence of a change (to not beating your wife) implies the previous existence of the state from which change took place. Again, this principle does not apply to the overt utterance, but to its conceptual content.

These sorts of principles, studied by logicians and semanticists, are rules of *rational* inference. However, one might conceive of using the same formal organization in rules of "irrational inference." Here is one candidate that seems characteristic of psychodynamic displacement, again stated very informally. (In many prominent cases, individual X tends to be self.)

Major premise (enduring attitude): "X has characteristic Z" is bad, to be avoided.
Minor premise (particular situation): X has characteristic Z.
Conclusion: X does not have characteristic Z—someone else does.

In other words, the situation "X has characteristic Z" is flatly denied, but the characteristic Z does not go away: it is displaced onto some other appropriate individual. Within the formal organization of conceptual structure, such an operation seems no harder to state than the displacement of a consonant into another word.

Given such a formulation of displacement, it is possible to ask what constraints exist on it (and they may be different in dreams than in waking life, I suppose). For instance, to what individuals is it possible (or likely) to displace Z, and to what individuals is it *impossible* (or unlikely)? As in phonology—and as in the case of rules of rational inference—such constraints can help reveal the unconscious organization of the structures to which the displacement process applies.

As in phonology, we can see process of regularization at work. In ordinary circumstances, the conceptual processes of regularization are the logical inferences and hypotheses that one makes to fill in otherwise undetermined information. However, when applied to the results of "irrational inferences" they appear as confabulation. For instance, when one's own aggression is displaced in paranoia, fear of others' aggression is a logical reaction—a confabulated regularization. That is, the reaction is perfectly reasonable, given the (false) premises, just as "an unkey's muncle" is phonologically perfect English. The interesting thing is that a simple formal change can, as a result of regularization, lead to a drastic change in superficial behavior.

In the sorts of situations described in Horowitz's paper, a confabulated view of the world, arising from regularization, may in its turn serve as a minor premise to another rule of irrational inference, leading to embedded or cyclic warded-off states. We can thus see in these complex psychodynamic chains of states a counterpart to an extended series of logical inferences, leading to a distant conclusion.

As in the phonological case, the applied processes of regularization tend to obscure the precise form of damage that has been inflicted on the original information. However, if these processes can be properly separated and independently explored, they can provide further evidence for the organization of the system as a whole.

I therefore find myself suggesting quite a different approach to studying psychodynamic phenomena from that of a number of authors in this volume. Rather than appealing to physiological measurements that reveal when psychodynamic inferences are taking place (Shevrin, Spence), or to techniques of data sampling that reveal the temporal extent of psychodynamic influence (Singer), I am trying to find ways to focus directly on the *content* of the mental states involved in psychodynamic phenomena. By treating such phenomena as subtly integrated into one's overall conception of the world, it is hoped that they can be treated as of a piece with the formal system underlying ordinary reasoning, which we are now beginning to learn to study in the rigorous way that phonology and syntax have been studied for some decades. As I emphasized in the opening section, the methodology does not call for direct introspection of the content, which is in principle impossible. Rather, one is to use whatever fragments of evidence appear in conscious judgments as clues to the underlying unconscious principles of organization.

I should be clear about the immediate limitations of such an approach. By concentrating on the formal organization of psychodynamic phenomena rather than processing, it offers no direct account of such mechanisms as repression and intrusion, so prominent in these phenomena—it may say at best what material is likely to be repressed or intruded. Similarly, it can say nothing about the processes involved in segregating information into multiple personalities—although it may shed light on what information may cluster together into such personality if such segregation takes place.

These qualifications may be seen by some as altogether damning, but I think the situation is not so bad. First of all, this approach does not *exclude* the description of process. Rather, as in linguistics, a description of formal organization is to be conceived of as an essential part of a full theory of process. In linguistics, moreover, it has always been the case that developments in the theory of form have inspired more sophisticated theories of processing; one might hope for the same result here. Thus I see a theory of the formal structure of psychodynamic states and inferences and their relationship to more everyday conceptualization at the core of an overall theory of these phenomena.

V

Horowitz's analysis of the defensive organization of Ann's states (Table 3.2) provides a sample of the kind of evidence out of which such a theory might develop. Without going into detail, let me make a few remarks on this analysis as an illustration of how one might begin.

Each line of the table associates an affect ("state") with a set of roles and relationships between self and other. For instance, the first line lists the affect "frightened yearning" in association with the self in the role of the abandoned child, supplicating the other in the role of neglectful caretaker. Preliminary examination suggests the following sorts of questions.

1. Does the affect depend systematically on the roles and relationships? Obviously yes, since the affect "explosive rage" would seem grossly out of place substituted for "frightened yearning" in the table.

2. Can this dependence be specified formally, so as to *predict* the association of affect with roles and relationships? In order to do so over an indefinitely large range of possible combinations (parallel to predicting linguistic intuitions over novel sentences), it is necessary to decompose the elements of affects, roles, and relationships into the constituents over which the principles governing associations can be formally defined. This does not necessarily mean that these constituents will be available to consciousness per se, any more than the constituents of language are.

3. Is there interdependence between the roles in any dyad? Intuition suggests again that there is. For example, self in the role of "wise and strong," supplicating other in the role of "weak and defective" seems like a combination close to "ungrammatical," with a bizarre effect not unlike sentence (3b).

4. What are the possible roles and combinations of roles into dyads? A number of dyads in Horowitz's table are implicitly relational; for instance, a "failed caregiver" must take care of *someone*, presumably the other member of the dyad, and a "child" stands in implicit relation to a parent. Moreover, a number of relational dyads are variants on a basic relation of social dominance: parents dominate children, mentors dominate students, caretakers dominate their charges, assailants dominate victims. Other roles such as "weak and defective" and "wise and strong" are not inherently relational. Do they function differently from relational roles in psychodynamic states?

5. Some of the roles, for example, "failed caregiver," have a great deal of information packed into them. A failed caregiver is someone who *should* have taken care of someone during some period in the past but has not done so adequately. Like the sentence "Have you stopped beating your wife?" this role carries an implied history and critical judgment. How do such "loaded" roles add to the complexity of psychodynamic states?

The goal of asking questions like these with respect to a large number of state-diagrams would be to discover the full range of unconscious postures available to an individual participating in human relationships and to elucidate their systematic organization. Such inquiry would lead in two directions. On one hand, it would send one back to the primary data, suggesting new analyses and refinements of previous analyses. On the other hand, broader issues might come to be addressable, for instance the possibility of differentiating personalilty types, both normal and pathological, in terms of an available repertoire of roles, relationships, and state-transitions. Turning back to the "displacements" discussed in the previous section, the formal elements discovered in role analysis might also be expected to be the sorts of elements over which principles of "irrational inference" operate. On an even more general plane, the goal would be to isolate the basic elements and combinatorial principles common to all psychodynamic phenomena, to discover how they come to shape social cognition, and through the Correspondence Condition, to discover how they come to shape conscious experience.

In the background all the time is the metatheory borrowed from linguistics: the entities that the theorist manipulates are not merely classificatory devices for expository convenience. They are intended as hypotheses about *psychologically real* elements of the computational mind. Their inaccessibility to awareness is not an argument against their existence or a proof that their proponents are tilting at windmills: the formal elements of language are in principle unavailable to awareness, too. Thus the outlook of linguistic theory not only confirms and refines the psychoanalytic view of the unconscious; it also provides an attractive precedent for pursuing and justifying a more fine-grained empirical analysis of the content of psychodynamic states.

References

Anderson, John. 1983. *The Architecture of Cognition*. Cambridge, Mass.: Harvard University Press.

Chomsky, Noam. 1965. *Aspects of the Theory of Syntax*. Cambridge, Mass.: MIT Press.

———. 1972. *Language and Mind*. San Diego: Harcourt Brace Jovanovich.

———. 1975. *Reflections on Language*. New York: Pantheon.

Dennett, Daniel. 1978. *Brainstorms: Philosophical Essays on Mind and Psychology*. Cambridge, Mass.: Bradford/MIT Press.

Fodor, Jerry. 1975. *The Language of Thought.* Cambridge, Mass.: Harvard University Press.

Fromkin, Victoria. 1971. The non-anomalous nature of anomalous utterances. *Language* 47:27–52.

Garrett, Merrill. 1975. The analysis of sentence production. In G. H. Bower, ed., *Psychology of Learning and Motivation,* vol. 9. New York: Academic Press.

Halle, Morris. 1978. Knowledge unlearned and untaught: What speakers know about the sounds of their language. In M. Halle, J. Bresnan, and G. Miller, eds., *Linguistic Theory and Psychological Reality.* Cambridge, Mass.: MIT Press.

Jackendoff, Ray. 1972. *Semantic Interpretation in Generative Grammar.* Cambridge, Mass.: MIT Press.

———. 1978. Grammar as evidence for conceptual structure. In M. Halle, J. Bresnan, and G. Miller, eds., *Linguistic Theory and Psychological Reality.* Cambridge, Mass.: MIT Press.

———. 1983. *Semantics and Cognition.* Cambridge, Mass.: MIT Press.

———. 1987. *Consciousness and the Computational Mind.* Cambridge, Mass.: Bradford/MIT Press.

Kosslyn, Stephen. 1980. *Image and Mind.* Cambridge, Mass.: Harvard University Press.

Lashley, Karl. 1956. Cerebral organization and behavior. In H. Solomon, S. Cobb, and W. Penfield, eds., *The Brain and Human Behavior.* Baltimore: Williams and Wilkins.

Lerdahl, Fred, and Ray Jackendoff. 1983. *A Generative Theory of Tonal Music.* Cambridge, Mass.: MIT Press.

Lightfoot, David. 1982. *The Language Lottery: Toward a Biology of Grammars.* Cambridge, Mass.: MIT Press.

Marcel, Anthony. 1983. Conscious and unconscious perception: An approach to the relations between phenomenal experience and perceptual processes. *Cognitive Psychology* 15:238–300.

Marr, David. 1982. *Vision.* San Francisco: Freeman.

Pylyshyn, Zenon. 1984. *Computation and Cognition.* Cambridge, Mass.: Bradford/MIT Press.

Rosch, Eleanor. 1978. Principles of categorization. In E. Rosch and B. Lloyd, eds., *Cognition and Categorization.* Hillsdale, N.J.: Erlbaum.

Schank, Roger, and Robert Abelson. 1975. *Scripts, Plans, Goals, and Knowledge.* Hillsdale, N.J.: Erlbaum.

Shepard, Roger, and Lynn Cooper. 1982. *Mental Images and Their Transformations.* Cambridge, Mass.: Bradford/MIT Press.

4 Omissions of the Expectable from Consciousness

Unconscious defensive processes have been discussed
as a debatable theoretical construct in the preceding
chapters. A concern for the validity of this type of
explanation led to a convergent view on the need for
further theory, in finer-grained detail, about how such
processes might operate in terms of what is known of
cognition and emotion. One of the phenomena of
omission that may allow such increases in specification
and the use of empirical research methods is that of
momentary forgetting. The interesting aspect of
momentary forgetting is that the conscious
representation sought was in awareness and probably
will return to awareness at some future time but is
unavailable for the time being. Chapters in this section
seek to explain this phenomenon in different ways, as a
product of motivated inhibition of emergent
representations and as a consequence of competition
between preconscious parallel processes that are not
intentionally inhibited for defensive reasons.

In Chapter 10, the next chapter, Luborsky presents a
long period of research on the phenomenon of
momentary forgetting and some evidence in support of
a theoretical model that includes the unconscious
anticipation of threat and defensive aims to avoid that
threat by inhibiting a mental content that has been
consciously represented but which the subject is afraid
of communicating. His point of view is challenged
from a psychodynamic perspective by Spence, who
describes in Chapter 11 the issues of demand set that
might effect the validity of the phenomenon itself.
Spence's equal ability as a cognitive psychologist also
allows him to present a counter-model that could

account for momentary forgetting without the construct of unconsciously motivated and active defensive processes. Luborsky responds to this challenge in Chapter 12.

Baars follows in Chapter 13 by elaborating a more detailed cognitive theory, one that attempts to give details about unconscious information processing in a way that describes how momentary forgetting takes place and why it does or does not occur at a given time. As an aspect of this model, he outlines a theory of consciousness as a global workspace. Like Mandler in Chapter 2, Baars in Chapter 13 considers that the "real mystery" may be how consciousness occurs in the first place and what its functions are in view of the apparent fact that so much information processing goes on unconsciously. He elaborates on a distinction between analog and digital information processing speculated on by Spence as differentiating conscious and unconscious mental processes. Baars sets the stage for a reconsideration of consciousness, and the empirical methods for studying it, in the next part of this book.

10 Recurrent Momentary Forgetting: Its Content and Its Context

Lester Luborsky, Ph.D.

William James ([1890] 1950) was struck by the marvel of our well-functioning "intentions to say thus-and-so" that fill a large portion of our waking lives. He observed that we form the intention to say something and launch into speech fulfilling it, although initially we have only a skeleton of an intimation about how the intention will be fleshed out into words; they are "rapid premonitory perspective views of schemes of thought not yet articulate."

James did not mention one occasional dysfunction of these intentions—momentary forgetting. In this form of forgetting the nascent to-be-said thought abruptly fades so that the awareness of what was to be said is gone. Afterward, only the awareness of having intended to say something remains. Because such forgetting typically happens during speaking, the loss may become embarrassing. The speaker may try to pass over the hiatus by persistent efforts to rekindle the memory of the snuffed-out thought or may give up and start a new train of thought. Although the momentary-forgetting experience is only an infrequent aberration of the intention to say "thus-and-so," it is common enough for all of us to have experienced or witnessed it. The experience slips by so quickly, however, that few of us have been able to pay much attention to it—anymore than any of us have had a good look at a hummingbird feeding.

The year 1984 marks the twentieth anniversary of the first published research observations about momentary forgetting (Luborsky 1964). Since those observations, only a tiny though steady stream of research has revealed evidence for both attentional and motivational contributors to momentary forgetting (as

Prepared with the assistance of Dr. Paul Crits-Christoph, Keith Alexander, Dr. Anita V. Hole, Dr. Kenneth D. Cohen, Dr. Frederic J. Levine, Stephanie Ming, and Roberta Bailey Harvey.

summarized in Luborsky, Sackeim, and Christoph 1979). Most of that research was based on studies of the immediate state just before, during, and after the forgetting. This article will add to what was known in 1979. Its aim is to identify the content of what is momentarily forgotten and the conditions that conspire to instigate such forgetting. The general goal of the research is to examine further the bases for momentary forgetting; this phenomenon involves a dramatic shift in memorability that may offer us a box seat to inspect the bases of conscious-unconscious interactions—the topic of this text.

This chapter will be in four parts. The first is a naturalist's account of the nature of the phenomenon and of our sample of it; it is a review of what was known and our method of proceeding. The second is an examination of the degree of consistency in the content of the recovered forgettings from occasion to occasion over a period of months or even years; it is new in its intensity of focus on the consistency of the recurrently forgotten content. The third is about the immediately proximal conditions in the symptom context; it is an exploration of what is evident just before and after the forgetting. The fourth is about the broader distal conditions in the session and in the treatment, especially the core conflictual-relationship theme (CCRT Luborsky 1977); it is most new in its attempt to understand this symptom within the objectively measured CCRT framework of conflicts within self and with others.

The Phenomenon and the Sample

Momentary forgetting behaves as its name suggests: a thought is in awareness, loses the attribute of awareness, and then regains the attribute. An example of this three-phase sequence is shown in Table 10.1 (from a set of sessions loaned to us by an analyst in another city who has been supportive of psychoanalytic research). The example of the forgetting experience is presented in the middle of three sections with the forgetting itself beginning with the first recognition that something was forgotten; in the "Before" section are the patient's 50 words before the forgetting, and in the "After" section are the patient's 50 words after.

The three typical phases in momentary forgetting are shown in this example: (1) a thought that is intended to be said is in awareness, for example, "Two things: . . ." (i.e., "two things" were in awareness); (2) the thought abruptly drops out of aware-

TABLE 10.1 The Recovered Forgetting and the Context Before and After
(Ms. A, Session #36)

#36 Before	Recovered Forgetting	After
Two things: One that I didn't, didn't mention, I was going to, uh, [4 sec.] mmm, why I feel better—I-I wonder whether it had something to do with the—with the fact that I, uh [2 sec.] this the business about, uh, "I present myself to you in such a way that I can't like you," whatever reasoning, uh, is behind that [2 sec.] that, uh, nonsensical statement, uh. [9 sec.]	Now I've lost the other thing that I was going to say [7 sec.]. Now it's, it's so s—I mean it's silly but I suppose [clears throat] it needs to be said, because it came to my mind, that, uh, [4 sec.] that, uh, either on Monday or Tuesday, I think—on Monday, probably, I-hah (snort) I became conscious, eh, uh, of these, I mean I hear a sound that I heard suggested that, uh, that you were brushing a spot off your, eh, off your trousers or something like, like your sleeve, uh [3 sec.] and that I recall that while I was talking I had, I mean the fee—it—it struck me that you, uh, that you weren't really listening . . .	. . . and I—you know, I rationalized it in my mind—well, some things—I mean a doctor can tell when to listen and when not to, so to speak, but [clears throat] I did—uh, I did notice it, and it came up in my mind again, so . . . [6 sec.] I'm really—I'm hard to please. [25 sec.]

ness despite the intention to say it. "Now I've lost the other thing
. . ."; (3) the thought is sometimes recovered and said after a
momentary delay. In this example, seven seconds later the patient again said, "Now," and then she recounted the thought that
she had recovered.

THE SAMPLE OF PATIENTS

A pilot sample of nineteen patients, chosen on the basis of the
therapist's process notes (Luborsky 1964, 1967), will be drawn
on only as a source for some of the main hypotheses about momentary forgetting. The main sample for this report consists of
seventeen tape-recorded patients (Table 10.2). At least one momentary forgetting per patient had been found for each of them.
It was necessary to secure such a sizable number of patients and
psychotherapy sessions in order to collect a sufficient sample of

TABLE 10.2 An Enlarged New Sample of Momentary Forgettings

Subject	Age	Sessions Observed	Instances Observed	Recovered	Rate (instance/session)
1. Mr. BG	20	15	2	1	0.13
2. Mr. PB	29	193	4	0	0.02
3. Ms. CG	23	230	2	2	0.01
4. Ms. MF	39	176	3	3	0.02
5. Ms. CH	27	146	2	0	0.01
6. Mr. MH	26	117	2	2	0.02
7. Ms. JP	23	205	2	1	0.01
8. Mr. JC	26	194	2	2	0.01
9. Ms. SE	19	68	2	1	0.03
10. Mr. RJM	29	66	2	1	0.03
11. Mr. AB	26	179	2	1	0.01
12. Mrs. MS	30	61	1	1	0.02
13. Mr. Q	24	225	1	1	0.00
14. Mr. TRK	35	31	1	1	0.03
15. Mr. D[a]	28	259	3	3	0.01
16. Mr. WS[a]	24	365	2	1	0.01
17. Ms. A[a]	31	296	13	8	0.04

[a]These patients were in psychoanalysis; the others were in psychoanalytic psychotherapy.

this infrequent phenomenon. The explanation for the use of patients is conveyed by the answer to this riddle: which people in which situation meet regularly over many months or years, talk almost without interruption for 50 minutes at a time, and are often willing to arrange to have a tape recorder present? Answer: patients in psychotherapy.

The patients were all nonpsychotic, with a global Health-Sickness Rating Scale (HSRS; Luborsky 1975) between 50 and 75, as rated by independent judges on the basis of the initial evaluation and the early sessions. Most patients were between twenty and thirty years of age.

Of the seventeen patients, nine were treated by myself and eight by other psychotherapists. These two subgroups of patients were carefully compared. They showed no obvious differences in HSRS, in the momentary-forgetting phenomenon, or in its associated conditions. As examples, there were no significant differences in the rate of the forgetting per session (0.2 vs. .03) or in the percentage of recoveries of the forgetting per patient (67% vs 70%). Since there were no significant differences in any area related to the main conclusions, these two subgroups are not distinguished in this presentation.

Three of the seventeen patients were in psychoanalysis; the others were in psychoanalytically oriented psychotherapy. These two subgroups also showed no relevant differences in the nature of the momentary forgetting nor in its associated conditions.

CHARACTERISTICS OF THE PHENOMENON

These are characteristics of momentary forgetting that illustrate the regularity of the phenomenon:

1. *"Goodness of fit" to an ideal form*

The instances included in the sample were those that fit the main defined criteria for momentary forgetting: (1) clarity of the thought—the more fully the thought was in awareness before the forgetting, the better it fit the ideal form; (2) suddenness of the loss of the thought—the more sudden the loss, the more likely the patient had been fully speaking his thoughts before the forgetting. These criteria were reliably judged. The correlation between two judges on the different criteria ranged from .63 to .83.

2. *Frequency*

Momentary forgetting occurred relatively infrequently. The rate for most patients was one to three per hundred sessions.

3. *Frequency of recovery*

Recovery occurred in about two-thirds of the instances.

4. *Degree of certainty about the recovery*

Certainty on the patient's part varied considerably from instance to instance according to the degree to which the patient experienced the recovery as a faithful rendition of the forgotten thoughts. Usually, however, the patients affirmed that the recovered thoughts were the forgotten thoughts.

5. *Elapsed time until recovery*

The median time was 26 seconds. If the recovery did not occur in approximately that time, the forgotten thoughts were progressively less likely to be recovered as the time interval extended.

6. *Genuineness of the momentary forgetting experience*

Is it likely that momentary forgetting is really a conscious experience in which the patient says that a thought is forgotten and acts as though it is forgotten but in fact remains aware continuously of the "forgotten" thought? Even such an alternative hypothesis as this needs to be entertained by any properly relentless researcher in this area. There is, however, no evidence to support this hypothesis; in fact, there is strong circumstantial evidence against it. Among the many patients with instances of reported forgetting over the past twenty years, none has ever intimated in any way that a forgetting experience was voluntary. Nor has there ever been an instance in which a patient, thinking back over the phenomenon immediately after it occurred or later, has recanted and confessed that it was anything other than the experience of an intrusive gap in recalling the thoughts that just occurred. On this issue the patient's own experience is unquestionably uniform.

The Recurrent Content of Recovered Momentary Forgetting

If a specific content is recurrently forgotten, it is then likely that the content has a specific meaning for the patient. It would also suggest that the meaning of the topic to the patient rather than an external distraction was involved in the forgetting.

An analysis of the consistency of recovered forgettings has never been done in a properly controlled fashion. When it was first tried (Luborsky 1967) on a pilot sample of patients, the data were the therapist's notes, not recordings. In that study, the comparison was between the recovered thoughts and control thoughts. The main discriminating variables found were (1) new attitude or behavior; (2) difficulty with attention; (3) guilt; (4) lack of control and competence; (5) oedipal conflict; (6) high level of abstraction; (7) observation about oneself; (8) references to an important relationship; and, (9) elated mood. The previous work with this sample compared the content before forgetting to the content after forgetting, where the "after" contained the momentary forgetting, which was not rated separately.

Recently, I began studies of the temporal consistency of the content of the recovered forgotten thoughts within the cases in the sample of seventeen patients. To study consistency from instance to instance requires a series of instances. Thus, I settled on a minimum of three or more instances of momentary forgetting per patient. Only four of the cases in the seventeen in the new sample qualified, and one of these had a severe limitation: there were no recoveries of the forgotten thoughts. The cases are (with the number of forgettings in parentheses): Ms. A (thirteen), Mr. D (three), Mr. PB (four, but no recoveries), and Ms. MF (three). For the sake of brevity I will give as an example the forgettings of Mr. D, since he had only three forgettings and all three were recovered.

My reading of instances in sessions #12, #68, and #137 (Table 10.3) suggests as a main consistency of content the imminence of the outbreak of anger at the therapist. It is absent from the segments from three control sessions of the same patient, that is, with no forgettings (Table 10.4). Another independent judge was given these six segments, in no special order, to rate a set of variables (see below). His ratings on a 5-point scale clearly confirmed the presence of this core content of anger (mean 3.5) and clearly indicated that the control sessions from the same patient did not have it (mean = 1).

My conclusion is that there is a patient-specific content in the recovered momentary forgettings for Mr. D. It appears to be the fear of expressing anger toward the therapist and receiving anger from the therapist. The anger may well be about feeling dominated by the therapist. The fact that this content is evident in all three of the recovered forgettings suggests that it may play a part in instigating the forgetting. We hope to estimate how much of a part when we know more about the nature of the associated conditions that are discovered in the context of the forgetting, which are analyzed in the next section.

The Immediate Context

The investigation of the symptom-contexts followed our usual research style of a sequence of three interconnected methods: (1) a review of the pilot data through clinical analyses; (2) the development of rating scales based on the review of the pilot data and the application of these scales to the new sample of tape-recorded sessions; and, (3) the development and application of objectively coded scales.

Of course we could not be sure in advance how broad a context to evaluate before and after the forgetting. On the basis of the experience with the pilot data, we settled on 550 patient-words before and 550 patient-words after the point of forgetting, to be judged in 50-word units for both the real forgetting instances and the control instances. This 1,100-word unit represented about 5 or 6 minutes before and 5 or 6 minutes after the onset of forgetting. That seemed a long enough period to catch the proximal conditions involved in the ups and downs of the immediate state.

Analyses of our data by independent judges rating the immediate state indicate that three associated conditions were prominent in the context. These may collaborate in setting the

TABLE 10.3 Mr. D: Three Recovered Forgettings

#12	#68	#137
Oh! I began having—resentment towards you, [2 sec.] [wheezes] having resentment, feeling resentment [3 sec.] and I had the feeling although there a—I didn't have, [2 sec.] I was very much aware at the time that there were, there was no—nothing you had done. [2.5 sec.] But I had the feeling [3 sec.] again that if I let loose [4 sec.] whatever there is inside me, here we go again, [2 sec.] I could almost kill you with my words, [2 sec.] that you couldn't stand the onslaught. [6 sec.]	It had something to do with letting go, that if I lower my guard [4 sec.] you will penetrate me, [2 sec.] rip me to pieces, tear me apart. [13 sec.] You're a nice guy. You wouldn't do that. [10 sec.] Again I have thought of—biting your genitals off.—It's a—terrible thought—being on guard here. [4.5 sec.] It's almost as if my mind becomes a sphincter and I've got to—tightly control that [hesitates] so that–you can't get in and all this shit can't come out. [2 sec.] It was that thought. [7.5 sec.]	Oh! and, and what investments can you possible have in my getting better. No, that isn't what I was g–[7.5 sec.]: If you don't want me to get better I'm pissed off and if you do I'm pissed off. [2 sec.] If you don't you don't care and if you do you want something from me. [15 sec.]

TABLE 10.4 Mr. D: Three "Controls" - Absence of Forgetting

#13	#70	#129
I want to smoke again. [*hesitates*] I'm getting anxious. I have another thought. Oh h– [*something bangs*] [*10 sec.*] I can't. I just can't. I'm sorry. [*18 sec.*] I also had the f–the fantasy last night—of being in bed with Phyllis, this girl that— I'm taking out this Friday. [*7 sec.*] In a way last night it was just good being in bed with somebody; I didn't care who. There was another person in bed with me. [*hesitates*]	something has to happen. [*4.5 sec.*] And again usually my–my fantasies are homosexual I don't consciously try to control them [*2 sec.*] and all I could think of was screwing the girl I'm taking out tomorrow night. [*2 sec.*] Of entering her fully erect pushing her lips— aside—and I suppose there's a reason for my—using that word. [*3 sec.*] And the thought came along now she's gonna suck me with her vagina [*2 sec.*] but that I wouldn't lose it—and that I would be erect and be able to take my time and really—get her so hot—and she could have such a glorious orgasm and it would be so great—it was a nice fantasy. [*6 sec.*]	I have a, the analysis is like coming off—filling the—I don't even know what I'm saying. [*T: It's like what?*] Coming off. Like ejaculating. [*2 sec.*] I don't know why I said that. I have no idea why. [*3 sec.*] But the fantasy was that it's really ejaculating.— Whole room, boy that's pretty grandiose.—This whole room—filled with semen. [*sharp intake of breath*] Oh! [*breathes out*] [*15.5 sec.*]

stage for a forgetting, probably along with the patient's response to the particular recurrent content (noted in the preceding section). These conditions are cognitive disturbance, involvement with the therapist, and core conflictual-relationship thoughts.

COGNITIVE DISTURBANCE

Momentary forgetting is also one of many possible cognitive disturbances. I therefore developed a scale (Luborsky 1966) that would measure twenty-five forms of such disturbance. These forms are grouped into three main types: (1) disturbances in the recall of memories (e.g., "I had a dream but now I can't recall it"); (2) disturbances in the certainty of thoughts (e.g., "My opinion may be, perhaps that. . . ."); and, (3) disturbances in the ability to express thoughts clearly (e.g., "My opinion is. . . . No, I meant to say instead it is. . . .").

The last two types were the most frequent disturbances and therefore the scale is essentially based on these last two. Two judges scored the other cognitive disturbances in each 50-word unit. The reliability of their scoring was high, ranging from 71% to 84% agreement with an overall figure of 78%. Our main expectation was confirmed; the cognitive disturbance did increase just before forgetting (Fig. 10.1). Differences between the groups before instances of momentary forgetting were crucial, an impression supported by a repeated measures analysis of variance for the scores of real and control groups for the three 50-word units before forgetting. These results indicate that momentary forgetting is temporarily associated with other cognitive disturbances expressed in the 150-word unit before forgetting (about 1 to 2 minutes) and especially in the 50 words before momentary forgetting. More specifically, before forgetting patients show greater uncertainty about their thoughts and greater disturbance in clearly expressing their thoughts.

The amount of cognitive disturbance is also involved in the recovery of the forgetting. A nonrecovery sample of $n = 10$ was

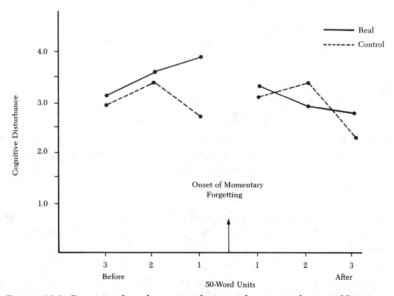

FIGURE 10.1 Cognitive disturbance in relation to the temporal onset of forgetting (real) and nonforgetting (control).

compared with a recovery sample of $n = 21$. A repeated measures analysis of variance (*recovered vs. nonrecovered groups* by *before vs. after forgetting* by *units*) on cognitive disturbance scores for the three units before and after forgetting showed a significant main effect for the recovery groups ($p < .05$). Therefore, greater cognitive disturbance is associated with the nonrecovery of momentarily forgotten thoughts.

These results about the relation of increased cognitive disturbance to decreased recovery may imply that the momentary forgetting occurs when there is an impairment of attention because of the cognitive disturbance. On the other hand, the cognitive disturbance itself may be a response to the buildup of awareness of a "danger signal" (Freud [1926] 1959) because of a recognition of the impending thought as threatening, and once the cognitive disturbance is present it sets the stage for the forgetting.

The implication of the last alternative is that the impairment of attention is mainly internally rather than externally determined. To explore this possibility, two judges rated (on a 5-point scale) the extent to which they could identify any external distraction during the real and control segments. The interjudge agreement of their pooled ratings was .77. The average rating for external distraction for all the instances was low. The mean on a 5-point scale was 1.8. In only seven of the thirty-one instances was there possible evidence of external distraction, and for all of these seven the ratings were only moderate. In conclusion, there was little evidence that external distraction played a part within the instances.

INVOLVEMENT IN THE RELATIONSHIP WITH THE THERAPIST

Two independent judges rated the degree of "involvement" (as the term is used in its everyday English meaning) with the therapist in the real and control instances for the three 50-word units before the forgetting. The interjudge agreement of these ratings was high (.91; two judges pooled; Luborsky and Mintz 1974); a recently added third judge agreed with the first two. Again, a marked peak in involvement was found preceding the real instances.

An even more objective measure of involvement was found: the number of explicit references to the therapist (correlation of judges .95; two judges pooled). A count of these references for the real and control instances showed the curve for explicit references in the real instances was similar to the curve for involvement with the therapist.

THREATENING THOUGHTS IN THE CORE CONFLICTUAL-RELATIONSHIP THEME

The sudden and large rise in involvement with the therapist preceding the forgetting is probably based on the patient's sudden realization that the set of threatening thoughts that have just come to awareness and are about to be expressed could endanger the relationship with the therapist. These suppositions are inferential. We only know that a recurrent content is thought at a time of elevated cognitive disturbance and heightened involvement with therapist.

THE TIME SEQUENCE

A note needs to be added now about the time intervals for the buildup and decline of the three immediate context conditions for momentary forgetting. We had examined an immediate context of 5 or 6 minutes both before and after the forgetting, which turned out to be more than enough time to catch some of the action of the associated conditions. In fact, the shape of the time curves is a peak that gets launched only about 200 words before (about 2 minutes) for cognitive disturbance and 150 words before for involvement with the therapist. The curves achieve their maximum height at the moment of forgetting and they decline afterward in about the same time to about their original level—the increase accelerates as it nears the symptom onset, and after that point its begins to subside in reciprocal symmetry to its ascending phase.

The Broad Context

I will consider here three kinds of observations about the "broad context," a term that refers to the remainder of the session beyond the immediate context: (1) the location of the forgettings within the sessions and within the treatments; (2) the ratings of qualities of the whole sessions; and (3) a comparison of the core content of the recovered forgetting with the core conflictual-relationship theme (CCRT) of the remainder of the session.

LOCATION OF MOMENTARY FORGETTINGS WITHIN THE
SESSIONS AND WITHIN THE TREATMENTS

The treatment lengths were divided into units of 10% of the sessions. More momentary forgettings occurred at the beginning of treatment, with a decrease in frequency as treatment proceeded and an increase again in the latter part of treatment.

The distribution of momentary forgetting was observed in ten units of 5 minutes each across the 50-minute therapy sessions. Forgettings were most likely to occur in the first and last 15 minutes of the session.

This distribution of forgetting both in the session and in the treatment suggests that the symptom's appearance is a function of the patient's sense of security about the relationship with the therapist. At the beginning and ending of the session and of the treatment, there may be higher levels of insecurity about the relationship. If this supposition is correct, the same pattern of increased symptom appearance should be found around other kinds of interruptions of the treatment. It is of interest that other types of recurrent symptoms show a similar distribution during psychotherapy; for example, the report of stomach pain in a stomach ulcer patient, the appearance of cluster headaches (Luborsky and Auerbach 1969), and petit mal epilepsy attacks (Luborsky et al. 1975).

Similarly, the distribution of occurrences of momentary forgetting follows a pattern that is familiar for certain psychophysiological measurements; that is, there is a decline during sessions and across the series of sessions. For example, decline effects for almost all patients have been reported for repeated measures of blood pressure (Luborsky et al. 1982), and such a decline is typically attributed to initially greater insecurity followed by habituation to the situation.

RATINGS OF SESSIONS

The qualities of sessions containing forgetting were investigated in a study of nine patients of one therapist. Just after the end of each session, the therapist rated forty-five qualities of the session. This is distinctly a pilot study since all judgments were made by the therapist. Be it said, though, that this therapist had made similar ratings on similar variables and shown high reliability with other judges in other studies. The across-patient analyses for the discrimination of the "real" from the "control" sessions yielded the following: attention difficulty ($p < .001$), elation ($p < .005$), and new attitude or behavior ($p < .05$). The first of these was successfully validated, as reported in the preceding section on cognitive disturbance; the other two are to be examined in future studies.

THE CORE CONTENT OF FORGETTING COMPARED WITH THE CCRT

A compelling observation drew our attention to the potential insights to be derived from comparison of the content of the forgetting with the content of the core conflictual-relationship theme. We observed that the patient's involvement with the therapist increased markedly during the period surrounding the momentary forgetting, as shown most dramatically in the rise in the number of explicit references to the therapist (Luborsky, Sackeim, and Christoph 1979). Furthermore, these references tended to occur during the telling of or the enactment of relationship episodes with the therapist, and these also include the instances of forgetting. Since most other relationship episodes about other people tended to have certain pervasive themes in common, the episodes dealing with the therapist should also involve similar themes that fit with the CCRT.

The four patients listed earlier can serve as the basis for the comparisons of the content of the forgetting with the CCRT because they had the highest frequency of forgetting in the sample of seventeen subjects: Ms. A (thirteen instances), Mr. D (three instances), Mr. PB (four instances), and Ms. MF (three instances).

The first research step, as described above, was to have judgments made of the content of the momentary forgettings, since the main themes of the momentary forgetting were recurrent for a particular patient and these main themes may be related to a central repressed-memory system for that patient. To explore this possibility, the next step was to compare the core content of each patient's forgetting with the CCRT formulation made by an independent set of judges following the CCRT procedures in Luborsky (1984). The CCRT is derived from guided clinical judgments of psychotherapy sessions. The narratives that are commonly told during sessions are the primary data for the judgments because these narratives, or "relationship episodes" (RE), are an especially fine source of information about relationship patterns. Each narrative contains a major other person (O) with whom the patient is interacting. The main other person most often is one of these: the patient's parents, siblings, friends, bosses, or the therapist. The CCRT scoring procedure begins by a judge going through the sessions and locating the most complete narratives. The judge then reads the transcript of the session and identifies in each narrative the patient's wishes, needs, and intentions toward the main other person (W), the responses of the main other person (RO), and the responses of self (RS). The combination of the most frequent of each of these components constitutes the CCRT. The steps in the method represent a formalization of the inference sequence used by clinicians in formulating the transference pattern (Luborsky et al. 1985; Luborsky, Crits-Christoph, and Mellon 1986). The clinician-judge first counts the wishes and the responses to the wishes in each of the REs and makes a preliminary CCRT formulation (Steps 1 and 2). Then the operation is repeated and the judge recounts and reformulates (Steps 1′ and 2′). The summary of the steps is as follows:

Step 1. Score wishes (W) and responses (RO, RS) in each relationship episode (RE).
Step 2. Count these. Review and make preliminary CCRT.
Step 1′. Rescore REs based on this CCRT.
Step 2′. Recount all W, RO, RS. Review and make final CCRT.

For the present study the CCRT judges also scored the session after omitting the relationship episode containing the forgetting. The yield from this comparison of forgetting and CCRT will be illustrated for two of the patients: Ms. A and Mr. D.

MS. A

Comparison of the Forgetting Theme with the CCRT.
At the time treatment started Ms. A was thirty-one years old and a graduate student and college teacher of French. She decided to undergo psychoanalysis because of her main symptom: she saw herself as stuck in a repetitive pattern—although she wanted to be married, she had had a series of attachments to unsuitable men; with each one she felt unfairly treated, and she then terminated the relationship. The immediate impetus for seeking treatment was an encounter with a young man, which followed the same pattern and left her in an "unusually emotional state with crying and depression." The treatment was in two parts—after the first year of treatment her male analyst had to break off treatment because of illness and she continued with a female analyst.

A large number of tape recordings of sessions of this treatment were obtained from another analyst. These sessions were searched, and thirteen instances found that fit the basic criteria of momentary forgetting. Brief contexts for each forgetting and for the matched controls are reproduced in Luborsky and Mintz (1974) and 50 words before the forgetting and 50 words after are given in Table 10.1.

Consistency Within the Forgettings.
The ratings show that the recovered forgotten thoughts contain a highly recurrent content: various versions of the idea of being rejected (as in Table 10.1). The rejection is usually experienced as coming from the therapist; sometimes as coming from mother, sister, or friends. In nine of the thirteen instances, the forgotten thoughts were recovered; all of them contained the idea of being rejected by someone.

Because this patient had two different analysts in succession, another very special data analysis was tried: a comparison of the four recovered forgettings for analyst A with the five recovered forgettings for analyst B. The fact that the two analysts were very different people (one a man and the other a woman) could have made an important difference in the content of the recovered forgettings. But it did not. Differences between the analysts were not sufficient to alter the major contents of the patient's momentary forgetting; obviously there are patient characteristics that remain unchanged by differences in the therapist's personality or therapeutic style.

It should be noted that the scale used for measuring rejection included a variety of evidence of the patient's experience of being rejected and of not being rejected. The common element in the rejection scale is the presence of the idea of being rejected, whether it is negative (rejection) or positive (avoiding rejection). Two of the instances were about the avoidance of rejection and both of these occurred with analyst B, which suggests that the relationship with her was somewhat more positive than the one with analyst A.

Comparison of the Segments Before, During, and After.
The thoughts in all three time segments reflect a progression of closely associated thoughts rather than an obvious dysjunction, even including the thoughts that comprise the forgetting: rejection content is in the thoughts before forgetting, in the forgetting thought, and in the thoughts after forgetting. There are some differences in quantity of some kinds of thoughts but the core

qualities of the content remains similar. Perhaps in some instances, however, the forgotten thought that is recovered might not have been exactly the thought that was forgotten, but rather a more abstract version of it.

Comparison of CCRT.
Each of the sessions in which the forgetting occurred was analyzed for the CCRT by two independent judges. To help make clearer how the CCRT is derived, Figure 10.2 gives an abbreviated-for-this-occasion list of the relationship episodes in session #36 in the order they were told in the session (in clockwise order). The CCRT in the center circle reflects the most repeated wishes, responses from others, and responses from the self in the five episodes in the session (and the CCRT is much the same in the other two sessions). The following is the CCRT as judged by two judges:

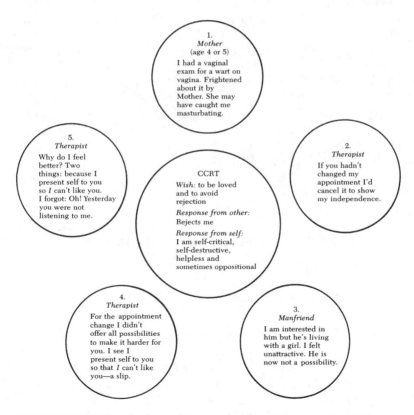

1.
Mother
(age 4 or 5)
I had a vaginal exam for a wart on vagina. Frightened about it by Mother. She may have caught me masturbating.

5.
Therapist
Why do I feel better? Two things: because I present self to you so *I* can't like you. I forgot: Oh! Yesterday you were not listening to me.

CCRT
Wish: to be loved and to avoid rejection
Response from other: Rejects me
Response from self: I am self-critical, self-destructive, helpless and sometimes oppositional

2.
Therapist
If you hadn't changed my appointment I'd cancel it to show my independence.

4.
Therapist
For the appointment change I didn't offer all possibilities to make it harder for you. I see I present self to you so that *I* can't like you—a slip.

3.
Manfriend
I am interested in him but he's living with a girl. I felt unattractive. He is now not a possibility.

FIGURE 10.2 CCRT and relationship episodes from Ms. A, session #36.

W: I wish to be loved and positively responded to and to avoid rejection
RO: Rejects and dominates me
RS: I am self-critical, self-destructive, helpless and sometimes oppositional (e.g., "I'd cancel. . . .")

Inspection of the core forgotten content alongside the CCRT indicates that what is forgotten is the most frequent version of the RO: "Rejects me."

MR. D

Comparison of the Forgetting Theme with the CCRT.
Mr. D. started psychoanalysis at age twenty-eight, while he was in training as a graduate student in one of the mental health professions. He was both homosexual and heterosexual, and his goal was to be able to remain consistently heterosexual. He was treated by an experienced analyst who, after the treatment, lent us a sample of sessions in which we found the three instances from sessions #12, #68 and #137 (Table 10.3).
Consistency Within the Forgettings.
All three contain a fear of expressing anger toward the therapist (Table 10.3). In session #12, it is, "Oh, I began having resentment toward you. If I let loose I could almost kill you with my words." In session #68, it is, "Oh, it had something to do with letting go. I've got to control so you can't get in and this shit can't come out." In session #137, "Oh, I'm pissed if you do and pissed if you don't," that is, show interest in my getting better. The three control (nonforgetting) segments (Table 10.4) do not contain this content; instead the content happens to be mainly sexual.
Comparison with the CCRT.
The CCRT formulation that emerges from the three sessions (by two independent judges; see the abbreviated relationship episodes in Figures 10.3 and 10.4) is the following:

W$_1$: I wish to be dominated
W$_2$: I wish to be close with someone
RO: Dominates and rejects
RS: Submissive, impotent, manipulated, frightened, angry

The core content of the forgotten thoughts, the imminence of anger at the therapist, is contained in the responses from self in the CCRT. This similarity may be based partly on the patient's anger and partly on the high degree of fearfulness the patient has about responding with anger to the therapist.

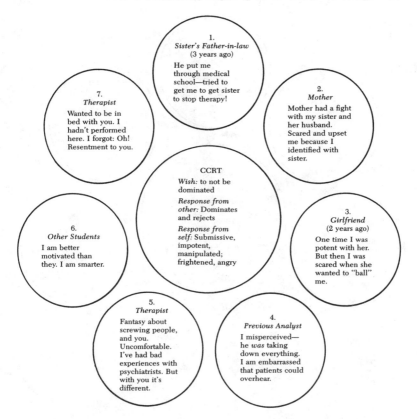

1.
Sister's Father-in-law
(3 years ago)
He put me
through medical
school—tried to
get me to get sister
to stop therapy!

2.
Mother
Mother had a fight
with my sister and
her husband.
Scared and upset
me because I
identified with
sister.

7.
Therapist
Wanted to be in
bed with you. I
hadn't performed
here. I forgot: Oh!
Resentment to you.

CCRT
Wish: to not be
dominated

*Response from
other:* Dominates
and rejects

*Response from
self:* Submissive,
impotent,
manipulated;
frightened, angry

3.
Girlfriend
(2 years ago)
One time I was
potent with her.
But then I was
scared when she
wanted to "ball"
me.

6.
Other Students
I am better
motivated than
they. I am smarter.

5.
Therapist
Fantasy about
screwing people,
and you.
Uncomfortable.
I've had bad
experiences with
psychiatrists. But
with you it's
different.

4.
Previous Analyst
I misperceived—
he *was* taking
down everything.
I am embarrassed
that patients could
overhear.

FIGURE 10.3 CCRT and relationship episodes from Mr. D, session #12.

Conclusions

The first five conclusions to follow are mostly based on reliable judgments of independent observers in our research, while the subsequent two conclusions are more inferential. These first conclusions derive from observations about the conditions for instigating the momentary forgetting. These conclusions all point to the existence of patient-specific thematic contents, which have their place within the overall CCRT. The final two conclusions take a broader perspective on needed research agendas for the future. The first of these suggests that the conditions setting off momentary forgetting would also be found for other symptoms as well. The final conclusion begins to sketch out where in the CCRT-forgetting system deficiencies in awareness are to be found.

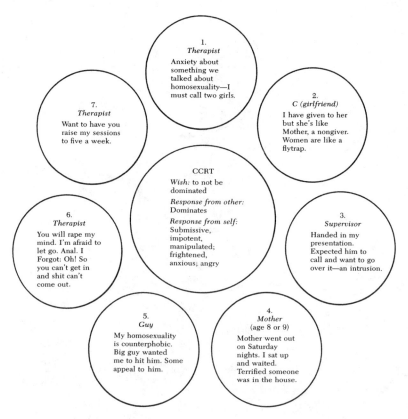

FIGURE 10.4 CCRT and relationship episodes from Mr. D, session #68.

CONCLUSIONS ABOUT CONDITIONS FOR
MOMENTARY FORGETTING

Conclusion 1.

One main recurrent forgetting content is especially prominent in the series of each patient's recovered momentary forgettings. The type of recurrent content and the degree of recurrence of the forgetting are summarized in Table 10.5 for the four patients with three or more forgettings in the sample of seventeen patients. For three of the four, the uniformity in the recurrent content is clear. For the other one, Ms. MF, the uniformity is only moderately evident.

Conclusion 2.

The type of recurrent forgetting content tends to be specific for each patient. As noted in Table 10.5, for Ms. A, the content is

TABLE 10.5 Recurrence of a Main Content in the Momentary Forgetting

	Content	Rate of Recurrence
Ms. A	Fear of being rejected	high
Mr. D	Fear of expressing anger	high
Mr. PB	Fear of expressing anger[1]	high
Ms. MF	Fear of expressing indulgence in forbidden gratification	moderate

[1]Since the forgetting was not recovered, this is an inference based on the immediate context.

fear of rejection; for Mr. D, it is fear of expressing anger; for Mr. PB, it is a similar fear of expressing anger; and for Ms. MF, it is a wish to indulge and a fear of indulging in and having to reveal forbidden sexual and oral gratifications.

Conclusion 3.

The type of recurrent content tends to maintain considerable temporal consistency through the adjacent segments: from before the forgetting, to the forgetting itself, to after the forgetting.

Conclusion 4.

The presence of the main recurrent forgetting content is a necessary but not sufficient condition for the occurrence of momentary forgetting. The shift in the threatening content from before forgetting to the forgetting itself can be only slight, and the thought can be present without triggering the forgetting. Both of these observations imply that what sets off the forgetting is not just the fear of expressing the threatening thought—but also the concomitant increased presence of other conditions, such as increases in cognitive disturbance, involvement with the therapist, and the experience of the core conflictual-relationships theme. However, even a slight shift toward a more specific version of the core content may be perceived as more dangerous and that perception may play a part in the recourse to forgetting.

Conclusion 5.

The core content of each person's forgetting is similar to one of the three components of the person's CCRT. This is very clear for three of the four patients and somewhat evident for the fourth as well. For the three clearest cases, the component is either the response from other or the response from self.

Why should the recurrent core content of forgetting be similar to a component of the CCRT? As was noted at the outset, the similarity may be partly understandable because the forgetting tends to occur during the relationship episodes with the therapist.

That relationship, as Freud ([1912] 1958) observed, is the hardest one for the patient to deal with since it involves expressing proscribed thoughts to the very person to whom the thoughts relate. Furthermore, the relationship episodes with the therapist have been shown to be similar in their content to the larger pattern of other relationships in the CCRT (Luborsky, Crits-Christoph, and Mellon 1986).

FURTHER CONCLUSIONS AND SPECULATIONS

Conclusion 6.

The three main symptom-context conditions for momentary forgetting (cognitive disturbance, involvement with the therapist, and CCRT activation) may be generally applicable to other types of psychological and psychosomatic symptoms (when the conditions for these are analyzed intraindividually by the symptom-context method).

Some evidence for this conclusion is already available for other recurrent symptoms when these are analyzed within each patient: momentary forgetting (Luborsky and Mintz 1974), petit mal attacks (Luborsky et al. 1975), stomach pains (Luborsky and Auerbach 1969), migraine headaches (Luborsky and Auerbach 1969), and precipitous depressed-mood shifts (Luborsky et al. 1984). In addition, one variable, helplessness, uniformly predicted symptom onset within each of the five intraindividually analyzed cases—one case for each of the different symptoms in the studies cited.

One of these cases, Mr. PB, even provided a comparison of two different symptoms within the same case: momentary forgetting and headaches. The three conditions, and helplessness as well, were evident for each of these symptoms but the content differed for each symptom. The context for momentary forgetting was the imminence of the possible expression of anger. The context for the headaches was the buildup of a feeling of tension and pressure in the relationship along with the helpless feeling that nothing could be done about it.

Conclusion 7.

Awareness of the forgetting content and of the related relationship conflicts is not a consistent attribute; it varies from patient to patient and, within patients, from occasion to occasion.

My initial intention was to discuss the conscious and unconscious bases of recurrent momentary forgetting and see how well the words come out to fulfill the intention. To try to expand knowledge in this area of unconscious processes is an awesome challenge—in the original sense of "awesome"—because of deficiencies of research methods and language. Much of what I have to say is consistent with "Freud's cognitive psychology," as Erdelyi (1985) presents it. What I have added comes from the observations from the CCRT and Symptom-Context methods. What I have subtracted comes from my preferred style to stay clear of certain words, even including the conscious and the unconscious used as mental locations, in order to stay closer to the descriptive level. Rather than speak of the conscious and the unconscious, I will refer to degrees of awareness. I am trying to heed Freud's (1937) self-admonition about the snares he suffered from getting too involved with "metapsychology," that is, abstract concepts that are distant from clinical observations. Although I listen to the caution, I am tempted recurrently into momentary romps with the ensnarer. For a measure of safety, I resolve at least to observe the rule of starting speculations from a solid platform of well-established observations.

So much for preliminaries. I am ready to start with an enlarged list of factors that combine to produce the advent of a momentary forgetting, since these can serve as stepping stones to discerning the location of gaps in awareness: (1) a particular type of thought, special for each person, comes to acquire increased awareness; (2) the person perceives the thought but also experiences a danger signal about thinking or saying it; (3) the thought is typically experienced as a danger in interpersonal terms, usually having to do with the relationship with the therapist, and therefore the involvement with the therapist increases; (4) the involvement with the therapist is an aspect of involvement in a larger conflictual relationship pattern (as measured by the CCRT); and, (5) various cognitive signs appear showing the person's difficulty in thinking or expressing the thought or related thoughts (and therefore cognitive disturbance increases). One of these signs is the momentary forgetting itself.

Now while these five factors are in awareness, I will tie them in with several propositions about the conscious-unconscious dimension of the content of recovered forgettings.

1. Much of the content of each patient's recovered forgetting is in awareness at one moment or another. In about two-thirds of the forgetting instances, the patient recovers a lost thought; obviously at that moment it is in awareness and the patient reports it.

2. It is harder for some patients to remain aware of a thought when it is about to be said to the therapist (note factors 2 and 3, above). As an example, Ms. A in the forgetting instance in session #36 had rehearsed the thought she had intended to say some days before the forgetting experience in which those thoughts were forgotten. It was when she realized she was about to say the thought to the therapist that awareness of it lapsed.

3. At times the patient (and even the therapist) may be unaware of the particular therapist behavior that began the inferential linkage with the thoughts that are part of the transference potential. Aspects of the therapist's behavior are often interpreted by the patient as evidence to further confirm negative expectations about the therapist. As Gill (1982) points out, there is often some reality basis in the therapist's behavior for the patient's experience of the relationship with the therapist. In the example below, the patient was aware of how she had found evidence for the therapist's attitudes toward her just before the forgetting instance in session #36: when the patient became "conscious" (her word) of a sound "that you were brushing a spot off your trousers." After that, her further inference involved a really threatening thought: "It struck me that you weren't listening," meaning that the therapist was really rejecting her. Such a thought is associated with her transference potential, as noted in factor 4. The same transference potential had been involved in a long series of similarly upsetting inferences she had made about the therapist and about other people, for example, about the basis for the therapist's missing an appointment with her and about the basis for her father's having been away by himself on trips when she was young. She interpreted much similar behavior of the therapist and other people in the same way as in session #36, as evidences of rejection.

4. The components of the theme of each patient's CCRT-forgetting system vary in the degree to which the patient can become aware of them. Some characteristics of this system imply that it resembles what Rapaport (1951) referred to as a "drive-organized memory system." The difficulty of achieving awareness of some aspects of this memory system is consistent with the possibility that these aspects are not passively out of awareness but, rather, actively kept out of awareness. For patient A the idea of saying to the therapist "you are not listening" was at least momentarily kept out of awareness by the forgetting. She may

have been afraid that saying the thought would stimulate the therapist to reject her.

The wish not to be rejected is one of her dominant ones in the CCRT and in the forgetting. Other thoughts that are only glimpsed, and then somewhat indistinctly, may also have been involved. One of these is a wish to be rejected, which appears to be involved in her attraction to men who are likely to provide her with extreme forms of rejection.

5. Deficiencies in awareness of the CCRT-forgetting symptom system may be particularly prevalent in the *relation among contents* rather than only affecting the awareness of individual contents. Some observations of these patients are consistent with this possibility. Several types of expansion in awareness of the relations among the content of the CCRT-forgetting symptom system appeared during the course of the sessions. These types are elaborated in Luborsky (1984), but only a brief sample of these examples from Ms. A are offered below:

Session #53: She began to see the generality of her CCRT pattern. She reported the experience of feelings of fear about the man's reactions and then realized the parallel feelings of fear about the therapist's reactions.

Session #91: She began to see her role in selecting the men who reject her. The change in awareness here involves the change from a passive to active position in relation to one of the components of the CCRT, for example, "The feelings [of rejection] are justified except that I do the choosing of the men."

Session #165: She began to be aware not only of the expectation of negative responses from others in the form of being rejected but also of the absence of (or maybe partly the denial of) the expectation of being rejected. She ventured then to acknowledge her positive expectations: "You never seize on remarks and embarrass me for having made them."

These examples serve to illustrate areas in which there were expansions in awareness of the relations among different aspects of the CCRT-symptom system: (1) the idea of the generality of the appearance of a particular content with different kinds of people (session #53); (2) the way wishes conflict with each other (session #91); (3) the idea of an association between the appearance of a symptom and the appearance of conflict between self and others; and (4) the emergence of a distinction between the patient's negative expectations of the therapist and the therapists's nonnegative behavior toward her (session #165).

Where to Remember to Go from Here

I will end now with some fond wishes for the future of this research on forgetting, together with some fairly good directions about how to go there from here.

To make further progress in the search for a deeper psychological understanding of the basis for the consistency in the content of recurrent forgetting and its place in the CCRT, these studies might be beneficial: (1) An obvious next step is to investigate other symptoms analyzed in the same fashion as the momentary forgetting in relation to the CCRT. (2) We should also try to learn even more about the degree to which the content and context of momentary forgetting are different from the content and context of other recurrent symptoms within the same patient. As noted earlier, this could be tried for patients with two recurrent symptoms, such as Mr. PB for momentary forgetting and headaches and for Mr. Q for momentary forgetting and precipitous depressions. Our impression, so far, is that the themes for each symptom appear to be distinguishable. (3) To determine whether laboratory research approaches would indicate thematic contents similar to those from forgetting studies, it could be helpful to try Baar's method of inducing slips of the tongue. (4) To determine whether the thematic contents of momentary forgetting for a subject would show up as a "complex" indicator in word associations, it will be valuable to have selected words from the CCRT-forgetting system added to the word association test. (5) To see even broader effects in each subject's stream of consciousness, we should sample each subject's thought stream by Singer's (1984) methods. (6) To learn more about the conscious-unconscious dimension, we should build on the beginnings in this working paper by further systematic observations about the vicissitudes of awareness of the momentary forgetting contents, using Crits-Christoph and Luborsky's (forthcoming) method.

To move to a "deeper" level—defining deeper as physical—it would also be illuminating to examine the concurrent psychophysiological substrate of momentary forgetting: (7) For patients who have provided instances of recurrent momentary forgetting, it would be valuable to have Shevrin's (1984) evaluation of cortical-evoked potentials (CEP). This procedure might show that words from the recurrent forgettings have a distinctive CEP. (8) Other measures of brain function could also be included along with Shevrin's, such as those used by Gur et al. (1983), of coritcal blood flow or nuclear magnetic resonance during various psychological states. However, since recurrent momentary forgetting is infrequent, instead of using measures concurrent with the forgetting it might be convenient to try a tachistoscopic presentation of content related to the forgotten content.

To carry out these seven types of studies it should help to bring closer together the two research styles represented here in the chapters of this text, the naturalistic-clinical and the laboratory-experimental, since they have complementary assets and liabilities. I will end with reflections about the relative virtues of the two research styles in offering suitable "preparations" for the investigation of factors influencing forgetting and recall: the systematic-naturalistic style, as reflected in our work on momentary forgetting, versus the laboratory style, which I have consorted with from time to time. What may emerge from such a tempting tango of the two together? The two may bump up against certain realities of their own limits. For the laboratory methods, the limits are that the clinical data are especially difficult to make sense of in relation to any clinical concepts. These are significant limits since it is clinical data that provided the source of most of the significant constructs about unconscious processes. Even my version of the systematic-naturalistic methods of utilizing clinical data has limits; for example, conditions cannot be varied at will, and the patients do not always reveal their thoughts fully. Yet the attraction that warrants putting up with each other's blemishes is that the systematic-naturalistic method offers for analysis a phenomenon involving both forgetting and remembering, while the patients are revealing many of their thoughts and while objective methods can simultaneously be applied to such data. A fitting resolution is to marry the two methods, as illustrated in the proposed studies, and see how their offspring develop.

References

Baars, B. J. 1985. Can involuntary slips reveal one's state of mind? In M. Toglia and T. Shlechtor, eds., *New Directions Cognitive Science*, Norwood, N.J.: Ablex.

Crits-Christoph, P., and L. Luborsky. Forthcoming. Development of a new type of measure of self-understanding of core relationship problems. In N. Miller et al. eds., *Handbook of Psychodynamic Treatment Research*. New York: Basic Books.

Erdelyi, M. H. 1985. *Psychoanalysis: Freud's Cognitive Psychology*. New York: Freeman.

Freud, S. [1912] 1958. The dynamics of transference. *Standard Edition, Vol. 12.* London: Hogarth Press.

―――. [1926] 1959. Inhibitions, symptoms, and anxiety. *Standard Edition,* vol. 20. London: Hogarth Press.

―――. [1937] 1964. Analysis terminable and interminable, *Standard Edition,* vol. 23. London: Hogarth Press.

Gill, M. M. 1982. Analysis of transference: Theory and technique. *Psychological Issues,* monograph 53: 1–193.

Gur, R. E., Brett E. Skolnick, Ruben C. Gur, S. Caroff, W. Rieger, W. D. Obrist, D. Younkin, and M. Reivich. 1983. Brain function in psychiatric disorders, 1: Regional cerebral blood flow in medicated schizophrenics. *Archives of General Psychiatry* 40: 1250–54.

James, W. [1890] 1950. *The Principles of Psychology,* vol. 1. New York: Dover.

Luborsky, L. 1964. A psychoanalytic research on momentary forgetting during free association. *Bulletin of the Philadelphia Association for Psychoanalysis* 14: 119–37.

―――. 1966. The cognitive disturbance scale. Manuscript.

―――. 1967. Momentary forgetting during psychotherapy and psychoanalysis: A theory and research method. In R. R. Holt, ed., *Motives and Thought: Psychoanalytic Essays in Honor of David Rapaport. Psychological Issues* 5, nos. 2–3, monograph 18/19, 177–217.

―――. 1975. Clinicians' judgments of mental health: Specimen case descriptions and forms for the Health-Sickness Rating Scale. *Bulletin of the Menninger Clinic* 35: 448–80.

―――. 1977. Measuring a pervasive psychic structure in psychotherapy: The core conflictual relationship theme. In N. Freedman and S. Grand, eds., *Communicative Structures and Psychic Structures.* New York: Plenum.

―――. 1984. *Principles of Psychoanalytic Psychotherapy: A Manual for Supportive-expressive (SE) Treatment.* New York: Basic Books.

Luborsky, L., and A. H. Auerbach. 1969. The symptom-context method: Quantitative studies of symptom formation in psychotherapy. *Journal of the American Psychoanalytic Association* 17:68–99. Abstracted in *Digest of Neurology and Psychiatry,* series 37 (May 1969): 156.

Luborsky, L., J. Docherty, T. Todd, P. Knapp, A. Mirsky, and L. Gottschalk. 1975. A context analysis of psychological states prior to petitmal seizures. *Journal of Nervous and Mental Disease* 160:282–98. Reprinted in L. A. Gottschalk, ed., *Content Analysis of Verbal Behavior: Further Studies.* New York: Spectrum, 1978.

Luborsky, L., P. Crits-Christoph, J. P. Brady, R. Kron, T. Weiss, M. Cohen, and L. Levy. 1982. Behavioral versus pharmacological treatments for essential hypertension: A needed comparison. *Psychosomatic Medicine* 44:203–13.

Luborsky, L., B. Singer, J. Hartke, P. Crits-Christoph, and M. Cohen. 1984. Shifts in depressive state during psychotherapy: Which concepts of depression fit the context of Mr. Q's shifts? In L. N. Rice and L. S. Greenberg, eds., *Patterns of Change*. New York: Guilford.

Luborsky, L., J. Mellon, K. Alexander, P. Van Ravenswaay, A. Childress, F. Levine, K. D. Cohen, A. V. Hole, and S. A. Ming. 1985. A verification of Freud's grandest clinical hypothesis: The transference. *Clinical Psychology Review* 5:231–46.

Luborsky, L., P. Crits-Christoph, and J. Mellon. 1986. The advent of objective measures of the transference concept. *Journal of Consulting and Clinical Psychology* 54:39–47.

Luborsky, L., J. Mellon, and P. Crits-Christoph. 1985. Tracking a social phobia with the CCRT and SC methods. Paper for MacArthur conference, Stanford, July 16–19.

Luborsky, L., and J. Mintz. 1974. What sets off momentary forgetting during psychoanalysis? Methods of investigating symptom-onset conditions. In L. Goldberger and V. Rosen, eds., *Psychoanalysis and Contemporary Science*, vol. 3. New York: International Universities Press.

Luborsky, L., H. Sackeim, and P. Christoph. 1979. The state conducive to momentary forgetting. In J. Kihlstrom and F. Evans, eds., *Functional Disorders of Memory*. Hillsdale, N.J.: Erlbaum.

Rapaport, D., ed. 1951. *Organization and Pathology of Thought*. New York: Columbia University Press.

Shevrin, H. 1984. Unconscious conflict: A convergent psychodynamic and electrophysiological approach. Workshop for MacArthur conference, Stanford, July 5–9.

Singer, J. 1984. Sampling ongoing consciousness and emotional experience: Implications for health. Workshop for MacArthur Conference, Stanford, July 5–9.

11 Momentary Forgetting: An Alternative Formulation

Donald P. Spence, Ph.D.

When the world was flat the sailor who ventured too far from port was taking the enormous risk of dropping off the edge and never being seen again. The visible horizon was taken to be the end of the world, and the way men saw the world was taken as isomorphic with the way it was. We are in danger of making a similar mistake in the way we study the problems of the mind, confusing experience with description and mistaking our introspections for the way things really are.

So it is in the case of forgetting. It "feels" as if what is forgotten has simply dropped out of sight, moved to a different "location" in the head and is resting there, more or less intact, waiting to be "recovered." Freud's emphasis on recovery, his frequent use of an archaeological metaphor, and his emphasis on reconstruction, all point to a kind of lost-and-found model of the mind. Not only does this way of thinking make dubious assumptions about mental space and the different kinds of locations in the mind, but it implies continuity between conscious and unconscious processes, which argues that a change in introspective status does not necessarily imply a change in form. This emphasis was particularly evident in the use of the unconscious to explain discontinuities in a patient's waking thoughts, and in the case of Dora, where Freud made repeated reference to the idea that the interpreted dreams supplied the missing links in her somewhat bizarre clinical history. We are also tempted by our introspections to assume continuity, because when the forgotten thought is "recovered," it feels familiar, as if it had never "left home." There are no tell-tale signs of travel or other kinds of wear and tear.

This peculiar innocence of our introspections is almost universal. With only a few exceptions, we are never aware of the workings of either our descriptive or our dynamic unconscious; we have no direct access to the deep structure of our grammar, to our primitive visual percepts, or to our successive visual fixations. This widespread lack of awareness argues strongly for a significant discontinuity between conscious and unconscious in both form and content and should make us suspicious when we impute familiar patterns to unconscious operations. Although it may feel comfortable and neighborly to assume that organized schemata, scripts, and other kinds of "look-up tables" are operating out of awareness, more or less intact, there is no direct evidence that this is the case; we may once again be making the mistake of confusing appearance with reality.

Although Freud was a part-time archaeologist (at least in a metaphorical sense), he also believed in discontinuity. In making the distinction between the primary and secondary processes of thought, Freud was making the assumption that the form of a representation may change when it moves out of awareness. Even though there are difficulties in developing the full grammar of the primary process—the rules were only roughly sketched out in the famous Seventh Chapter of *The Interpretation of Dreams*— and many of these rules may be completely wrong, the assumption of discontinuity may be one of his most important contributions. To think in these terms is to become aware of the fact that many different combinations of unseen operations may produce the same final product. What might be called introspective bootstrapping may sometimes only get us into trouble. And last but not least, it is clear that computer models do *not* make this assumption and should be particularly suspect for that reason alone.

A close inspection of the vicissitudes of momentary forgetting may give us important clues about possible discontinuities between conscious and unconscious processes. To be sensitive to the scope of this important phenomenon, so carefully isolated by Lüborsky in his trail-breaking series of experiments, it is particularly important that we become aware of our implicit assumptions and not fall too readily into assuming a standard lost-and-found model of forgetting. To give only one possible alternative: it may be that forgetting comes about not because of a specific loss or a specific failure of "recovery," but because we lack the means of putting the pieces together. We may be faced not so much by failures of *repression* as by failures of *expression*. This view of forgetting may remind you of Schachtel's (1947) famous analysis of infantile amnesia. He claimed that early experiences are not repressed so much as they are coded in an infantile and primitive symbol system that is not accessible to the average adult; therefore, we may have all the raw materials we need to describe the early years of infancy, but since we lack the proper code, we have no "memory" of childhood events. Hypnotic recovery of childhood scenes may, in this view, be less mysterious than many people think; perhaps hypnosis provides access to the necessary code, which can be used to integrate the fragments and flesh out the details.

Or take another example—the notorious unreliability of eyewitness testimony (see Loftus 1979). This unreliability is often correlated (inversely) with the meaningfulness of the event. Unreliability comes about because the witness may try to impute meaning to the scene and generate his own script, which then takes over to organize and give context to the individual episodes. Naturally, each witness will have his own script, despite the fact that they were all present at the event; hence, conflicting testimony will result.

Finally, consider the Case of the Impulsive Programmer. He writes a program in some high-level computer language that leaves few clues as to its overall goal or strategy, and he neglects to add explanatory comments along the way. Suppose he comes back to the program four months later—he will very likely be unable to "remember" its purpose. But what is forgotten? The details are still the same; no erasures have taken place. He is missing the embedding context, the organizing rules that link them together. Yet it would seem absurd to claim that these rules are buried somewhere by themselves, waiting to be reunited with the manifest program. The lost-and-found model simply does not apply.

What does this tell us about momentary forgetting and Luborsky's specimens? If the details of the forgotten thought are, in fact, available to consciousness all the time, we may expect to see them emerge in other contexts, inadvertently expressed in metaphors or double entendres or slips of the tongue. Secondly, we can assume that the so-called "recovery" of the forgotten idea may mark the point at which a new organizing framework has been supplied that will make sense of the particulars, and this new scenario may be triggered by mood as well as idea. Thus, a growing feeling of sadness during the hour may allow the patient to recognize an isolated image as not just a mask but a *clown's* mask; once this detail is set in place, he may recover the fact that he had been to the circus and was unpleasantly reminded of a childhood unhappiness when he was separated from his parents and was found, lost and miserable, by the police. The growing feeling of sadness gives context to the mask and the bare bones of the incident can be reconstructed.

Given this view of forgetting, we can see the role of free association in a different light. Rather than provide us with privileged access to some nether region of the mind, perhaps it allows the patient the freedom to try out different contexts and to bring unfamiliar ideas together in new ways; from these first-time meetings, new light can be shed on old assumptions. (The well-known role of dreams in aiding and abetting creativity may follow similar principles: the dream allows for a recombination of old ideas, and the new insight or discovery represents a first-time fabrication rather than the "emergence" of something already formed and waiting in the unconscious.)

What does Luborsky's data tell us about this model of forgetting? We can look first at the target incident—the place where the patient says, "I was about to tell you something, but I forgot what I was going to say." If we assume that nothing is really forgotten but that the organizing code—the macroprogram—has been mislaid, then we would assume that the patient may be remembering more than he claims and that the region of forgetting can be searched for signs of displacements and other derivatives of the forgotten material. Both Baars (Chapter 13 of this volume) and I have pointed to the similarity of momentary forgetting and Brown and McNeill's (1966) tip-of-the-tongue phenomenon (TOT); building on the findings of the TOT work, we could look for similarities in word length, number of syllables, initial letters, and various kinds of paraphrase with respect to the forgotten item and the remembered sentences. Of particular interest are those cases where the "forgotten" thought is distributed over five or more minutes of seemingly irrelevant discourse, with the target words (the "forgotten thought") appearing in passing and out of context and thus giving no clue to their real significance. What I am suggesting is that we look at those cases where the forgotten thought has been recovered, go back to the initial forgetting, and then systematically search for derivatives of the thought in as many ways as we can imagine. Perhaps in this procedure we will uncover ways in which the patient is "confessing" even as he is "forgetting."

Freud had a patient who spoke with her fingers and "chattered at every pore" while being unable to remember an incident in so many words; when she was forgetting or misunderstanding on one level, she was loquacious and transparent on another. Did her nonverbal hand-waving supply a natural organization to her utterance that words could not? Do our momentary-forgetting patients also remember in body language or somehow speak in other tongues? Plans might be made to look for target instances among the sessions stored in a video data bank—Horowitz and his group may have some useful specimens—and in the lucky event that examples could be found that fit Luborsky's criteria, we would be in a position to look for correlates of momentary forgetting in the patient's body language. Does the body become more active when the patient starts to forget? Does it lag behind the target (verbal) forgetting? Does it come before? If hand movements take over, do they favor the preferred or nonpreferred hand? To ask this kind of question is to embed the target happening in the vast literature on body language, paying particular attention to the study of affective and lexical leakage, which has been studied by Ekman and Friesen (1969) and Spence (1977, 1980). One would think that momentary forgetting would be particularly rich in these kinds of leakages.

In looking for displacements and derivatives, I would pay particular attention to metaphor. In our study of cervical cancer patients who were coming in for cone biopsies, we found that the best predictor of a positive diagnosis (unknown to either patient or doctor at the time of the interview) was the single word *death*. Patients with positive diagnoses used this word significantly more often than controls. We also found that this word tended to appear significantly often as a figure of speech—"I almost froze to death," "I was scared to death," and similar expressions. Metaphor gives us a way of speaking in tongues, as it were; we can take the metaphor off the shelf, say it with almost no knowledge that it is being said, and in the process, tuck in a number of highly loaded words without taking responsibility for them. What better way to inadvertently express conflict-laden material, while all the while claiming to have forgotten it?

To put the phenomenon in this context is to make a link with the class of clinical events described by Roy Schafer (1976) as "disclaimed actions"—cases where words are used to conceal or belittle what is taking place. The patient may say that something "slipped his mind" in order to put emphasis on his passive role rather than underline the fact that he participated in the forgetting.

To appreciate this context would suggest that Luborsky might want to distinguish between cases of real forgetting and what might be called pseudo-forgetting, where the patient uses the

same words but where no real loss has taken place (see Luborsky's Ms. A, session #36, where only 16 seconds elapsed between
"forgetting" and "recovery"). This example might be better classified as a momentary disturbance in which the patient is searching for ways to say something without saying it, stalling and
dissembling before finally admitting to the thought about the
therapist. On the other hand, it could be argued that both kinds
of forgetting show the same loss of overall organization and that
what is important in both cases is the subjective sense of confusion and loss of purpose that comes about when the organizing
principle disappears. Whether this is done "consciously" or in
some other ways may be less important than the fact that a momentary loss of pattern or framework can produce a major disruption in communication.

Perhaps more fundamental is the distinction between the cases
of momentary forgetting collected by Luborsky and those collected by other therapists. Luborsky tells us that there were no
significant differences between the two samples in either the
rate of forgetting per session or in the percentage of recovery per
patient. But it might be interesting to look more carefully at
differences in function—differences in the way in which forgetting comes to pass or, to use a better model, differences in kinds
of disorganization.

To merge the samples too soon is to lose clues about an important question: does Luborsky bring about momentary forgetting in a particular way, perhaps by leaking—in a very subtle
manner—some expectation of what should occur? Consider one
possible difference between the two samples. When Luborsky
is the therapist, he may be eagerly awaiting the appearance of a
specimen disturbance and his eagerness may be communicated
to the patient, perhaps counteracting the patient's anxiety and
confusion.

Given this line of reasoning, we would expect that the disturbance might last for a shorter period and that the derivatives
might be more easily tracked because they were somehow being
rewarded (reinforced) by the expectant therapist. When someone
else is the therapist, the forgetting takes place in a more neutral
surrounding, and the size and shape of the envelope of disturbance would be more likely to follow some natural law. Both
classes of events should be studied, but they should not be confused; differences between classes would be just as informative
as similarities.

With a neutral therapist, the forgetting might be harder to understand because it was taking place in a somewhat foreign context; the disorganization might be more prolonged, the derivatives harder to track, and the lag between forgetting and recovery might be appreciably longer. With Luborsky as the therapist, the phenomenon is presumably better understood as well as more warmly anticipated; in this more hospitable surrounding, with a more benevolent "host," the organism has a better chance to develop and prosper. (One can think of the difference in dreams told to a sympathetic therapist and those told to a therapist who thinks that all dreaming is random discharge.)

There is an interesting paradox in Luborsky's own cases that should also be considered. Luborsky has argued that, in the general case, forgetting takes place because a thought emerges that arouses some interpersonal anxiety and the patient is uneasy about a negative reaction from the therapist (see Ms. A, session #36). But with Luborsky's patients, a different model may be needed because the momentary disturbance will provoke a positive reaction—it is just what this particular therapist had been hoping to hear! Does this subliminal welcome somehow eliminate the patient's interpersonal anxiety? If he feels that he is saying just the right thing, does the momentary disorganization disappear? Does the subliminal welcome somehow take away the uneasy sense that something forbidden is being expressed? These and other possibilities point to the need to look separately at the two classes of events.

We next come to the second phase—the so-called recovery of the forgotten memory. Under what conditions does it reappear? Here it might be useful to borrow from the recovery studies of Erdelyi (1974) and Zeigarnik (1927), some of Neisser's more naturalistic investigations of early memories (1982), and from Loftus and her work on eyewitness testimony (1979).

Erdelyi has taught us that free association does wonders for picture fragments but has next to no influence on verbal memory. Given that finding, it might be useful to categorize the forgotten (or disorganized) memory as either pictorial or verbal and to look for different rates of recovery across the two classes of events. We might also find that the kind of inadvertent confessing I referred to above would happen more often with a *verbal* memory and that "leakage" of body language would happen more often with a *pictorial* memory. Once you classified memories into these two groups, a whole host of interesting patterns might emerge.

Turning to Loftus, we find that subjects' memories of accidents (which are partly random events and therefore susceptible to retrospective "smoothing") can be significantly biased by cuing questions and that the content of these questions may sometimes turn up in the original "memory." Thus, a subject is first shown a film of a traffic accident involving a school bus and a brown car; she is then asked, "Did you see the yellow Volkswagen come around the corner?" A week later, when asked to remember the film, she describes a scene with a school bus and a *yellow* car. Leading the patient in this way may happen sometimes in psychotherapy, and it would be interesting to study the examples of momentary forgetting to determine how frequently the therapist's comments either triggered the recovery of the target thought or in some way shaped the recollection. This point has obvious implications for the difference between the two samples discussed above and provides another reason why we should study Luborsky's own cases separately from those of the other therapists. If he is more invested in the phenomenon, he may be more interested in its "recovery" and provide subtle kinds of prompts that will aid the patient in reorganizing the material.

Loftus's experiments help support the thesis that we are dealing with organization rather than problems of loss and/or recovery. When asked to remember the accident, her subjects seem to use whatever information they have available to help flesh out the details of a somewhat vague frame. In the process, they do not distinguish between what was originally perceived in the film and what was added later—either explicitly or implicitly—in the form of questions. In other words, they have no record of where the information comes from; whatever is available is put to the task of telling a reasonable story. If we run this process backward, we have a model of momentary forgetting, which is best illustrated by the case of Ms. A in session #36. In the section labeled *Before*, she does a good job of talking around the point, telling and yet not telling what is on her mind. Consider the confused syntax and the ambiguous references in this fragment:

Two things: One that I didn't, didn't mention, I was going to, uh [4 sec.] mmm, why I feel better—I-I—wonder whether it had something to do with the—with the fact that I, uh [2 sec.] this the business about, uh, "I present myself to you in such a way that I can't like you, whatever reasoning, uh, is behind that [2 sec.] that, uh, nonsensical statement, uh [9 sec.]. Now I've lost the other thing that I was goin to say [7 sec.].

This fragment could be described as an attempt to talk in such a way that the underlying organization of the thought will not emerge, much as if a picture were being described by listing its main objects rather than by describing its organizing theme (thus, Mona Lisa—a half-smile in a face with a vague landscape in the distance). The patient finally "recovers" the thought—she heard a sound in a recent session that made her think that the therapist was not really listening.

I would argue that the thought was never lost but that the patient was having great difficulty in expressing it (probably because it implied a criticism of the therapist) and that this difficulty generates a confusion of syntax that allowed her to say the words without saying the thought. Syntax, after all, is directly linked to organization; we choose our grammar depending on the point we want to make or the point we want to avoid, as the case may be. Such an essentially syntax-free utterance strongly suggests that organizing themes are being denied expression; the patient pays lip service to the idea of free association while not revealing the one idea that would allow the associations to make sense. (To the extent that she is taking responsibility for this omission, she is performing one of Schafer's disclaimed actions.)

It might be argued that this particular sample of free association gives us a glimpse of primary-process thinking—a direct upsurge of unconscious or preconscious material. To reason in this manner is to mistake appearance for reality and to assume a continuity between the form of the contents of consciousness and the way it has been stored. To take a more parsimonious position, I would argue that the fragment gives us evidence for a particular kind of strategy, a strategy of concealment and delay, and that the loss of syntax is as much imposed by the patient as it was missing in the unconscious.

If the rules of the primary process are incomplete and in many ways unsatisfactory, can we arrive at a more general way of describing the discontinuity? It may be useful to consider the more traditional distinction between analog and digital representations and to think of the process of becoming conscious as performing some kind of A-to-D transformation (this position has been elaborated by Spence [1973] and more recently by Marcel [1983]). This formulation would suggest that what is represented out of awareness is continuous rather than discrete and that what is selected at any particular time (what "comes to mind") represents only a one-time sampling of a continuous data base. Such a model would also allow for information storage in a wide range of modalities. It could accommodate Reich's character armor (1949) and Zajonc's more recent elaboration of this theme (Chapter 15 of this volume) because "muscle memory" would seem to consist of graded patterns of continuous rather than discrete sensations. Different "memories" of the same event could be understood as different samplings of a continuous gradient; conversely, forgetting might be represented as the removal of the digital and oppositional distinctions that underlie our grammar and our sharp-edged ways of describing the world. (Saussure's [1973] emphasis on the oppositional standing of the elements of language—*hot* is defined in contrast to *cold*—can be seen as consistent with this argument.)

The patient in session #36 could be described as trying to make continuous what should be discrete; and she does this by omitting the normal distinctions between subject and object, noun and verb, and past and present. We might represent her utterance before the momentary forgetting as a partial analogic representation of her experience, and as such, it is ambiguous both to her and to her listener. The addition of various organizing principles in the recovered-forgetting section produces a more recognizable structure in the form of sentences, syntax, and specific events; we begin to have a clearer understanding of what took place earlier in the week and how this event was represented by the patient. Notice the many distinctions needed (Monday or Tuesday but not other days; brushing, not mopping or cleaning; sleeves or trousers, not necktie) to bring "reality" into focus. Also notice that the A-to-D transformation is not complete: was it Monday or Tuesday, the therapist's sleeve or his trousers? Additional distinctions—this, not that—are a necessary part of successful reporting (and remembering); conversely, a vaguely worded report is often equivalent to (and confused with) a "bad" memory.

Whether analog-digital or primary-secondary process is the more useful distinction remains to be seen. The former, because it is more general, allows us to draw data from a wide range of different experiments and embed the clinical phenomena in a set of much broader formulations. Luborsky's carefully collected specimens can be further studied to look for residual signs of analog operations during the "forgetting" stage of the process and the substitution of digital distinctions during the remembering stage. Whether or not this formulation proves superior to others, we can be assured of new discoveries and new surprises.

References

Baars, B. J., and M. T. Motley. 1976. Spoonerisms as sequencer-conflicts: Evidence from artificially elicited errors. *American Journal of Psychology* 89:467–84.

Brown, R., and D. McNeill. 1966. The "tip of the tongue" phenomenon. *Journal of Verbal Learning and Verbal Behavior* 5:325–37.

Ekman, T., and W. V. Friesen. 1969. Non-verbal leakage and clues to deception. *Psychiatry* 32:88–105.

Erdelyi, M. H. 1974. A new look at the "New Look": Perceptual defense and vigilance. *Psychological Review* 81:1–25.

Erdelyi, M. H., and J. Becker. 1974. Hypermnesia for pictures: Incremental memory for pictures but not words in multiple recall trials. *Cognitive Psychology* 6:159–71.

Loftus, E. F. 1979. *Eyewitness Testimony.* Cambridge, Mass.: Harvard University Press.

Marcel, A. J. 1983. Conscious and unconscious perception: An approach to the relations between phenomenal experience and perceptual process. *Cognitive Psychology* 15:238–300.

Neisser, U., ed. 1982. *Memory Observed.* San Francisco: Freeman.

Reich, W. 1949. *Character Analysis.* New York: Noonday Press.

Saussure, F. de. 1973 (orig. publ. 1916). *Cours de linguistique générale.* Tullio de Mauro, ed. Paris: Payot.

Schachtel, E. 1947. On memory and childhood amnesia. *Psychiatry* 10:1–26.

Schafer, Roy. 1976. *A New Language for Psychoanalysis.* New Haven: Yale University Press.

Spence, D. P. 1973. Analog and digital descriptions of behavior. *American Psychologist* 28:479–88.

———. 1977. Lexical derivatives in patients' speech: Some new data on displacement and defense. In N. Friedman and S. Grand, eds., *Communicative Structures and Psychic Structures.* New York: Plenum.

———. 1980. Lexical leakage. In R. W. Rieber, ed., *Applied Psycholinguistics and Mental Health.* New York: Plenum Press.

Wilden, A. 1977. *System and Structure: A Phase in a Communication and Exchange.* London: Tavistock Publications.

Zeigarnik, B. 1927. Das Behalten erledigter und unerledigter Handlungen [The remembering of completed and uncompleted tasks]. In K. Lewin, ed., Untersuchen zur Handlungs und Affektpsychologie. *Psychologische Forschung* 9:1–85.

12 Take a Moment to Really Look at the Little Lawful World of Momentary Forgetting— A Reply to Spence

Lester Luborsky, Ph. D.

My venture into the little world of momentary forgetting seems to Spence to require big reminders to beware of seeing things that may not be there or of not seeing things that are there. He offers me at least four caveats to help guide me safely on my way: (1) when the patient says that he or she has momentarily forgotten something, the patient may be "dissembling"; (2) the momentary forgettings and their contexts that were collected from my patients may be different from those that other therapists collected from their patients; (3) the therapist's behavior may trigger the recovery of the lost thoughts or shape their recollection; (4) because of possibilities 1, 2, and 3, I may be overinterpreting the patient's "momentary forgetting" behavior. I may not have a basis for my inference that the patient may be afraid to reveal the context of the thought to the therapist and may show some repressionlike phenomena that are involved in the momentary forgetting.

1. In the first warning, Spence surmised that the patient may be "dissembling before finally admitting the thought about the therapist." I reviewed the evidence for Spence's scary scenario and decided that it seems highly speculative for several reasons.

First, if dissembling were to be taken seriously as an explanation, one would expect some evidence for it either at the time, later on, or in the sessions thereafter. One would expect that some patients at some time would have recanted their dishonest behavior and acknowledged, or at least implied, that it was not a true experience but a made-up one. This has never happened. After having assembled a collection of scores of momentary forgettings and after having many other judges review these momentary forgettings and the sessions in which they occurred, I can report as a direct observation that neither I nor any of the judges ever read a momentary forgetting and the patient's discussion of it that conveyed any experience on the patient's part of dissembling when he said he had momentarily forgotten something. Patients always described their experience as forgetting, both at the time of the experience and thereafter forever. But all of us researchers should take such possibilities of prevarication seriously because they may ultimately advance our science. The other presenters at this conference should also consider the possibility of their patients having dissembled, for example, Shevrin's patient who screamed at the sight of blood may have been putting on an act, Horowitz's patients whose symptoms were pathological bereavement reactions may also be dishonestly presenting symptoms.

Second, I discovered evidence in the sessions that the recurrence of each instance of momentary forgetting was associated with a recurrent content that was specific and individual for each patient. Still, if the patient were dissembling the patient could have chosen to dissemble only with a particular patient-specific content. But this is unlikely.

Third, there was a regular buildup of cognitive disturbance, as measured by the cognitive-disturbance scale, in the several minutes before each momentary forgetting. There are two main interpretations for this: (a) that the patient was having some conflict about the intention to be dishonest or (b) that the patient was already having trouble with knowing what he was intending to say and saying it. I consider that a conceptualization in terms of motivated forgetting has some fit to the phenomenon. Spence considers a safer conceptualization is in terms of motivated dissembling.

2. Spence's second suggestion is that there might be differences between momentary forgettings presented to me and to other therapists. Spence had told me about this before the conference, and so I compared the data from my patients with instances of momentary forgetting taken from the patients of other therapists, who were not familiar with my interest in or conceptualization of momentary forgetting. In the data that I have presented using a variety of comparisons, I reported that no significant differences were found. Spence believes that other as-yet-undetermined differences may still exist.

3. The same negative results apply to his third suggestion. Analyses have been made to try to trace the therapist's behavior as an unwitting stimulus for the patient's momentary forgetting behavior. Certainly the therapist's behavior could, in theory, involve a stimulation of momentary forgetting. But so far we do not see any signs of instigations to forgetting that are immediately

prior to it. What we do see is that often the patient's momentary forgetting occurs within an extended period of the patient's speech rather than immediately following what the therapist said. Furthermore, we have shown that within the period of the patient's speech, the higher the rate of cognitive disturbance the less recovery of the forgotten memory (Luborsky, Sackheim, and Christoph 1979). One way to make sense of this observation is that it is the meaning to the patient of the about-to-be-presented content that is generating the high rate of cognitive disturbance and is also involved in the forgetting and the difficulty of recovering the lost thought subsequently. In fact, a review of these transcripts and a relistening to the tapes show that either the therapist said nothing when the forgetting was reported or that the therapist may after a while have asked what was forgotten. Nothing more. Neither Luborsky nor the other therapists made comments about the content of the forgetting or why it appeared or when it appeared. The patient reported it, and either nothing was said by the therapist or occasionally a nondirective question was asked when it was unclear what was forgotten. In essence, this kind of examination failed to find any specific actions provided by the therapist that might have triggered the forgetting or the recovery or the shape of the recollection.

4. Spence's suggestions have resulted in a considerable review of some very important issues. However, not much new has been unearthed in these areas. But the re-search on one suggestion is still being continued. Spence's suggestion takes up the observation of Luborsky (1967) that the recovered memories tend to be more concrete than abstract. His suggestion is to try a classification of pictorial versus nonpictorial or verbal content. It may be that the recoveries expressed in the pictorial content are of a different kind or amount than in the nonpictorial content.

As a whole, Spence's discussion does not really spend much time with the attempt to understand the lawfulness of the findings that have been reported about momentary forgetting. I wish more of his discussion had done that, especially for these findings: the considerable consistency of recurrence of the content and context is each of the momentary forgettings for each patient (for example, Ms. A's expectation or fear of rejection by the therapist), the momentary forgettings' content in relationship to the patient's independently established core conflictual-relationship theme, the buildup of cognitive disturbance before the momentary forgetting, and the relation of the level of cognitive disturbance to the ultimate recovery of the forgetting. Instead, his "alternative formulation" turns out to be a general warning: "Whoa, don't speculate about motivated forgetting until you are sure you have a data foundation established." His concern has been with the necessity to answer basic questions about the unreliability of testimony because momentary forgetting could be a product of therapist behavior or of the patient's unreliable productions. It has been and can be a support to this research on momentary forgetting to deal with these speculative possibilities.

References

Luborsky, L. 1967. Momentary forgetting during psychotherapy and psychoanalysis: A theory and research method. In R. R. Holt, ed., *Motives and Thought: Psychoanalytic Essays In Honor of David Rapaport*. New York: International Universities Press. Also in *Psychological Issues* 5, no. 2–3, monograph 18/19.

Luborsky, L., H. Sackeim, and P. Christoph. 1979. The state conducive to momentary forgetting. In J. Kihlstrom and F. Evans, eds., *Functional Disorders of Memory*. Hillsdale, N.J.: Erlbaum.

13 Momentary Forgetting as a "Resetting" of a Conscious Global Workspace Due to Competition between Incompatible Contexts

Bernard J. Baars, Ph. D.

Professor Luborsky has done an admirable job of taking the fathomless complexity of the psychoanalytic interview, abstracting a simple, repetitive, and observable phenomenon from it, and relating that to the fundamental workings of the transference. As a cognitive psychologist I am presumed to know something about forgetting, momentary and otherwise. I shall start with one of my favorite passages from William James describing the state of momentary forgetting; this will have several important theoretical implications. Next, I will sketch a theoretical framework that I have been developing since 1978, which unifies in a sensible way a very large number of empirical properties of conscious and unconscious processes: the "global workspace theory of consciousness" (Baars 1983, 1986a, 1986b, 1986c, 1987a, 1987b, forthcoming.) I will briefly show how a global workspace (GW) theory can represent the "dynamic" as well as the "cognitive unconscious" and will refer to ways in which the theory is hospitable to issues raised by several other workshop participants, including Luborsky, Singer, Marcel, Spence, Shevrin, Jackendoff, Erdelyi, and Spiegel.

Finally, I will return to James's ideas about momentary forgetting, attempt to model them in terms of the global workspace theory, and show one way to think about the very interesting phenomena uncovered by Luborsky and his co-workers. My main purpose is to demonstrate how the global workspace theory can comfortably accommodate most of the good ideas we have about conscious and unconscious processes.

William James on Momentary Forgetting

In 1890 William James observed the state of attempting to recall a forgotten word and asked whether such a state is truly conscious or not:

Suppose we try to recall a forgotten name. The state of our consciousness is peculiar. There is a gap therein: but no mere gap. It is a gap that is intensely active. A sort of a wraith of the name is in it, beckoning us in a given direction, making us at moments tingle with the sense of our closeness, and then letting us sink back without the longed-for term. If wrong names are proposed to us, this singularly definite gap acts immediately so as to negate them. They do not fit into its mould. (James [1890] 1981, 1983)

Clearly something is going on. We are conscious of some sort of definite state; if someone suggests the wrong word to us, we know immediately that it is the wrong word. We also immediately recognize the right word when it comes to mind. In modern terms, we can successfully recognize matches and mismatches of the state of looking for a forgotten word—and the ability to accurately detect matches and mismatches implies that this state involves a *representation* of the words that come to stand for it. Since words vary along many dimensions, it must be a complex representational state, much like a mental image or a percept.

Further, this "tip-of-the-tongue" (TOT) state resembles a mental image or a percept, because having it excludes other conscious contents. We cannot search for a forgotten word and at the same time contemplate a picture or think of yesterday's breakfast or do anything else that involves conscious experience or mental effort. The TOT state competes for central limited capacity.

In one respect the TOT state differs from mental images, feelings, inner speech, and perceptual experiences. All these conscious events have experienced qualitative properties—qualities like size, color, warmth, or location. The TOT state, however, does not have experienced qualities (see Natsoulas 1982). Two different TOT states are not experienced as having different semantic properties, syntactic roles, connotations, or other abstract properties that characterize different words. In some ways, therefore, the TOT state is like other conscious states such as percepts and images; in other ways, it is not like these conscious experiences at all.

The same may be said whenever we intend to speak a thought that is not yet clothed in words; as James ([1890] 1981, 1983) described it:

And has the reader never asked himself what kind of a mental fact is his intention of saying a thing before he has said it? It is an entirely definite intention, distinct from all other intentions, an absolutely distinct state of consciousness, therefore; and yet how much of it consists of definite sensorial images, either of words or things? Hardly anything! Linger, and the words and things come into the mind; the anticipatory intention, the divination is there no more. But as the words that replace it arrive, it welcomes them successively and calls them right if they agree with it, it rejects them and calls them wrong if they do not. It has therefore a nature of its own of the most positive sort, and yet what can we say about it without using words that belong to the later mental facts that replace it? The intention to-say-so-and-so is the only name it can receive.

James suggests that perhaps one-third of our psychic life consists of states like this; further, he seems to say that this state itself triggers retrieval processes that produce the words that will clothe the intention. In other words, the TOT state is active; it initiates a conscious display of a series of candidate words, and "it welcomes them . . . and calls them right if they agree with it, it rejects them and calls them wrong if they do not."

In modern terms we can summarize the theoretical claims made by James about the state of momentary forgetting as follows.

1. The TOT state involves a complex representation of the missing word. (As shown by the fact that it accurately matches and mismatches candidate words.)

2. The TOT state competes for central limited capacity, like other conscious states. (Witness the fact that the TOT state excludes other conscious events.)

3. It helps trigger word retrieval processes, so that candidate words come to consciousness as long as the TOT state dominates our limited capacity.

4. The complex representation of the desired word serves to evaluate each conscious candidate word to see if it will match its own representation, and the TOT state only stops dominating our central limited capacity when the right word is found.

5. Yet, in spite of all these properties, the TOT state does not have experiential qualities like color, warmth, flavor, location, and intensity. It is therefore radically different from other conscious experiences like mental images, feelings, inner speech, and percepts. Nevertheless, James suggests that states like this occupy perhaps a third of our mental lives.

Given these theoretical implications, let me sketch out a way in which the global workspace theory can help to model the TOT state, its antecedents, and its consequences.

The Global Workspace Theory

The Global Workspace Theory suggests a certain overall system architecture for the nervous system (Baars 1983, 1986abc, forthcoming-b). First, it suggests (along with a growing number of neuroscientists and psychologists) that the nervous system is largely a collection of highly efficient, specialized systems, which often operate independently from each other as well as from centralized control. These are known technically as "parallel distributed processors" (PDPs); such systems are currently the focus of much interest in cognitive science (cf. Rummelhart, McClelland, and the PDP Group 1986). PDPs have interesting properties and also some drawbacks. In particular, they are very good at solving complex, routine problems. If a set of PDPs is given a new problem that it cannot solve, its component specialists must communicate with each other to try to solve it cooperatively. (This is often called cooperative computation.) In order to cooperate in a new way with each other, these independent specialists need some central information exchange, some small memory that may be accessed by any system that needs to communicate with others, and whose contents are made available to the other systems. This central information exchange is called a global workspace. Figure 13.1 shows a diagram of a parallel distributed system equipped with a global workspace.

This system operates very much like a roomful of human experts who work together to solve a problem that no single expert can solve alone. Their meeting room is equipped with a blackboard that everyone can see, but upon which only one expert can write at any single time. That is to say, there is competition for access to the blackboard (the global workspace), and any message written on the blackboard is broadcast globally so that it becomes available to all experts able to understand it. A group of experts may cooperate with each other to gain access to the blackboard; the more experts decide to cooperate to gain access, the more likely they are to compete successfully with other expert coalitions that also attempt to write on the blackboard.

This system architecture has been used fairly widely in the field of artificial intelligence (Reddy and Newell 1974; Erman and Lesser 1975), especially in cases where there is no single known algorithm for solving a given kind of problem. It has clear advantages and disadvantages (Baars 1983). Baars explores the claim that conscious processes require three properties: they must be globally distributed, internally consistent, and informative, in

Competing Input Systems

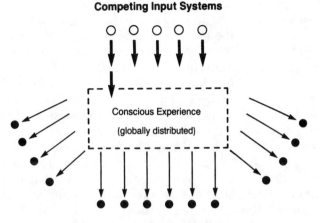

Specialized Distributed Processors

FIGURE 13.1 A first approximation Global Worksapce model, showing the role of conscious limited-capacity mechanisms.

The assumption is that the nervous system can be treated as a collection of specialized unconscious processors, including perceptual analyzers, output systems, action schemata, syntax systems, planning and control systems, etc. In general, these specialists are highly efficient in their own domains, but not outside of them. The system is fundamentally decentralized or "distributed." Interaction, coordination, and control of the unconscious specialists requires a central information exchange, a "global workspace." Input specialists can cooperate and compete for access to the workspace; once there, the message is broadcast to the system as a whole.

the sense that they trigger widespread adaptation in the nervous system. If any of these properties fail, the process will not be conscious (see especially Baars forthcoming-b).

One may think of the Global Workspace Theory as a "publicity metaphor" for consciousness. That is, the theory suggests that consciousness is the publicity organ of the brain. Publicity—systemwide broadcasting of some particular message—in parallel distributed systems has advantages and disadvantages similar to those of publicity in society. One disadvantage is that it is expensive to make information available to all parts of society. Publicity may also interfere with local functions or arouse contradictory tendencies. There are advantages, too: publicity may help activate the solution to a problem stemming from an unpredictable source. In the case of novel problems, this is especially important. (This is, of course, why widespread publicity is so important for scientific progress—precisely because the course of scientific research is inherently unpredictable.)

One of the inevitable drawbacks of a global workspace is that
it imposes a bottleneck on global processes, since only one message can dominate the global workspace at any one time. From
a psychological point of view, however, this is very realistic.
Conscious processes are indeed serial, one-at-a-time processes.
They are slow and inefficient compared to unconscious specialized processes like syntactic parsing, visual analysis, and motor
control. If we only considered conscious processes, we would
scarcely suspect that the cerebral cortex alone has some 500 bil-
lion neurons, that each of these neurons fires on the average of
40 times per second, up to 1000 times, that each neuron has about
10,000 dendritic synapses with other neurons, and that the system
is so interconnected that one can go from any neuron to any other
neuron in the nervous system in less than 7 synapses! This is a
very big, complex, parallel system. But the conscious component
of it is comparatively slow, simple, and unified. I am not aware
of any other theory that gives a functional account of the well-
known limited capacity processes that emerge out of such an
immense parallel system.

Shallice (1976) and Norman and Shallice (1980) discuss the
way in which action control systems can gain access to central
limited capacity by competing with other action systems. Their
work has a great deal in common with my own, but it does not
give a functional reason why it is important for action systems to
dominate central limited capacity. The global workspace theory
suggests an answer: if some goal system needs to recruit other
systems to carry out its goal, it must be able to dominate the
global workspace long enough for the appropriate effector systems to organize to carry out the goal. (This is indeed very similar
to William James's "ideomotor theory" of voluntary control of
action, which suggests that one is conscious momentarily of a
goal before unconscious effector systems begin to carry out the
goal [Baars 1987b, forthcoming]).

From a psychodynamic point of view, the idea that different
goal systems must compete for access to consciousness is also
important. It creates a natural way in which we can speak of
conflicts between unconscious emotions and motivations, which
always involve goals. Competition for access to consciousness is
one way in which dominant systems can also drive out or "re-
press" disturbing goals.

Figure 13.2 shows how two goal systems may compete for
access to the conscious global workspace. Figure 13.3 indicates
that we tend to be primarily conscious of goals in the middle

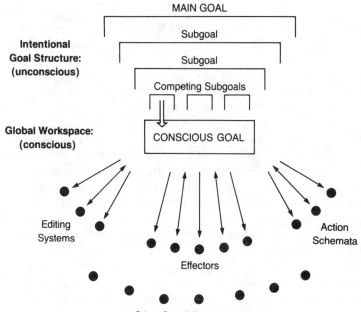

FIGURE 13.2 Intentions can be viewed as multileveled goal structures that are not conscious in detail, but which do compete against incompatible intentions and conscious contents for access to the global workspace.

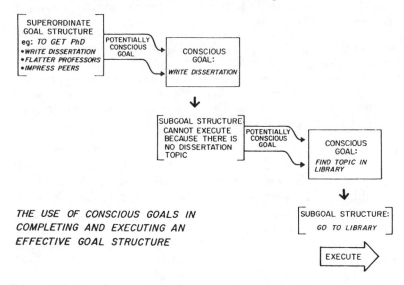

FIGURE 13.3 Use of conscious goals in completing and executing an effective goal structure.

level of a complex hierarchical goal structure; the highest-level goals tend to be presupposed, while the lowest-level goals tend to be automatic (Baars 1987b, forthcoming; Baars and Mattson 1981).

It is surprisingly easy to represent the dynamic unconscious in a global workspace model of consciousness. Indeed, the "publicity metaphor" may be thought of as the flip-side of Freud's "censorship metaphor." How does the global workspace theory relate to dynamic notions of unconscious and preconscious processes? First, it is important to consider that for all his genius, Freud does not provide us with a theory of unconscious (or conscious) processes. Rather, he makes a number of persuasive arguments in favor of *motivated* unconscious processes, which presuppose and make use of the existence of conscious and unconscious events. A complete psychological theory would have to account for unconscious processes due to, say, distraction, forgetting, automatization, and habituation and also incorporate the dynamic unconscious, which presumably *makes use of* these cognitive processes to hide unpleasant thoughts from executive systems.

So how do the cognitive and dynamic unconscious relate? One of Freud's metaphors for repression, the metaphor of newspaper censorship, suggests an answer. In the *Interpretation of Dreams* Freud drew an analogy between repression and censorship of the news:

The political writer who has unpleasant truths to tell to those in power . . . stands in fear of the censorship; he therefore moderates and disguises the expression of his opinion. The stricter the domination of the censorship, the more thorough becomes the disguise, and, often enough, the more ingenious the means employed to put the reader on the track of the actual meaning. ([1900] 1938:223)

Censoring the news in society limits the distribution of disturbing information; it becomes "dissociated," confined to only a few people. Making things unconscious also means limiting its distribution. Conversely, the Global Workspace Theory (GW) suggests that making things conscious may be analogous to making information public in society—consciousness is the publicity organ of the nervous system. This suggests that the "publicity metaphor of consciousness" is indeed the flip-side of the "censorship metaphor of the dynamic unconscious."

Making disturbing information public in society may lead to unforeseen consequences, which are out of the control of any government. Of course, one of the major functions of a global workspace is to make information available to processors whose actions cannot be foreseen (this is, after all, how a global workspace helps to deal with novel information). Thus the function of repression follows naturally from the characteristics of a global workspace: it is to confine the disturbing information to some small, dissociated domain, lest it trigger unexpected and uncontrollable consequences in the rest of the system.

A psychodynamic theoretician might protest that we fail in this model to make a distinction between *unconscious* and *preconscious* processes, that is, between recallable and hard-to-recall material. It seems to me that this distinction was never hard-and-fast for Freud. Material that is unconscious today may be recalled, with effort and against resistance, by next week, and then it will be preconscious rather than unconscious. So I would favor expressing the preconscious-unconscious distinction in terms of "difficulty of retrieval"—that is, as a continuous variable rather than a sharp delineation between two types of unconsciousness. As Erdelyi (1985) has shown so persuasively, even difficult-to-retrieve information can often be retrieved with enough time and effort. Once it is retrieved, it can be recalled again with much less effort: so the "unconscious" becomes "preconscious," and presumably vice versa.

Note well that the global workspace theory was not developed primarily with an eye to psychodynamic concepts, nor were the neurophysiological facts discussed in Baars (1987a, forthcoming) considered at first. The global workspace notion was initially designed to deal with the psychological evidence summarized in Baars (1983, forthcoming). That the theory naturally seems to incorporate psychodynamic and neurophysiological findings provides another hint that we may be on the right path.

SURPRISE AS A "RESETTING" OF CONSCIOUS CONTENTS

Surprise often seems to be accompanied by a moment of conscious "emptiness," somewhat similar to the TOT experience discussed in the quote by James presented earlier. It is a function of novelty, and novelty is associated with conscious functioning in numerous ways. Several psychologists have suggested that surprise may have the function of resetting consciousness (e.g., Underwood 1982; Grossberg 1982). It is a plausible idea, which can be readily interpreted in terms of the GW theory.

In a sense, every time a new conscious content comes up, the global workspace is "reset." In other words, it allows conscious processes to start anew, uninhibited by previous contents. Most of the time the bulk of contextual constraints remain the same (Fig. 13.2), so that recovering from a momentary "resetting" of conscious content will be easy and quick. The previous conscious experience is probably not lost completely in this case. Thus, if we are pursuing a Ph.D. and we are surprised to find that a book that should be in the library is not there, most of our contextual assumptions and goals remain constant; our topmost goal is still the same, and it is easy to adapt to the surprising circumstance. On the other hand, if we suddenly lose interest in gaining a Ph.D., this change of context requires major changes throughout the system. Presumably we get serious "blank-outs" of conscious processing only when some rather fundamental context is violated.

THE ROLE OF CONTEXTS

In global workspace theory a *context* is simply *a representation that shapes a conscious experience without itself being conscious.* It is closely related to the idea of "set" and "adaptation level" in perception (Bruner 1957; Helson 1947; Allport 1955) and to various proposals for knowledge structures and "frames" in cognitive psychology and artificial intelligence (Minsky 1975; Schank and Abelson 1977; Clark and Carlson 1981). Contexts are responsible for fixedness in problem solving, an extremely common phenomenon, which may indeed be defined as a case where we are controlled by unconscious assumptions that make it impossible for us to see the answer to a problem. They are also similar to ideas like expectancy, priming, and preparedness in all mental activities. But a context is not just any knowledge representation, because some aspect of a knowledge structure might be at some specific time either conscious or unconscious— and "context" is unconscious by definition. Thus in the Global Workspace Theory the word "context" is always used relationally: it is an unconscious representation that is acting to influence another, conscious representation. (Figure 13.4 shows our convention for diagramming active contexts as rectangular "frames" embracing the global workspace and its conscious contents.)

When we have some conscious content—a percept, an image, or even an abstract concept—it is always influenced by numerous contextual representations that are currently not conscious. It is well established, for instance, that:

1. Our experience of a visual scene is controlled by unconscious assumptions about space, about the direction and intensity of the incoming light, and about the typical size of objects (e.g., Rock 1983).

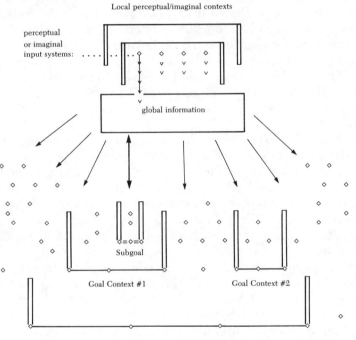

FIGURE 13.4 Conscious contents bounded by unconscious local and global contexts.

Global contexts from committed processors impose constraints on possible actions and representations. Goal contexts constrain conscious plans for action, and the model permits competition between different goal contexts. Competition between goals can represent the psychodynamic notion of unconscious imotional conflict.

2. Our understanding of a conversation is profoundly influenced by what we assume to be the "given" versus the "new" information at any point in the discourse (Clark and Carlson 1981). In most cases, given information is unconscious while new information is conscious.

3. Similarly, we can use many unconscious contexts to help resolve the numerous ambiguities contained in every sentence we read or hear. In essence all words in English are ambiguous and can only be understood relative to a context involving syntax, semantics, morphology, phonology, the acoustic environment, discourse relations, shared particulars between speaker and listener, knowledge of the domain of reference, knowledge of the intentions of the speaker, conversational conventions, etc.

4. Our experience of social relationships is deeply dependent on what sociologists have called "primary frameworks or schemata of interpretation" (Goffman 1974), frameworks of which we are typically unaware at the time when we operate under their influence.

5. Scientific discussion of any topic provides another case in which our experience is profoundly influenced by its presuppositions, for better and for worse, as the history of psychology so amply illustrates. Such unconscious presuppositions may never become conscious—but even if they are discussed consciously at some point, they will continue to influence subsequent work long after fading from the daily conscious experience of working scientists.

In sum, conscious experience and consciously accessed knowledge are continually shaped and molded by contexts that are not conscious at the time when they do this shaping and molding.

Bear in mind that we cannot experience contexts directly, so that they are tricky to think about. If we look at work in cognitive science on the knowledge structures involved in everyday life, we find that we can make aspects of this contextual everyday knowledge conscious (e.g., Schank and Abelson 1977). Yet even as we make one aspect of context conscious, our experience of it is shaped and bounded by other, unconscious knowledge structures. We can never really "undo" context. (We become spontaneously conscious of contextual assumptions when they are severely violated. This often occurs among anthropologists studying a different culture who suddenly realize their own cultural presuppositions, which were unconscious before.)

INTERPRETATION IN PSYCHOTHERAPY

Consider the problem raised by Erdelyi in his recent book, *Psychoanalysis: Freud's Cognitive Psychology* (1985). He points out that the process of analytic interpretation is highly context-dependent. Thus, interpreting quite obvious sexual symbolism in liquor advertising is difficult to do explicitly, because the bottle growing out of the model's groin could be interpreted, well, as just a bottle, in only a slightly different context. And if the people who look at the ad are primarily affected unconsciously, they can give us no reliable report of their own reaction.

If the symbolism is truly sexual, it should prime the interpretation of subsequent ambiguous stimuli, just as any notable conscious stimulus primes the interpretation of subsequent processes (Baars 1983, forthcoming). That is, the sexual symbol should create a context for the processing of subsequent experience. Therefore, to decide whether the ad is interpreted, even unconsciously, as a sexual symbol, we need only follow it with an ambiguously sexual sentence with a known probability of the sexual interpretation. That probability should shift in the direction of the sexual interpretation if the ad is truly sexual.

The same method can presumably apply to the analysis of a neurotic symptom, the interpretation of which is also heavily context-dependent (viz., Chapter 10 in this volume and Erdelyi 1985). With this reasoning, indeed, one should be able to design individualized diagnostic tests for patients with highly idiosyncratic symptoms.

Conscious contents may trigger a new, dominant context; conversely, contexts can trigger new conscious contents. We will look at each of these complementary claims.

CONSCIOUS CONTENTS AS TRIGGERS OF NEW CONTEXTS

If someone yells "Fire!" this conscious stimulus is not just a momentary event: it will structure a number of future conscious events, evaluations of credibility, plans for action, and so forth. That is, it tends to trigger a set of contexts that will constrain future conscious events.

Beginning a new topic is a good example of accessing a context. Asking a question creates a set of constraints on subsequent conscious events: for at least a few seconds, conscious thoughts are constrained to be responsive to the question. This is indeed how

Brown and McNeill (1966) elicited TOT experiences experimentally, by asking subjects to find a fairly rare word corresponding to a definition. Examples of conscious contents triggering contextual constraints on later conscious experiences are extremely common (see Bransford 1979 for numerous examples).

Conscious events that are experienced as incomplete seem to set up very active contexts. They may vary from incomplete sentences to the conscious accumulation of constraints on the solution of a mathematical or scientific problem. In each case, the conscious experience appears to establish a set of unconscious constraints on future conscious events. This "Zeigarnik effect" was demonstrated directly by Klos and Singer (1981) in the case of emotional conflict in adolescents. For adolescents with persistent parental conflicts, a dramatic reenactment of an unresolved conflict situation caused more conflict-related spontaneous thoughts afterwards than did dramatic reenactments of resolved conflict situations (Singer 1984).

CONTEXTS AS TRIGGERS OF NEW CONSCIOUS CONTENTS

The TOT state may be viewed as "a context looking for the right content." We have already analyzed one example in which a dominant context triggers new conscious contents. The "Aha!" experience in problem solving is another example, as is the conscious "popping-up" of answers to questions, the emergence of thoughts in free association, and the like. Examples abound in all parts of psychological study.

Since dominant contexts shape subsequent conscious experiences, we can easily access the operation of a context by means of ambiguous stimuli, which are consciously experienced in only one way although there is in fact an unconscious choice-point in the input processing (Baars 1986b, forthcoming). Thus we would expect a depressed state of mind—a context that controls many conscious contents—to "prime" only one interpretation of ambiguities like the following:

(1)   The entire office of the President is a mess. (i.e., the Presidency? Or the room?)

(2)   She could not bear children after the accident. (i.e., she could not give birth? Or she did not like children any more?)

(3)   My ex-wife hates spinach as much as me. (i.e., we both hate spinach? Or she hates me?)

Given specified probability of a sad interpretation of such sentences in a normal population, we would expect to find even higher probability in a depressed population—again, because each sentence presents a person with an unconscious choice that she or he is likely to decide according to any dominant state of mind (context). This is of course the rationale behind classical projective tests, but a technique like this is immune to the usual criticisms of projective techniques: the interpretation of the stimulus is very straightforward, it has face and content validity, and it is very easy to quantify the differences between a normal and a pathological population.

I have argued elsewhere (Baars 1980, 1986b, forthcoming) that slips of the tongue also represent unconscious choice-points in information processing. Our work with experimentally elicited slips shows that, with the proper choice of materials, we can elicit essentially any kind of meaningful slip we want to, and this makes it possible to show that slips, too, are affected by dominant context (Motley and Baars 1979). Thus, aspects of speech production and speech perception seem highly constrained by context.

CONTEXTS AND THE STREAM OF CONSCIOUSNESS

The stream of consciousness can be viewed as a complex, multi-thematic dialectic between conscious events and their contexts, which are triggered and shaped by conscious events, and which, in their turn, shape subsequent events in the stream. Figure 13.5 models this process in terms of the GW theory.

The superficial purposelessness of much of the stream may in fact be quite purposeful, as suggested by Singer's work (e.g., 1984). As he has written:

"Current concerns"—unfulfilled intentions, hierarchically organized in terms of closeness to fulfillment or personal value . . .—make up a goodly share of the conscious content derived from thought sampling. Our basic "rules" for admission of material to consciousness seem to involve a screening strategy that is especially sensitive to our current concerns even in dichotic listening experiments or during sleep. . . . As we gain more information of this kind, it is my personal guess that we will find that a great deal of respondent (spontaneous) or playful fantasy has long-term planning, decision-making, and self-schema formation functions (p. 25).

Indeed, personality patterns can be viewed as a circular pattern of conscious contents triggering certain contextual frames,

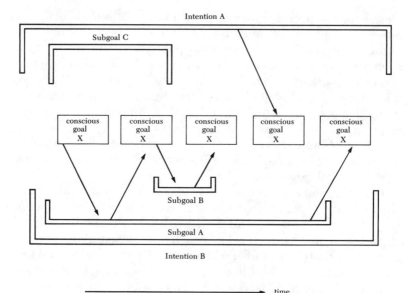

FIGURE 13.5 William James's stream of consciousness can be modeled as a flow of conscious contents that act to trigger unconscious intentions which in turn result in conscious thoughts or images farther downstream. Nested frames represent goal-subgoal relationships, while frames at the same level, as in fig. 13.4, compete against each other. As Freud suggested, any single conscious content is multiply determined by many levels of the goal hierarchy.

which trigger new conscious contents, which then trigger more of the contextual frames, and so on. This is one way to think about Luborsky's work on "core conflictual-relationship themes" (1977) and the work of Horowitz et al. (1984) on the interaction between personality and effective therapeutic strategies.

Compatible contexts can cooperatively constrain conscious contents. Although we started discussing contexts that compete for access to consciousness, it is clear that many of our contexts must be compatible. In Figure 13.5, nesting of contexts is intended to show symbolically that the contexts involved are compatible and, indeed, may be mutually supportive, while competing contexts are shown operating at the same "level."

Some direct evidence for the operation of compatible contexts developed from our experimental studies of unconscious *double entendres* (Motley, Camden, and Baars 1982). Double entendres, are, of course, ambiguous words and phrases that are compatible with two contexts of interpretation. Thus, if male subjects are presented with a sentence-completion task (context A), and if there is an attractive female confederate in the same room (context B), the number of unconscious double entendres (starred items [*]) will rise considerably, as follows:

1. With the telescope, the details of the distant landscape were easy to: (a) see clearly (b) determine (c) make out* (d) pick out
2 The lid won't stay on regardless of how much I . . . (a) turn it (b) screw it* (c) twist it (d) tighten it.

Incompatible contexts will tend to compete for the ability to constrain conscious contents. Perhaps the best example of contexts competing for access to consciousness would come from conflicts between different goals. In fact, in the following structure we will see how the pattern of free association in one of Luborsky's subjects can be modeled as competition for access to consciousness between two different goal contexts.

Application to Luborsky's Findings

Now we have the theoretical tools needed to examine the situation studied by Luborsky and his co-workers and to relate this work to a vast number of other studies in psychology and neurophysiology. The situation of patients in psychotherapy, especially classical psychoanalysis, can be modeled as constrained by two kinds of overarching contexts (Figure 13.6): context A: the "relationship context" vis-à-vis the therapist (who becomes the object of transference); and context B: the manifest "topical context," having to do with the overt tasks of therapy (discussing problems, engaging in "proper" free association, etc.).

From the client's point of view, we might say:

1. Context A (relationships theme): I want the therapist to love me and take care of me; since he will not do so, I often feel angry at him (etc.).

2. Context B (compatible therapy theme): I want to behave like an adult; but I can also enjoy absolute positive regard in therapy, as long as I am a "good patient," that is, attempt to free associate persuasively, make some progress, etc.

Much of the time, these two contexts are in fact compatible, but Luborsky's findings suggest that just prior to an instance of momentary forgetting, competition occurs between contexts A and B. They tend to become inconsistent, presumably, toward

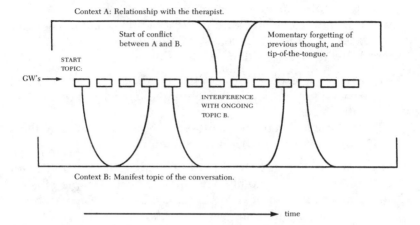

Context A: Relationship with the therapist.

FIGURE 13.6 Hypothetical interaction between two contexts just before an instance of momentary forgetting.

Patient D, reported in Luborsky, Sackeim, and Christoph (1978). Context A is the overarching relationship theme that is developing over time in therapy, including classical infantile transference themes, desire to be loved and cared for by the therapist, anger, fear of anger, fear of rejection and abandonment, and sexual feelings. This context is often compatible with context B (the overt task context of the therapy, including normal adult conversation and "being a good patient"). To the extent that the patient satisfies the goals of context B, he often also satisfies the goals of context A—he keeps the attention of the therapist, all of his thoughts are tolerated, he can freely express relationship fantasies, and so on. However, sometimes A and B are at odds—perhaps when the patient has the impulse to express a very peremptory desire. At that point context A may disrupt the conscious flow controlled by B, leading to a case of momentary forgetting.

the end of therapy, when context A, the relationship goal context, is threatened with the possibility that it will not be satisfied in the near future. It therefore competes with context B, the "act like a good, adult patient" context. Figure 13.6 models the following situation of patient "D" whose words before and after momentary forgetting are cited by Luborsky, Sackeim, and Christoph (1979: 348)

Discussion of a problem (context B):
    ... boy in high school—was brighter than I and it always used to bother me that my mother compared us—and now when I feel in this group of students that I am—the brightest [*hesitates*] that I am number one, it bothers me [*hesitates*].

Intrusion of context A, the relationship context:
    Maude [?] is the name of a homosexual magazine [*pause of 7.5 seconds*].

Intrusion of self-monitoring context (B):
> Just had a thought [*wheezes*] you know, I've got to preface things by "I've just had a thought"—I'm picking it up myself—that this is a way of leading into—something which is embarrassing for me. [*hesitates*] I don't know why it sort of displaces the thought but it does. . . .

Return to context A, the relationship context:
> But I wanted to be in bed with you. Crikes.

[*Therapist makes remark about patient's resistance to free association.*]

Expressions of relationship theme alternating rapidly with self-monitoring remarks (A and B):
> Yes, that's what I was trying to say. [*pause, 8.5 secs.*] I'm still not free associating well. [*pause, 3 secs.*] That gives me some element of control. [*pause, 3 secs.*] I was thinking—the other day that [*hesitates*] when I—the day that I—I walked out of here I felt so shitty that I hadn't performed or that—nothing had come out—[*hesitates; slight wheeze?*] God I—everything's coming out in anal terms. . . .

Expression of relationship theme, context A:
> And I felt [*pause, 2 secs.*] that you just—eh—just—hated me [*pause, 4 secs.*]

Momentary forgetting, expressing tip-of-the-tongue feeling:
> [*bangs table*] I forgot what I was going to say. I just forgot what I was going to say again.

Finally, a clear expression of the relationship theme (context A):
> I began having—resentment towards you . . . I had the feeling [that] . . . I could almost kill you with my words . . . and I don't want to do that to you . . . It's much harder for me to dislike you [*hesitates*] than anybody . . . 'Cause you're such a decent guy. . . .

TESTING THE HYPOTHESES

Theory must be anchored to empirical operations. Each of the constructs I have mentioned so far—context, conscious experience, limited capacity processes, and the like—can be tied to fairly adequate operational definitions. Let me suggest a few more possibilities, especially those relevant to Luborsky's chapter (chapter 10 of this volume).

MONITORING UNCONSCIOUS CHOICE-POINTS

We have already mentioned that, since dominant contexts determine what will become conscious, ambiguous sentences make natural test stimuli for assessing a dominant contextual state of mind (see above). Similarly, experimentally elicited, predictable slips of the tongue have been used for this purpose and appear to be quite effective (Baars 1986b, forthcoming-b).

QUASI-EXPERIMENTAL INTERVENTION IN THE THERAPEUTIC DIALOGUE

Momentary forgetting could be induced quite easily in a therapy situation by overloading the patient's immediate memory. For example, one might ask the patient "to say three sentences about the three most important things on his mind"—some reasonable percentage of the time, patients will certainly forget the third idea by the time they have expressed the first two.

However, this would not quite tap the variables Luborsky and his co-workers are primarily interested in—after all, momentary forgetting is only a way of accessing motivational variables for these researchers. However, being able to get a high rate of TOTs would be a step in the right direction: if that were possible, one might systematically vary the conditions in which subjects were asked to do the task. For instance, independent observers of therapy might be able to agree on those times when the relationship theme became especially prominent. If those times could be reliably spotted, the patient could be asked to do the three-sentence task mentioned above at those times, compared to other times when the relationship theme was latent. One could make predictions both about the likelihood of momentary forgetting in those two conditions and about the likely topics to be expressed in the three-sentence task.

SUPPRESSED EMOTIONS APPEAR TO INVOLVE DISJUNCTIONS BETWEEN VOLUNTARY AND INVOLUNTARY EXPRESSIONS OF THE EMOTION

In several studies, we have noticed that denied emotions like anger, sexuality, and depression appear to be expressed involuntarily through experimentally elicited slips and other means, more often than voluntarily expressed emotions (Baars 1986b, forthcoming). This kind of disjunction between voluntarily and involuntarily expressed emotion should appear in Luborsky's subjects at times of conflict between different contexts. Since this work is entirely under experimental control, it would be fairly simple to test this hypothesis with a particular patient who displays a consistent pattern over time.

Summary

I have tried in this paper to view the work of Luborsky and his colleagues on momentary forgetting in analytic psychotherapy from a cognitive point of view. In particular, I have tried to show how a Global Workspace Theory of consciousness can handle a great deal of cognitive and neurophysiological evidence and can incorporate Luborsky's findings in a very natural way.

Starting from a consideration of William James's description of the tip-of-the-tongue (TOT) state, I noted that there are complex representational states that dominate our central limited capacity but which are not conscious in the sense that there are conscious qualities (Natsoulas 1982); these states are experienced differently from percepts, images, and the like. One can view such states as "contexts looking for conscious contents." Contexts can be defined as representations that shape and evolve conscious experiences, but which are not themselves conscious when they exercise this influence.

All of these notions can be modeled in terms of a Global Workspace Theory of consciousness, which views the nervous system largely as a collection of unconscious specialized processors that can interact in novel ways through a central information exchange. This system architecture has been used in artificial intelligence, and parallel systems in general are currently the subject of intensive study in cognitive science. Many neuroscientists have also viewed large parts of the nervous system in this way, as have an increasing number of cognitive psychologists. Such a system can also interpret psychodynamic ideas in a very natural way. Further, one can treat "momentary forgetting" as a "resetting" of a global workspace due to competition between incompatible contexts, followed by a TOT, which is a dominant context looking for conscious contents to express it in words.

We can interpret Luborsky's findings within this theoretical framework. When one patient's words are analyzed, just before and after the experience of momentary forgetting, it appears that contexts that are compatible during most of therapy may begin to compete at certain points resulting in a rapid alternation of topics in the patient's words; this is followed by momentary forgetting, which in turn is followed by a clear expression of the interrupting context. Finally, this approach suggested some ways of testing these notions empirically.

References

Allport, F. 1955. *Theories of Perception and the Concept of Structure.* New York: Wiley.

Anderson, J. 1983. *The Architecture of Cognition.* Cambridge, Mass.: Harvard University Press.

Arbib, M. A. 1980. Perceptual structures and distributed motor control. In V. B. Brooks, *Handbook of Physiology,* vol. 3. Bethesda, Md.: American Psychological Society.

Baars, B. J. 1980. On eliciting predictable speech errors in the laboratory: Methods and results. In V. A. Fromkin, ed., *Errors of Speech and Hearing.* New York: Academic Press.

———. 1983. Conscious contents provide the nervous system with coherent, global information. In R. Davidson, G. Schwartz, and D. Shapiro, eds., *Consciousness and Self-Regulation,* vol. 3. New York: Plenum Press.

———. 1986a. *The Cognitive Revolution in Psychology.* New York: Guilford.

———. 1986b. Can involuntary slips reveal one's state of mind?—with an addendum on the problem of assessing repression. In M. Toglia and T. M. Shlechter, eds., *New Directions in Cognitive Science.* Norwood, N.J.: Ablex.

———. 1986c. What is a theory of consciousness a theory of? Some constraints on theory. *Consciousness, Imagination, and Personality* 1:1–35.

———. 1987a. Biological implications of a global workspace theory of conscious experience. In G. Greenberg and E. Tobach, eds., *Language, Cognition, Consciousness: Integrative Levels.* Englewood, N.J.: Erlbaum.

———. 1987b. What is conscious in the control of action? A modern ideomotor theory of voluntary control. In D. Gorfein and R. R. Hoffmann, eds., *Learning and Memory: The Ebbinghaus Centennial Symposium.* Hillsdale, N.J.: Erlbaum.

———. Forthcoming. *A Cognitive Theory of Consciousness.* London: Cambridge University Press.

Baars, B. J., and Mattson, M. E. 1981. Consciousness and intention: A framework and some evidence. *Cognition and Brain Theory* 4, no. 3:247–63.

Baddeley, A. D. 1976. *The Psychology of Memory.* New York: Basic Books.

Boden, M. 1977. *Artificial Intelligence and Natural Man.* New York: Basic Books.

Bransford, J. D. 1979. *Human Cognition.* Belmont, Calif.: Wadsworth.

Brown, R., and D. McNeill. 1966. The "tip of the tongue" phenomenon. *Journal of Verbal Learning and Verbal Behavior* 5:325–37.

Bruner, J. S. 1957. On perceptual readiness. *Psychological Review* 64:123–52.

Chase, M. M., ed. 1974. *Operant conditioning of brain activity.* Berkeley and Los Angeles: University of California Press.

Clark, H. H., and T. B. Carlson. 1981. Context for comprehension. In J. Long and A. Baddeley, eds., *Attention and Performance,* vol. 9. Hillsdale, N.J.: Erlbaum.

Dixon, N. F. 1971. *Subliminal Perception: The Nature of a Controversy.* London: McGraw-Hill.

Erdelyi, M. 1985. *Psychoanalysis: Freud's Cognitive Psychology.* San Francisco: Freeman.

Erman, L. D., and V. R. Lesser. 1975. A multi-level organization for problem solving using many, diverse, cooperating sources of knowledge. *Proceedings of the Fourth Annual Joint Computer Conference.* Georgia, USSR.

Fodor, J. A. 1983. *The modularity of mind: An essay on faculty psychology.* Cambridge, Mass.: Bradford/MIT Press.

Freud, S. [1900] 1938. The interpretation of dreams. In A. A. Brill, trans. and ed., *The Basic Writings of Sigmund Freud.* New York: Random House.

——. [1901] 1938. The psychopathology of everyday life. In A. A. Brill, trans. and ed., *The Basic Writings of Sigmund Freud.* New York: Random House.

Geschwind, N. 1979. Specializations of the human brain. *Scientific American* 241, no. 3:180–201.

Goffman, E. 1974. *Frame Analysis.* New York: Harper.

Grossberg, S. 1982. *Studies of Mind and Brain.* Boston: Reidel.

Helson, H. 1947. Adaptation-level as a frame of reference for prediction of psychophysical data. *American Journal of Psychology* 60:1–29.

Horowitz, M., et al. 1984. *Personality Styles and Brief Psychotherapy.* New York: Basic Books.

Jackendoff, R. Forthcoming. *Awareness and Understanding.* Cambridge, Mass.: Harvard University Press.

James, W. [1890] 1981, 1983. *The Principles of Psychology.* Cambridge, Mass.: Harvard University Press.

John, E. R. 1976. A model of consciousness. In G. Schwartz and D. Shapiro, eds., *Consciousness and Self-Regulation.* New York: Plenum Press.

Kahneman, D. 1973. *Attention and Effort.* Englewood Cliffs, N.J.: Prentice-Hall.

Klos, D. S., and J. L. Singer. 1981. Determinants of ongoing thought following simulated parental confrontation. *Journal of Personality and Social Psychology* 41:168–77.

Libet, B. 1978. Neuronal vs. subjective timing for a conscious sensory experience. In P. A. Buser and A. Rougeul-Buser, eds., *Cerebral Cor-*

relates of Conscious Experience. INSERM Symposium no. 6. Amsterdam: N. Holland/Elsevier.

Luborsky, L. 1977. Measuring a pervasive psychic structure in psychotherapy: The core conflictual relationship theme. In N. Freedman and S. Grand, eds., *Communicative Structures and Psychic Structures*. New York: Plenum Press.

———. 1984. *Principles of Psychoanalytic Psychotherapy: A Manual for Supportive-Expressive Treatment*. New York: Basic Books.

Luborsky, L. H. Sackeim, and P. Christoph. 1979. The state conducive to momentary forgetting. In J. Kihlstrom and F. Evans, eds., *Functional Disorders of Memory*. N.J.: Erlbaum.

Magoun. H. W. 1963. *The Waking Brain*. 2nd ed. Springfield, Ill.: Thomas.

Mandler, G. A. 1975. *Mind and Emotion*. New York: Wiley.

———. 1983. Consciousness: Its function and construction. Presidential Address to the General Psychology Division of the American Psychological Association.

Marcel, A. J. 1983a. Conscious and unconscious perception: An approach to the relations between phenomenal experience and perceptual processes. *Cognitive·Psychology* 15:238–300.

———. 1983b. Conscious and unconscious perception: Experiments on visual masking and word recognition. *Cognitive Psychology* 15:197–237.

Minsky, M. 1975. A framework for representing knowledge. In M. Winston, ed., *The Psychology of Computer Vision*. Cambridge, Mass.: MIT Press.

Morokoff, P. 1981. Female sexual arousal as a function of individual differences and exposure to erotic stimuli. Ph.D. diss., SUNY at Stony Brook.

Motley, M. T., and B. J. Baars. 1979. Effects of cognitive set upon laboratory-induced verbal (Freudian) slips. *Journal of Speech and Hearing Research* 22:421–32.

Motley, M. T., C. T. Camden, and B. J. Baars. 1979. Personality and situational influences upon verbal slips: A laboratory test of Freudian and prearticulatory editing hypotheses. *Human Communication Research* 5, no. 3:195–202.

———. 1982. Polysemantic lexical access: Evidence from laboratory-induced *doubles-entendres*. *Communication Monographs* 50:193–205.

Mountcastle, V. B. 1978. An organizing principle for cerebral function: The unit module and the distributed system. In G. M. Edelman and V. B. Mountcastle, eds., *The Mindful Brain*. Cambridge, Mass.: MIT Press.

Natsoulas, T. 1982. Dimensions of perceptual awareness. *Behaviorism* 10:85–112.

Newell, A., and H. A. Simon. 1972. *Human Problem Solving*. Englewood Cliffs, N.J.: Prentice-Hall.

Norman, D. A. 1981. *Perspectives on Cognitive Science*. Norwood, N.J.: Ablex.

Norman, D. A., and T. Shallice. 1980. Attention to action: Willed and automatic control of behavior. CHIP Document no. 99. San Diego: University of California, Center for Human Information Processing.

Posner, M. 1982. Cumulative development of attentional theory. *American Psychologist* 37, no. 2:168–79.

Reddy, R., and A. Newell. 1974. Knowledge and its representation in a speech understanding system. In L. W. Gregg, ed., *Knowledge and Cognition*. Potomac, Md.: Erlbaum.

Rock, I. 1983. *The Logic of Perception*. Cambridge, Mass.: Bradford/MIT Press.

Rozin, P. 1976. The evolution of intelligence and access to the cognitive unconscious. In J. Sprague and A. Epstein, eds., *Progress in Psychobiology and Physiological Psychology*. New York: Academic Press.

Rummelhart, D. E., J. L. McClelland, and the PDP Research Group. 1986. *Parallel Distributed Processors: Studies in the Microstructure of Cognition*. Cambridge, Mass.: MIT Press.

Schank, R. R. and R. P. Abelson. 1977. *Scripts, Plans, Goals, and Understanding*. New York: Halsted.

Scheibel, M. C., and A. B. Scheibel. 1967. Anatomical basis of attentional mechanisms in vertebrate brains. In G. C. Quarton, T. Melnechuk, and F. O. Schmitt, eds., *The Neurosciences: A Study Program*. New York: Rockefeller University Press.

Shallice, T. 1976. The dominant action system: An information-processing approach to consciousness. In K. S. Pope and J. L. Singer, eds., *The Stream of Consciousness: Scientific Investigations into the Flow of Experience*. New York: Plenum Press.

Shevrin, H., and S. Dickman. 1980. The psychological unconscious: A necessary assumption for all psychological theory. *American Psychologist* 35, no. 5:421–34.

Singer, J. L. 1984. The private personality. *Personality and Social Psychology Bulletin* 10, no. 1.

Spiegel, D. 1984. Multiple personality as a post-traumatic stress disorder. *Symposium on Multiple Personality: Psychiatric Clinics of North America* 7, no. 1.

Szentagotai, J., and M. A. Arbib. 1975. Conceptual models of neural organization. *Neurosciences Research Bulletin* 12:307–510.

Thatcher, R. W., and E. R. John. 1977. *Foundations of cognitive processes*. Hillsdale, N.J.: Erlbaum.

Underwood, G. 1982. Attention and awareness in cognitive and motor skills. In G. Underwood, ed., *Aspects of consciousness*, vol. 3: *Awareness and Self-Awareness*. New York: Academic Press.

5 Understanding Conscious Experience

The previous section ended with Baars's discussion of consciousness as a special set of representations that might allow a transformation of information across channels for the unconscious processing of information. The unique property of conscious representation would be the availability of the information contained to systems that otherwise might not have access to the meanings. This discussion prepared the way for a reconsideration of just what information might be available by sampling conscious experiences in an empirically based manner. This is done in Chapter 14, where Singer reviews methods and findings for the study of ongoing streams of conscious representations.

The issue of defensive inhibitions of representations is discussed in terms of its stylistic facet, in the concept of repressive personality traits. The emphasis on study of the ongoing stream of consciousness and the reconsideration of schemas as organizers of conscious knowledge leads Singer to describe a program of research that would find out how extensively conflictual issues might be consciously represented but obscured by devaluation and later obscurities of recall.

In Chapter 15, Zajonc discusses Singer's emphasis that conscious representation contains a great deal of present but incompletely integrated self-knowledge. He calls attention to the importance of emotional consciousness through motoric representation. He also reviews much of what has been said about the importance of the currently active schema of self in organizing what memories may be available to formation as current conscious representations.

14 Sampling Ongoing Consciousness and Emotional Experience: Implications for Health

Jerome L. Singer, Ph.D.

Sigmund Freud and William James met in the United States at Clark University in 1909. The brief encounter of the two great pioneers of the scientific study of the flow of human thought processes symbolizes the task that modern students of consciousness now must confront. William James, using introspection, clinical observation (Taylor 1983), and the kind of interpersonal sensitivity that also characterized his brother Henry, described the critical properties of ongoing conscious thought as a basic dimension of human psychology. Sigmund Freud used the characteristics of the thought stream as verbalized in the free associations of his patients to identify—through blockages of verbalizations, diversions in sequence, and momentary forgettings of the type studied quantitatively by Luborsky (1977b)— the operation of a set of thought activities that were unconscious or preconscious. Much of the modern psychoanalytic theorizing about the ways in which presumably unconscious wishes, fantasies, conflicts, or interpersonal attitudes (transferences and object-representations) influence adult behavior continues to be derived from anecdotal accounts of psychoanalysts who are assumed to be trained to make observations and to draw inferences from samples of the free associative thought. Indeed, to the extent that one can assert that psychoanalysis meets the criteria of eliminative inductionism and remains a viable scientific method for investigating the possibility of unconscious influences on the public personality of an individual (Edelson 1984), one must confront the method's reliance upon ongoing associative thought as its information base.

Although the hypotheses about unconscious thought activity derived from psychoanalysis reflect sweeping insights, we may have underemphasized the valuable harvest to be gleaned from studying the domain of normal conscious thought. In this domain are found waking interior monologues, reminiscences, mental rehearsals of future acts, the speculative forays into possible and impossible futures—what we call daydreams or fantasies. They are all part of the ongoing flow of consciousness first identified formally by William James.

Curiously, Freud and many subsequent psychoanalytic theorists have paid little attention to the structural characteristics of naturally occurring associative thought despite their dependence on the content of such material in drawing inferences about unconscious mechanisms. My own hypothesis, which someday I hope to elaborate, is that psychoanalysts have tended to cast the childish, trivial, slimy, salacious, self-serving, and hostile qualities of ordinary conscious thought down to the limbo or hell of an unconscious mind. Rather than confront the full absurdity of much of our ongoing consciousness, Freud emphasized the secondary process or logical-sequential processes of ego-oriented consciousness and studied the primary processes as manifestations from the nether regions, discernible in occasional peremptory ideational upsurges, in transference fantasies, and, especially, in night-dreams.

While psychoanalysis was forging its elaborate topography of the unconscious and general psychology was ignoring consciousness by recording overt behavior in rats and pigeons, the psychology of ongoing thought was explored primarily in the literary genre of stream-of-consciousness fiction by Dorothy Richardson, Marcel Proust, Edouard Dujardin, James Joyce, Virginia Woolf, William Faulkner, and, more recently, Saul Bellow. The ambitious, sweeping effort of James Joyce, especially, in capturing in richest detail the natural flow of the daily natural stream of consciousness evokes a shock of recognition from us. With incomparable honesty, introspection, and literary skill, Joyce sets before us in *Portrait of the Artist as a Young Man* and *Ulysses* remarkable examples of human conscious thought that we can identify as often typical of our own ordinary conscious activity. The interior monologues, reminiscences, and occasionally playful fantasies of Herzog or Mr. Sammler in the novels of Saul Bellow, while designed for literary and aesthetic effect, also reflect qualities of ordinary waking consciousness that are quite comparable to the tape-recorded thought samples one obtains in the laboratory from participants in research.

With the emergence of the cognitive movement in the behavioral sciences in about 1960, we see a paradigm shift toward a view of the human being as an information-seeking, information-processing organism rather than as the hydraulic-energy machine described in the writings of psychoanalysts and learning theorists of the 1930s, 1940s, and 1950s. Even so, the cognitive movement, with its focus on the active sequence of information organization, is uncomfortable with the problem of the natural stream of thought. Most cognitive research assigns to people circumscribed, well-defined problems to solve, usually in the form of the identification of rapidly presented letters, shapes, or pictures. The revival of interest in private imagery has chiefly emphasized its role in the direct reduplication of objective, circumscribed external stimuli, as in the experiments of Segal (1971), Shepard (1978), or Kosslyn (1981), rather than addressing self-generated fantasies and daydreams. Yet much naturally occurring imagery is more dynamic and fluid than the well-controlled mental cube rotations of Shepard and, indeed, it is probably much more about people in relationships or about buildings, shops, or nature scenes rather than the geometric shapes we can manipulate so easily in the laboratory. In a sense, a painting such as Picasso's *Guernica* with its fragmented bodies, distorted horses, and emotional impact captures the *memory images* of a spectator of the village bombing better than a moving picture of the scene would. Our great artists and writers have pointed the way for us in describing the role of conscious thought in the human condition. We now must move toward meeting that challenge by developing methods and theories that make possible a fuller description of the functioning organism as one that not only processes environmentally presented information about physical objects and people but also processes and reshapes a continuing flow of stimulation generated from the long-term memory system.

A Cognitive-Affective Perspective

It has become increasingly clear to cognitive psychologists that our ways of knowing the world are intrinsically bound up with our ways of feeling or, indeed, our moral and aesthetic evaluations (Rychlak 1977, 1981; Tomkins 1962, 1963; Zajonc 1980). Philosopher Robert Neville's "reconstruction of thinking" points to the centrality of some inherent valuation process in imagination (Neville 1981). In effect, in the very act of organizing our experiences we introduce a sense of positive or negative value.

Significant advances have been made in the past decade in empirical studies of the specific emotions with which we seem "wired." Excitement-interest and joy are positive emotions that, when invoked, are usually positively reinforcing. Fear-terror, distress-sadness, anger, and shame-guilt-humiliation are negative affects, generally serving as punishing experiences (Izard 1977; Singer 1974; Tomkins 1962, 1963). Tomkins's proposal is that humans are inherently motivated by four implications of the positive and negative emotions. We maximize experiences we expect to generate positive affect and minimize the likelihood of experiencing negative affect; we experience and express emotions as fully as possible; and, finally, we control emotions as it becomes adaptively necessary. The emotions are explored in detail elsewhere; here I will point to the close link of emotions with the cognitive system amd with the information-processing sequence. In effect, in studying the private personality, we need to recognize that we can be startled and intrigued by our own thoughts, that waking as well as nocturnal fantasies of betrayal or humiliation may have important bodily feedback implications even if (or sometimes because) they are never translated into overt action. The quiet, "nonemotional" scholar can react with private experiences of intense joy to a humorous passage in one of Aristophanes' plays or with intense excitement at the realization of the relationship between two previously obscure readings of an ancient text. The hypertensive adult has been shown to be characterized specifically by recurrent aggressive daydreams (Crits-Christoph 1984).

A key concept in the paradigm shift from a stimulus-response (S-R) to a cognitive perspective in psychology is the notion of a temporarily extended, if very rapid, "sequence" in information processing. Cognitive psychologists like to draw flow charts representing the interplay of anticipation, identification of features, "gating out" or filtering of irrelevances or threatening material, retention in short-term memory, movement of new material (under the direction of some kind of central executive or rule-making system) to long-term memory for further rehearsal, and so forth. The close tie between information processing on the one hand and emotional experience on the other pointed to by Tomkins (1962, 1963), Izard (1977), Mandler (1975), McClelland (1961), and Singer (1973, 1974) has greatly expanded our ability to relate motivation to cognition.

Most cognitive theories tend to emphasize consciousness as a feature of the private personality. They do not preclude, however, the possibility that many of our plans and anticipations may have become so automatic that they unroll too rapidly for us to notice them in the flurry of events. Thus, when we first learn to drive, we must consciously think of each step to be taken: "depress the clutch, shift the gear, gradually release the clutch, slightly feed the gas by the gas pedal." When we have carried out a sequence like this often enough, we can then engage in the complex motor and perceptual acts necessary for driving a car *and,* simultaneously, talk, think of other events, listen to music, or observe the scenery. Langer's notion of mindlessness, or overlearned mental action sequences, is relevant here (Langer 1983). Meichenbaum and Gilmore (1983) have further developed the viewpoint that unconscious processes reflect well-established or overlearned constructs, schemata, or metacognitions (e.g., rules of memory retrieval and various biasing rules about material accepting or threatening to self-beliefs), a position similar to Tomkins's (1979) theory of nuclear scenes and scripts.

Cognitive theories often make the assumption that private experiences such as conscious thoughts, fantasies, or images provide an alternative environment to the continuous processing of material from the external world (Singer 1974). Thoughts may be reshaped and reorganized and acted on by further thought in much the same way as our experience is modified by new inputs from the physical or social environment. Thus, there is a constant restructuring of material in the memory system: memory is never simply a process of passive storage.

Additionally, cognitive theories assume that certain attitudes, beliefs, or patterns of information are more central or self-oriented than others and are more likely to evoke complex affective responses. In this view the self can be regarded as an object of cognition or as a part of perceived experience rather than as an agent. Because our most personal schemata are associated both with a·long background of memories from childhood and with our most recent experiences, they are linked to the most complex network of related images, memories, and anticipations. Novel material that does not fit in with beliefs about the self will generate a sense of incongruity. In the face of persisting incongruity, an experience relating to the self will evoke greater intensities of distress or anger than a thought that relates to other persons or stems from news of other countries. The following vignette may help to illustrate these points:

A young man coming home to his apartment house late one evening sees a couple kissing in the hallway. Ordinarily he might find this a bit surprising and mildly amusing as he walks past. If, however, he suddenly realizes that the woman is his wife, this new and surprising information arouses a great range of memories of closeness with this woman as well as anticipations and images of future closeness. All these anticipations and images are suddenly threatened. In addition, a whole set of private beliefs influencing his self-esteem, which depend upon the fact that someone loves him and is faithful to him, are suddenly incongruous with this new information. First, the man is startled. Then, as the situation persists and the couple either keeps on kissing or refuses to explain what happened, the young man is confronted with a continuous incongruity between this new information and all his prior expectations and memories. He is likely to experience anger or despair.

Certain events are clearly more central to this man's self, not because there is any inherent mystical quality about the self but because of the greater network of private experiences relating to self-esteem and positive emotions connected to his relationship with his wife. An environmental cue, a scene in a film, may also trigger a *fantasy* of such a kissing scene and evoke much the same sequence of emotional arousal without such a direct experience. This has been suggested by recent studies of jealousy (Salovey and Rodin 1984).

In summary, the human being is regularly confronted by two major sources of stimulation: the complex physical and social characteristics of the surrounding environment, which make demands for "channel space" on one's sensory system, and an alternative, competitive set of stimuli (some form of "recycled" memory material) generated by the brain, which may also impact the sensory system. Such centrally generated stimulation may have somewhat less urgency when one is in the highly activated and aroused condition of wakefulness. A third source of stimulation (weaker in its demand for conscious processing, but often no less important) is the signaling system from the ongoing machinery of our bodies, a system of great importance in health but not yet well-enough researched and, certainly, except under great pain or fatigue, often ignored. We shall consider later some of the implications of the link between bodily cues and the stream of consciousness. I would suggest that as far as we can tell, most people are carrying on some kind of ongoing interior monologue, a kind of gloss on immediately occurring events that also engages in associations of these events. Under circumstances in which the external stimulus field involves sufficient redundancy or familiarity that one can draw on automatized cognitive and motor processes, one may become aware of a continuing array of memories or fantasies unrelated to the immediate environment. Since, as I will argue below, much of our stream of thought is made up of unfinished intentions of long-standing as well as current concerns, the attention to such stimulation often provokes negative emotions of fear, sadness, shame-guilt, or anger and has generally a mildly aversive quality. Thus we often prefer to turn on the radio or television, do crossword puzzles, or, if in an elevator with a stranger, talk about the weather rather than stay with the thought sequence.

There are, however, great individual differences in the extent to which people choose to control and indeed play along with their ongoing thought streams, or to engage in self-monitoring (Snyder 1979). The well-established psychometric dimension of introversion-extraversion identifies the range from those who, like Walt Whitman "loaf and invite their souls," to those who constantly seek new external stimulation, whether socially or from the electronic media, in order to avoid self-awareness.

Attention to self-generated stimulation seems to involve, at least temporarily, a shift to a "different place" and the use of the same sensory systems, sometimes in parallel, sometimes in sequential fashion (Antrobus et al. 1970; Singer, Greenberg, and Antrobus 1971). The complex interaction of both hemispheres of the brain necessary for such a mixture of sequential thought and automatic verbal-chain or intended action-sequence processing (left hemisphere) and the more parallel, global, novelty-seeking, and perceptual orientation (right hemisphere) has been documented in an impressive review by Tucker and Williamson (1984). I will focus the balance of this paper on a series of methods that have emerged for providing systematic data on ongoing thought and will not further address the presumed brain mechanisms that may underlie the recurrent generation of stored "material" that provides us with a phenomenal but very "real" experience of a stream of consciousness.

Experimental Laboratory Studies of Ongoing Thought: Stimulus-Independent Thought in Signal-Detection Studies

Beginning in 1960 John Antrobus and I developed a series of experiements designed to determine if we could in some way tap into ongoing thought. Our intention, in effect, was to capture the daydream or fantasy as it occurred, or come as close to doing so as possible. The model grew out of the vigilance and signal-detection studies developed in World War II to study how individuals could adjust to tasks that required considerable attention under monotonous conditions or environments of minimal complexity and stimulation.

In this model the subject has different degrees of demand made upon him or her for processing externally derived information under conditions of reasonably high motivation. Since the amount of external stimulation can be controlled, the study determines to what extent individuals will shift their attention away from processing external cues in order to earn money by accurate signal detections and toward the processing of material that is generated by the presumably ongoing activity of their own brains. Our attempt was to demonstrate whether we could ascertain the conditions under which individuals, even with high motivation for external signal processing, would still show evidence that they were carrying on task-irrelevant thought and imagery (TITR) or stimulus-independent mentation (SIM).

A participant is seated in a sound- and light-proof booth. The task is to report whether tones coming at 1 per second are louder or softer than the one before. If, while detecting signals, an individual is interrupted every 15 seconds and questioned about whether any stimulus-independent thoughts occurred, a "yes" response would be scored as TITR or SIM. By establishing in advance a common definition between subject and experimenter as to what constituted such task-irrelevant thought, one could have at least some reasonable assurance that reports were more or less in keeping with the operational definition established. Thus, a thought that went something like the following, "Is that tone louder than the one before it? It sounded like it was," would be considered stimulus-dependent or task-relevant and would elicit a "no" response even though it was indeed a thought. A response such as "I've got to remember about picking up the car keys for my Saturday night date" would, of course, be scored as task-irrelevant or stimulus-independent mentation. A thought about the experimenter in the next room, "Are they trying to drive me crazy?" even though in some degree generated by the circumstances in which the subject found himself, was nevertheless scored as SIM because it was not directly relevant to the processing of the signal that was defined for the subject as his or her main task.

While keeping the subjects in booths for 45 minutes, we obtained 180 reports of the occurrence of stimulus-independent thought through queries after each 15 minutes of signal detection. It is possible to build up rather extensive information on the frequency of the occurrences of SIM and their relationship to the speed of signal presentation, the complexity of the task, and other characteristics of the subject's psychological situation. Indeed, as Antrobus (1968) showed, it was possible to generate a fairly precise mathematical function of the relationship of stimulus-independent thought to the information load confronted by the subject in the course of ongoing processing.

By using periodic inquiries for content (obtained either by recording verbalizations or by having subjects press appropriate buttons on a panel) as well as for the presence or absence of SIM, it is also possible to examine the range and type of content available and to score this material along dimensions similar to those also used for night-dream research, for example, vividness of imagery, modality of imagery, degree of personal content versus impersonal content, future or past references. The alternative method of establishing content is to make use of continuous free association by the subject during a vigilance task (Antrobus and Singer 1964).

In one study, it was possible to show that while subjects spoke continuously in a varied and undirected fashion (with white noise piped into their ears so they could not hear their own verbalization), they were more likely to maintain arousal during a lengthy session in a darkened booth detecting visual signals (Antrobus and Singer 1964). In contrast, counting from one to nine repetitively during the same situation led to actual sleep, sleepiness, and, indeed, irritability and gross discomfort. Some arousal effects of continuous free association were at the cost of accuracy, for when arousal was maintained artificially by periodically piping marching-band music into the subject's ears, the accuracy rate of the counting condition was significantly greater than for the free-association condition. In other words, responding to one's inner experiences provides a varied internal environment that maintains moderate arousal under conditions of a fairly routine or boring task. This is at the cost, however, of some accuracy. If external situations are sufficiently arousing, then a restricted internal focus of attention, as in the counting task, may actually lead to a more accurate response to the environment. Daydreaming may be one way we maintain interest and arousal in boring or redundant situations, with the likelihood that because the situations are to redundant we will not miss too much of what happens. The situation is analogous to that of driving on a well-

306 JEROME L. SINGER

known, relatively untraveled highway. Clearly, under conditions of driving in heavy traffic in a midtown area, daydreaming would be less functional than almost complete concentration on the physical environment. Experimental research with driving simulators to test out some of these implications, however, remains to be done.

A number of generalizations have emerged out of the signal-detection experiments. It was possible to indicate that stimulus-independent thought could be reduced significantly if the amount of reward paid subjects or the complexity of the task were systematically increased. As a matter of fact, although significant reductions in stimulus-independent thoughts did occur, it turned out to be difficult to reduce reports of stimulus-independent thought to zero unless signals came at such irregular intervals that subjects apparently could not learn to pace themselves. Although this would suggest that the general pattern of dealing with stimulus-independent thought involves a sequential style, there has been evidence in a study by Antrobus, Singer, Goldstein, and Fortgang (Antrobus et al. 1970) that, under certain circumstances, it is possible to demonstrate parallel processing, that is, stimulus-independent thought occurring even as the subject was accurately processing signals.

When new, potentially personal information is presented to the subjects just prior to a signal detection "watch," there is a greater likelihood of an increase in stimulus-independent thought. However, errors may not necessarily increase for some time. It is as if subjects are not consistently using their full channel capacity for processing private as well as external cues during tasks of this kind. The model of examining how newly presented information, usually of a more emotional nature, becomes incorporated into the ongoing stream of thought has been adapted for a series of studies by Horowitz and various collaborators, to which we will soon refer.

The signal-detection method for tapping into ongoing thought presents some elegant opportunities for more precise measuring of the odds that any task-irrelevant mentation will take place at all. Fein and Antrobus (1977) were able to demonstrate that even though the pace of signal detections was increased, the relative frequency of reports of stimulus-independent mentation was capable of being described by a Poisson distribution *once* the subject had made an *initial* report of an SIM. (An increase from 1 to 2 minutes, for instance, with signals coming every second, would require 60 to 120 detections of the subject.) In other words, even though there might be as many as 8 "no" reports of SIM in a given trial of 1 or 2 minutes of signal presentation, once the subject reported a positive occurrence of stimulus-independent thought, the frequency of such reports was describable by a Poisson distribution rather than by a binomial distribution.

A procedure such as this provides an opportunity for us to see exactly what inherent capacities there are for processing private as well as public material. We can also study the extent to which there may actually be inherent brain rhythms that play a role in the pattern of the sequential shifting that can occur, or in the emergence of parallel processing. It has also been possible to show, by a systematic division of reports according to whether the signal presented was visual or auditory, that the visual system is implicated in the production of visual SIM whereas the auditory system is implicated in the production of sounds in the "mind's ear." This study provides evidence that privately generated phenomena are closely related to the basic imagery modalities implicated in the perceptual process as well as in the thought process (Antrobus et al. 1970).

The signal-detection model also permits the study of some degree of individual differences. Antrobus, Coleman, and Singer (1967) demonstrated that subjects already predisposed to be imaginative (by self-reporting on a questionnaire) were more likely as time went on to report more stimulus-independent thought than subjects who reported that they were little given to daydreaming. The differences between the two groups expanded as the number of errors did. Initially, the frequent daydreamers reported a considerable amount of stimulus-independent thought without differing in the level of errors from the less frequent daydreamers. As time went on, however, there was a suggestion that they seemed to prefer to respond to stimulus-independent mentation, and their error rate increased significantly compared with the relatively stable rate of errors for the subjects who showed little stimulus-independent mentation.

The cognitive processing model has a great many other implications that have not been examined fully. In addition to studying individual differences and the processing of information between the external environment and self-generated material, we can also look at the task of processing in relation to the kind of priorities the individual may set more generally for processing information in life situations. We may stress either internally generated material or externally generated signals. We can also look at the role of private material in generating specific emotional reactions. The same signal-detection task has been used in several studies to which we will refer in order to establish the implications of positive and negative affect.

In various studies we have regularly found evidence that individuals show a fairly consistent rate of stimulus-independent thought, even when they are paid for correct signal detections, penalized for errors, or forced to maintain a rapid pace of response (e.g., 1 per second; Antrobus et al, 1970).

An attempt was made to observe the relative frequency of two types of thought content, both unrelated to an immediate task (auditory signal detections). Four persons participated in eleven consecutive daily 2-hour signal-detection watches with interruptions after each 16-second trial for reports of occurrences of task-irrelevant thought. Subjects maintained an 80% accuracy detection level throughout. They reported the occurrence of stimulus-independent thought in more than 55% of the trials, a figure that was remarkably stable across the eleven daily sessions. Within the category of stimulus-independent thought, thoughts of a general nature about the experiment but not about the detection of signals (e.g., "I'm imagining what the experimenters are doing in the next room while I'm in here") are experiment-related but task irrelevant; they may be compared with more remote task-irrelevant thoughts such as "I'm picturing meeting my roommate Joe's sister next week." Although experiment-related thought constituted up to 40% of all task-irrelevant thought in the first four sessions, it dropped off drastically during the remaining days, while more remote thought increased considerably (Antrobus et al. 1984; see Figure 14.1).

In yet another study, reports of stimulus-independent thought characterized more than 50% of eighty trials of random lengths in four daily signal-detection watches. Female participants reported a higher overall length of such responses; both males and females reported more task-irrelevant thought when the experimenter was of the opposite sex, but the effect was clearly greater for females (Algom and Singer 1984).

Controlled studies of ongoing thought during signal-detection watches afford a continuing rich opportunity for estimating the determinants of the thought stream. We know that the introduc-

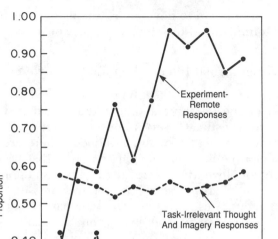
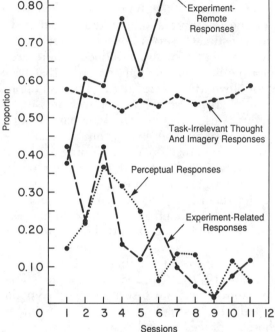

FIGURE 14.1 Proportions of various types of thought or perceptual responses reported following interruptions after every 15 seconds of signal detections during each of 12 daily periods of one-hour laboratory watches.

tion of unusual or alarming information prior to entry into the detection booth (overhearing a broadcast of war news) can increase the amount of stimulus-independent thought even though the accuracy of detections may not be greatly affected. A series of studies directed by Horowitz (1978) has demonstrated that specific emotional experiences of an intense nature prior to engaging in signal detections lead to the emergence of material in the form of stimulus-independent ideation when thought is sampled during the detection period. Such findings have suggested a basis for understanding clinical phenomena such as "unbidden images" (Horowitz 1978) or "peremptory ideation" (Klein 1967). I believe, however, that we can go even further with such a procedure and begin to develop a systematic conceptualization of the determinants of the stream of consciousness.

Experimental Interventions and Thought Sampling

Even though the signal-detection procedure gives us a powerful control over the environmental-stimulus input and affords an opportunity to estimate very precisely the lengths of specific stimulus-independent thought sequences, there are somewhat less artificial methods of thought sampling that have been increasingly employed in the development of an approach to determining the characteristics and determinants of waking conscious thought. These involve: (1) asking participants to talk out loud over a period of time while in a controlled environment and then scoring the verbalization along empirically or theoretically derived categories; (2) allowing the respondent to sit, recline, or stand quietly for a period of time and interrupting the person periodically for reports of thought or perceptual activity; (3) requiring the person to signal by means of a button press whenever a new chain of thought begins and then to report verbally in retrospect or to fill out a prepared rating form characterizing various possible features of ongoing thought.

Klinger (1977a, 1977b, 1978, 1981) has employed thought sampling in the above forms to test a series of hypotheses about ongoing thought. He has made an interesting distinction between operant thought processes and respondent thought processes. The former category describes thoughts that have a conscious instrumental property—the solution of a specific problem, the analysis of a particular issue presently confronting one, the examination of the implications of a specific situation in which one finds oneself at the moment. Operant thought is active and directed, with the characteristics of what Freud called "secondary-process thinking." As Klinger has noted, it is volitional; it is checked against new information concerning its effectiveness in moving toward a solution or the consequences of a particular attempted solution; and there are continuing efforts to protect such a line of thought from drifting off target or from the intrusion of distraction either by external cues or extraneous, irrelevant thought (Klinger 1978). Operant thought seems to involve a greater sense of mental and physical effort, and it probably has the property that the neurologist Head (1926) called "vigilance," Goldstein (1940) the "abstract attitude," and Pribram and McGuinness

(1976) "effort," a human capacity especially likely to suffer in the event of massive frontal brain damage. Klinger's research involving thought-sampling methods has suggested that operant thought is correlated to some degree with external-situation-related circumstances. It involved higher rates of self-reports about thought-evaluation progress toward the goal of the thought sequence as well as of efforts to resist drift and distraction (Klinger 1978).

Respondent thought in Klinger's terminology involves all other thought processes. These are nonvolitional in the sense of any conscious direction of a sequence, and most are relatively noneffortful (Bower 1982–83). Respondent processes include seemingly unbidden images (Horowitz 1978) or peremptory thought (Klein 1967), which are the mental distractions one becomes aware of when trying to sustain a sequence of operant thought (analyzing the logic of a scientific or legal argument or simply trying to concentrate on writing checks to pay bills). Most of what we consider daydreams and fantasies (and, of course, nighttime dreams) are instances of respondent thought.

One can further classify thought into stimulus-dependent or independent (Singer 1966; Antrobus et al. 1970); thought identifiably relevant to external cues or to processing environmentally operated cues is, at least to some degree, stimulus-dependent. In a sample of 285 reports from a dozen subjects, Klinger reported a significant correlation between the environmental setting and reports of operant or directed thought. A broader percentage of the variance of both operant and respondent thought seemed independent of the physical or social milieu, but we shall return to this point later when we relate waking thought to night-dream reports.

The use of thought-sampling in a reasonably controlled environment permits the evaluation of a variety of conditions that may influence or characterize ongoing consciousness. One can score the participants' verbalizations on dimensions such as (1) organized-sequential versus degenerative, confused thought; (2) use of imagery or related episodes or event memory material versus logical-semantic structures; (3) reference to current concerns and unfulfilled intentions; (4) reminiscence of past events versus orientation toward the future; (5) realistic versus improbable content, and so forth. A study by Pope (1978) demonstrated that longer sequences of thought having greater remoteness from the participants' immediate circumstances were obtained from respondents who were reclining rather than walking freely and alone rather than in an interpersonal situation. Zachary (1983) evaluated the relative role of positive and negative emotional experiences just prior to a thought-sampling period. He found that the intensity of an experience rather than its emotional nature, and, to a lesser extent, the relative ambiguity rather than the clarity of the material, determined recurrence in the thought stream.

Studies reviewed by Klinger, Barta, and Maxeiner (1981) point to the relative importance of the following current concerns as determinants of the material that emerges in thought sampling. These concerns are defined as "the state of an organism between the time one becomes committed to pursuing a particular goal and the time one either consummates the goal or abandons its objective and disengages from the goal" (Klinger, Barta, and Maxeiner 1981). Such current concerns as measured by a well-thought-out psychometric procedure make up a useful operationalization of the Freudian wish in its early (prelibido theory) form (Holt 1976). They may range from an unfilfilled intention to pick up a container of milk on the way home to a long-standing unresolved desire to please a parent or to settle an old score with a parent or sibling. In estimating current concerns at a point prior to thought-sampling sessions, one obtains scale-estimates of the valences of the goals, the relative importance of intentions in some value and temporal hierarchy, the person's perception of the reality of goal achievement, and so forth. It seems clear that only after we have explored the range and influence of such current consciously unfulfilled intentions in a sampling of the individual's thoughts and emotional and behavioral responses can we move to infer the influence of unconscious wishes or intentions.

The possibilities for controlled, hypothesis-testing uses of laboratory thought-sampling are exemplified in a recent study of the determinants of adolescents' ongoing thought following simulated parental confrontations (Klos and Singer 1981). In this study we set up a hierarchy of experimental conditions prior to a thought sampling, which were expected to yield differential degrees of recurrence in the consciousness of the participants. We proposed that, even for beginning college students, parental involvements were likely to prove especially provocative of further thought. We chose to evaluate the relative role of (1) generally fulfilled versus unresolved situations, the old Zeigarnick effect (Lewin 1935); (2) a mutual nonconflictual parental interaction; (3) a confrontation or conflict with a parent that involved a collaborative stance by the adult; and (4) a comparable confrontation in which the parents' attitude was clearly coercive rather than collaborative. We proposed that exposure (through a simulated interaction) to each of these conditions would yield differences in the later recurrence of simulation-relevant thoughts in the participants' consciousness. For example, we believed that unresolved situations would more likely recur than resolved situations but that the incompletion effect would be less powerful than a collaborative confrontation and, especially, than a coercive confrontation. We hypothesized that the coercive parental-conflict simulation when unresolved would lead to the highest frequency of recurrence in the thoughts of the adolescents. We went a step further, however, in the light of the research just mentioned on current concerns. We proposed that a history of long-standing stress with parents would constitute a major current concern and that this factor would amplify the effect on later thought of the simulated parent interactions. Thus, frequency of recurrence in later thought of a simulated parent interaction would be highest for those participants with a history of long-standing parental conflict undergoing an unresolved coercive confrontation.

After providing, some weeks earlier, questionnaire responses regarding parental stress, 96 men and women participated in the study and were assigned to one of six conditions: (1) collaborative decision-making with parent, resolved; (2) collaborative decision-making with parent, unresolved; (3) collaborative confrontation with parent, resolved; (4) collaborative confrontation with parent, unresolved; (5) coercive confrontation with parent, resolved; (6) coercive confrontation with parent, unresolved.

Participants engaged in carefully developed imaginary simulated interactions with one of their parents (seated in an "empty chair") while an experimenter read a predeveloped parental script appropriate to each situation. Three rather typical parent-child situations were used in each simulation condition. Subsequent to the simulations subjects were taken to another room and over a period of 20 minutes thought samples were obtained at twenty random-interval interruptions (45–75 secs.). Their reports were tape-recorded and then scored by experimentally naive judges who rated whether verbalized content was related to definitions of the simulation settings. The participants had also made ratings of their involvement in the task, the specific emotions experienced, the relative vividness of imagery during simulation, their perception of the relative similarity of simulations to their own early experience with parents, and so forth. Manipulation checks failed to suggest condition differences other than those experimentally defined and supported the relative involvement and "reality" of the experience for this sample.

Figures 14.2 and 14.3 provide a graphic means of evaluating the findings. First of all, Figure 14.2 is included to demonstrate how meaningful estimates of emotion can be obtained in thought sampling. Although the conditions differed in the directions expected with respect to emotions such as joy and discomfort (distress), the emotion of anger showed a specific relationship to the coercive confrontation conditions and to the subject's history of stress with a parent (see Fig. 14.2).

Figure 14.3 provides clear support for our major hypotheses, that recurrence of thoughts will be strongest for most conflictual material that is unresolved, next for conflictual material that is resolved, next for an unconflictual simulation that is unresolved, and negligible for nonconflictual material that is resolved. The frequency of recurrences of simulation-condition-related thought

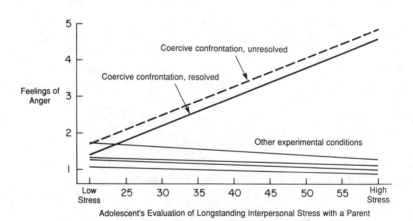

Regression lines showing the interaction of coercive confrontation and long-standing interpersonal stress on anger arousal. (Feelings of Anger is a self-rating immediately after the simulation on a 5-point scale from "Not at all angry" to "Very angry".)

FIGURE 14.2 Reported feelings of anger during thought samples obtained subsequent to simulated parental interactions by adolescents. Scores on stress based on questionnaire administered at outset of study.

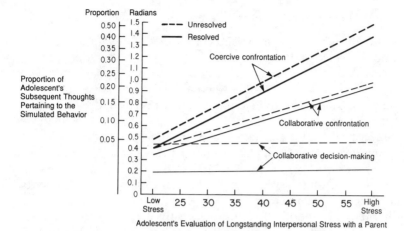

Regression lines showing the interaction of confrontation process and long-standing interpersonal stress on subsequent thoughts about the simulation. (Proportion (p) of subject's 20 thoughts sampled during 20 minutes subsequent to simulation. Radian is a 2 arcsine $\sqrt{p}$ transformation to stabilize the variance of p.)

FIGURE 14.3 Proportion of thought samples rated as reflecting recurrence in thought of a prior simulated parental interaction as a function of type of interaction and of adolescents' scores on a measure of experienced stress with their parents. Scores on stress based on questionnaire administered at outset of study.

occur in the predicted order with the effects clearly amplified by a history of long-standing interpersonal stress with a parent. The incompletion effect is a modest one, mainly in evidence in the nonconflictual situation. It is overridden to some degree by the increasing coerciveness of the imaginary conflict situations. Of special interest is the fact that, once exposed to a simulated parent conflict, the young people who had a history of stress showed as much as 50% of their later thought reflecting this brief, artificial incident. One might surmise that, if we generalize from these results, the thought world of adolescents who have had long-standing parent difficulties may be a most unpleasant domain since many conflictual chance encounters or even film or television plots might lead to recurrent thoughts to a considerable degree. The implications of a method of this kind (combined with estimates of personality variables or of other current concerns) for studying various groups—clinical, postsurgical, hypertensives, etc.—seem very intriguing.

Thought and Experience Sampling in Daily Life

It is obvious that laboratory-based methods present some difficulties because of their artificiality and because the very controls
on physical movement and restrictions on novel sensory input
that are necessary for their effectiveness may lead to overesti-
mations of the naturally occurring fantasy and daydreaming. An
approach to thought sampling that circumvents some of these
problems calls for participants to carry signaling devices in pock-
ets or purses or on belts as physicians do. These "beepers" go
off at random during the ordinary activities of participants; at
once they fill out a special card that asks for reports of activity
just prior to the signal, the environmental setting, their current
thoughts and emotional states. Typically these are carried for a
week and they go off on the average of 2-hour intervals permitting
an accumulation of 50–60 reports per participant. Studies by Klinger (1978), Hurlburt (1978, 1979), McDonald (1976) and a whole
series directed by Csikszentmihalyi (1982; Csikszentmihalyi and
Graef 1980; Csikszentmihalyi and Kubey 1981; Csikszentmihalyi
and Larson 1984) all demonstrate the feasibility of this method,
its potential for reliable results, and its suitability for hypothesis
testing as well as for the accumulation of normative data. In a
recent study with seventy-five adolescents in a suburban community, self-reports were obtained for 69% of the signals sent,
leading to an accumulation of almost 4,500 reports. Missed signals were chiefly attributable to travel outside the 50-mile signal
range, "beeper" malfunctions, or sleep. Reports included such
potentialy censorable events as parental quarrels, sexual inti-
macies, or drug and alcohol abuse. The evidence of consistency
and reliability is impressive in most of these studies.

Figure 14.4 presents a sample information sheet derived and
modified from Csikszentmihalyi and Larson (1984). By including
specific references to a limited group of emotions and to *types*
of operant and respondent thought processes, one can apply such
an activity sheet to a large sample of respondents and to clinical
patients as well and thus accumulate data on ongoing private
experiences as well as public action. The implications of such a
monitoring procedure for developing both normative and ideo-
graphic data in the health field seem very exciting. Elaborate
code sheets for scoring self-reports using trained judges are available but one can also simplify the participants' task (at the risk
of some data loss) by providing them with empirically derived

Daily Thought and Experience Diary   Code #_____

Circle Time Completed: Morning   Midday   Afternoon   Evening

Name:_____ Date:_____Time:_____

1. Please write briefly an account of the main things you were doing at the time you
stopped to fill this out, where you were, and what your main activity was during the
previous 1-2 hours.

_____
_____
_____

2. What were some of the thoughts you were aware of? Include any fantasies, memories
or daydreams as well as planful or direct problem-solving thoughts. Use back of paper
for additional space if needed.

   1._____
   2._____
   3._____
   4._____

3. Please check your emotional reactions during the previous 1-2 hours. Please check all.

		not at all			extremely				not at all			extremely
1.	Relaxed	1 2 3 4 5 6 7				8.	Sad/depressed	1 2 3 4 5 6 7
2.	Fearful	1 2 3 4 5 6 7				9.	Joyful/happy	1 2 3 4 5 6 7
3.	In-control	1 2 3 4 5 6 7				10.	Restless,bored	1 2 3 4 5 6 7
4.	Surprised	1 2 3 4 5 6 7				11.	Guilty	1 2 3 4 5 6 7
5.	Shy;ashamed	1 2 3 4 5 6 7				12.	Cautious	1 2 3 4 5 6 7
6.	Interested-Excited	1 2 3 4 5 6 7				13.	Angry at self	1 2 3 4 5 6 7
7.	Angry(at others or events)	1 2 3 4 5 6 7				14.	Self-conscious	1 2 3 4 5 6 7
						15.	Disgusted/ humiliated	1 2 3 4 5 6 7

4. Please check some of the activities you engaged in that might possibly bear on
your physical health or energy level. Circle as applies:

1.	Regular exercise	Yes	No		11.	Drinking fruit juice	Yes	No
2.	Smoking	Yes	No		12.	Smoking marijuana	Yes	No
3.	Eating balanced diet	Yes	No		13.	Using "hard" drugs	Yes	No
4.	Eating desserts & cookies	Yes	No		14.	Using non-prescription medication	Yes	No
5.	Using beer/alcohol	Yes	No		15.	Taking prescription medication	Yes	No
6.	Washing/showering	Yes	No		16.	Using sleeping pills	Yes	No
7.	Brushing teeth	Yes	No		17.	Gorging and purging	Yes	No
8.	Heavy physical work	Yes	No		18.	Skipping meal(s)	Yes	No
9.	Sports activity	Yes	No		19.	Relaxation/leisure	Yes	No
10.	Drinking soda	Yes	No		20.	Took it easier while working	Yes	No

FIGURE 14.4 Daily thought and experience diary.

categories for checking off their experiences as predefined for
them in training sessions.

    The "beeper" method can also be used to evaluate the relevant
influence of long-standing traits and momentary environmental
circumstances on emotional response and on the train of thought.
Johnson and Larson (1982), for example, used the experience-

sampling method with bulimics and a normative group and demonstrated that bulimics showed more dysphoric moods and also greater mood variability. Bulimics spent far more time alone at home and reported their highest levels of distress under such circumstances. In a European investigation employing a variation of this method, twenty-four housewives who had already taken personality tests were studied over a month. Their attributions for what "caused" their moods in various settings could be ascertained as a function of the personality characteristics of the respondent and of the situation. Thus, imaginative women attributed the causes of their moods to themselves; self-confident women were more likely to attribute positive moods to their own actions than to others (Brandstatter 1983). In another study participants whose Thematic Apperception Tests pointed to greater motivation for intimacy showed more interpersonal thoughts and more positive emotional responses in interpersonal situations than did low-intimacy-motive scorers, based on a week-long accumulation of eight daily reports (McAdams and Constantian 1983). The relationship between accumulated daily reports about thought patterns and a self-report questionnaire, the Imaginal Process Inventory (Singer and Antrobus 1972; see below), was evaluated by Hurlburt (1980). He reported significant correlations between the retrospective questionnaire scales for frequent daydreaming, acceptance of daydreaming, and low distractibility, and the accumulated daily reports of daydreaming based on 2 days of dozens of interruptions. The scale on the IPI of sexual daydreams was significantly correlated ($r = +.40$) with the accumulated record of sexual fantasies. Similarly, those persons who reported more future-oriented daydreaming on the IPI questionnaire scale actually were engaged significantly more often in such fantasies of the future ($r = +.39$) when interrupted by an electronic pager during the 2 days sampled.

Behaviorally oriented psychologists have been increasingly interested in thought-sampling methods to identify the negative self-attributions continually linked to depression and to determine the specific coping strategies used by persons experiencing severe pain (Kendall and Hollon 1981; Turk, Meichenbaum, and Genest 1983). It remains to be seen whether such data accumulated into empirically derived or theoretically relevant categories serve to predict future thought and, especially, behavior in particular health-relevant situations. Of special interest is whether thought samples can identify differential patterns of response to body signals and, further, whether they can predict the course of physical illness as well as emotional or mental status.

Psychometric Assessments

ESTIMATING CURRENT CONCERNS

The procedures of thought sampling thus far described have involved some degree of investigator control and intervention, either in the laboratory or with paging devices in the field. Another approach to estimating patterns and content of the private thought stream uses self-reports by participants who, in effect, summarize their accumulated experience in this domain by responses to carefully designed questionnaires. Klinger's Concern Dimensions Questionnaire has proven useful in predicting how much time people actually spend thinking about something (Klinger, Barta, and Maxeiner 1981). Respondents list items they have thought about in the past few days, rank them in terms of how much time they estimate they have spent on the subjects, and then rate the thoughts on four factor-analytically derived dimensions: (1) valence (positive or negative); (2) value (emotional investment in goal or general affective intensity); (3) probability of successful goal attainment and (4) imminence of goal or of resolution of the situation.

A "beeper" study with eleven participants who were interrupted at about 40-minute intervals for the day following the completion of one of these questionnaires provided evidence that at least 62% of the thoughts obtained from the sample were judged by "blind" raters as semantically related to questionnaire-derived thoughts, especially to those given highest rank. An even more intriguing study using this procedure (and linked to the relation between daytime thought and night-dream content, which will be discussed below), was the finding that sleeping subjects given verbal cues during Stage 1-REM sleep were more likely to incorporate current-concern-related cues into their dream content (determined from later ratings of similarity from their laboratory-awakening dream reports) than cues about thought material not listed by themselves but by other respondents (Hoelscher, Klinger, and Barta 1981).

A more ambitious effort to establish lists of significant current concerns, assign them to major life-area categories such as home and family, love and sex, etc., and determine valences, values, per-

Excerpts of Main Interview Questionnaire Scales

Step Number	Step Description
1	[Written brief description of current concern]
2	S's Role: (1) take part, (2) observe only but would like to take part, (3) observe only, (4) observe, but an important other in your life is actively involved, (5) neither take part nor observe, but an important other in your life is actively involved
3	Valence:...whether each thing you listed is mainly positive or negative...
4	Verb[b]: (1) get, (2) keep, (3) restore, (4) do, (5) get rid of, (6) avoid, (7) prevent, (8) escape, (9) attack, (10) find out more about
5	[Optional written longer description of current concern]
6	Commitment: (6) I fully intend to if I possibly can (or would if I could), (5)...(4) I will (or would) make a moderate effort, (3) I will (or would) try only if it is convenient and if it fits in with my other plans, (2)...(1) I do not (or would not) intend to...
7	Positivity: How much joy or relief will (or would) you feel when you first (get, keep,...) the thing? [Prothetic scaling, see text]
8	Negativity: Sometimes even successes bring some unhappiness with them. How much unhappiness will it bring you when you (get, keep,...) the thing? [Prothetic scaling]
9	Loss: How sorry will you feel (how much sorrow) if you find you cannot (get, keep,...) the thing? [Prothetic scaling, see text]
10	Probability of Success: Overall, how likely are you to succeed in (getting, keeping,...) the thing? (9) Almost certain--at least 90% sure, [anchored intermediate numbers 8 to 1]..., (1) almost no chance--0-9%
11	Confidence in Probability of Success:...(1) Pretty confident--at least 75% sure, (2)..., (3)..., (4) Very doubtful--0-24% sure
12	Nearness: Do you have a particular time in mind when you next expect to (get, keep,...) the thing? If yes, how soon is that? [Answer in number of days, X if inapplicable]
13	Time Available: How soon must you start acting if you are to (get, keep,...) the thing? [Same answer format as in previous step]
14	Ways: Below are a number of different ways you might view each thing you have listed in Step 1. ...[W]rite its number...opposite the thing[s] that it fits.[Apply each "Way" to all things in succession before going on to the next way.] (1) The thing represents a significant change in the kinds of goals you strive for... (2)...is something that you have lost or failed with, or been separated from, or you are in process of losing..., but you have not yet been able to resign yourself to losing.... (3) Same as Way 2, except that you have resigned yourself emotionally.... (4)...[Y]ou are currently concerned about whether you will be able to keep your relationship with that person the way you want it. (5) In your efforts to (get, keep,...) the thing, you are currently experiencing unexpected difficulties or special demands on your energies or resources (6) The thing constitutes a special, nonroutine challenge for you .... (7) The thing is simply a routine part of your life.... (8)...happened in the recent past (last few days or so).

The Interview Questionnaire is copyrighted by Eric Klinger.

FIGURE 14.5 Excerpts of main Interview Questionnaire scales. The interview Questionnaire is copyrighted by Eric Klinger.

Categories	Step 1 — List your particular concerns, goals, interests, or activities here	Observe or take part Step 2	Step 3 or	Step 4 Verb	Step 5 Commitment	Step 6 Positivity	Step 7 Negativity	Step 8 Loss	Step 9 Prob. of Success	Step 10 Cost, in	Step 11 Nearness	Step 12 Time Available	Step 13 How
Family and Home													
a immediate family and other relatives (for example, problems and achievements of children, sister's upcoming confirmation, gift for mother-in-law)	*I take pleasure of grandmother's items / Good relation with my? / Aunt visit, went to... / Spend more time w/ her.*	1	—	9	6	10	0	10	1	1	7300	0	5
		2	—	7	5	8	0	8	5	1	165	0	2
		2	—	7	5	8	0	9	1	1	X	0	2
		2	+	1	6	10	0	11	5	2	365	0	2
b roommates and nonrelatives (for example, roommate who is never home, noisy people who live upstairs you are trying to get rid of, needing to find a roommate)	*Noisy people downstairs, muddle too loud, late. / Landlord is a pain. / Can't help by anything*	2	—	5	1	5	1	1	0	1	X	0	7
		—	—	—	—	—	—	—	—	—	—	—	—
		1	—	5	1	5	1	1	0	1	X	0	7
c home and housekeeping (for example, raking the yard, planting a garden, painting the woodwork, buying a house, grocery shopping)	*Fixing + repairing window / Want to move / Cooking meals — boyfriend / Chamber - party*	1	+	5	3	0	0	0	1	1	X	0	7
		2	+	4	5	20	0	20	5	1	165	0	7
		1	+	4	6	10	1	10	8	1	0	0	7
		1	+	4	6	2	1	0	2	1	0	0	7
d sexual intimacy (for example, particular sexual techniques or experiences of a particular kind or with particular people, results of intimacy, sexual problems)	*Can't achieve orgasm / don't enjoy sex - like fo... / Need closeness*	1	—	5	5	20	0	20	3	1	365	0	5
		1	+	5	5	20	0	20	4	1	365	0	5
		1	+	1	6	10	0	10	5	1	100	0	5
Friends													
a friendships (for example, particular people who are friends or you would like to have as friends, problems with friends, events with friends)	*F. is seeing my ex-boyfriend*	1	—	7	4	3	0	2	6	1	100	0	7
Mental and Emotional Health													
(for example, emotions, maintaining mental health)	*Get jealous too easy / Can't express anger*	1	—	5	4	4	0	3	5	2	100	0	5
		1	—	5	4	4	0	3	8	1	100	0	5

Excerpts from the Interview Questionnaire answer sheet of a female college student.

FIGURE 14.6 Excerpts from the Interview Questionnaire answer sheet of a female college student.

sonal estimates of probabilities of success, etc., involves a self-administered interview questionnaire (see Figures 14.5 and 14.6 for samples from Klinger, Barta, and Maxeiner 1981, 177–78).

A device like this questionnaire provides a wealth of information about conscious current wishes and their apparent importance to the individual. Although the research and clinical possibilities of such a procedure seem to be great, there is little systematic evidence available as yet. The assessment of current concerns and their valences, values, proximity to resolution, and subjectively estimated probability of attainment seems an important basis for evaluating the conscious content of thought linked to a fairly sophisticated quantitative motivational theory such as that of Heckhausen (1977). It also points up the necessity for a systematic exploration of conscious contents, Freud's "day residues," from whose workings out in fantasy and night-dreaming we may attempt to infer unconscious schemata or scripts. As Klinger, Barta, and Maxeiner (1981) point out:

The question of accessibility of conscious evidence about current concerns can be approached from yet another perspective, that of "unconscious motivation." The history of psychotherapy strongly suggests that clients are sometimes consciously oblivious to the environmental effects—to their effective goals—that their behaviors, to the outside observer, seem obviously directed at achieving. The case for unconscious motivation has most likely been overstated and misstated. The situation in which unconscious motivation is attributed to a client arises when the client and therapist in some way disagree about the client's goals. The client and therapist may agree on the client's immediate goal but disagree on the presence of an ulterior goal (for instance, drinking too much in order to have fun versus doing so as a way of satisfying unmet oral-stage needs), disagree on the label to apply to the goal ("just friendly teasing" versus wishing to distress a sibling), disagree on the nature of a conflict (too attracted to going out with friends the evening before a test to stay home versus wanting to fail the test), and so on.

Much also depends on the way people are asked to account for their behavior. When people are asked directly "why" they performed some act (for instance, 'Why did you break all those windows in the school?'), the answer is often "I don't know." However, this answer may generally be taken as signifying that the respondent has no socially acceptable, reasonable explanation, and "It felt good to do it" is rejected by the respondent as not providing the requested depth of analysis. Yet this may often be the only correct answer, short of a theoretical analysis of aggression. The vandal may in fact be acting in a context of severe frustration or humiliation against a symbol of the frustrators, but it takes

an arguable leap of inference to assert that the vandal is "really" ag-
gressing against the school principal or against the vandal's father, although unconscious of that fact.

Doubtless, people do sometimes misrepresent their goals to themselves and to others. However, the nature, prevalence, and conditions
of this distortion have by no means been definitively established. Almost
certainly, some of the history of "unconscious motivation" can be ascribed to misperceptions on the part of therapists regarding clients'
goals, the extent of their information about these goals, or the intended
meaning of the clients' self-descriptions.

In any case, human life would be far more chaotic than it is if substantial portions of people's goal striving were for goals about which the
striver was unconscious. Empirical investigations of choice undertaken
by expectancy-value and "intention" theorists report a respectable degree of predictability on the basis of self-reports of value and expectancy.
However, the accessibility of "current concerns" to conscious inspection
remains an uninvestigated empirical question—perhaps best operationalized in the question of how helpful self-report assessments of current
concerns prove to be to the therapists that use them. (Klinger, Barta,
and Maxeiner 1981, 170–71).

IDENTIFYING PATTERNS OF DAYDREAMING AND
ATTENTION TO PRIVATE EXPERIENCE

Another approach to describing private experience is to rely on
the self-awareness of each individual's own continuing thought
patterns. These self-reports can be accumulated in the psychometric questionnaire format that has served personality researchers
fairly well when properly employed. I will mention just a few
of many possible research approaches in this area.

Factor analyses with large numbers of respondents generally
yield three second-order factors that seem to underlie scales characterizing inner experience (Imaginal Processes Inventory [IPI];
Singer and Antrobus 1972; Segal, Huba, and Singer 1980; Isaacs
1975; Giambra 1980; Huba et al. 1982; Huba 1980). One factor
can be labeled positive-constructive orientation of inner experience: it includes scales tapping positive emotions and events
in daydreams, an acceptance and enjoyment of daydreams, vivid
visual and auditory imagery in fantasies, and a generally future-
oriented and problem-solving quality to fantasy. A second dimension can be characterized as guilty-dysphoric daydreams or
unpleasant, emotionally toned fantasies. Scales such as guilty
content in daydreams, hostile-aggressive daydreams, fear-of-
failure fantasies, and so forth load highest in this factor. The third

pattern that we identify really represents a negation of an extended, elaborated inner experience. It reflects poor attentional control and is characterized by high loadings of such scales as distractability, susceptibility to boredom, and other scales suggesting an inability to sustain an extended skein of private imagery or, for that matter, to maintain a prolonged internally oriented concentration without reacting to the continuous stimulation in the physical environment.

Some examples of correlates of these daydreaming styles can be cited briefly. Maddi (1976) proposed a tridimensional personality classification: high-low activation, high-low active-passive control, and internal-external event orientation. Data from a sample of one thousand respondents using the Jackson Personality Research Form, Zuckerman's Sensation-Seeking Scales, the Imaginal Processes Inventory, and Rotter's Locus of Control Inventory seemed to offer evidence of at least two of Maddi's combinations, high-activation, internal focus, active control, and low activation, internally oriented, passive control (Segal, Huba, and Singer 1980). In another study employing Fenigstein, Scheier, and Buss's (1975) scales of Public and Private Self-Consciousness and Tellegan and Atkinson's Absorption Scale, a distinct cluster of measures included positive-constructive daydreaming, guilty-dysphoric daydreaming, private self-consciousness, and absorption emerged (suggestive of thinking introversion). Poor attentional control, public self-consciousness, and social anxiety formed a separate cluster reflecting something more like an emotional instability dimension (Barrios and Singer 1981). In studies of hypnotic susceptibility or of the use of daydreaming scales to predict waking imagery methods of helping people to overcome creative blocks, there is further evidence that a predisposition to positive, planful daydreaming is consistently tied to measures of absorption, imagery vividness, and hypnotic responsiveness (Crawford 1982; Barrios and Singer 1981). Golding and Singer (1983) reported on data linking guilty daydreaming to one style of depression (self-critical and guilt-oriented) and poor attentional control to another depressive style (dependency and shame-oriented).

The three patterns of inner experience constitute a separate domain of measurable psychological response from personality trends and more public behavior, but they are linked systematically to such behaviors, probably in a transitional two-way interactive fashion (Segal, Huba, and Singer 1980). Recent studies by McIlwraith and Schallow (1983a, 1983b) found that adults and children who were heavy viewers of television and especially of the more violent programming were also characterized by higher scores on the guilty-dysphoric daydreaming dimension. The data are correlational and cross-sectional, but other evidence suggests that persons with unpleasant and distressing inner experiences may seek distraction and passive escapes from such thoughts in television (Csikszentmihalyi and Kubey 1981). Once exposed to the violence and disaster that characterizes daily TV fare, they may find their later conscious experience increasingly characterized by frightening, hostile, or fearful fantasies (Kubey 1982).

With the availability of psychometric instruments such as the IPI, Bower's (1982–83) Effortless Experiencing Scale (which taps somewhat related aspects of respondent thought), the Public and Private Self-Consciousness Scales, the Absorption Scale, a complex questionnaire and thought-sampling method designed to estimate alternate states of consciousness (Pekala and Levine 1981, 1982), and a number of other new and promising questionnaires for scoring imagery vividness and control (Cartwright, et al. 1983; Tower and Singer 1981), we can set up experiments or naturalistic studies that examine such long-standing predispositions along with thought samples and measures from outcomes of experimental interventions.

OTHER METHODS FOR ESTIMATING
PRIVATE EXPERIENCES

Johnson and Raye (1981), in a thoughtful paper reflecting a cognitive experimental orientation, have identified a process they term reality monitoring. It refers to the relative ability of individuals to identify events as having occurred in the "real world," that is, in their physical environment of words or pictures shown them by an experimenter, and similar stimuli as generated by their own imagery and memory systems. They point to specific processing and structural differences that lead to the correct differentiation of such experiences as long as a week following their occurrence. They do not, however, examine patterns of individual differences in imagery vividness, attention, enjoyment of self-generated processes, and so forth. The patterns of questionnaire responses described above and data from a burgeoning group of new questionnaire or assessment devices (Bower 1982–83; Pekala and Levine 1982; Tower and Singer 1981) suggest that many individuals learn during their lifetime to tune into and out of the private stream of thought, to direct or control it, and to engage in a variety of cognitive operations that may actually help them make more precise discriminations between "reality and fantasy" or at least to control their attention.

It has been proposed that one major outcome of the subtle training one undergoes in psychoanalysis or in the more explicit rehearsal procedures of cognitive therapies is to learn to "rerun" the mental "film" of a series of experiences, identifying gaps, moments of anger or anxiety, and, ultimately, the overlearned cognitive structures (schemata, scripts, or transferences) that may represent the unconscious motivations for thought or behavioral sequences (Meichenbaum and Gilmore 1984; Singer 1974). Measures of imagery-vividness abilities, controllability, self-monitoring (Snyder 1979), and absorption in one's experiences provide an exciting possibility for identifying persons who may prove especially adept at monitoring their thought streams or benefiting quickly from training in this area and persons who may show real difficulties in identifying or controlling their thought patterns. The latter group is of special interest in view of some evidence that "repressors" or "alexithymia" may be more susceptible to a variety of health difficulties (Jensen 1984; Schwartz 1983; Sifneos 1972).

An area of relevance to the measurement of absorption in fantasy is that of hypnosis. A good deal of evidence is accumulating to suggest that measures of hypnotic susceptibility and some of their cognitive or childhood correlates are also associated systematically with the capacity for vivid imagery and the enjoyment and use of daydreams in a positive manner (Barber 1984; Barrios and Singer 1981; Crawford 1982; Spanos and Radtke 1981; Wilson and Barber 1983). Indeed, one might take the position today, building upon Hilgard's (1965, 1977) extensive research on hypnosis, that entering a "deep" hypnotic state may not reflect a weakness or even a "susceptibility," to use the term still current, but a basic human capacity. It was once thought that introverted subjects, persons given to imagery and fantasy, were less hypnotizable. I propose, however, the hypothesis that a necessary intervening variable to test such a view would involve the evaluation of personal beliefs that "being hypnotized" represented a human weakness, a surrender of autonomy. Introverts could distract themselves by tuning out the phrases of the hypnotist and attending to their private thought stream, thus not accepting the psychological "contract" of the trance situation. Once having modified their "fear" of hypnosis, however, such thought-oriented persons ought to be the best candidates for hypnosis since, in effect, they often already engage in the self-hypnosis of extended reverie states or absorption in books (Singer and Pope 1981).

In summary, there seems a considerable and growing availability of reasonably sophisticated measures for assessing ongoing thought in the laboratory or the field. Additionally, there are increasingly numerous measures to estimate for individuals and groups, through questionnaires, the traitlike patterns of current concerns, styles of daydreaming, imagery use, and absorption capacities in private experience, even to the point of trance-like states. What we have not done yet is examine in more systematic ways the links between these data derived from conscious report and the kinds of inferred unconscious schemata, motivational structures, and special processing patterns beneath awareness that have made up the bulk of the clinical literature on the unconscious dimension of human experience.

Ongoing Thought in the Formation and Maintenance of Schemata: Self-Concepts and Action-Scripts

Methods are increasingly available, then, for capturing ongoing thought as it occurs, for identifying the personality variations of self-monitoring thought (Snyder 1979) or styles of ongoing thought (Tower and Singer 1981). We have good support now for the possibility of using concurrent physiological measurement to identify bodily correlates of some mental activity through cardiovascular measures (Bowen 1984; Schwartz, Weinberger, and Singer 1981; Weinberger, Schwartz, and Davidson 1979; Qualls, 1982–83), facial muscle activity (Brown 1978; Ekman, Levenson, and Friesen 1983) and brain wave patterns (Ahern 1982). Of special interest is the evidence that we can identify a group of individuals sometimes termed "repressors" because their conscious reports that they do not feel anxious, worried, or tense are belied by strong physiological patterns suggestive of fear and distress. These physiological reactions are similar to or even greater than those obtained from participants who admit consciously to a good deal of anxiety (Weinberger, Schwartz, and Davidson 1979; Weinberger 1983). We shall shortly consider some of the health implications of this repressive style.

Let me now outline some major speculations, hypotheses, and possibilities for research that stem from my emphasis on the importance of the ongoing stream of consciousness.

IMPLICATIONS FOR AFFECT AND COGNITION

Following Tomkins's (1962) theoretical proposals I have suggested that most people are motivated to enhance circumstances for experiencing positive emotions. The two major positive emotions are (1) interest-excitement, generated by a *moderate* level of novel stimulation or complexity and ambiguity in one's environment, and (2) the joy one experiences by matching or assimilating such novel or complex information with previously well-established schemata. I propose that one major function of ongoing consciousness may be to react to new information by reflection and matching against previous schemata. The duplication of experience by imagery and an interior monologue may reduce the fear associated with extreme novelty but allow for a curious, interested continued search until the information is fully assimilated. Broadbent (1958) has described two forms of processing styles: "short-processing," in which each stimulus is reacted to with the most immediate previous or nearly automatic overlearned association, thus yielding a rapidity of reaction; and "long-processing," which involves an extended reaction involving a fuller survey of possible long-term memory match-ups before a response is produced. I have elsewhere proposed some links between extraversion, the cognitive style of field-dependence, the "neurotic" style of hysteria (Horowitz, et al. 1984), and short-processing and thinking introversion, field-independence, the obsessional neurotic pattern, and long-processing (Singer 1984a, 1984b). It is my hypothesis that reflective awareness and longer processing may slow down reactivity, lead to some loss of information (but most of our environments are highly redundant anyway), and establish a sense of *control* over input that maintains an emotional stance of interest and even excitement or joy. The inner environment of the short processor may lack a complexity and richness or depth of processing, which may lead to a lack of complicated emotionality. Because of the lack of preparatory rehearsal of material, it may also result in a vulnerability to sudden fear or distress when extremely novel or complex *external* information is presented.

The practiced long-processor may show less fluctuation in mood but may experience more continuing blends of the interest and joy of controlled processing with mildly dysphoric moods. After all through reflection one necessarily confronts one's unfinished business, such as unfulfilled intentions or the various possibilities of "real world" tragedies (e.g., death, nuclear war, injustice), toward which any sequence of associations will lead the knowledgeable individual. Studies by Linville (1982) suggest that persons identified as showing self-complexity do demonstrate less variability in mood over several days' sampling. (Self-complexity refers to a measure of more differentiated self-description, acceptance of somewhat contradictory beliefs, recognition of weaknesses as well as strengths, etc.) It is my proposal that this more differentiated belief structure about one's self emerges from greater reflection and mental replay in the form of ongoing rumination—in effect, a habitual or stylistic pattern of long-processing. A pattern of long-processing in the healthy personality configuration can be recognized as an adaptive form of a thinking-introversive or (following Witkin's extensive research) field-independent cognitive style (Witkin and Goodenough 1981). In its more pathological extreme, such an elaborate set of self-beliefs may be a feature of the obsessive-compulsive style described by Horowitz ([1976] 1986).

The patterns of response to stimuli from long-term memory as they emerge spontaneously (especially in less novel, "busy," or life-endangering physical and social environments) may also reflect the styles of long- and short-processing and the attempt to maintain a positive affective tone either by exploration, search, and "play" with thought (the long-processing mode) or by rapid shifts of attention to new external material (the short-processor's method). Such styles involve the individual in varying degrees and qualities of rehearsal of current concerns, as well as in the projections of self into different situations. Gradually they become the basis for forming sets of organized beliefs about the self or about the environment, which have special properties that, I believe, form a tie between the conscious representations of the stream of thought and those relatively unconscious schemata, scripts, and prototypes that unroll automatically to expedite cognitive matching and information-processing.

KNOWLEDGE STRUCTURES: SCHEMATA AND SCRIPTS ABOUT SELF AND OTHERS

The use of schemata as organizational structures that encapsulate knowledge about self or the world is traceable in psychology to the concepts of Jean Piaget, Kurt Lewin, Edward Tolman, and George Kelly. This concept of schemata reflects the psychoanalytic notions of unconscious fantasy, object representations, (Blatt and Wild 1976) and transference. It is only during the last decade that systematic efforts at operationalizing and experimenting with such notions have proliferated (Hollon and Kriss 1984; Turk and Speers 1983). Schemata may serve to filter the complex new information our senses confront; they are also continuously strengthened when similar information is processed ("Dogs bark when someone is at the door") or when one reflects on new, slightly divergent information ("Why isn't Fido barking when the bell rings? Is he sick?").

Self schemata, as operationalized and investigated systematically by Markus (1977) and Bandura (1977) and, in work with depressed patients, by Beck et al. (1979), represent a special case of beliefs about one's self. Beliefs about other people, fuzzy set "prototypes," such as "a typical businessman" or "the usual politician," have also been identified and studied (Cantor and Mischel 1979). The term "scripts," originally proposed by Tomkins (1962, 1963), has been developed by researchers in artificial intelligence in a specialized way to define organized belief-systems about action-sequences in the "real world," sequences that unroll relatively automatically like a well-programed series (Schank and Abelson 1977). A model for a similar schema in dealing with the imaging process was developed by Minsky (1975). Recently, Tomkins has proposed a theory that scripts about self or about especially important interpersonal interactions are frequently organized out of fairly specific childhood "scenes" that are associated with either strong positive or negative emotions (Tomkins 1979). The work of Rae Carlson (1981) and L. Carlson and R. Carlson (1984) exemplifies the way in which positive or negative affective "scenes" and scripts are differentially influential in current behavior and in the interpretation of new information. The semantic and practical relationship of schemata, scripts, and prototypes to the transference phenomenon identified in psychoanalytic sessions deserves much more extensive attention. It is increasingly clear that the long-standing dilemma of social psychology, the "why don't attitudes predict behavior?" question, has been resolved when the careful measurement of schemata about self and about others are considered separately and combined to predict overt actions (Kreitler and Kreitler 1976, 1982).

This very brief review of a major area of development in the lively field of social cognition is designed to suggest that if we wish to understand unconscious processes we will, first of all, have to seek them in the relatively automatic unrolling of scripts, the filtering processes of schemata, or in the inherent rules for evaluating information and making judgments described as *availability, representativeness,* and *anchoring with adjustment* heuristics by Tversky and Kahnemann (1974). Yet, so far such patterns of relatively automatic sequences have been explored chiefly in the framework of assigning individuals rather specific tasks to accomplish or problems to solve. The thrust of my earlier presentation leads me to propose that schemata, scripts, or prototypes are not static, even though they are certainly well-organized structures. They are constantly subject to reexamination and reshaping during waking conscious thought or even in the course of rumination about night-dreams, especially if one approaches such a process, as a psychotherapy patient might, with a particular schema for interpretation. If we are ultimately to understand the workings of "the unconscious," we will have to "unpackage" the various individual schemata, prototypes, scripts, "core organizing principles" (Meichenbaum and Gilmore 1984) or behavior heuristics by using types of systematic questioning or forms of thought sampling that can permit us to observe how they are used in ordinary daily life. Of course, psychoanalysis has been engaged in such a task, although in an often-unwitting and diffuse fashion. More recently, cognitive behavior therapists have begun addressing this task quite directly in treatment (Meichenbaum and Gilmore 1984; Singer 1984a). Luborsky's (1977b) demonstration of reasonably reliable methods for identifying "core conflictual themes" (surely close relatives of schemata and scripts) within psychoanalytic sessions could also be applied to more extensive samples of nontherapeutic ongoing thought sequences in daily life or in laboratory settings, as well as to samples of patients' communication in various forms of psychotherapy.

In view of the great importance assigned to beliefs about self by both psychoanalysts oriented toward object relations theory and cognitive researchers, special attention should be paid to how such schemata become organized by ongoing interior monologues. Tomkins's notion of positively or negatively laden nuclear scripts (which usually involve the self) implies differential filtering processes for new information in relation to expectancies based on such scripts. He suggests hypersensitivity to possible analogies in new settings for negative nuclear scripts, or efforts to "reshape" new information to enhance its similarity to positive nuclear scenes. Can we identify such processes by extended samples of thought or self-monitoring procedures? Certainly no one would seriously claim, nor could they prove, that the "objects" of object relations are permanently crystallized in the original pregenital schemata. Very likely they emerge again and again into conscious ruminations, tested and elaborated in mental rehearsals or reminiscences and "acted out" in transferential encounters in daily life as well as in analysis. As we shall consider in the next section, they may also be replayed and reshaped further in what we remember of our sleep mentation. An individual stylistic variable worth exploring is the way that "repressors" seem to have developed long-standing strategies to avoid extended attention to ongoing thought. Thus, they may have differentiated and reshaped earlier schemata, prototypes, and scripts less than other individuals. When such material subsequently emerges into their consciousness, it may surprise them more or seem alien and peremptory, and it may remain more global, childlike, and rigid in structure. Recent work by Bowen suggests that such undifferentiated patterns may also be evident in their cardiovascular response to emotional arousal.

The relative importance of self schemata has implications for general emotional patterning. It can be argued (as in the example of the jealous husband presented at the outset) that there is a more complex set of associative links and schemata about self or scripts involving self-directed actions than for many other situations of daily life. Experimental studies designed to arouse emotions or to alter moods have generally shown mixed results because they have failed to separate self-involving instructional sets or experimental manipulations from other-oriented procedures. A thorough review of dozens of available studies on mood induction indicates that where self-oriented situations are presented, strong and more persisting emotional arousal is obtained. Other-oriented instructions or sets, on the other hand, evoke mild and transient mood changes (Salovey and Singer forthcoming). Here again I would propose that extensive samplings of ongoing thought would demonstrate how often our ruminations and daydreams turn on a range of possibilities bearing on self so that the ultimate associate network of self-related images and semantic links is broad and deep, as in Anderson's sense (Anderson 1983).

WAKING THOUGHTS AND DREAM CONTENT

I have already suggested that we begin to structure the content and organization of sleep mentation in the "day residues" or, as

Klinger (1971) has proposed, in the current concerns of waking life. Although Freud regarded the dream as the royal road to the unconscious, I suggest that increasing evidence from comparisons of daydream and night-dream samples (Starker 1978) or from the accumulation and analysis of sleep mentation reports in EEG Stage 1-REM and EEG Stage 2-NREM from laboratories, points to a continuity between dreams and conscious thought. The studies of Breger, Hunter, and Lane (1971) indicate that even specific phraseology occurring in presleep verbalizations emerges as presumably visual images in subsequent dream reports of participants who sleep in the laboratory. Recent careful work by Antrobus (1983) and his co-workers has shown that very precise quantitative analyses of REM and NREM sleep mentation reports point much more to continuities and similarities in content and patterns of thought than to differences between these stages. Antrobus's analysis of the metaphoric structure of waking thought and how metaphors may be formed by semantic generalization in dreams further suggests a continuity of day and sleep mentation. In a recent analysis, Antrobus, Reinsel, and Wollman (1984) compared night-dream reports from Stage 1-REM and Stage 2-NREM with reports obtained from waking subjects in a normally stimulated environment as well as one in which sensory input was relatively reduced. The researchers hypothesized that two properties of Stage 1-REM sleep might account for the major difference consistently obtained between dream reports from that sleep stage and those from Stage 2-NREM: (1) a higher level of cortical activation (that is, a more wakeful brain) and (2) a higher perceptual threshold for awareness of one's physical surroundings. Indeed, this combination has led to the general term *paradoxical sleep* for Stage 1-REM. In the waking state, even in relatively understimulated environments, one usually is processing external material. Daydream material seems therefore to lack the vividness, sense of reality, and figure-ground differentiation of the night-dream report. The study found that the major differences in the reports obtained from a series of participants was that Stage 1-REM and sensory-restricted wakeful free associations were characterized by more words, longer sequences of thought, and less reference to the physical environment. One might surmise that the long, storylike quality of the "classical" Stage 1-REM dream is a function of an extended response to long-term memory material uninterrupted by any notice of the participants' surroundings, (e.g., bed, laboratory). Such references are more frequent in both the waking "noisy" environment reports and the Stage 2-REM reports. Similarly, the waking mentation reports from a less busy setting reflect extensive response to self-derived thought and minimal reaction to the physical environment. Comparable waking data of longer sequences of thought, more remote from present concerns, as the social situation of respondents was reduced, were obtained in a thought sampling study by Pope (1978). A remarkable literary demonstration of this result can be seen in Molly Bloom's soliloquy in bed at the end of James Joyce's *Ulysses* (Humphrey 1968; Steinberg 1979).

The data on the comparability of waking reverie and night-dreaming suggest an extended continuity between conscious mentation and night-dream content. I propose that the images and metaphors of many dreams are already prepared in waking rumination but such thoughts are frequently forgotten because we have no purpose in remembering them. Dream interpretation in psychoanalysis draws on after-the-fact associations. What would we find if we sampled the patients' thoughts beforehand?

Here is an example of such an instance, the dream and then the prior thought samples of an individual who carried a pager for a week:

I am in Canada visiting Bill, a younger former associate of mine. We are on an extremely steep mountain. There are dozens of skiers who are coming down this incline with great speed, often taking long leaps before coming back down to earth. Bill points upwards and says "Let's keep walking up there and we can get some skis and ski down." I find myself appalled as I see the steepness of the mountain. As we climb higher I become more and more aware that I am not a good enough skier to come down at the rate of other skiers.

I put on some skis and am trying in my slow fashion to cut slowly sideways across the mountain face rather than schussing straight downhill. I notice my friend Bill whizzing by with great confidence. Suddenly, however, he takes a very bad fall and lies in the snow, obviously having hurt his leg.

Later I am visiting Bill and another, even younger man who now shares an apartment with him. I realize that both Bill and his new roommate have recently had marital problems and are living bachelor lives. I say to them that while I appreciate some of the advantages of bachelorhood, I am really quite happy with my own wife after twenty years of marriage.

A surprising number of details from this man's recent waking thoughts turned up in the dream. The dreamer was a middle-aged man who was an executive in a well-established engineering company. He seriously questioned his ability to master the required technology (to schuss downhill) as the firm moved into new areas of engineering. He had also been examining in his thoughts the value of his intensive work for the company. He wondered whether he could keep up the pace, considering his apparently diminishing physical strength and skill.

Several events in recent days had triggered some of these thoughts. In one of them, he and his wife had set out on a quiet walk on a marked trail in the woods. They took the wrong path and ended up climbing a mountain; they then had to retrace their steps down a steep incline. Despite what seemed at times an impossible climb, they both emerged none the worse. He had also been watching the Olympic games on television, with many thoughts and conversations about the intensity and determination required for the athletes to reach the levels of skill necessary for international competition.

The man's dream can be understood as a representation in visual form of a whole series of questions and thoughts that had been going on in his conscious mind. These included intense emotions as well as unfinished business and current concerns. There were fears and doubts associated with the difficulty of maintaining his standards of scientific work as his company moved toward more technological development. This thought brought to mind his former colleague, Bill. Although younger, Bill had always seemed more technically competent, but in recent years he had suffered setbacks at work and in his personal life. A new, younger colleague also seems likely to have greater professional skills, but again (and here the dream fades over in a wish), perhaps the older man can say, "Well, I can still climb that mountain, and I can also say that I have a more fulfilled personal life."

Thus, the symbolism of the dream was probably not created completely within the dream but was already anticipated in the man's daytime thoughts. Usually psychologists do not have daytime records and samples of ongoing thought as in this case. And in a psychotherapy session a patient's associations to a dream are after the fact. The likelihood is that many of our daytime thoughts contain symbolic or allegorical associations, which we may store and think about further during the day. But the press of daily affairs may prevent us from noticing how much time we spend in self-reflection, and we are therefore surprised by the symbolism and imagery of our dreams (Singer 1984a).

Thought and Health: Some Research Directions

Some implications for physical health have been emerging from studies of thought. I have already indicated that the ongoing machinery of the body represents a signaling system that competes weakly (except for massive pain or severe stress or fatigue) for channel space at the focus of conscious awareness with environmental stimuli and reverberating material from long-term memory. The process is cyclical and interactive. As systems theorists point out, our mental awareness of body signals produces thought sequences that, if in the form of pleasant, relaxing imagery or in the form of frightening scripts about serious illness, surgery, or death, may generate quite specific neurotransmitter reactions in the central nervous system and particular autonomic, muscular, or cardiovascular reactions (Schwartz 1982). Researchers are increasing their efforts to identify general kinds of self-communications that aid people in coping with particular kinds of pain or physical stress and that may also promote longer-term strategies of adherence to medical regimens, self-care, or disease-preventive life-styles (Turk, Meichenbaum, and Genest 1983).

Probably the most persuasive evidence of how some form of thought activity can almost at once influence physiological functions or disease processes has come from clinical and experimental studies with hypnosis. A recent review by Barber (1984) documents dozens of examples of bodily changes produced by suggestion and intense imagery absorption. Perhaps most dramatic are the cases of relatively rapid clearing of loathsome fish-scale dermatological conditions with brief hypnosis. Since current research suggests that persons under hypnotic directions continue to show self-monitoring and ongoing thought, we might want to sample more extensively over time some of their images and self-directions to determine what the "active ingredients" at the mental level are for suggestion effects and to correlate those with specific bodily changes linked to physical improvement.

In a study carried out in Japan on contagious dermatitis produced by contact or proximity to the lacquer and wax trees, the investigators studied adolescent boys who had on previous occasions shown considerable sensitivity when exposed during hikes to these trees (somewhat like our poison oak or sumac). Using extracts and hypnotic suggestion, they exposed participants to either harmless leaves identified as noxious or to noxious leaves identified as harmless. Within less than an hour, flushing and papules appeared on the arm exposed to the actual poisonous extract. Within half a day, erythema, papules, edema, serious exudate, and vesicles appeared on the suggested arm (Ikemi and Nakagawa 1962). Although such results were strongest in especially sensitive persons, effects were evident even in persons only moderately sensitive from past history. Only 13% of the subjects were unresponsive either to the suggestion or the extract.

A serendipitous exemplification of this effect emerged when my research assistant read the above paper. She had recently returned from a two-week wilderness vacation very pleased that despite a history of poison-ivy sensitivity she had emerged without any signs of the condition. Within a few hours after reading Ikemi and Nakagawa's lengthy (and illustrated) report, she developed skin flushing and papules on her arm and in the next day they spread, a clear manifestation of poison ivy but fortunately a mild one. It seems certain that while reading the article she had brief reminiscent images of her own earlier exposures to poison ivy and to scenes involving the consequences or body images of the pain. Very likely such images mimicked direct ideomotor instructions (even if not consciously *desired*) and the autonomic nervous system and skin receptors responded. Perhaps the skin, like the old dictum about the unconscious, knows no negatives.

On a more serious note, there is a sizable and growing literature linking major illness, either in onset or in course, to particular psychological orientations. I will mention here only a few instances of studies at Yale in which specific thought processes have been linked to such illness or their outcomes. A very careful recent study by Crits-Christoph (1984) examined the thought patterns (based on questionnaire responses) of normal individuals whose blood pressure was known and clinical hypertensives. For these groups, contrary to some early beliefs, it could be shown that a history of consciously experienced anger, not suppression or repression of anger, predicted hypertension. Anxiety, direct or suppressed, served as a control emotion to anger and it did not predict hypertension. Thus, the effect was specific to a *particular* emotion, anger, and was even more specifically linked to hostile, angry fantasies as measured from the Imaginal Processes Inventory.

A more extensive study carried out by Jensen (1984) sought to determine if psychological measures could predict the course of neoplastic disease, specifically breast cancer. Very carefully matched groups were set up of women having cancer-free breasts, breast cancer that had been remitted for two years, and recently diagnosed breast cancer. They were matched on a very extensive array of physical, hereditary, sociocultural, and treatment variables. A group of psychological tests as well as extensive physiological and blood-chemistry measures were administered, and the groups were followed for two years. In conformity to a good number of earlier studies, both cancer groups showed a greater proportion of women who could be classified as repressors, that is, persons who report no anxiety but who score higher on a measure of social conformity or defensiveness than the control group. The repression variable, as well as a measure of positive daydreaming, proved to be a strong predictor of a poor treatment course for the patients. The latter variable was especially predictive for nonrepressors; that is, women who did not show a repressive style but who reported a good deal of positive, playful, or escapist daydreaming, obtained as poor scores on disease status after two years as did the repressors. As predictors, the psychological variables were as good as or better than the blood chemistry measures. The implications of these findings (in conformity with clinical reports) is that better health outcomes may emerge, at least for some forms of cancer, if the patient concentrates on angry and resolute fantasies rather than denying concern or escaping into pleasant fantasy. A recent study by Felton and Revenson (1984) also found a poor outcome for escapist, wish-fulfilling fantasy in chronic illness. In the words of Dylan Thomas to his dying father, "Do not go gentle into that good night. . . Rage, rage against the dying of the light."

Note the contrast between the two studies by Crits-Christoph and Jensen. In one, angry fantasies seem correlated with pathological trends; in the second, the absence of conscious anger, determination, and concern seems more associated with a disease process. In a controlled study just now completed by William Polonsky, images involving positive effects on the immune system of asthmatics were specifically associated with subsequent actual improvements in the immune system, although not nearly so strongly with symptomatic relief. We will need a great deal more careful work, it appears, tying specific kinds of self-generated images to specific ongoing physiological changes. An exciting opportunity lies ahead. To what extent are conscious thoughts functioning like ideomotor suggestions? Or are they merely translating into conscious reports some as yet not understood "body machinery" communication? Are the relatively automatic, out-of-awareness operations of our body scripts and schemata crucial here, or are conscious reports the critical factors? I would suggest that research may support the latter option.

In conclusion, I have suggested that we have not given sufficient thought to the operation of conscious, continuing thought as an influence on our behavior or physiological states. We have, I believe, delegated important effects to presumed unconscious fantasies or to complex unconscious dynamics before exploring fully enough the extent to which the ordinary stream of consciousness reflects the concerns, intentions, long-term wishes, and conflicts that recur regularly to us. Such conscious intentions or fantasies are reshaped and symbolized so that they form organized schemata, scripts, or person prototypes that, when over-learned, operate almost automatically and outside awareness, as many motor habits do under some conditions. Until we examine conscious thought more extensively—and, as I have suggested, improved methods are now available—I propose that we remain cautious about assigning a major role to the complex unconscious mechanisms, as psychoanalytic theory has in the past. We need to sample waking, natural thought if we are to understand how repressors evade an awareness of problematic issues, how repressors ignore body cures, or how wishful fantasizers may relax and enjoy life in some circumstances and endanger themselves in others. Perhaps attention to consciousness lacks the aura of mystery, of cave exploration, that is conveyed by talk of uncovering the secrets of the unconscious. But when I contemplate the great riches of waking imagery—our conscious capacity to journey to many worlds, play different parts, and live many vicarious lives in narrative lines of thought—I am happy to follow that sunlit road.

References

Ahern, G. L. 1982. Differential lateralization for positive and negative emotion in the human brain: EEG spectral analysis. Ph.D. diss., Yale University.

Algom, D., and J. L. Singer. 1984. Interpersonal influences on task-irrelevant thought and imagery in a signal-detection task. *Imagination, Cognition, and Personality,* vol. 4, 69–83.

Anderson, J. R. 1983. *The Architecture of Cognition.* Cambridge, Mass.: Harvard University Press.

Antrobus, J. S. 1968. Information theory and stimulus-independent thought. *British Journal of Psychology* 59:423–30.

———. 1983. REM and NREM sleep reports: Comparison of word frequencies by cognitive classes. *Psychophysiology* 20:562–68.

Antrobus, J. S., R. Coleman, and J. L. Singer. 1967. Signal detection performance by subjects differing in predisposition to daydreaming. *Journal of Consulting Psychology* 31:487–91.

Antrobus, J. S., G. Fein, S. Goldstein, and J. L. Singer. 1984. Mindwandering: Time-sharing task-irrelevant thought and imagery with experimental tasks. Manuscript.

Antrobus, J. S., R. Reinsel, and M. Wollman. 1988. Dreaming: Cortical activation and perceptual thresholds. In S. Ellman and J. S. Antrobus, eds., *The Mind in Sleep*. 2d ed. Hillsdale, N.J.: Erlbaum.

Antrobus, J. S., and J. L. Singer. 1964. Visual signal detection as a function of sequential task variability of simultaneous speech. *Journal of Experimental Psychology* 68:603–10.

Antrobus, J. S., J. L. Singer, S. Goldstein, and M. Fortgang. 1970. Mindwandering and cognitive structure. *Transactions of the New York Academy of Science*, 2d series 31:242–52.

Bandura, A. 1977. Self-efficacy: Toward a unified theory of behavioral change. *Psychological Review* 84:191–215.

Barber, T. X. 1984. Changing "unchangeable" bodily processes by (hypnotic) suggestions: A new look at hypnosis, cognitions, imaging, and the mind-body problem. In A. A. Sheikh, ed., *Imagination and Healing*. Farmingdale, N.Y.: Baywood.

Barrios, M., and J. L. Singer. 1981. The treatment of creative blocks: A comparison of waking imagery, hypnotic dreams, and rational discussion techniques. *Imagination, Cognition, and Personality* 1:89–116.

Beck, A. T., A. J. Rush, B. F. Shaw, and G. Emery. 1979. *Cognitive Therapy of Depression*. New York: Guilford.

Blatt, S. J., and C. M. Wild. 1976. *Schizophrenia: A Developmental Analysis*. New York: Academic Press.

Bowen, W. 1984. Cardiovascular rigidity and flexibility: Relationship to affect and cognition. Ph.D. diss., Yale University.

Bower, P. B. 1982–83. On *not* trying so hard: Effortless experiencing and its correlates. *Imagination, Cognition, and Personality* 2:3–14.

Brandstatter, H. 1983. Emotional responses to other persons in everyday life situations. *Journal of Personality and Social Psychology* 45:871–83.

Breger, L., I. Hunter, and R. W. Lane. 1971. *The Effect of Stress on Dreams*. New York: International University Press.

Broadbent, D. 1958. *Perception and Communication*. London: Pergamon Press.

Brown, S. L. 1978. Relationships between facial expression and subjective experience of emotion in depressed and normal subjects. Ph.D. diss., Yale University.

Cantor, N. and W. Mischel. 1979. Prototypes in person perception. In L. Berkowitz ed., *Advances in Experimental Psychology*, vol. 12. New York: Academic Press.

Carlson, L., and R. Carlson. 1984. Affect and psychological magnification: Derivations from Tomkins' script theory. *Journal of Personality* 52:36–45.

Carlson, R. 1981. Studies in script theory, 1: Adult analogs of a childhood nuclear scene. *Journal of Personality and Social Psychology* 4:533–61.

Cartwright, D., J. L. Jenkins, R. Chavez, and H. Peckar. 1983. Studies of imagery and identity. *Journal of Personality and Social Psychology* 44:376–84.

Crawford, H. J. 1982. Hypnotizability, daydreaming styles, imagery vividness, and absorption: A multidimensional study. *Journal of Personality and Social Psychology* 42:915–26.

Crits-Christoph, P. 1984. The role of anger in high blood pressure. Ph.D. diss., Yale University.

Csikszentmihalyi, M. 1982. Toward a psychology of optimal experience. In L. Wheeler ed., *Review of Personality and Social Psychology*, vol. 3. Beverly Hills, Calif.: Sage.

Csikszentmihalyi, M., and R. Graef. 1980. The experience of freedom in daily life. *American Journal of Community Psychology* 8:4101–4414.

Csikszentmihalyi, M., and R. Kubey. 1981. Television and the rest of life: A systematic comparison of subjective experience. *Public Opinion Quarterly* 45:317–28.

Csikszentmihalyi, M., and R. Larson. 1984. *Being Adolescent*. New York: Basic Books.

Edelson, M. 1984. *Hypothesis and Evidence in Psychoanalysis*. Chicago: University of Chicago Press.

Ekman, P., R. W. Levenson, and W. V. Friesen. 1983. Autonomic nervous system activity distinguishes among emotions. *Science* 221:1208–1210.

Fein, G. G., and J. S. Antrobus. 1977. Daydreaming: A Poisson process. Manuscript.

Felton, B. J., and J. A. Revenson. 1984. Coping with chronic illness: A study of illness controllability and the influence of coping strategies on psychological adjustment. *Journal of Consulting and Clinical Psychology* 52:343–53.

Fenigstein, A., M. Scheier, and A. H. Buss. 1975. Public and private self-consciousness: Assessment and theory. *Journal of Consulting and Clinical Psychology* 43:522–24.

Giambra, L. M. 1980. Sex differences in daydreaming and related mental activity from the late teens to the early nineties. *International Journal of Aging and Human Development* 10:1–34.

Golding, J. M., and J. L. Singer. 1983. Patterns of inner experience: Daydreaming styles, depressive moods, and sex roles. *Journal of Personality and Social Psychology* 45:663–75.

Goldstein, K. 1940. *Human Nature in the Light of Psychopathology.* Cambridge, Mass.: Harvard University Press.

Head, H. 1926. *Aphasia and Kindred Disorders of Speech.* 2 vols. Cambridge: Cambridge University Press.

Heckhausen, H. 1977. Achievement motivation and its construction: A cognitive model. *Motivation and Emotion* 1:283–329.

Hilgard, E. R. 1965. *Hypnotic Susceptibility.* New York: Harcourt, Brace and World.

————. 1977. *Divided Consciousness: Multiple Controls in Human Thought and Action.* New York: Wiley.

Hoelscher, T. J., E. Klinger, and S. G. Barta. 1981. Incorporation of concern- and nonconcern-related stimuli into dream content. *Journal of Abnormal Psychology* 90:88–91.

Hollon, S. D., and M. Kriss. 1984. Cognitive factors in clinical research and practice. *Clinical Psychology Review* 4:35–76.

Holt, R. R. 1976. Drive or wish? A reconsideration of the psychoanalytic theory of motivation. In M. M. Gill and P. S. Holzman, eds., Psychology Versus Metapsychology: Psychoanalytic Essays in Memory of George S. Klein, *Psychological Issues,* monograph 36. New York: International Universities Press.

Horowitz, M. J. [1976] 1986. *Stress Response Syndromes.* 2d ed. New York: Aronson.

————. 1978. *Image Formation and Cognition.* New York: Appleton-Century-Crofts.

Horowitz, M., C. Marmar, J. Krupnick, N. Wilner, N. Kaltreider, and R. Wallerstein. 1984. *Personality Styles and Brief Psychotherapy.* New York: Basic Books.

Huba, G. J. 1980. Daydreaming. In R. H. Woody, ed., *Encyclopedia of Clinical Assessment.* San Francisco: Jossey-Bass.

Huba, G. J., J. L. Singer, C. S. Aneshensel, and J. S. Antrobus. 1982. *The Short Imaginal Processes Inventory.* Port Huron, Mich.: Research Psychologists Press.

Humphrey, R. 1968. *The Stream of Consciousness in the Modern Novel.* Berkeley and Los Angeles: University of California Press.

Hurlburt, R. T. 1978. Random sampling of cognitions in alleviating anxiety attacks. *Cognitive Therapy and Research* 2:165–70.

————. 1979. Random sampling of cognitions and behavior. *Journal of Research in Personality* 13:103–11.

————. 1980. Validation and correlation of thought sampling with retrospective measures. *Cognitive Therapy and Research* 4:235–38.

Ikemi, Y., and S. Nakagawa. 1962. A psychosomatic study of contagious dermatitis. *Kyushu Journal of Medical Science* 13:335–50.

Isaacs, I. 1975. Self reports of daydreaming and mindwandering: A construct validation. Ph.D. diss., City University of New York.

Izard, C. E., ed. 1977. *Human Emotions.* New York: Plenum Press.

Jensen, M. 1984. Psychobiological factors in the prognosis and treatment of neoplastic disorders. Ph.D. diss., Yale University.

Johnson, C., and R. Larson. 1982. Bulimia: An analysis of moods and behavior. *Psychosomatic Medicine* 44:341–51.

Johnson, M. K., and C. L. Raye. 1981. Reality monitoring. *Psychological Review* 88:67–85.

Kendall, P. C., and S. D. Hollon. 1981. Assessing self-referent speech: Methods in the measurement of self-statements. In P. C. Kendall and S. D. Hollon, eds., *Assessment Strategies for Cognitive-Behavioral Interventions*. New York: Academic Press.

Klein, G. 1967. Peremptory ideation: Structure and force in motivated ideas. In R. R. Holt, ed., *Motives and Thought*. New York: International Universities Press.

Klinger, E. 1971. *Structure and Functions of Fantasy*. New York: Wiley.

———. 1977a. *Meaning and Void: Inner Experience and the Incentives in People's Lives*. Minneapolis: University of Minnesota Press.

———. 1977b. The nature of fantasy and its clinical uses. *Psychotherapy: Theory, Research, and Practice* 14:223–31.

———. 1978. Modes of normal conscious flow. In K. S. Pope and J. L. Singer, eds., *The Stream of Consciousness*. New York: Plenum Press.

———. 1981. The central place of imagery in human functioning. In E. Klinger, ed., *Imagery*, vol. 2: *Concepts, Results, and Applications*. New York: Plenum Press.

Klinger, E., S. Barta, and M. Maxeiner. 1981. Current concerns: Assessing therapeutically relevant motivation. In *Assessment Strategies for Cognitive-Behavioral Interventions*. New York: Academic Press.

Klos, D. S., and J. L. Singer. 1981. Determinants of the adolescent's ongoing thought following simulated parental confrontations. *Journal of Personality and Social Psychology* 41:975–87.

Kosslyn, S. M. 1981. The medium and the message in mental imagery: A theory. *Psychological Review* 88:46–66.

Kreitler, H., and S. Kreitler. 1976. *Cognitive Orientation and Behavior*. New York: Springer.

———. 1982. The theory of cognitive orientation: Widening the scope of behavior prediction. Ed. B. Maher. *Experimental Personality Research* New York: Springer.

Kubey, R. 1982. Recuperative leisure and the psychic economy: The case of television. Ph.D. diss., University of Chicago.

Langer, E. 1983. *The Psychology of Control*. Beverly Hills, Calif.: Sage.

Lewin, K. 1935. *A Dynamic Theory of Personality*. New York:McGraw-Hill.

Linville, P. W. 1982. Affective consequence of complexity regarding the self and others. In M. S. Clark and S. T. Fiske, eds., *Affect and Cognition: Seventeenth Annual Carnegie Symposium on Cognition*. Hillsdale, N.J.: Erlbaum.

Luborsky, L. 1977a. Measuring a pervasive psychic structure in psychotherapy: The core conflictual relationship theme. In N. Freedman and S. Grand, eds., *Communicative Structures and Psychic Structure*. New York: Plenum Press.

————. 1977b. New directions in research on neurotic and psychosomatic symptoms. In I. L. Janis, ed., *Current Trends in Psychology: Readings from the American Scientist.* Los Altos, Calif.: Kaufman.

McAdams, D., and C. A. Constantian. 1983. Intimacy and affiliation motives in daily living: An experience sampling analysis. *Journal of Personality and Social Psychology* 4:851–61.

McClelland, D. C. 1961. *The Achieving Society.* Princeton: Van Nostrand.

McDonald, C. 1976. Random sampling of cognitions: A field study of daydreaming. M. A. prediss., Yale University.

McIlwraith, R. M., and J. Schallow. 1983a. Adult fantasy life and patterns of media use. *Journal of Communications* 33:91–99.

————. 1983b. Television viewing and styles of children's fantasy. *Imagination, Cognition, and Personality* 2:323–31.

Maddi, S. 1976. *Personality Theories: A Comparative Analysis.* Homewood, Ill.: Dorsey.

Mandler, G. 1975. *Mind and Emotion.* New York: Wiley.

Markus, H. 1977. Self-schemata and processing information about the self. *Journal of Personality and Social Psychology* 35:63–78.

Meichenbaum, D., and J. B. Gilmore. 1984. The nature of unconscious processes: A cognitive-behavioral perspective. In K. Bowers and D. Meichenbaum, eds., *The Unconscious Reconsidered.* New York: Wiley.

Minsky, M. 1975. A framework for representing knowledge. In P. H. Winston, ed., *The Psychology of Computer Vision.* New York: McGraw-Hill.

Neville, R. C. 1981. *Reconstruction of Thinking.* Albany: State University of New York Press.

Pekala, R., and R. Levine. 1981. Mapping consciousness: Development of an empirical-phenomenological approach. *Imagination, Cognition, and Personality* 1:29–47.

————. 1982. Quantifying states of consciousness via an empirical-phenomenological approach. *Imagination, Cognition, and Personality* 2:51–71.

Pope, K. S. 1978. How gender, solitude, and posture influence the stream of consciousness. In K. S. Pope and J. L. Singer, eds., *The Stream of Consciousness.* New York: Plenum Press.

Pribram, K., and D. McGuinness. 1976. Arousal, activation, and effort in the control of attention. *Psychological Review* 82:116–49.

Qualls, P. J. 1982–83. The physiological measurement of imagery: An overview. *Imagination, Cognition, and Personality* 2:89–101.

Rychlak, J. 1977. *The Psychology of Rigorous Humanism.* New York: Wiley.

————. 1981. Logical learning theory: Propositions, corollaries, and research evidence. *Journal of Personality and Social Psychology* 40:731–49.

Salovey, P., and J. Rodin. 1984. Some antecedents and consequences of social-comparison jealousy. *Journal of Personality and Social Psychology* 47:780–92.

Schank, R. C., and R. P. Abelson. 1977. *Scripts, Plans, Goals, and Understanding.* Hillsdale, N.J.: Erlbaum.

Schwartz, G. E. 1982. Cardiovascular psychophysiology: A systems perspective. In J. T. Cacioppo and R. E. Petty, eds., *Focus on Cardiovascular Psychopathology.* New York: Guilford.

———. 1983. Disregulation theory and disease: Applications to the repression/cerebral disconnection/cardiovascular disorder hypothesis. *International Review of Applied Psychology* 32:95–118.

Schwartz, G., E. Weinberger, and J. A. Singer. 1981. Cardiovascular differentiation of happiness, sadness, anger, and fear, following imagery and exercise. *Psychosomatic Medicine* 43:343–64.

Segal, B., G. J. Huba, and J. L. Singer. 1980. *Drugs, Daydreaming, and Personality: A Study of College Youth.* Hillsdale, N.J.: Erlbaum.

Segal, S. J. 1971. Processing of the stimulus in imagery and perception. In S. J. Segal, *Imagery.* New York: Academic Press.

Shepard, R. N. 1978. The mental image. *American Psychologist* 33:125–7.

Sifneos, P. E. 1972. *Short-Term Psychotherapy and Emotional Crisis.* Cambridge, Mass.: Harvard University Press.

Singer, J. A., and Salovey, P. Forthcoming. Mood and memory: Evaluating the network theory of affect. *Clinical Psychology Review.*

Singer, J. L. 1966. *Daydreaming.* New York: Random House.

———. 1973. *The Child's World of Make-Believe.* New York: Academic Press.

———. 1974. *Imagery and Daydreaming Methods in Psychotherapy and Behavior Modification.* New York: Academic Press.

———. 1984a. *The Human Personality: An Introductory Text.* San Diego, Calif.: Harcourt Brace Jovanovich.

———. 1984b. The private personality. *Personality and Social Psychology Bulletin* 10:7–30.

Singer, J. L., and J. S. Antrobus. 1972. Daydreaming, imaginal processes, and personality: A normative study. In P. Sheehan, ed., *The Function and Nature of Imagery.* New York: Academic Press.

Singer, J. L., S. Greenberg, and J. S. Antrobus. 1971. Looking with the mind's eye: Experimental studies of ocular mobility during daydreaming and mental arithmetic. *Transactions of the New York Academy of Sciences* 33:694–709.

Singer, J. L., and K. S. Pope. 1981. Daydreaming and imagery skills as predisposing capacities for self-hypnosis. *The International Journal of Clinical and Experimental Hypnosis* 29:271–81.

Snyder, M. 1979. Self-monitoring processes. In L. Berkowitz, ed., *Advances in Experimental Social Psychology.* New York: Academic Press.

Spanos, N. P., and H. L. Radtke. 1981. Hypnotic visual hallucinations as imaginings: A cognitive-social psychological perspective. *Imagination, Cognition, and Personality* 1:147–70.

Starker, S. 1978. Dreams and waking fantasy. In K. S. Pope and J. L. Singer, eds., *The Stream of Consciousness: Scientific Investigations into the Flow of Human Experience.* New York: Plenum Press.

Steinberg, E. 1979. *Stream of Consciousness Technique in the Modern Novel*. Port Washington, N.Y.: Kennikat Press, National University Publications.

Taylor, E. 1983. *William James on Exceptional Mental States: The 1896 Lowell Lectures*. New York: Scribner.

Tomkins, S. S. 1962. *Affect, Imagery, Consciousness*, vol. 1. New York: Springer.

————. 1963. *Affect, Imagery, Consciousness*, vol. 2. New York: Springer.

————. 1979. Script theory: Differential magnifications of affects. In H. E. Howe, Jr., and R. A. Dienstbier, eds., *Nebraska Symposium on Motivation, 1978*. Lincoln: University of Nebraska Press.

Tower, R. B., and J. L. Singer. 1981. The measurement of imagery: How can it be clinically useful? In P. C. Kendall and S. Hollon, eds., *Assessment Strategies for Cognitive-Behavioral Intervention*. New York: Academic Press.

Tucker, D. M., and P. A. Williamson. 1984. Assymetric neural control systems and human self-regulation. *Psychological Review* 91:185–215.

Turk, D. C., D. Meichenbaum, and M. Genest, M. 1983. *Pain and Behavioral Medicine: A Cognitive-Behavioral Perspective*. New York: Guilford.

Turk, D. C., and M. A. Speers. 1983. Cognitive schemata and cognitive processes in cognitive-behavioral interventions: Going beyond the information given. In P. C. Kendall, ed., *Advances in Cognitive-Behavioral Research and Therapy*, vol. 2. New York: Academic Press.

Tversky, A., and D. Kahnemann. 1974. Judgment under uncertainty: Heuristics and biases. *Science* 135:1124–31.

Weinberger, D. A. 1983. Distress, suppression of desire and the classification of personality style. Ph.D. diss., Yale University.

Weinberger, D. A., G. E. Schwartz, and J. R. Davidson. 1979. Low-anxious, high-anxious, and repressive coping styles: Psychometric patterns and behavioral and physiological responses to stress. *Journal of Abnormal Psychology* 88:369–80.

Wilson, S. C. and T. X. Barber. 1983. The fantasy-prone personality: Implications for understanding imagery, hypnosis, and parapsychological phenomena. In A. A. Sheikh, ed., *Imagery: Current Theory, Research, and Application*. New York: Wiley.

Witkin, H. A., and D. R. Goodenough. 1981. *Cognitive Styles: Essence and Origins*. New York: International Universities Press.

Zachary, R. 1983. Cognitive and affective determinants of ongoing thought. Ph.D. diss., Yale University.

Zajonc, R. B. 1980. Feeling and thinking: Preferences need no inferences. *American Psychologist* 35:151–75.

Prolegomena for the Study of Access to Mental Events: Notes on Singer's Chapter

R. B. Zajonc, Ph.D.

In the natural sciences there are probably no topics more difficult to study than consciousness and unconsciousness. It is easier to find out what the world is like than to find out *how* we come to know it and to know that we know it. It is this sort of puzzle that we must solve if we are to understand conscious and unconscious processes.

In the study of natural phenomena, the epistemological question of how we can be sure of our knowledge is treated by the assumption that, aided by instrumentation and logic, our sources of knowledge must be considered reliable and trustworthy. For those of us who study consciousness and cognition, or perception, the problem is much more serious because we are required to make *premature* epistemological assumptions about the very phenomena that we seek to explain.

Jerome L. Singer's assertions about the importance of studying consciousness might well be viewed in this light, for if anyone succeeds in solving the question of mental processes, not only will that particular problem be solved but the *general* epistemological problem will have been solved as well. A profound revolution in all science may take place depending on the nature of the answer, thus changing the meaning of all that we know or do not know about life and the universe.

Singer's article contains many rich ideas. I shall confine my discussion to four main issues raised by his work: (1) reactivity of reporting ongoing thought; (2) access to ongoing conscious and unconscious thought; (3) access to memories: the nature of representations; (4) the role of self in conscious and unconscious processes.

Reactivity of Reporting Ongoing Thought

We are not aware of most aspects of sensing, perceiving, and cognizing as these processes take place *here and now*. As they go on, these processes are only partly accessible to consciousness. The first general issue brought up in Singer's article concerns the nature of the subject's report of the contents of an *ongoing* conscious process. Ericsson and Simon (1980) have recently examined the usefulness of such reports in subject's protocols obtained for the analysis of problem solving. They have identified many useful and reliable features of the protocol in which subjects disclosed how they went about solving a given problem, especially a fairly well-defined one. Singer's procedure is admirably careful and the consistency of his results indicates that, in all likelihood, they are reliable. Nevertheless, the question arises about the effects of having subjects *themselves* (without a convergent backup procedure) indicate the presence and content of thoughts.

Rousseau, Johnson, and Stevens (1984) have recently examined the possible reactive effects of a protocol (thinking aloud) on the cognitive process that is itself the subject of the protocol. The results are somewhat disquieting. In comparing subjects who did and did not give protocols of the way they dealt with simple problems, considerable differences were found, even though no *systematic* trends emerged. In one task, for example—mental addition of three three-digit numbers—the performance of subjects thinking aloud was 14% *poorer* and 31% slower than that of subjects performing silently. However, when subjects were comparing gambles (e.g., What is a *better* bet—.5 chance on $1.00 or .20 chance on $2.60?), there was a 20% *better* performance accuracy for subjects thinking aloud, although they were 17% slower than subjects working silently. These differences are troublesome because we cannot assume that the effects of protocols will always be harmful (or beneficial).

Rousseau and his colleagues distinguish five causes of reactivity, some that may enhance, others that may impair cognitive performance that is carried out aloud.

1. *Auditory feedback*
Performance may benefit because one hears oneself say items to be operated on and thus the memory for these items might be enhanced. But *delayed* auditory feedback has been known to impair performance.

2. *Protocols necessarily use up processing capacity*
The same task may take longer or be otherwise interfered with when thinking aloud about it.

3. *Errors become public*
Because the cognitive process is now available for public inspection, various motivational factors might enter that are nor-

mally absent in covert cognitive thought. Social desirability factors may prompt subjects to select methods that appear elegant but are inefficient. They might try to justify steps without sufficient grounds. Very often subjects do not know what prompted them to go from one step to the next in analyzing a problem. The subject may simply invent reasons for his or her actions. Also, the performer might hesitate lest errors be detected by the recipient of the protocol.

4. *More time for reflection*
Since thinking aloud is slower than silent mental work, there is time to reflect on the quality of the method and the accuracy of the solution.

5. *Recoding the internal process into communicable form*
For purposes of describing to someone else one's own mental content, internal representations must be recoded into a transmittable, usually verbal, form. Not all images, tastes, or feelings are readily transformed into a verbal form. And this feature of thinking aloud is especially troublesome when components of the problem-solving activity are unconscious or are represented in a form that does not lend itself readily to a verbal translation. (Try to describe the taste of truffles to someone who has never tasted them.)

We do not know if the subjects in the Singer study, sampling their ongoing thoughts, were affected by having to report periodically the state of their minds; it is possible, however, to verify if they were. Such an experiment would require another task, which is. *adversely* affected by a stimulus-independent thought. Then, comparisons could be drawn between the quality of the performances on such a competing task when it is given with and without a beeper that tracks stimulus-independent thought.

The systematic and careful procedures of the Singer study should eventually allow us to compare reactive and nonreactive methods. This would help determine what portion of the variance (and what sorts of variations) in subjects' thoughts is to be attributed to their measurement.

Access to Ongoing Conscious
and Unconscious Thought

For purposes of this discussion, and perhaps for the purposes of analysis in general, it is useful to distinguish between access to an *ongoing* mental process and access to the residues that it leaves, that is, to *memories*. We can be aware of an aspect of a cognitive process as it is taking place, even though we are not aware of many stimuli that impinge on our senses. In fact, as mentioned previously, it is an obvious fact that we are unaware of most aspects of our sensations, perceptions, and cognitions. However, these processes, whether they are conscious or not, leave traces—memories. And these memories can, under different conditions, become conscious or resist access to awareness. At the very least, the methods employed for the study of access to an ongoing process and for the study of retrieval from memory are different. I do not wish to imply, however, that different theories should be developed to explain these two forms of access. On the contrary, I hope that one theory would apply to both.

Singer argues convincingly that if we are to understand unconscious processes we need to study the conscious ones. In seeming contradiction, Shevrin and Dickinson (1980) claim, with equal conviction, that if we are to understand conscious processes we need to study the unconscious ones. Moreover, it could probably be argued that one theory should explain both arguments within one set of concepts and axioms. Such a theory would rely on the assumption that the access to internal cognitive processes and contents varies in degree, from direct and clear access to zero access, with the latter representing what would be considered unconscious. If access varies in degree and if unconscious process and content represent only one particular point on the continuum of access, then the theory of conscious and unconscious processes should consider above all the conditions that facilitate and inhibit access to internal states.

According to various articles in this book—and judging from the results of the Singer studies—mentation seems to be a flow consisting of many streams of varying vigor, which run in parallel. Most of these streams flow "underground"; only a few flow "on the surface" and are accessible to awareness. Sometimes a conscious thought submerges itself momentarily, sometimes it disappears for a longer time, and sometimes it does not reappear. If the problem is formulated in this way, what questions can be asked to guide research? The very first question is, what happens to a conscious mental process that becomes *momentarily* submerged?

For some problems (and we should eventually discover what kind they are) the process initiated at the conscious "level" (or in a conscious "form") continues when submerged into an unconscious "level" or "form." We all must have had instances of being interrupted while working on a problem and coming back to it later, discovering that we are several steps ahead, sometimes coming to the complete solution. Such "sudden" insights must indicate either a miraculously instantaneous problem-solving ability or the fact that when conscious process is interrupted it may continue in some form as an unconscious one. Perhaps this unconscious continuation is slower, less efficient, or noisier. Under some circumstances, however, it is conceivable that it could be more efficient, faster, and cleaner.

More important, the general hypothesis of the continuation of submerged ongoing conscious processes is systematically verifiable. Thus, for example, we might ask a subject to count by threes for a short period of time. At a predetermined point, say when the subject reaches "46," we interrupt and ask the unsuspecting subject to sing the national anthem. We then interrupt the anthem and ask the subject to resume counting. Is the next number called out "49," "52," "55," or "76"? If it is "49," then the process may have been arrested upon interruption. Any higher number would mean that some counting went on "underground."

Should it be true that the individual continues counting "unconsciously" or "subconsciously," or in some other fashion not accessible to immediate awareness, then it should also be true that the longer the interruption, within some limits, the further along the "underground" counting would have gone. Also, the more similar the intrusion task to the starting task, the less should be accomplished "underground." Thus, if the intrusion task is counting by twos, there might even be a setback, and when asked to resume, the subject might go back to "46," "43," or even an earlier point.

Another method is to compare the output rate before and after an interruption of a listing task. We ask the person to list his or her friends and classmates or to name the states of the union. We interrupt for the national anthem, with the expectation that if the listing continues "underground" and if it is "saved," the output rate (items per unit of time) after resumption will be higher than immediately beforehand. Furthermore, the greater the difference in the two rates, the poorer will be the singing of the national anthem. These ideas are similar to Singer's use of the Zeigarnik effect in studying unresolved tensions in recurrent thought and could possibly be used in conjunction with the Klos-Singer procedure.

The question arises about the nature of the cognitive processes that are interrupted: are they conscious, semiconscious, subconscious, or altogether unconscious? Clearly, the surface activity performed overtly—counting—is suppressed, but is there access to it *at the time* of the ongoing interruption? It is likely, I believe, that the easier and more automatic the interpolating task, the easier it is to access the suppressed one. This presents the possibility that we could *teach* the subject to continue counting even during an interruption.

The above experimental paradigm relies on the assumption that we are capable of processing several items and kinds of information *simultaneously* and that some of these processes go on without conscious monitoring.

It is customary in cognitive psychology today to speak of consciousness in terms of channel capacity. Since we can process just "so much" information at any given time and since we are continually bombarded by an awesome quantity of stimulation, some of it cannot be processed. What is not processed is considered unconscious. However, this principle often sounds as if we were capable of doing just one thing at any one time—of processing only one item of information and no more. Clearly this is a gross underestimation of the human channel capacity.

The conscious channel is not as narrow as cognitive psychology tends to suppose. Rather, it is probably quite flexible and may be quite broad. Consider, for example, the task of a conductor performing a Wagnerian opera. There are an enormous number of events that must be attended to, and the time intervals are short. There are frequently ten or even twelve lines in the score that must be followed *in anticipation* of the actual execution by the performers; there is the totality of the orchestra and of the chorus that must be monitored in relation to the soloists. Yet conductors do not collapse from mental exhaustion; on the contrary, many seem to enjoy exceptional longevity! Since it is possible to simultaneously perform several conscious tasks, is it not also possible to do so below the level of consciousness? It is likely that the conductor does not track all the sections at the same time; at times he pays less attention to one section than to some others. For example, he might make eye contact with the concert master in anticipation of an important part for the violins, ignoring his basses. But when the time approaches for the part that the basses must perform, he turns his attention to them. All the while his singers are entering and disappearing from his span of attention. Therefore, in principle, it is possible to probe the fate and course of "submerged" cognitive processes simply by overloading the subject to such an extent that some of the processes cannot be consciously monitored and must be relegated to an "automatic pilot."

Access to Memory:
The Nature of Representations

The distinction between access to an ongoing mental process and access to memory brings up several interesting questions. Are the mental processes of an ongoing cognitive performance that have been momentarily submerged qualitatively the same as momentarily inaccessible memories? Are we speaking of the same type of "unconscious" when we speak of an inadvertent slip of the tongue, for example, which we have not noticed, and when we deal with a name that we know we knew but have forgotten? Is the nature of the unconscious that accompanies the unnoticed slip of the tongue *formally* the same as that which accompanies a memory that cannot be retrieved at a given time? In order to answer these questions we shall require the understanding of representational functions.

Just as there is a multiplicity of simultaneously ongoing mental processes, so there must be a multiplicity of representations. The conductor not only attends to the timpanist visually, he listens to see if his drums have been properly tuned, he indicates meter by his entire body, has some thoughts about how the trombones will come in on top of the percussion, and worries about the way a given phrase will carry into the vocal duet. He hears, sees, and thinks about the timpanist, not only hearing the sound of the kettledrums but noticing that the timpanist's jacket is wrinkled and that he looks too often at the harpist. All these perceptions and cognitions may deposit residues—memories. Thus, for any object and event there are multiple, partially redundant representations formed at the time of their encoding, which probably remain in memory. Any internal event that "stands for" another event or object, external or internal, is a "representation" of that internal event. A one-to-one correspondence between the referent and its representation is not necessitated, nor is isomorphism. Direct correspondence or isomorphism do not apply to language and there is no reason to suppose that they need to hold for other forms of cognitive activity.

There may be, therefore, various subjective representations—semantic, for example, or iconic—and several of each kind for any one object, such as "timpanist." But the conductor also has an auditory representation of the timpanist's notes before the vocal duet and of his own hand movement pointing the baton in the timpanist's direction. I wish especially to draw attention to a particular form of representation other than the subjective, verbal, or iconic, namely, *motor* representation. Largely ignored for decades, motor representations were clearly seen by Freud, Reich, and others as having an important mental role. Since John B. Watson, motor theories of thought or speech perception have taken an extreme position. Thought, for example, has been considered by several theorists to be nothing more than subvocalization. These theories were easily disproved. There is no reason to suppose that the motor system is the exclusive and unique source of representation. And for the identical reason—namely, the provision for redundancy—it is unnecessary to suppose that the realm of subjective experience is the exclusive and unique source of representation.

There is sufficient evidence now to demonstrate the utility of the motor system in encoding and retrieval (Zajonc and Markus 1984). Orienting behavior, including peripheral acts such as accommodation, head movement, or more extensive locomotion have generally been reputed to serve *only* direct ongoing behavior. But it is clear that it, too, leaves traces that aid retrieval. Animals raised in darkness and subsequently allowed to explore a novel environment on their own learn to operate in that environment much better than animals that are carted around and allowed only to view the environment from their cart (Held and Hein 1963).

The motor system can provide a source of representation to the extent that the individual engages in distinctive behavior in addressing the object or otherwise having contact with it. Thus, my having sat on a particular chair in a particular way, stumbling over it on the way to the kitchen, painting it, pushing it too close to the table, having it recovered, and so forth, may constitute retrievable parts of my representation of that CHAIR and serve to enhance recall and recognition. However, many motor acts are too vague, diffuse, and insufficiently distinctive to serve representational or mnestic functions. Of course, I am not implying that one must reproduce the original muscular reaction in its entire complexity and intensity. What is necessary is simply low-voltage muscular reaction patterns that correspond to the original in configuration but are reduced very much in intensity, perhaps so much that they cannot be seen by a naked eye.

The motor system is not always diffuse in its representational function. There is an area where the motor system does provide a useful and efficient additional means of encoding and retrieval. It is in the area of face perception. People are remarkably good at recognizing faces. For example, if in a typical recognition memory experiment we show subjects some (say fifty) picture stimuli, such as houses or trees, and then we show the same items interspersed among an equal number of similar but previously not seen items, then the subject can recognize accurately as "old" or "new" only about 60%. However, a similar experiment with faces may generate up to 80% recognition memory. It is also interesting that the decrement in recognition memory for faces that are presented upside down is four times as large as it is for upside-down houses and trees.

When viewing another face, especially under everyday circumstance, our own face does not remain passive. There is a rich activity and reactivity, and a good portion of it matches or mimics the target face. We smile at a smiling face and frown at an angry one. This is less so when viewing faces on television or in the movies, and even less when viewing photographs of faces. Dimberg (1982) has found that the subject's major zygomatic muscle (the one involved in smiling) shows considerably increased EMG activity when viewing photographs of happy faces and that the corrugator (the muscle involved in frowning) shows increased activity when the subject is viewing angry faces. If we imitate faces in encoding, then we can understand why it is so difficult to recognize upside-down faces. We cannot easily imitate an upside-down face.

In one such experiment we investigated the role of facial musculature in the recognition memory of faces presented under various conditions. One group of subjects was shown a large set of photographs of faces, one at a time, with the instructions to pay attention to each photograph. Each photo was shown for 17 seconds. Another group was shown the same set with the instructions to imitate six features of the face (vertical and horizontal orientation of the head, orientation of the eyes, form and movement of the mouth, etc.) A third group was told to attend to the same six features, but these subjects only noted (on 6-point scales) the states of features without a requirement to mimic. A fourth group viewed the photographs while chewing gum. The assumption for the last group was that their muscles—zygomaticus, risorius, orbicularis oris and oculi—would be so occupied by chewing gum that mimicry would be seriously interfered with. The results confirmed this supposition. Only 59% of this last group gave correct responses, while the imitators did the best by far with nearly 80% correct responses.

The point of this study to understand unconscious mental processes is that the motor responses that serve encoding and retrieval are not attended to by the individual or monitored as much as subjective, verbal or iconic representations. Motor responses are usually not accessed and are perhaps not easily accessible. Consequently, they might constitute an unconscious part of the memory trace. Because muscular movements can now be quite precisely measured by fine EMG recording, an objective study of these inaccessible processes that are significantly involved in cognitive work is now possible. Tics are an example of a muscular habit that may have been acquired to interfere with a muscular movement that retrieves a painful memory.

Self in Conscious and Unconscious Processes

Singer and Horowitz both note in their chapters the important role of the self in conscious and unconscious processes. Singer points to the growing sophistication in social psychology that has developed in studying the self, and Horowitz stresses the subject-object aspects of consciousness that are embedded in the self as it participates in our cognitions about the world. Clearly, a reflective consciousness must include the self as an object and the self as a subject, and this role is yet to be clarified. The communicative aspect of consciousness—what Singer refers to as the internal monologue—implies that there is a sender and a receiver. Such processes are known as "rehearsal" in memory and in problem solving, and they, too, involve the self as an object and the self as a subject. Here the self often acts as a monitor and a censor.

If retrieval involves the reinstatement of original muscular reactions of the subject, then the self may play a more important representational and mnestic function than we suspected. It is taken for granted that what one remembers is information or traces of stimuli of words, pictures, propositions, and so forth. When we ask what it is that one stores, the answer is that the individual stores "information."

This was not always the fashionable way of thinking about memory. In the S-R decades, we believed that it was an association between the stimulus and the response that was retained; according to the classical conditioning paradigm, the subject retains not the conditioned stimulus but the conditioned *response*. What he remembers is *how* he reacted to the conditioned stimulus. Of course, he must somehow remember the stimulus, too, but just remembering the stimulus is insufficient for conditioning. It is the specific association between the stimulus and the response that matters.

In attempting to understand memory, modern cognitive science pays more attention to the properties of the stimulus than to the subject's reaction. There are grounds to believe that the reaction of the subject plays a much more important role than we suspected. It might be noted in this respect, for example, that Edward B. Titchener expected the analysis of how the external world is perceived and represented would generate sensory or stimulus dimensions and qualities. But it did not. On the contrary, the semantic space of any set of concepts, which was obtained in the hundreds of studies summarized by Osgood (1962), generates the three dimensions of evaluations, activity, and potency, with the first dimension explaining 50% of the variance. None of these three reveals much about the stimuli. In contrast, all have to do with the reactions of the person.

More important, if reactions of the subject are in fact significant aspects of the memory trace, then we might ask *how* or in *what way* the person remembers his reaction or response to the object. My memory of the Eiffel Tower is not an image of the tower in the abstract but an image of *my* standing in the Champs de Mars by a particular bench on a gravel path near a tree, *looking* and *seeing* and *reacting* with pleasure at this fine and delicate, yet immense structure. I believe that many—perhaps most—things are remembered that way. I do not remember a particular passage in a book—but I remember *myself* reading that passage and myself *reacting* to it. I don't just remember Mr. X or Ms. Y, but I remember meeting them on a specific occasion in a specific place, and above all, I remember how I reacted to them on that occasion, how I shook hands with them, whether I had to look up because they were taller or bend down because they were sitting, and what my impression was.

Thus, a part of the self is very much involved in the trace. It might be only the part that observed the object or event, perhaps only the part that processed the information, or perhaps only the part that reacted. But any combination of these elements may be retrieved.

How is the self involved in forgetting and in the unconscious? My "now" self may well be a different self from the self that originally encountered the given object. I may have changed between the time of the original encounter and the time of the retrieval. Or it is equally possible that different aspects of my self were activated on these two occasions. If these conditions prevail, then perhaps the reaction that occurred originally cannot be readily retrieved or reproduced.

These considerations imply that retrieval may be facilitated if the self present upon original encoding of the object or event is somehow reinstated. These considerations also imply that if we wish to have a biographical description of a given past experience of an individual, it might be useful to start the interview by asking the subject (or patient) to first retrieve the self structure (schema) of that period. Primed in this way, the events that occurred might be viewed in their original perspective and reported more accurately, because the configuration of all the subject's reactions that occurred with respect to the original object or event would also be brought back.

Conclusion

Singer presented us with a rich body of material and a method that reveals the ongoing conscious processes of an individual in his daily routines. His method can be applied very well to the study of the unconscious. In fact, in order to collect any data of an ongoing unconscious process we must have complete control and information about all the conscious processes that take place at that time. Singer provides us with a useful technique to do so. Even if the method of self-monitoring distorts certain mental processes, it can still be useful in revealing all that is conscious at the moment. If there is independent evidence that the individual has acquired some information or processed some items during that interval of time, then we will know that it had to happen at the level of the unconscious.

References

Dimberg, U. 1982. Facial reactions to facial expressions. *Psychophysiology* 19:643–47.

Ericsson, K. A., and H. A. Simon. 1980. Verbal reports as data. *Psychological Review* 87:215–51.

Held, R., and A. Hein. 1963. Movement-produced stimulation in the development of visually guided behavior. *Journal of Comparative and Physiological Psychology* 56:872–76.

Osgood, C. E. 1962. Studies on the generality of affective meaning systems. *American Psychologist* 17:10–28.

Rousseau, J., E. Johnson, and D. Stevens. 1986. The validity of verbal protocols. Manuscript.

Shevrin, H., and S. Dickinson. 1980. The psychological unconscious: A necessary assumption for all psychological theory? *American Psychologist* 35:421–34.

Zajonc, R. B., and H. Markus. 1984. Affect and cognition: The hard interface, in C. E. Izard, J. Kagan, and R. B. Zajonc, eds., *Emotions, Cognitions and Behavior*. Cambridge: Cambridge University Press.

6   Conclusions

The brief, final chapter sums up the main points of this volume.

16   Agreements and Disagreements: Indications for Research

Mardi J. Horowitz, M.D.

The existence of unconscious systems for organizing meaning and guiding information processing is a relatively recent scientific discovery (Ellenberger 1964). Mesmerists, hypnotists, then psychoanalysts, and later clinicians described relevant phenomena and gave varied explanations for them. The explanations, much more than the phenomena, are still in dispute (e.g., Grünbaum 1984). More recently, cognitive psychology has developed theory about unconscious formative processes that construct conscious representations. The present convergence of cognitive science and psychodynamics on issues of unconscious meaning structures and information processing offers an opportunity to reexamine, revise, and test theories of classification and explanation.

This task requires inference. Unconscious meaning structures are intangible. No direct materialistic assessment is possible, and the structures and processes are not directly experienced by the subject. Even the designation of a psychological phenomenon as such is the result of inferences constructed by observers. The observers are outsiders except in the case when self observes self. Both situations are potentially biased, as emphasized by Spence in Chapter 11. The external observer is biased by preexisting theories and the mental set operative at the time of observation, while the internal observer is biased by a different set of motives and intentions. It may be possible to triangulate inferred aspects of unconscious structures and processes by taking advantage of the differences in these points of view. Such a method would require future efforts to carefully record reports of streams of conscious experience in a communicative context of enough richness of signals that observers could repeatedly review such records and draw their own independent inferences. One potential method is to video-record psychotherapy sessions and amplify them by concurrent research-oriented interviews and experimental probes, making such an archive available to multiple scientists. State-altering situations such as hypnosis, sensory deprivation, and guided imagery may all deserve a new look.

In such situations one can record and then study behavior, communication, and reports of conscious experience. How much about unconscious processes can one infer from conscious experience? Contributors to this volume agree about the usefulness of such study and about its possible limitations. On the most positive side, Singer favors an extensive research approach to sampling thought and suggests that many theories that place conflicted motives in the dynamic unconscious may seriously underestimate the degree to which ideas about these motives are quite conscious but pushed to a periphery of awareness by inattention, communicative reluctance, and subsequent nonrecollection. Consistent with this view, Luborsky's studies of momentary forgetting and Horowitz's studies of states of mind show that an idea that is conscious under some conditions may be forgotten under others. Spence warns that if a model of unconscious operations looks similar to a model of conscious ones, it is likely to be a fallacious model. Working from differing perspectives, both Shevrin and Marcel emphasize the view that conscious and unconscious processes and structures are likely to turn out to be very different in nature, once we understand them scientifically.

Conscious Representations

The careful study of conscious phenomena means a focus not only on why certain *contents* are or are not represented, but on how and why certain *qualities* of thought occur. One example of such a quality is the feeling that a specific conscious representation is intrusive, as in the unbidden images discussed in Chapters 1 and 3. Another example of quality is the shift in the mode of representation during a stream of conscious thought from primarily lexical to primarily visual image representation. The interruptions of the flow of conscious thought described by Mandler in Chapter 2, and the experiences that omit an expectable representation in thought, as in the tip-of-the-tongue phenomenon described by Baars and Jackendoff, and instances of momentary forgetting described by Luborsky, are further examples of a focus on qualities. If videotape archives of psychotherapies, research evaluations, and thought samples are promising resources for refining observation, operational definition, and anchored theory in this domain, then patients with intrusive or omissive phenomena might prove of special interest. Experimental situations for increasing such episodes in normal subjects would also be of use and might be more systematically explored.

To model consciousness, we need a better theory of representation. Several chapters contain references to differences between image, lexical, and enactive modes of conscious representation. Different modes might have different kinds of formative preconscious computations, different schemas, and perhaps differential access to diverse, modular, unconscious streams of information processing and motivation. Whether these various modes for conscious representation all represent a global work space that allows translation between nonconscious models of information processing, as suggested by Baars, requires further theoretical analyses and empirical studies. Whether supraordinate schemas organize consistency and coherent meanings across modes of representation also needs to be theoretically explored to see if there is a route to empirical studies.

Image-representation systems have a property of dual input, from inner schemas and from the excitations derived from external stimuli. Expectations, intentions, social situations, and emotions color the sequence. The combination of external, perceptual, and internal schematic input allows various kinds of transformation of meanings, among them symbolic distortions of reality. The recurrence of systematic, patterned distortions allows observers to form inferences about unconscious meaning structures. For this reason, experiments involving variously ambiguous stimuli may be useful, as described for subliminal stimuli by Shevrin and Baars. These stimuli can be composed of contents inferred to be very high in relevance to the individual subject or to a given type of subject, as in Shevrin's chapter on the paradigm used by him and his colleagues. Conscious responses following stimuli related to inferred unconscious conflicts involving, for example, negative affect can be compared to responses to stimuli related to inferred conscious concerns of similar degrees of emotional saliency. Ambiguous stimuli can be given not only visually by subliminal, peripheral, or embedded perceptions, but in the auditory mode as in dichotic listening and shadowing tasks. Eventually a medley of such experimental approaches might be used with single subjects, studied intensively, to see if cross-modal coherences of findings occurred.

Unconscious Defensive Processes

Some omissions of conscious representations have been called the result of repression so often that the term *repression* has become reified. Intrusive episodes of conscious representation are then explained as a failure of such repressive mechanisms. Erdelyi points out that if repression is a mechanism, we do not adequately know how it operates. He calls for a much closer examination of the concept of unconscious defense and asks that we consider carefully how defensive motives relate to a general methodology for the study of human purposiveness. Many of the authors call for a more detailed, microgenetic, cognitive theory of defense, which they see as a necessary prelude to the operational definition of theoretical constructs; they also call for empirical studies to examine the psychodynamic hypotheses of unconsciously determined defensively aimed controls of how information is processed and represented.

In psychoanalytic theory, a variety of defenses have been postulated and used to explain neurotic psychopathology. Every new text attempts a list of defenses, but the same list is seldom repeated exactly (e.g., Freud 1936; Sandler et al. 1980; Vaillant 1986; Haan 1977; Horowitz et al. forthcoming; Horowitz forthcoming). Defenses are not simply inhibitions placed against elements otherwise on the route to conscious representation. As Knapp describes it, unconscious defensive operations involve complex transformations of meaning before conscious representation occurs. We need to model the way these processes operate and also to classify warding-off phenomena—those behaviors that indicate an aim at nonexpression of themes. The terms that are used to label the postulated intrapsychic defensive processes should not be used to describe warded-off behavioral phenomena. Otherwise, the concept of unconscious defenses could be supported by circular reasoning rather than submitted to potential invalidation or useful revision. What is required, then, as a useful next step, is an improved classification system of manifest signs and research manuals for how to score them reliably. With this in hand, flurries of the increased use of warding-off behaviors could serve as indicators of what passages or segments in recorded reports of conscious experience would be most valuable to study closely.

Luborsky presents an example of the relationship between the phenomenon of momentary forgetting and an explanation of unconscious defensive purposes in Chapter 10; the case illustration involves a spontaneously emerging and anxiety-inducing thought. This idea became conscious and then was forgotten at the very instant when the patient thought she was just about to tell the idea to her therapist. The statement "I forgot," in context, was taken as a sign of the kind of warding-off just mentioned. This episode of momentary forgetting required a multi-level explanatory model of defensive processes that included a rather "intelligent" unconscious, one that could compute what might happen if verbal expression were to occur and could differentiate the consequences of telling socially from those of thinking consciously. Another example of a warding-off phenomenon or sign was the rapid shifting between communicative, emotional themes evident in the case of Ann in Chapter 3. Neither Ann's rage theme nor her guilt theme was fully represented in her conscious thought, but her juggling of ideas was apparent in some states. A fairly "intelligent" nonconscious appraisal of the consequences of expression was again postulated, one that would involve interactive defensive processes serving defensive aims and leading to the outcome of juggling and shifting themes and stances of the self in relation to these themes.

These signs, which suggest unconscious "intelligent appraisals" of anticipated consequences of conscious representation, seem to support the concept of unconscious defense, yet the proofs of this hypothesis are not yet sufficiently strong. Some phenomena that appear to be the consequences of defensive processes may be explained by an alternative hypothesis. Phenomena believed to be signs of warding-off behavior, such as the speech disruptions described by Luborsky, Jackendoff, and Baars, may be due to internal information-overload and the competitions of parallel, distributed processes. That is, as emotions are activated by the progress of a train of thought, other trains of thought associated with that emotion may be activated. The increasing rate of thought with emotional arousal, adding to the direct consequences of the emotional excitation, may lead to the disruption of computational unconscious processes and associations in a memory network. The results would be interferences in the clarity of conscious thought sequences and communicative expressions. The multiplication and intensity of parallel, distributed, unconscious processes might also join channel capacity at the point of reduction required to generate serial conscious episodes of representation, as described by Mandler.

Both cognitive and dynamic theories agree on this point: emotional stress may induce a disruptive effect on computational processes. The dynamic theory postulates an additional factor, the occurrence of computations anticipating possible futures and future self-views that may lead to *active inhibitions* and other defensively motivated regulations. Active inhibitions would *add* effects to the effects that were the consequence of dysregulations and failures of essential clarity in the series of conscious representations and the sequence of communicative expressions, such as speech and gesture. Whether phenomena mandate this addition as essential is not known for certain, as Spence discusses in Chapter 11. Thus, more attention to phenomena that seem to represent warding-off behaviors and to the validity of such a label of classification is indicated. These signs could be studied in multiple channels of communication including the face, the autonomic arousal of the skin and circulatory system, vocal qualities, and other verbal and nonverbal systems. Methods for coordinating such multiple channels for co-occurrences and sequential patterns can now be developed because of modern computers, software, and across variable statistical analyses using Z-scoring procedures. This would permit a finer analysis of the concept of different states governed by different schemas and perhaps manifesting varied types and frequencies of warding off, as discussed especially by Erdelyi, Baars, Jackendoff, and Horowitz.

The recollection of important memories after a period of forgetting them has been described as a "lifting of repression." Conscious reminiscences of a traumic memory after a period of repressing it are one example. This phenomenon of forgetting and then recalling clearly important life events is very impressive, but does it necessarily mean there has been an active inhibition of the memory or of the processes of reconstructing a memory into conscious representation? Spence argues that the procedures facilitating such recollections (hypnosis, suggested effort at recall, hints, free association) may provide access codes that *permit* motivated expressions. This is a different process than postulated in the hypothesis that such procedures reduce defensive aims and operations. With further theoretical modeling, it may be possible to test empirically whether the active, unconscious, defensive inhibition theory is really a necessary addition to our view of stress-induced loss of access codes and competitive, parallel, distributed processes overloading the channels for conscious representation. Possibly, experimental tests of the neurophysiology of information processing, following such paradigms as presented by Shevrin, can eventually validate or invalidate the defensive-inhibition theory.

Unconscious Processes

Although all the contributors attest to the importance of unconscious mental processes, there are disagreements about how to model the structures that go beyond the issue of unconscious defensive processes. Jackendoff formulates a model of unconscious mental processes and calls it the *computational mind,* the body of *propositional* as opposed to *declarative* knowledge. It is the same "mind" that behaviorists allude to in their theories of *operant* and *classical conditioning.* But the theoretical linguistic models derived from studies of phonology and syntax add much more flesh to the model and provide a third perspective to the dynamic and cognitive theories emphasized in the book.

The mind may be modular for different types of computations, as illustrated by Jackendoff in his examples from linguistics and music. Such examples demonstrate how varied unconscious computations lead to a conscious contemplation of options for action without any conscious access of the person to the knowledge of the rules and regulations that govern his or her choices. Marcel adds the phenomenon of blind sight to this domain. Knapp refers to all such systems of unconscious computation as "pure cognitive" processing. He differentiates "pure cognitive" processing from "protocognitive" processing, or unconsciously made decisions on how to maximize pleasure and minimize pain. Protocognitive processing is also called the dynamic unconscious.

The participants agree on the theory that most stimuli are processed in the computational unconscious. The additive nature of the dynamic unconscious and how to model interactions of conscious representations, the organizational and computational unconscious, the inhibited dynamic unconscious, and the deep dynamic unconscious remain topics for future theoretical work. The concept of the "dynamic unconscious" has to be reevaluated using a clear, more contemporary theoretical language (and linked to well-recorded clinical phenomena, as already mentioned).

Knapp, Shevrin, Luborsky, and I describe the deep dynamic unconscious as including the core of instincts, drives, and interpersonal appetites. This set of deep dynamic unconscious processes might have different access to conscious representations and use different schemas than the inhibited dynamic unconscious. The inhibited dynamic unconscious contains codings that were once consciously represented, such as memories of traumatic perceptions that press toward repeated representation but are actively inhibited. Raw urges of the deep dynamic unconscious, in schemas of how self would interact with others, might not be so directly inhibited, since they might have poor access to high-level, rationally sequenced, conscious representations in the first place. Defensive operations involving such urges might operate at a different level than the repression, suppression and disavowal of representations.

Such passions might gain representation first through motoric-emotional forms, as suggested by Zajonc, or as images during dreaming sleep. Lexical representation in words and rational serial organization of ideas in conscious thought might occur only by translation from these developmentally more primitive modes of enactive and image representation (Horowitz 1983). This speculation is consistent with Marcel's suggestion that computational unconscious systems are not linked to deep dynamic unconscious systems. He asserts that the entry of information from one system into the other occurs only with episodes of conscious representations. This view accords with the global workspace theory of consciousness described by Baars.

In contrast, Shevrin sees the computational and dynamic unconscious processes as directly interactive. For him, the processing of visual subliminal stimuli combines computations and dynamic meanings without any intervening conscious representation. He views subliminal stimuli as unconsciously understood and given emotional valences resulting in varied types of information processing, manifested by different electrophysiological responses. If replicated and validated, his approach suggests that subliminal stimulation and other cognitive science methods such as dichotic listening and masked stimuli can be incorporated into designs that use subjects who have active unconscious conflicts. By using experimental and control stimuli, related or not to these clinically inferred conflicts, it might be possible to validate or invalidate the hypothesis that unconscious computational processes are affected by anticipations of pleasure or displeasure and resultant defensive or impulsive choices. Such experiments probably should be done with neurotic rather than normal subjects, since the locked-in nature of neurotic schemas might lead to the clearest manifestations of unusual responses when information is related to these schemas.

To a large extent all the authors agree that person schemas, that is, schemas of self and others, may be an especially important research topic to pursue. Some supraordinate person schemas such as those of self might operate to produce coherence in meaning across modes of representation. This focus on person schemas—on self concepts and role-relationship models—allows one to postulate another type of defensive regulation, one inhibiting and facilitating schemas in an unconsciously coded repertoire, just as other control operations facilitate or inhibit specific elements such as words, images, or enactions.

Research with Psychiatric Patients

Issues of defense, person schemas, the organization of the conscious stream of thought, and the modes of representation are important areas for theoretical effort and dialogue between psychodynamics and cognitive psychology. The classical topics of perception, memory, symbolism, and volition could be usefully reexamined with a focus on issues where high emotion and conflict prevail. In doing so, a careful reexamination of particular clinical phenomena such as intrusions and omissions of conscious representations may be indicated.

Since these conscious experiences are more common in persons with mental disorders, a suitable context for such investigations would be psychiatric patients involved in exploratory psychotherapies. This context is useful because it both provides for the possible relief from unwanted experiences and creates a situation where the person will want to disclose conscious ideas and feelings that are often shielded from communications to others. Since it would be important to study person schemas, the kind of symptom pictures selected could emphasize intrusive maladaptive views of self and others. Therapy situations with such patients often contain transference reactions; these could be a context for a here-and-now study of neurotic interpersonal patterns.

It would be important to carefully record such sessions, including videotaping to get at nonverbal communications, and recording pulse, blood pressure, skin resistence, and skin temperature to get at autonomic nervous system arousals. By retaining such records and coordinating parallel records through appropriate computer-based codes, it would be possible to have multiple reviews of the information by the same and by collaborating groups of investigators. Repeated reviews would allow a gradual linkage between theoretical constructs and operational definitions of those reliably recognized features in the recordings that were thought to signify such constructs.

Such a call for intensive case studies, using many variables and many reviews, has been heard before. Murray (1938) conducted such a multifaceted project with normal subjects and emphasized the importance of "themas," rather than what was anticipated to be primary, individual needs and presses. These "themas" are rather like what we have been discussing as "schemas" as they involve the self and other configurations of recurrent motives. Working with psychiatric patients, efforts led independently by Shakow and Alexander (both unpublished as far as I know) piled up wire-recorded or movie-based records of many therapy sessions. The amount of raw information and raw data contained therein was overwhelming and the records were never successfully examined. Human beings emit so much information in every channel of expression that such records may exceed available logistics for analyses. In order to solve this problem, methods of data-base management must be imposed, and advanced technology now permits this. Murray's group of scientists might also choose, now, to study fewer subjects more intensively than they could when examining fifty subjects.

The computer allows us to develop the power over data that is required. By data reduction and use of parallel visual-display formats, we can examine multiple channels at once. Symbols of a set of data that show where there is great change from baseline activity can be developed. The computer can be used to unpack a symbol, showing more detailed displays of what is not shown at the data-reduced level. It will take time and patience to develop such data-base management systems, but it is quite worthwhile if it can open up this important area.

The psychotherapy context, while useful for the above reasons, should be expanded to produce a maximum data base for this type of methodological effort. The subjects of such research will be, to an extent, altruistic in the sense of wanting to aid science; they will also be willing to participate in order to know more about themselves. These supplementary research sessions could have investigative rather than therapeutic purposes, allowing a variety of questions and experimental stimuli of the kind described as useful in this volume. The recorded data could be managed along with the therapy data, and the effects on therapy and research could be assessed.

The work to unpack such a data base would include the development of new methods of the human judgment of others. This requires attention to the problem of inference by observers when patterns are described as unconscious in a subject. Positive reports of solving this consensus problem (Malan 1963, 1976; Weiss et al. 1986) must be balanced with negative findings (e.g., Seitz 1966; DeWitt et al. 1982). Furthermore, vigorous efforts are needed to develop a methodology of multiple judges with varied mental sets to provide a systematic review of the recorded information.

Summary

This book focuses on issues of emotion, conflicts between wishes, fears, and defenses, and themes of interpersonal memories and fantasies. It aims at a dialogue on unconscious mental processes between the fields of psychodynamics and cognitive science. The contributors have found such dialogue to be fascinating and useful. There is much greater agreement on the usefulness of the theoretical constructs of unconscious mental processes than might have been true in previous decades. They see the hypothesis of unconscious defensive operations as interesting, debatable, and worthy of testing against alternative explanations of intrusive and omissive phenomena.

In cognitive psychology there is a call for models that go beyond existing theories of memory networks and associational processes. Schema theory has been utilized as an aspect of what is needed, but this theoretical construct itself needs work to become more than a mere label for a sector of mystery. Psychodynamics requires a schema theory that deals with whole people and scripts of emotional exchange, including the multiple self-schemas that may characterize even a single individual, and the defensive regulations of schemas.

Advances in research on this topic could lead to quite a change in the sector of psychiatry that deals with the personality disorders. The nosology of abnormal mental conditions is especially weak in the area of recurrent, maladaptive patterns of interpersonal behavior and self-esteem. A good theoretical framework could lead to an entirely new diagnostic and classificatory approach to personality assessment as well as to case formulation, one that reflects different sets of traits for different states in one person. Such a theory would be a vital contribution to understanding change processes, especially in murky areas such as the utility or harmfulness of therapy techniques that promote corrective emotional experiences or encourage regressive transference reactions. The processes underlying identification, mourning, and transference are important to change the individual and might be understood in terms of alterations of existing schemas.

As we close this book, it may be useful to close a loop to its beginning. In the first chapter I wrote that given a phenomenon of consciousness such as a recurrent unbidden visual image, a psychodynamic approach might focus on why it occurred, and cognitive psychology on how it occurred. From what we have seen, the psychodynamic approach might focus on why the image was intrusive and describe motives for and against expressing its contents. The cognitive science approach might focus on how the image was constructed from perceptual and internal schematic input and how the mode of visual representation occurred in terms of underlying modules of information processing. The kind of convergence hoped for by the contributors to this volume and many others in the field can be seen as a focus on regulation— on how the processes leading to representation are regulated and why the degree of control varies from state to state.

I also raised the problem of the omission of learning about opportunities clearly present in a new interpersonal situation. The psychodynamic approach would focus on why a person persisted in seeing this new situation according to some previous pattern. It would include hypotheses about the developmental reasons for persisting in the inappropriate use of some earlier view of situations and reproducing a neurotic pattern. The cognitive approach would focus on how the individual was able to perceive the other and how previously acquired beliefs biased thinking. A convergence would not sacrifice any essential ingredient in either approach but would centralize on the regulation of person schemas. If anything comes of such a dialogue, the fields of abnormal personality, neurotic psychopathology, and psychotherapy research will become open to useful revitalizations.

References

DeWitt, K., et al. 1982. Judging change in psychotherapy: The reliability of clinical formulation. *Archives of General Psychiatry* 40:1121–28.

Ellenberger, H. F. 1964. *Discovery of the Unconscious.* New York: Basic Books.

Freud, A. 1936. *The Ego and the Mechanisms of Defense.* London: Hogarth Press.

Grünbaum, A. 1984. *The Foundation of Psychoanalysis.* Berkeley and Los Angeles: University of California Press.

Haan, N. 1977. *Coping and Defending.* New York: Academic Press.

Horowitz, M. J. 1983. *Image Formation and Psychotherapy.* New York: Aronson.

———. Forthcoming. Controls of the level of experienced stress. In *Introduction to Psychodynamics.* New York: Basic Books.

Horowitz, M. J., H. Markman, J. Ghannam, C. Stinson, and S. Tunis. Forthcoming. A classification theory of defense. In J. Singer, ed., *Repression.* Chicago: University of Chicago Press.

Malan, D. 1963. *A Study of Brief Psychotherapy.* London: Tavistock Press.

———. 1976. *Frontier of Brief Psychotherapy.* New York: Plenum Press.

Murray, H. A. 1938. *Explorations in Personality.* New York: Oxford University Press.

Sandler, J., et al. 1980. *Technique of Child Psychoanalysis.* Cambridge, Mass.: Harvard University Press.

Seitz, P. F. 1966. Consensus problem in psychoanalytic research. In L. A. Gottschalk and A. H. Auerbach, eds., *Methods of Research in Psychotherapy.* New York: Appleton-Century-Crofts.

Vaillant, George E. 1986. Empirical studies of ego mechanisms of defense. *Clinical Insights Monograph.* American Psychiatric Association.

Weiss, J., and H. Sampson. 1986. *Psychoanalytic Process: Theory, Clinical Observation, and Empirical Research.* New York: Guilford.

Author Index

Abelson, R., 183, 214, 278, 280, 330
Ahern, G. L., 327
Alberts, W. W., 128
Algom, D., 308
Allport, D. A., 173
Allport, F., 278
Alvarez, W., 50
Anderson, J., 214
Anderson, J. R., 11, 56, 332
Andrews, G., 124
Antrobus, J. S., 51, 303, 305, 306, 307, 308, 311, 318, 323, 333
Appelbaum, G. A., 85
Arzumanov, Y., 128
Asch, S., 13
Atkinson, R. C., 25n
Auerbach, A. H., 235, 244
Aunon, J. I., 146, 163

Baars, B. J., 25n, 100, 134, 256, 269, 272, 273, 274, 276, 277, 281, 282, 283, 284, 288
Bandura, A., 13, 330
Barber, T. X., 326, 336
Barkoczi, I., 128
Barrios, M., 324, 326
Barta, S., 312, 319, 322, 323
Bartlett, R. C., 13
Beck, A. T., 330
Becker, S., 52
Begleiter, H., 127
Benjamin, L. S., 76
Bevan, W., 134
Blatt, S. J., 329
Block, N., 95
Blumenthal, D., 85
Bolton, W., 186
Boomer, D. S., 100

Bowen, W., 327
Bower, G. H., 11
Bower, P. B., 311, 325
Bowers, K. S., 3
Brandeis, D., 128
Brandstatter, H., 318
Bransford, J. D., 282
Breger, L., 333
Brenner, C., 125, 154
Breuer, J., 11, 50, 89, 90n, 92
Broadbent, D., 328
Brown, R., 256, 282
Brown, S. L., 327
Brown, W. S., 127, 200
Bruner, J. S., 278
Burke, K., 109
Burns, T. E., 85
Buss, A. H., 324

Camden, C. T., 284
Cantor, N., 330
Carlson, L., 330
Carlson, R., 330
Carlson, T. B., 278, 280
Cartwright, D., 325
Castellano, M., 13
Chapman, R. M., 127, 130, 135, 146, 200
Cherry, C., 102
Childers, D. G., 163
Chomsky, N., 203, 204
Christoph, P., 86, 91, 224, 236, 267, 286
Clark, H. H., 176, 278, 280
Coleman, R., 307
Constantian, C. A., 318
Cooper, L., 208
Crawford, H. J., 324, 326

Crits-Christoph, P., 237, 244, 248, 300, 337
Crocker, J., 13
Csikszentmihalyi, M., 316, 325

Dahl, H., 147
Dalkey, N. C., 129, 156
Davidson, J. R., 327
Dell, G. S., 100
Dennett, D., 207
DeWitt, K., 373
Diaconis, P., 147
Dickinson, S., 350
Dickman, S., 126, 133, 177
Dimberg, U., 355
Dixon, N. F., 56, 83, 134, 172

Eagle, M., 192
Edelson, M., 3, 192, 297
Efron, B., 147
Ekman, P., 51, 327
Ekman, T., 257
Ellenberger, H. F., 11, 95, 363
Ellis, A. W., 100
Erdelyi, M. H., 3, 83, 84, 85, 86, 87, 89, 91, 96, 97, 126, 171, 187, 245, 259, 277, 281
Erickson, E. H., 56
Ericsson, K. A., 348
Eriksen, C. W., 83, 86
Erman, L. D., 272
Evett, L. J., 171

Fairbairn, W., 12
Fein, G. G., 306
Feinstein, E., 128
Felton, B. J., 338
Fenichel, O., 87
Fenigstein, A., 324
Fisher, C., 96, 126
Flores, F., 197
Fodor, J. A., 120, 175, 207
Fowler, C. A., 26
Frank, J. D., 124
Freud, S., 6, 11, 25, 50, 82, 87, 88, 90n, 99, 184, 233, 244, 245, 276, 366
Friesen, W. V., 257, 327
Fritzler, D., 128
Fromkin, V. F., 100, 213, 214

Galanter, E., 186
Garozzo, R., 127
Garrett, M., 213
Gedo, J., 12
Gelade, G., 26n, 172
Genest, M., 318, 336
Giambra, L. M., 323
Gill, M. M., 246
Gilmore, J. B., 301, 326, 331
Gleitman, H., 39
Gleitman, L. R., 39
Goffman, E., 280
Goldberg, A., 12
Goldberg, B., 84, 85, 91, 126
Golding, J. M., 324
Goldstein, K., 310
Goodenough, D. R., 329
Goodman, N., 102
Graef, R., 316
Graesser, II, A. C., 34n
Graf, P., 83
Gray, J. A., 22
Greenberg, J. R., 4
Greenberg, S., 51, 303
Gregory, R. L., 25
Grossberg, S., 278
Grünbaum, A., 185, 192, 194, 363
Gur, R. E., 248

Haan, N., 366
Halle, M., 203
Harnad, S., 23n
Harré, R., 185
Hartmann, E. von, 21
Harvey, R., 124
Hastie, R., 13
Head, H., 310
Heckhausen, H., 322
Hein, A., 354
Held, R., 354
Helson, H., 278
Hilgard, E. R., 11, 96, 326
Hillyard, S. E., 127
Hoelscher, T. J., 319
Holender, D., 83
Hollon, S. D., 318, 330
Holmes, D. S., 85
Holt, R. R., 312
Horowitz, M. J., 4, 12, 13, 50, 52, 53, 55, 56, 57, 62, 76, 96, 155, 284, 309, 311, 328, 329, 366, 370

Horwitz, L., 104
Huba, G. J., 323, 324
Humphrey, R., 334
Humphreys, G. W., 171
Hunter, I., 333
Hurlburt, R. T., 316, 318

Ikemi, Y., 337
Isaacs, I., 323
Izard, C. E., 300

Jackendoff, R., 203, 205, 208, 209, 214
Jacobson, E., 12, 56
James, W., 223, 270
Jensen, M., 326, 337
Johnson, C., 317
Johnson, E., 348
Johnson, M., 88
Johnson, M. K., 325
Jung, C. G., 12

Kahnemann, D., 331
Kaltreider, N., 50
Kaufman, E. L., 34n
Kazdin, A. E., 125
Keet, C. D., 96
Kelly, G. A., 76
Kendall, P. C., 318
Kernberg, O., 4, 12, 56
Kihlstrom, J. F., 11
Klein, G., 309, 311
Klein, M., 12
Klinger, E., 310, 311, 312, 316, 319, 322, 323, 333
Klos, D. S., 282, 312
Knapp, P. H., 12, 56, 103, 104, 107, 108, 110, 111
Köhler, W., 26
Kohut, H., 12
Komlosi, A., 128
Kosslyn, S. M., 208, 299
Kostandov, E., 128
Kreitler, H., 330
Kreitler, S., 330
Kris, E., 110
Kriss, M., 330
Krumhansl, C., 13
Krupnick, J., 55
Kubey, R., 316, 325
Kunst-Wilson, W. R., 126
Kutas, M., 127

Lakoff, G., 88
Lane, R. W., 333
Langer, E., 301
Langer, S., 102
Lapointe, F. H., 187
Larson, R., 316, 317
Lashley, K. S., 25, 208
Laver, J., 100
Lazarus, R. S., 51, 96
Leach, E., 182, 183
Lehmann, D., 127, 128, 200
Lerdahl, F., 208
Lesser, V. R., 272
Levenson, R. W., 327
Levine, R., 325
Lévi-Strauss, C., 181, 183
Lewin, B. D., 110
Lewin, K., 312
Libet, B., 128
Lightfoot, David, 203
Lindawood, T. E., 127
Linville, P. W., 329
Loevinger, J., 76
Loftus, E. F., 85, 255, 259
Luborsky, L., 13, 56, 76, 84, 86, 91, 102, 110, 124, 126, 155, 223, 224, 225, 226, 228, 231, 233, 235, 236, 237, 238, 244, 247, 267, 284, 286, 297, 321

McAdams, D., 318
McClelland, D. C., 300
McClelland, J. L., 272
MacCormac, E. R., 101
McDonald, 316
McGillem, C. D., 146, 163
McGuinness, 310
McIlwraith, R. M., 325
Macmillan, N. A., 83
McNeill, D., 256, 282
Maddi, S., 324
Malan, D., 373
Mandler, G., 23, 26, 34n, 35, 39, 83, 300
Mandler, J. M., 27
Marcel, A. J., 13, 25, 26, 98, 126, 170, 171, 173, 186, 187, 212, 261
Margolin, S. G., 98
Marks, I. M., 148
Markus, H., 13, 330, 354
Marmar, C., 55, 76, 106

Marr, D., 170, 208
Marshall, R., 131, 192
Matthews, A. M., 148
Mattson, M. E., 276
Maxeiner, M., 312, 319, 322, 323
May, W. H., 127, 129
Meichenbaum, D., 3, 301, 318, 326, 331, 336
Mellon, J., 237
Merikle, P. M., 83
Miller, G. A., 25, 33n, 34n, 186
Minsky, M., 278, 330
Mintz, J., 233, 238, 244
Miron, M. S., 127, 129
Mischel, W., 330
Mitchell, S. A., 4
Motley, M. T., 100, 134, 283, 284
Murray, H. A., 372

Nakagawa, S., 337
Natsoulas, T., 289
Neely, J. H., 42
Neisser, U., 13, 126, 186, 259
Neville, R. C., 299
Newell, A., 272
Nisbett, R. E., 29, 126
Nishihara, H. K., 170
Norman, D. A., 25, 29, 41, 274

Oatley, K., 186
Ogden, C. K., 102
Opton, E. M., 51
Ortony, A., 101
Osgood, C. E., 127, 129, 192, 357
Ostrom, T. M., 13

Parloff, M. B., 124
Patterson, E. K., 170
Pekala, R., 325
Piaget, J., 13
Poetzl, O., 96
Polanyi, M., 170
Polonsky, W., 338
Pope, K. S., 311, 327, 334
Porjesz, B., 127
Posner, M. I., 25, 126
Pribram, K. H., 132, 186, 310
Pryor, J. B., 13
Purcell, D. G., 83
Pylyshyn, Z., 95, 207

Qualls, P. J., 327

Rachman, S., 124
Radtke, H. L., 326
Rao, C. R., 147
Rapaport, D., 120, 174, 185, 246
Raye, C. I., 325
Reddy, R., 272
Reich, P. A., 100
Reich, W., 262
Reinsel, R., 333
Rennick, P., 128
Revenson, J. A., 338
Reza, F. M., 158
Richards, I. A., 102
Ricoeur, P., 185
Rock, I., 279
Rodin, J., 302
Rosch, E., 214
Rosenberg, M., 76
Rousseau, J., 348
Rummelhart, D. E., 12, 13, 272
Rychlak, J., 299
Ryle, A., 76

Sackeim, H., 86, 91, 224, 236, 267, 286
Salovey, P., 302, 332
Sambursky, S., 194
Sandler, J., 366
Saussure, F. de, 262
Sayre, K. M., 132, 137
Schachtel, E., 254
Schafer, J., 156, 157
Schafer, R., 257
Schallow, J., 325
Schank, R., 183, 214
Schank, R. C., 330
Schank, R. R., 278, 280
Scheibe, M., 156, 157
Scheier, M., 324
Schilder, P., 98
Schmidt, H., 42
Schneiderman, S., 40
Schwartz, G. E., 326, 327, 336
Segal, B., 324
Segal, S. J., 299, 323
Seitz, P. F., 373
Sera, L., 128
Shallice, T., 25, 29, 172, 173, 274

Shannon, C. E., 157
Shebo, B. J., 34n
Shepard, R., 95, 208, 299
Shevrin, H., 84, 120, 126, 128, 131, 133, 134, 177, 192, 248, 350
Shiffrin, R. M., 25n
Shipley, E. F., 39
Shortliffe, E. H., 129, 156
Sifneos, P. E., 326
Simon, H. A., 348
Simpson, D. D., 13
Singer, B., 124
Singer, J., 248
Singer, J. A., 318, 323, 324
Singer J. L., 51, 282, 283, 300, 301, 303, 305, 307, 308, 311, 312, 323, 325, 326, 327, 328, 331, 332, 335
Skinner, B. F., 24
Skutsch, N., 156
Smith, W. H., 128
Snyder, C. R. R., 25
Snyder, M., 303, 326, 327
Spanos, N. P., 326
Speers, M. A., 330
Spence, D. P., 257, 261
Squire, L. R., 83
Stanovich, K. E., 83
Starker, S., 333
Steinberg, E., 334
Stevens, D., 348
Stewart, A. L., 83
Swets, J. A., 83
Szasz, T. S., 185

Taylor, E., 297
Taylor, S. E., 13
Teele, A. S., 56
Tomkins, S. S., 299, 300, 301, 328, 330
Tower, R. B., 325, 327
Treisman, A. M., 26n, 42, 172

Tucker, D. M., 303
Tukey, J. W., 160
Turk, D. C., 318, 330, 336
Tversky, A., 331

Underwood, G., 278

Vaillant, G. E., 366
Vidal, J. J., 130, 159

Wachtel, P., 89
Wallerstein, R., 192
Warrington, E. K., 26
Wegman, C., 3
Weinberger, G. E., 327
Weiskrantz, L., 42, 170
Weiss, J., 373
Westercamp, J. J., 146
White, P., 82
Whyte, L. L., 97
Wiggens, J. S., 76
Wilcoxon, L. A., 125
Wild, C. M., 330
Wilkins, A. J., 170
Williams, W., 131, 192
Williamson, P. A., 303
Wilner, N., 50, 52, 55, 76
Wilson, D. D., 126
Wilson, G. T., 124
Wilson, S. C., 326
Wilson, T. D., 29
Winograd, T., 197
Witkin, H. A., 329
Wollman, M., 333
Wright, E. W., 128

Zachary, R., 312
Zajonc, R. B., 127, 262, 299, 354
Zeigarnik, B., 259
Zilberg, N., 13

Subject Index

Absorption Scale, 318, 319
Activation theory, 41
Adaptation, and consciousness, 36–39
Aesthetical evaluations, and
  perceptions of the world, 299
Affect, and cognition, 127
Age regression, 8
"AM" (case study), 118–19, 134–54, 180
Amnesia: and conscious construction,
  38; infantile, 254. *See also*
  Forgetting
Analog and digital representations,
  301
Anger, and involuntary expressions,
  288
Animal consciousness, 39
"Ann" (case study), 57–75, 217–18
Artificial intelligence, 23, 95, 272, 330
Atkinson's (and Tellegan's)
  Absorption Scale, 324
Attention, 126
Awareness: dissociative episodes in,
  8; repressive episodes in, 8;
  segregated episodes in, 8

Belief systems, effect on phenomenal
  experience, 173
Bellow, Saul, 298
Bereavement reactions, 56
Body image, 98
Body language, 257
Breuer, Joseph, 89; source of
  psychoanalytic data, 96

Case studies: "AM," 118–19, 134–54,
  180; "Ann," 57–75, 217–18; "Little
  Hans," 96; "Magistrate Schreber,"
  96; "Rat Man," 96

Cathartic technique, 89
Cathexes, 87
Censorship metaphor, 276
Children, development of
  consciousness in, 39
Choice, and consciousness, 29
Codes, genetic, 12
Codings, defined, 17
Cognition, and affect, 127
Cognitive disturbance, 231–32; and
  memory recovery, 267
Cognitive performance, effects on,
  348–49
Cognitive processes: bodily correlates
  of, 327; conscious content of, 322;
  and conscious reports, 30–33; and
  dream content, 332–35; and health,
  336–39; operant and respondent,
  310; and pain, 336; and priority
  setting, 308; stimulus dependent vs.
  independent, 311; and stress, 336
Cognitive psychology: and computer
  sciences, 95; emergence of, 298–
  99; and emotional conflict, 4; and
  process descriptions, 182; and
  psychodynamics, 16–18; and study
  of unconscious emotional conflict,
  3; and unconscious information
  processing, 5
Cognitive science: and
  psychoanalysis, 191; and
  psychodynamic psychology, 184
Completion tendency, 54
Complex theory (Jungian), 89
Computation, cooperative, 272
Computational mind, 209–12, 369
Computational processes, and
  emotional stress, 368

Computer processing, analogies of consciousness to, 212
Computer sciences, and cognitive psychology, 95
Conceptual structure, 214–22
Concern Dimensions Questionnaire, 319
Configurational analysis, 56–57
Conflict, unconscious, 150–51
Conscious contents: contexts as triggers of, 281–82; as triggers of contexts, 282–83
Conscious experience: constructivist approach to, 25–26; limitation of, 33–35, 34n
Consciousness: during acquisition of new behavior, 27; during acquisition of new knowledge, 27; adaptiveness of, 36–39; analogies to computer processing, 212; animal, 39; behaviorist analysis of, 24; and channel capacity, 352; and choice, 29; consequences of, 35–36; conservative nature of, 36; continuity and flow of, 34n; current attitudes towards, 23–25; development in children, 39; evolution of, 37; and experiential report, 30–33; and information processing models, 25n; and language behavior, 209–22; and limited capacity concept, 33n; mythology of, 98; and neuroscience studies, 23n; organized nature of, 35n; periods of, 27–30; in prehuman phase of evolution, 38; psychology of, 21; as publicity organ for the brain, 273; selective nature of, 32; serial nature of, 33; in troubleshooting, 28; and unconscious, 349–53; William James on, 33n
Conscious phenomena, study of, 364–69
Conscious processes, self in, 356–58
Conscious self-awareness, 6
Constructivism, and conscious experience, 25–26
Contexts: conscious contents as triggers of, 281–82; role of, 278–81;

and stream of consciousness, 81; and the stream of consciousness, 283–85; as triggers of conscious contents, 282–83
Coping strategies, 318
Core Conflictual-Relationship Theme, 224, 234–49, 284, 329
Cybernetics, 95

Daydreaming, as predictor of poor treatment course, 338
Daydreams, 323–25; and night dreams, 85, 334
Deep dynamic unconscious, defined, 18
Defense: perceptual, 85; and recollection avoidance, 50
Defense mechanisms, 5–7, 83–86, 105–12
Defensive operations, unconscious, 4
Defensive regulation, 66–68
Denial, 5
Depression, and negative self-attribution, 318
Digital and analog representations, 301
Diseases, and cognitive processes, 336–39
Displacement, 214–16
Double entendres, 284
Doubt, paroxysms of, 9
Dream content, and cognitive processes, 332–35
Dreams, 85
Drive, 57
Dujardin, Edouard, 298
Dynamic unconscious, 6, 10, 57, 171; and perceptual nonconscious, 174

Ebbinghaus, Hermann, 84
Effortless Experiencing Scale, 325
Ego, 82
Ego defense mechanisms, 99. See also Defense mechanisms
Electrophysiological studies. See Event-related potential
Emotion, 110
Emotional conflict, and cognitive psychology, 4

Emotional disorders, psychodynamic model of, 125
Emotional experiences, interruptions as source of, 40
Emotional stress, and computational processes, 368
Emotions: patterning, 332; and perceptions of the world, 299–303; suppressed, and involuntary expressions, 288
Enactive systems, in repression, 7
Epilepsy, 244
Event-related potential (ERP), 127–55, 191–96
Evolution, prehuman, and development of consciousness, 38
Expectancies, violation of, 39–40
Experience, prior, importance of, 38
Experimental psychology, 83
Expression, failures of, 252
Extraversion, 303
Eyewitness testimony, unreliability of, 255, 260

Facial muscle activity, 327
Fantasies, 108–10; unconscious, 10
Faulkner, William, 298
Focal attention, 26n
Forgetting, momentary, 223–49, 253–62, 265–68
Free association, 259
Freud, Sigmund, 95; and behavior, 184; case studies, 96; censorship metaphor, 276; defense mechanisms, 84; *Interpretation of Dreams*, 276; materialistic explanation of mind, 184; as precursor of psychodynamic theory, 3; on repression, 6; second theory of anxiety, 11; source of psychoanalytic data, 96; "Studies on Hysteria," 96; and the unconscious, 41, 82; on unconscious mentation, 81; view of man as animal, 99–100; and William James, 297
Fugue states, 8

Generative grammar, 203
Genetic codes, 12

Gestalt structuring processes, 187
Global workspace theory of consciousness, 269, 272–77, 289
Grammar, 205; generative, 203
Grief reactions, 67
Guilt, 60

Health, and cognitive processes, 336–39
Hedonism, 82
Helplessness, 244
Hesse, Herman, 89
Hypnoid state, 11
Hypnosis, 96; age regression in, 8; and capacity for vivid imagery, 326; and disease processes, 336–39; susceptibility to, 324, 326
Hysteria, neurotic style of, 328

Id, 4, 82
Ideation, peremptory, 9
Identity, assignment to objects, 216
Image representation systems, 365, 370
Imagery, capacity for, and hypnotic susceptibility, 326
Image systems, in repression, 7
Imaginal Process Inventory, 318, 323, 324
Infantile amnesia, 254
Inference, rational, 215–16
Information, organization of, in brain, 207
Information processing, 95; cognitive psychology use of, 5, 126; electrophysiological manifestation of, 175; and emotional experience, 300; and human beings, 299; models, view of consciousness, 25n; and motor system, 354; neurophysiological basis for, 210; sequence in, 300; structure and process, 208–9; styles, 328–29; unconscious nature of, 208–9; unconscious systems for, 363
Information structure, conscious and unconscious, 209
Inhibited dynamic unconscious, 13; defined, 18

Inhibition, pathological vs. nonpathological words, 145
Instantiated schemas, defined, 17
Instinctual drives, unconscious, 4
Interpersonal behavior patterns, maladaptive alterations in, 16
Interpretation of Dreams (Freud), 276
Interruptions, and creative endeavors, 40
Introversion, 303, 328
Intrusive phenomena, 9, 60, 217
Irrational views, repetitive, 9
Isolation, 5

Jackendoff, Ray, 98
Jackson Personality Research Form, 324
James, William, 33n; flow of consciousness, 298; ideomotor theory, 274; on momentary forgetting, 269–71; and Sigmund Freud, 297: stream of consciousness, 81; tip-of-the-tongue phenomenon, 289
Jealousy, 302
John (film), 51
Joyce, James: *Portrait of the Artist as a Young Man*, 298; *Ulysses*, 298, 334
Judgment, 126
Jung, Carl, 89

Kelly, George, 329
Knowledge structure, 276

Lacan, Jacques, 40
Language: and conscious/unconscious processes, 209–22; oppositional elements of, 262; rule system, 205–7. *See also* Grammar; Speech
Language learning, 203
Learning, sequence in, 27
Lewin, Kurt, 329
Lexical systems, in repression, 7
Life events, and stress, 53
Limited capacity concept, 33n
Linguistics. *See* Language
"Little Hans" (case study), 96
Locus of Control Inventory, 324

"Magistrate Schreber" (case study), 96
Marcel, Anthony J., 83
Memory, 83, 126, 357; access to, 353–56; long-term, 329; and repression, 368; traumatic, 90n, 368
Meringer, R., 100
Metaphor, 101, 257
Migraine headaches, 244
Mind, computational, 209–12
Mindlessness, 301
Mood shifts, 244
Mood states, 16, 110
Moral evaluations, and perceptions of the world, 299
Motivation, unconscious, 322
Motivational theory, 322
Motives, defined, 17
Motor system, encoding and retrieving of information, 354
Multiple personality, 8
Muscle memory, 262
Musical cognition, 208

Natural sciences, positivist tradition in, 184
Natural world, cultural divisions of, 181
Neuroscience studies, on consciousness, 23n
Neurotic psychopathology, 366
Night dreams, and daydreams, 85, 334
Nonsense syllables, 84
Nuclear scenes, 301

Object relations school, 4
Object relations theory, 331
Obsessional neurotic pattern, 328
Obsessional worries, 9
Omission, errors of, 41
Omissive phenomena, 7–8, 60
Operant thought processes, 310
Organizational and computational unconscious, defined, 18
Organizational unconscious, 10
Osgood Semantic Differential, 127

Pain, and cognitive processes, 336
Paradoxical sleep, 333

Parallel distributed processing, 12, 153, 232–33, 367
Pathological grief reactions, 67–71, 73
Perception, 98, 126
Perceptual defense, 85
Perceptual nonconscious, and dynamic unconscious, 174
Perceptual processes, and phenomenal experience, 170
Peremptory ideation, 9, 309
Personality, interaction between therapeutic stages, 284
Personality patterns, 283–84
Personality Research Form, 324
Petit mal attacks, 244
Phantasies. *See* Fantasies
Phenomenal experience, effects of belief systems on, 173
Philosophy, romantic, 95
Phobias, 154, 180
Piaget, Jean, 109, 329
Pleasure-unpleasure principle, 82
Politzer, 187
Portrait of the Artist as a Young Man (Joyce), 298
Positivist tradition, in the natural sciences, 184
Post-Traumatic Stress Disorders, 50
Pragmatic meanings, 103
Preconscious, 82
Primary process thinking, 82
Prior experience, importance of, 38
Problem solving, 35, 272
Projection, 5
Projective tests, rationale behind, 283
Protocognitive operations, 98–99
Psychiatric patients, research with, 371–73
Psychic determinism, 184
Psychoanalysis: and cognitive science, 191; experiments in, 96; French School, 185; source of primary data for, 96
Psychoanalytic theory, 3
Psychodynamic configuration, defined, 17, 49
Psychodynamic phenomena, 217–18
Psychodynamics: and cognitive psychology, trial lexicon, 16–18;
defined, 5; and object relations perspective, 4; relationship to cognitive science, 183–86; theory, roots of, 3
Psychology: cognitive, 95; experimental, 83; scientific, and conscious experience, 81; shift from stimulus response to cognitive perspective, 300
Public and Private Self-Consciousness Scales, 324, 325

Rational inference, 215–16
"Rat Man" (case study), 96
Reaction formation, 5
Reactivity, causes of, 348–49
Reality monitoring, 325
Regression, 5
Regularization process, 216
Representations, defined, 17
Repression, 5, 6–7, 84, 85, 217, 276; defined, 17; enactive systems in, 7; failures of, 254; Freud's cognitive model of, 6; and memory, 368; predictor of poor treatment course, 338; and signal anxiety, 10–11
Richardson, Dorothy, 298
Role–relationship models, 11–12, 65–66; defined, 17
Role reversal, 5
Rotter's Locus of Control Inventory, 324
Rule systems, for language, 205–6

Sartre, Jean Paul, 187
Schemas: defined, 17; inhibitions of, 13; self, 12, 371; in the unconscious, 4
Schema theory, 13–14, 41; and consciousness, 26
Schematic repertoire theory, 11–12
Scientific psychology, and conscious experience, 81
Scripts (organized belief systems), 330; defined, 17
Self-attribution, negative, 318
Self-awareness, 6, 323
Self-communication, 336
Self-esteem, maladaptive alterations in, 16

Self-monitoring process, 303, 327
Self-schemas, 12, 371; in the
  unconscious, 4
Semantic meanings, 103
Sensation-Seeking Scales, 324
Sexual drives, in unconscious
  processes, 210–11
Sexuality, and involuntary
  expressions, 289
Signal anxiety theory, 10–11, 57
Singer, Jerome, 85
Sleep, paradoxical, 333
Slips of the tongue, 283
Social cognition, 330–31
Social relationships, 280
Social world, cultural divisions of,
  181
Speaking, automatic nature of, 210
Special states theory, 11
Speech: errors, 213; production of,
  100, 213
States of mind ("Ann" case study),
  59–62, 110–12
Steppenwolf (Hesse), 89
Stimulation, sources of, 302–3
Stimulus homogeneity, 176
Stomach pains, 244
Stream of consciousness, 81; and
  contexts, 283–85; determinants of,
  308–9; in fiction, 298
Stress, 112; clinical investigations of
  responses to, 53–56; and cognitive
  processes, 336; and computational
  processes, 368; effect on intrusive
  thinking, 50–57; in life events,
  intrusive repetition after, 49–57;
  and problem solution, 36
"Studies on Hysteria" (Freud), 96
Subliminal effects, 83
Subliminal perception, 96, 126
Subliminal stimuli, 133–36, 172, 370
Subliminal transinformation patterns,
  153–54
Sublimation, 106
Suppression, defined, 17
Surprise, and resetting of
  consciousness, 277–78
Survivor-guilt theme, 55
Symbolic transformation, 101

Symbolism, sexual nature of, 281
Systemic Unconscious, 82

Telegan's (and Atkinson's) Absorption
  Scale, 324
Thematic Apperception Tests, 318
Therapists: anger towards, 240;
  patient involvement with, 233–40
Thought: intrusive, 50–57;
  peremptory, 311; rationality of, 42
Thought processes. See Cognitive
  processes
Thought sampling, 310, 316–22
Thought stream, determinants of,
  308–9
Tip-of-the-tongue phenomenon, 8,
  256, 270–271, 289
Titchener, Edward B., 357
Tolman, Edward, 329
Transference, 102, 108, 330
Transference potential, 246
Transinformation, 130–33, 152–54,
  157–63, 175–76
Treatment, nature of, 55

Ulysses (Joyce), 298, 334
Unconscious: analogies to computer
  processing, 212; and consciousness,
  81, 349–53; deep dynamic, defined,
  18; defense systems, 366–69;
  defensive operations, 4; differing
  concepts of, 82; dynamic, 6, 10;
  emotional conflict, study of, 3;
  fantasies, 10; forms of, 98–116;
  Freud's concepts of, 81, 82;
  inhibited dynamic, 13, 18;
  instinctual drives, 4; and language
  behavior, 209–22; mental
  processes, 4; motivation, 322;
  motives, 6; organizational, 10, 18;
  processes, 369–72; conceptions of,
  121–23; self in, 356–58; schemas of
  self, 4; systemic, 82
Undoing, 5

Verbal behavior, automatic nature of,
  210
Verbal memory, and free association,
  259

Vision, theory of, 208
Visual illusions, 173
Visual information structure, 208
Visual perception, 169–70

Watson, John B., 354
Wolpe, Joseph, 91
Woolf, Virginia, 298

Word categories, conscious and
  unconscious, 154–55
Word selection, 155–56
Wundt, William, 81

Zeigarnick effect, 312
Zuckerman's Sensation Seeking
  Scales, 324